Essentials of Sport Leadership

This is a complete, step-by-step, reader-friendly introduction to leadership theories and their application in sport organizations. It outlines key concepts and approaches to leadership, clearly explains how they relate to sport, and shows how sport managers can use leadership theory to develop and improve their professional practice.

This book covers leadership and management across all sectors of sport, including for-profit, non-profit, and public, and adopts an international perspective that reflects the globalized reality of contemporary sport business. It explores key topics, including behavioural theories, transformational leadership, culture, self-leadership, ethics, and women in sport leadership, and encourages the reader to develop critical thinking skills that are essential in the modern workplace. Each chapter contains a selection of real-life examples, review questions, case studies, self-assessment exercises, topics for seminars and workshops, and suggested readings.

This is an essential textbook for any sport leadership course, valuable reading for anybody with an interest in leadership theory or contemporary sport management, and a useful handbook for anybody working in sport or event management who wants to become a better manager.

Online support material includes quiz-style questions and other resources for tutor use or adaptation.

Majd Megheirkouni is Senior Lecturer in strategy and leadership at Leeds Trinity University, UK. He is a Certified Management and Business Educator (CMBE), awarded by the Chartered Association of Business Schools, and a Chartered Manager, awarded by the Chartered Management Institute (CMI).

Peter Norrington is a freelance editor, working mainly on business management, leadership, and project management topics. While in academia, he was a PRINCE2 Practitioner and Fellow of the Higher Education Academy.

.

Essentials of Sport Leadership

THEORY AND APPLICATION

Majd Megheirkouni and Peter Norrington

Routledge
Taylor & Francis Group

LONDON AND NEW YORK

Designed cover image: Getty Images / Digital Vision.

First published 2025
by Routledge
4 Park Square, Milton Park, Abingdon, Oxon OX14 4RN

and by Routledge
605 Third Avenue, New York, NY 10158

Routledge is an imprint of the Taylor & Francis Group, an informa business

British Library Cataloguing-in-Publication Data
A catalogue record for this book is available from the British Library

ISBN: 978-0-367-25900-6 (hbk)
ISBN: 978-0-367-25901-3 (pbk)
ISBN: 978-0-429-29044-2 (ebk)

DOI: 10.4324/9780429290442

Typeset in Palatino
by codeMantra

Access the Support Material: www.routledge.com/9780367259013

"Learning from action is the key to building your leadership experience."

Majd Megheirkouni

CONTENTS

FIGURES

TABLES

ACKNOWLEDGEMENTS

This book would not have been possible without the contributions of academics and consultants who have an interest in sport leadership, human resource management, national and international sport organizations, and other areas of sport business. Also, this book is made meaningful with ever-present regard for sport students, participants, spectators, and the wider public.

Majd recognizes and thanks Mr. Samih Moudallal, Member of the International Olympic Committee and of the Culture and Olympic Heritage Commission, and Amanda Bond, formerly CEO, British Dressage, for the valuable ideas they have provided.

The authors thank all managers, board members, and chief executives of sport organizations in the UK, Europe, the Middle East, and Asia who responded to Majd's research surveys.

The authors are indebted to the anonymous reviewers who provided feedback, which has greatly improved the quality of this book.

They also acknowledge the superb assistance received from their editorial team at Routledge, from the formative stages of this project to the publication of this book. The guidance, flexibility, support, and professionalism of Simon Whitmore (Sport & Leisure Editor), Rebecca Connor (Senior Editorial Assistant), the copyeditor, indexer, and publication team have all been invaluable to the completion of this work.

Majd wants to acknowledge much love and wonderful support and understanding from his wife, Lorin, and sons, Danial, Arwa, and Saleh.

Peter wants to acknowledge the contributions of his brother and family, David, Rachel, Alex, and Tasha, to his self-reflection and self-development, both in sport contexts – which might surprise them – and as family.

1

INTRODUCTION

INTRODUCTION

This overarching goal of this sport leadership book is reflected in its subtitle: *Theory and Application*. The authors have developed the material to support students learning the essentials of sport leadership, to improve their capabilities of applying theory through critical thinking, and to develop leadership behaviours and capabilities in sports organizations. We would like this book to become a main textbook for sport business and sport management courses, because it provides step-by-step support to sport business, management, and leadership students, using specific and supported activities from the field. In turn, these will enable students to understand how to transfer leadership theory into your own practice.

This chapter introduces the four parts of this book, covering the concepts of sport management and leadership, sport leadership in different settings (for-profit, non-profit, public), leadership theories, and sport leadership learning and development. It covers the how and why we wrote it, this book's goals, who it is for, what it covers, its distinguishing features, and some notes on key terms across this book.

ABOUT THIS BOOK

The genesis of this book emerged from our review of numerous published works on sport leadership, aiming to serve as a fundamental resource for our undergraduate and postgraduate students. Our observations revealed that existing literature in this domain insufficiently covers the broad spectrum of leadership and its application within sport contexts. Consequently, our students may supplement their studies with resources from the broader fields of business and management. Leveraging our diverse blend of academic and non-academic expertise across multiple disciplines, we embarked on crafting a comprehensive book. Our objective was to provide students with a singular source that adeptly elucidates sport leadership theory and its practical applications, reducing the need for additional supplementary materials or resources.

Our research draws from diverse sources to ensure a well-rounded perspective, including publications, national and international networks, and virtual learning and training workshops. In the initial stages, we extensively surveyed respondents from various sport backgrounds, ranging from academic staff, students, athletes, coaches, administrators, to other stakeholders within the sport industry, from varied nations and regions. These surveys formed the

DOI: 10.4324/9780429290442-1

bedrock of our publications, allowing us to glean first-hand insights and experiences directly from people actively engaged in the sport settings. Furthermore, the implementation of our surveys was conducted through a collaborative effort involving experts, academics, and former and current leaders and governors possessing specialized knowledge in sport. Their contributions in executing these surveys added depth and authenticity to the material underpinning our publications, ensuring that the content is robust and reflective of real-world experiences within the sport landscape.

WHAT ARE THIS BOOK'S GOALS?

The goals of this book are:

- To make a clear distinction between sport in management, sport in sociology, sport in psychology, sport in physiology, sport exercise, and sport in education and development. This book offers an approach to assist understanding the differences between sport leadership and sport management.
- To offer strong coverage of the significant notions of sport leadership and sport management in a variety of sport settings, whether for-profit, non-profit, or public. This book will help students develop their critical-thinking skills, by presenting divergent and convergent facets of sport leadership across these settings.
- To make an early contribution to sport leadership textbooks and materials, comprising three approach strategies: making a clear distinction between coverage of theories and approaches, their applications, and the development of behaviours and capabilities based on these concepts in sport contexts.
- To stimulate students' development individually and in groups through checking knowledge, discussion questions, case studies, self-assessments, and developing self-awareness and sharing real experiences.

WHO IS IT FOR?

This is an essential textbook for any sport leadership course, valuable reading and reference for anybody applying contemporary theory and practice to successful sport leadership or sport management, and a useful handbook for anybody working in event management and business.

WHAT DOES IT COVER?

This book consists of four parts, comprising 16 chapters (this chapter apart), covering the concepts of sport leadership and management, sport leadership in different settings (for-profit, non-profit, public), leadership theories, and sport leadership learning and development.

Part I discusses some introductory issues for terminology in this book, here in Chapter 1. Chapter 2 covers the main topic of 'sport' and how it is defined in different fields, addresses the differences between management and leadership, and distinguishes between sport management and sport leadership.

Part II, Chapter 3, addresses the notion of sport leadership in three settings: for-profit, non-profit, and public. It discusses the convergent and divergent facets of leadership in these settings. This is important mainly because when approaching leadership theories, it is essential to be familiar with the similarities and differences between the three sport settings, regarding the nature of the leadership required.

Part III, Chapters 4–16, addresses the main, traditional, and contemporary, leadership theories and approaches and their application in sport settings. Each chapter explains the main characteristics of relevant theory and introduces the reader to the most important scholars, debates, and models on the theory with specific activities, such as open discussions, self-assessment, case studies, and general discussion topics. In addition, each chapter evaluates theories or approaches to give the reader a 'big picture' on their strengths and weaknesses. Also, and importantly, the classification of leadership theories and approaches in this book offers a good opportunity for scholars and researchers in the area of sport leadership to explore and investigate neglected aspects of leadership in sport settings.

Part IV, Chapter 17, perhaps uniquely at the time of writing, addresses learning and development in sport leadership in depth. It defines the terms 'education', 'training', and 'development' before introducing learning theories and approaches that will enable students to identify their own learning styles. It also helps students understand the major requirements to transfer learning and development in sport settings, with detailed information on the process.

DISTINGUISHING FEATURES

This book has several specific features that are designed to make the material accessible and valuable to students. These include:

- **Case studies**: These cases are based on personal and professional experiences of many leaders in sport and are drawn from a wide variety of sport organizations in for-profit, non-profit, and public settings. These cases test the student's ability to apply concepts when dealing with real-life leadership issues. The studies have been created by the authors: some are self-contained; others can be extended by tutor-led or student-led research.
- **Self-assessments**: These provide opportunities for students to learn and experience leadership theories and approaches in a personal way. Self-assessment can challenge the student's cognitive understanding of most ideas and concepts in real-life leadership. Self-assessment can take the form of scenarios, questionnaires, and personal reflections on experiences in sport.
- **Open discussion questions**: Each chapter contains several questions designed so that students can tackle them with each other outside the class or inside it as part of a group activity. These topics help students apply the chapter concepts in their own lives and leadership activities, as well as supporting students to learn through peer- and self-assessment.
- **General questions**: Each chapter also includes questions to help students reflect or check knowledge on the sport leadership concepts and ideas related to a chapter.

ONLINE MATERIALS

Quiz-style questions: For instructors and lecturers who have adopted this book, there is an online resource: multiple-choice questions (and answers) covering material across the whole book, enabling students to test their integrated understanding.

- **Slides**: Figures and tables from this book are presented on slides for use in lectures.
- **Editable documents with additional notes**: These contain the case studies, self-assessments, and questions from this book, so tutors can adapt them for their own use.
- **Resource guides**: These collect materials across different chapters and extend them for quick use with students: some key journals in sport and leadership, some key UK sport organizations, and some which provide support and development for sport issues.

SOME NOTES ON KEY TERMS

Throughout this book, we have used the terms 'public', 'for-profit', and 'non-profit' to distinguish between broad categories of organization. We realize that any terms we choose would carry different political, economic, and research meanings for readers with different backgrounds. So, we ask you to treat these terms as 'usefully fuzzy'.

The terms are used both for the idea of 'sector' – which carries meaning in economic analysis – and 'setting' which we intend to mean the particular 'nature' of an organization or the 'nature' of an event. For example, a for-profit (business) may run a not-for-profit event (even though the business may derive non-tangible benefits, such as brand awareness). However, the reader may find considering other terms used in different texts, and indeed countries, interesting – e.g., industry, voluntary, charity, informal, street, social enterprise, competitive, sponsored, fun: how does a change of term change what people expect in a particular context?

Focusing on women here is important. Women have been deliberately excluded from sport in general 'merely' or specifically for being women. They have been excluded from specific sports that some people consider 'unfeminine', channelled into sports considered 'appropriate' for women, and excluded from the same levels of recognition and reward as men. While there is a chapter dedicated to this, all the other material must be held to apply for women. This point needs raising as much of the literature in the various disciplines – business, management, human resources, etc. – and certainly the foundational literature has been written by men, about men, and often for men.

However, we have not – at this point – included material that explicitly covers all genders and gender identities. The public and political debates are fierce – often unpleasant – and theorizing about people is not what this book is for. We have retained some non-gender-neutral fictional names and pronouns in some exercises: this may stimulate debate – in safe learning environments – rather than pretend that gender has no effects – on experiences, perceptions, or identities.

Of course, throughout this book, we have had to make choices: for length, consistency, and readability. Do read critically, withhold judgement, find evidence. Perhaps, be surprised. We hope you will find this book useful – and also that you'll enjoy it.

We hold that sport is something everyone can do – and should be able to do.

Part I

INTRODUCTION TO SPORT LEADERSHIP

2 CONCEPTUALIZING **SPORT** MANAGEMENT **AND** SPORT LEADERSHIP

Learning Outcomes

After reading this chapter, you will be able to:

- Understand the meaning of 'sport' from different perspectives
- Identify the differences and similarities between leadership and management
- Identify the differences and similarities between sport leadership and sport management
- Understand your own, current positions on sport leadership and sport management

INTRODUCTION

This chapter reviews common definitions of sport to develop a specific definition that fits and focuses the purposes of this book. This draws on the significance of sport in our lives and cultures, and the value of integrating academic study of leadership and management specifically into a discipline for sport, and the resulting value for practitioners. The differences between the concepts of 'leadership' and 'management' are presented. Material from various disciplines presents common debates and arguments, enabling transfer of established knowledge into the sport leadership and management discipline and showing that the emergent sport leadership and management literature is a coherent discipline. Then, 'sport management' and 'sport leadership' are outlined.

DEFINING SPORT

Definitions of sport are common. Readers may find it useful to list and discuss definitions from sources you already know, as well as ones you come across later.

Here, we provide definitions drawn from different sport sub-disciplines – as practised and discussed socially and in academic literature – that may advance our general understanding of the notion of sport. However, the reader may note that in many sport management journals, ideas around sport often intertwine management and business, and these are researched as an interdisciplinary field despite any differences. For our purposes, we look at seven sub-disciplines: sociology, psychology, physiology, exercise, education and development, management, and business.

Elvin (1993) suggested that sport includes four key elements: competition, physical activity, aspects of organization, and the influence of outcome on quality of experience. He differentiated between recreation and sport by linking recreation specifically with the satisfaction that is gained from the quality of the experience and focusing on the activity for itself. Chernushenko et al (2001: 10) argued that the term 'sport' is "sustainable when it meets the needs of today's sporting community while contributing to the improvement of future sport opportunities for all and the improvement of the integrity of the natural and social environment on which it depends".

SOCIOLOGY

Sociology discusses sport in terms of issues, processes, and patterns, such as race, ethics, religion, gender, media, family, organizational culture and structure, competition, and how these influence groups and individuals. Sociological theories are widely adopted by sport sociologists to examine these concerns. For example, Coakley defines sport sociology as the "sub-discipline of sociology that studies sports as social phenomena" (2009: 11). This means that sociology investigates how sport reflects and changes socio-cultural contexts.

PSYCHOLOGY

Psychology discusses sport in terms of the ways in which we perceive, think, and feel about, and behave in our environment and activities in sport contexts, such as pressure in competitions, participating in an opening ceremony of the Olympic Games, and training in sessions and camps. For participants – whether we see ourselves as athletes or not – this can help improve performance, whether in training, competition, or rehabilitation, or when using sport, rather than exercise, as a means for health care, such as reducing work and life stresses, maintaining our bodies to the extent we are able as they change through life, or simply to improve our enjoyment. For example, for athletes, Nicholls and Callard (2012) suggest that the primary goals of sport psychology are to improve athletes' performance and reinforce the psychological well-being of athletes, particularly in specific events.

PHYSIOLOGY

Physiology discusses the application of physiological knowledge to specific sports, so it refers to the examination of how sports influence our bodies' movement and functioning. The focus may be on understanding a particular part of our body: e.g. nervous system, musculoskeletal system, cardiorespiratory system, digestive system, and red blood cells for oxygen transport. For example, Weinberg and Gould (2007: 4) define it as "the scientific study of people and their behaviours in sport and exercise activities and practical application of that knowledge".

EXERCISE

Sport exercise covers physical activities used for improving our physical fitness for leisure or competition purposes. We use physical activities or 'informal exercise' daily, but these are not sport exercise: e.g. walking to school, running for transport, gardening, fitness centre activities, work, and shopping. For Birch et al (2004), sport exercise is physical action aimed at improving fitness. It can be defined as a set of specific physical activities used for specific short- and long-term purposes, implemented through specific schedules, programmes, coaching, and plans to achieve specific results.

EDUCATION AND DEVELOPMENT

To describe sport in education and development, there is a need to understand the meaning of each concept. Based on human resource development literature, education refers to learning that prepares the person for a job whether or not it is related to a specific present or future job; whereas development refers to learning for growth whether or not related to a specific current or future job (Nadler and Nadler, 1990). In general, sport education – in school contexts usually known as 'physical education' – refers to content and learning relevant to one or more sports, as well as being relevant to exercise or health more generally. Sport education from an academic perspective provides guidance on how sport can be researched, discussed, or described for educational purposes: for example, developing a curriculum model. Siedentop (1994) was the first to develop a curriculum model in sport education to counter the criticisms of academics concerning how sport is presented in (school-level) physical education.

Sport development, in general, refers to helping individuals or communities regardless of their backgrounds and circumstances to start playing a sport, to select one sport (or perhaps more) to stay engaged in, and also to succeed at it (or them). Specifically, for example, Collins et al (1995: 3) defined sport development as:

> a process of effective opportunities, processes, systems and structures
> that are set up to enable people in all or particular groups and areas
> to take part in sport and recreation or to improve their performance
> to whatever level they desire.

However, this description does not reflect the whole sport environment. For example, Houlihan and White (2002) distinguished between 'development through sport' where the emphasis is on social objectives and sport as a tool for human development, and 'development of sport' where sport is perceived as having value in its own right.

Significantly however, the perspectives of the general public and people entering 'sport and exercise' in the most general sense depend on when, and where, formative school experiences happened and how they have been reinforced or changed by later experiences. The balance of content within the curriculum subject of Physical Education has changed, with more explicit emphasis over the years on personal aspects of health and exercise for health, rather than exercise as an obligatory 'good-for-you' activity or playing specific sports. It is important to consider that changing and contemporary academic discussion of sport may not match individuals' or groups' experiences.

BUSINESS

Although an emerging field, sport business is one of the biggest sport-related disciplines, with many sub-disciplines, with their own strategies, employees, consultants, and experts – and of course, participants. Sport in business refers to commercial activities that take place in the sport industry, usually intended to make a profit, or at least bring some benefit to an organization, such as brand awareness. There are fundamental factors that cannot be ignored which contribute to making a profit. Obvious factors are, for example, marketing, finance, media, law, human resource, information technologies, public relations, management, and strategy. The perhaps less obvious factors relate to the wide range of stakeholders that form the skeleton of sport business, such as athletes, agents for players and clubs, owners and operators of clubs and stadiums, sport event organizers, national sport governing bodies, sport equipment manufacturers, sponsors, and international sport federations (Beech and Chadwick, 2013), local and national public authorities, and local or wider communities of, for example, fans and people living, working, or travelling through a club's physical location. Therefore, sport business is a multidisciplinary field, involving participants who often work separately to achieve their own purposes whilst influencing the main purpose of a business that delivers sport experiences. Idealistically, it might seem that internal and external stakeholders would work together in harmony at individual, team, and organizational levels. Practically, such harmony is unlikely, as it may be even theoretically very difficult to achieve, particularly in large or interacting socio-economic systems, and wherever sub-systems develop in different ways or at different speeds.

MANAGEMENT

Although investigation of sport in management is still young in academic research (Masteralexis et al, 2012), the concepts and ideas around sport in management were initially drawn from business contexts (Gillentine and Crow, 2005). Sport in management can refer to how to manage sport activities, people, or organizations. In this regard, DeSensi et al (1990: 33) defined it as "any combination of skills related to planning, organizing, directing, controlling, budgeting, leading, and evaluating within the context of an organization or department whose primary product or service is related to sport and/or physical activity". Additionally, sport in management can refer to how to manage sport resources, such as Talavera-Gonzales et al's (2008: 286) definition of it as "the process of utilizing the least resources, materials, and facilities to accomplish the purpose of sports promotion and development".

LEADERSHIP AND MANAGEMENT

Leadership literature demonstrates continuing discussion, clarification, and dissent in what is meant by leadership and management, and continuing controversies regarding what count as proper differences between management and leadership.

Some researchers argue that management and leadership are qualitatively different (Bennis and Nanus, 1997; Maccoby, 2000; Daft, 2022). The leading debate about the difference between leadership and management has been derived from extant research, informed especially by reviews (e.g. Yukl, 2013; Daft, 2022; Kotter, 1990, 2001; Bennis and Nanus, 1997; Barker, 1997; Conger, 1992). According to these reviews and meta-analyses, some scholars support the view that leadership is different from management in terms of the nature of roles in each one.

Kotter (1999) emphasized that one of the main differences between management and leadership lies in their primary roles. It is argued that leadership is about building commitment and about changes that begin with developing and achieving a new vision of the future. This is achieved by putting strategies in place to create the change required in an organization (Kurland et al, 2010, Bennis and Nanus, 1997); this means implementing the strategies, not just having them. In contrast, management is a complex process involving functions that centre on organizing individuals, human resource, control, and organizational systems; and delegating responsibilities to subordinates for performing plans, finances, and structure (Saxena and Awasthi, 2010; Maccoby, 2000). Other debates go further, arguing that different leaders are for different roles across organizational levels (Champoux, 2010), because the role of top leadership is mainly responsible for developing organizational culture and human capital; exploiting competencies; creating organizational control, coordination, and ethical processes; determining the organization's purpose; improving the mission of the organization; and translating strategies into actions (Phipps and Burbach, 2010; Ireland and Hitt, 1999).

Leadership is also considered a social influence process that takes place among individuals through complex relationships (Northouse, 2021; Vroom and Jago, 2007; Pearce and Conger, 2003). According to this view, any individual may exhibit leadership in a social system at different organizational levels. The differences between followers and leaders of the social system of the organization are complex in terms of the nature of influence. This is because leaders influence their followers and followers also influence their leaders. Consequently, both influence each other in changing or keeping the organizational culture and developing the vision of collectivism (Crow et al, 1996).

It is important to bear in mind that influence may also come from factors such as personal characteristics of an individual, interpersonal power relations, team relationship skills, and power due to organizational position or relative position. However, if followers do have the ability to choose without influence whether they follow their potential leader, this might suggest the idea that leadership results when a leader influences followers without exercising any power. In any case, a leader exercises the power that is received from their followers by influencing others (Bertocci, 2009; Afolabi et al, 2008). Leadership and management may be considered in terms of authority and influence (Megheirkouni et al, 2018). In this regard, Rost (1998) defined management as an authority relationship that is noted between managers and their subordinates to produce services from coordinated activities, and leadership as an influence relationship between leaders and their followers to perform change through their shared purposes.

Some may argue that when an individual exercises power through positive or negative motivation – reward or punishment – to influence followers' behaviour, this may seem to be an exercise of power rather than leadership because power may be viewed as unethically exercised; and an individual is able to exercise power over followers. However, this does not mean that a leader is able to control followers (Burns, 2010; McMahon, 2004). For some, leadership takes place when followers are affected to do what is ethical for their organization (Lussier and Achua, 2010). However, we should be careful when applying our own judgements (biases or prejudices) of what is ethical to other people's circumstances, without discussion or negotiation. It is also possible that leadership may consider all ways to affect behaviour and attitudes of followers in the organization regardless of the purpose or the outcome.

Given that leaders are the major source of influence for social processes and tasks, the role of leaders may also be shared with team members or a (looser) group (Solansky, 2008; Hackman and Wageman, 2007; Ensley et al, 2003; Drath and Palus, 1994). This view is supported by Yukl (2013) who emphasized the distinction between leadership and management with the idea that managers are oriented towards stability and leaders are oriented towards innovation. So, Yukl adopted the term 'managerial leadership' to describe the overlap between management and leadership in the literature.

Although the concepts of management and leadership may be interchangeably utilized in (academic) literature (Hernon, 2010; McKenna and Maister, 2002) and elsewhere, however confusing this may be, we contend, there are indeed different roles for managers and leaders. This is supported by Grint's model (2005) that distinguishes between three types of authority for solving problems: management, leadership, and command.

SPORT MANAGEMENT AND SPORT LEADERSHIP

The Sport and Recreation Alliance[1] – the representative body for national sport organizations in the UK – has long identified management-related concerns or challenges for sport, which have not abated, including the sale and subsequent loss of school playing fields; competitive tendering, contract management, and the effect on public facilities; taxation on national governing bodies of sport; developing the role of sponsorship; the potentials of central government funds; the structure of sport; and other issues (Elvin, 1993). Their website is an excellent source for further, contemporary issues, such as the decline in children's health, abuse of participants in sport, tackling social loneliness through sport, various anti-discrimination and pro-engagement campaigns, and of course, the Covid-19 pandemic, while the usually annual, serious flu epidemics are not forgotten.

We suggest that these and many other issues have ensured that the need for sport leadership, as well as sport management, is clearly visible and vital across society for both sport and the many sports and interests that comprise it.

For at least the last decade, authors such as Hoye et al (2012) have highlighted the concept of specific sport management and claim that sport managers utilize management techniques and theories that are similar to managers of other organizations, such as hospitals, government departments, banks, mining companies, car manufacturers, and welfare agencies.

Yet, we must still address the need for sport management, and the variety of definitions and descriptions of its whole and parts. There are some aspects of strategic management, organizational structure, human resource management, leadership, organizational culture, governance, and performance management that are unique to the management of sport organizations (Hoye et al, 2012). For Chelladurai (1994: 15), sport management was already "a field concerned with the coordination of limited human and material resources, relevant technologies, and situational contingencies for the efficient production and exchange of sport services". According to Pitts and Stotlar (2007: 4), sport management is "the study and practice of all people, activities, businesses, or organisations involved in producing, facilitating, promoting, or organizing any sport-related business or product". Lussier and Kimball (2009) described sport management as a multidisciplinary field that integrates the sport industry and management. They indicated that the key reason for its growth in academic programmes is based on its value, which relies on the ways by which it is managed. Thus, they conclude that sport management programmes serve to train individuals for managerial positions in different areas, including professional teams, college athletics, fitness and recreation centres, coaching, officiating, sport marketing agencies, youth organizations, sporting goods manufacturing and retailing, and stadiums and arenas.

Some researchers argue that an active engagement with sport business practices would help to emerge new theories (Chalip, 1990) and help real-world testing of sport theories (Chelladurai, 2014; Cunningham, 2013; Doherty, 2013; Fink, 2013; Irwin and Ryan, 2013; Chalip, 2006). This may suggest that the field of sport business concerns implementing its own theories. Additionally, the sport field offers a fertile ground for deriving and generating theories. However, this argument is criticized on the basis of whether sport business is a unique field or derives practices from the original theories of other research disciplines (Arnold and Fletcher, 2012; Zanger and Groves, 1994). This concern is manifested by the lack of effective role for academic sport institutions (Megheirkouni, 2018b; Banks, 1983). Three situations exacerbate this concern.

1. **Business and management background**: The sport labour market at national and international levels mostly prefers recruiting individuals who have graduated from law, media, accounting, finance, human resource management, or other professional subject areas to occupy sport managerial roles, rather than selecting graduates from the area of sport business.
2. **Context-specific approaches**: Confusion is exacerbated by relying variously on business, media, law, or medical schools for developing sport research or focusing on sport as a dependent area for research.
3. **Sport and non-sport discipline journals**: Where can and should researchers, theoretical or practitioner, publish? Which readerships will or might be reached? What impacts are there for author recognition? What impacts will there be on quantity and more importantly, quality of sport research? Taking one aspect in more detail: there remains a need for reviewers and experts specializing in established business and management and related areas. Yet, there arises a need for reviewers and experts specializing in sport-focused issues, as sports have participant profiles that do not necessarily match with business terminologies of customers, consumers, or clients.

As a result, growth of leadership and management literature in the field of sport business begins with the application of leadership theories and approaches in the discipline of sport as a context-specific area within other disciplines and then learns from those applications and approaches how to find itself as a new, distinctive, central area, with the other disciplines, and perhaps new ones, becoming its own sub-areas. It has been noted that the numbers of papers and citations have grown at an increasing rate, not only in established fields like management and social psychology but also in other disciplines such as nursing, education, and industrial engineering (Antonakis, 2012). This has helped to strengthen their own literatures through specific debates, arguments, evidence, and frameworks; however, such activities are still limited in the field of sport business. This is supported by Chalip (2006: 3) who claimed that "If the study of sport [business] is to position itself as a distinctive discipline, then it must take seriously the possibility that there are distinctive aspects of the management of sport". Research evidence supports this argument and goes further to reveal that there is a need to apply leadership theories, approaches, and all organizational aspects in sport settings if we want to develop the field of sport business in general and the areas of sport leadership and sport management, in particular (Megheirkouni, 2018a, 2017a, b; Megheirkouni and Roomi, 2017).

COMPARING LEADERSHIP AND MANAGEMENT ROLES IN SPORT SETTINGS

This section addresses the roles of leaders and managers in sport settings. Daft (2022) identified five areas crucial to organizational performance: providing direction, aligning subordinates, building relationships, developing qualities, and creating leader outcomes.

Table 2.1 provides a generalized, comparative overview of management and leadership, and the following sections give substance to the comparisons.

PROVIDING DIRECTION

Leaders and managers are concerned with providing direction for their sport organizations, but there are differences. A management role is usually linked to a formal title within a department, established to carry out specific activities within a hierarchical organizational structure (e.g. HR manager, general relationship manager, marketing manager, and finance manager). Good managers bring calmness and stability to their sport organizations and bring a degree of order and consistency to the quality of product or services. Often, managers keep an eye on the bottom line and focus on short-to medium-term results. Leadership, by contrast, is about creating and developing 'vision': the desired future state at which a sport organization hopes to arrive (Goethals et al, 2004). The notion of vision includes seeing the big picture, communicating that vision or path to the future, then guiding and shepherding the sport organization to move towards achieving that vision. Leaders often keep an eye on the horizon and focus on the long-term future.

Table 2.1 Comparison of Features of Leadership and Management

Feature	Management	Leadership
Providing direction	Planning and budgeting	Establishing direction by creating vision and setting strategies
Aligning subordinates	Organizing people and job assignments by establishing rules and providing structure	Creating common culture and values by supporting learning and communicating goals
Building relationships	Focusing on providing good services and productivity using 'position power' as well as acting as a head	Focusing on people's needs using 'personal power' and acting as a coach, a facilitator, and a supporter
Developing qualities	Passive emotions and feelings Talking to employees Asking for work needs Intolerance of mistakes Tough-minded	Active emotions and feelings Listening to employees Asking for personal needs Tolerance of mistakes Open-minded
Creating outcomes	Focusing on current rules and procedures for completing works	Supporting new rules and procedures for completing innovative works

Source: Adapted from Daft, R. (2022). *The Leadership Experience*. (8th ed.). Boston, MA: Cengage Learning.

ALIGNING SUBORDINATES

The organizational structure of any sport organization requires a sport manager over the subordinates or employees, who have little alternative but to comply with a manager's orders and directives (Bertocci, 2009). Often, the concept of management refers to organizing by separating individuals in the sport organization into functions and specialities with boundaries by sections, departments, divisions, or centres; thereby managers simply direct and control subordinates and employees to achieve specific results. Leadership, in contrast, means creating shared culture and values. Unsurprisingly, leaders shape organizational cultures by creating shared practices in sport organizations (Hofstede et al, 1990). Leadership also means reducing boundaries and seeking to align individuals with broader ideas of what the sport organization should be and why. The concept of leadership means helping subordinates grow and succeed through ongoing advising and supporting, seeking organizational commitment and loyalty, and developing teams and building coalitions, alliances, and partnerships outside the sport organization (Northouse, 2021).

BUILDING RELATIONSHIPS

Leadership in terms of relationships focuses on people in a sport organization, such as inspiring and motivating subordinates through using their 'personal power', the influence capacity a sport leader derives from being seen by
subordinates as knowledgeable (Northouse, 2021; Yukl, 2013). Personal power
includes referent and expert power types (see Chapter 8). When sport leaders
act in ways that are important to subordinates, it gives sport leaders power.
Management, on the other hand, focuses on objectives such as managing daily
tasks and taking the required steps for improving existing performance and services in sport organizations. This takes place through using 'position power',
the power a person derives from a particular office or rank in a formal organizational system (Northouse, 2021). Position power includes legitimate, reward,
and coercive power types. For example, team players accept that a manager of
a professional football team can tell all players to be at training sessions twice
a day or they will stay on the bench, or even be sold or have their employment
terminated.

DEVELOPING QUALITIES

Undoubtedly, leadership is not only a set of behaviours and capabilities in a
sport organization but a set of personal qualities that give sport leaders more
power and influence. Some of the personal qualities used to identify sport leaders include personality features (e.g. self-confidence, independence, tolerance of
stress, and enthusiasm) and other characteristics (e.g. knowledge, intelligence,
and fluency of speech). Leadership generally encourages emotional connections
to others because great sport leaders are honest with themselves to the point of
inspiring trust, listen to subordinates, and share love and respect with them. The
leader's role is to ask the right questions rather than provide the right answers.
Management, on the other hand, means emotional distance because sport managers talk to people, give advice and orders more than they listen, and discern
what people want or need in the sport organization. In addition, the notion of
management means being an expert in understanding details within the section,
department, or division and being able to provide appropriate processes to solve
a problem (Grint, 2005).

CREATING OUTCOMES

The differences between leaders and managers in sports can create different outcomes. Leadership refers to challenging the status quo, so that old strategy, useless plans, and irresponsible norms can be replaced to meet any new challenges
(Daft, 2022). Good sport leaders bring valuable changes to sport organizations.
These can be new services and products that expand markets and increase sales;
new strategies focusing on participants' performance and achievement; new
directions for the organization within a sport or sport generally; and adapting
an organization towards futures that lie undetailed on the horizon, even creating the detail desired. Additionally, good sport leaders help sport organizations
promote openness and honesty, positive relationships, and long-term strategies.

Management, on the other hand, focuses on short-to-medium term outcomes, results, and current commitments and meeting the expectation of internal and external stakeholders of the sport organization.

SUMMARY

The purpose of this chapter was to give the reader a view of the topic by focusing on the notion of sport, the meaning of sport from different perspectives, how sport fits within various disciplines, and how it can have a special span of its own. This was followed by discussion of the differences between management and leadership and various ideas around these concepts. The discussion included the concepts of and differences between sport management and sport leadership.

GENERAL QUESTIONS

1. What can you identify as common or divergent characteristics of the various meanings of sport in this chapter – and your wider experience of definitions of sport?
2. How do you define 'management'? Why?
3. How do you define 'leadership'? Why?
4. What are the similarities between management and leadership?
5. What are the differences between management and leadership?
6. How do you define 'sport management'? Why?
7. How do you define 'sport leadership'? Why?
8. What are the similarities between sport management and sport leadership?
9. What are the differences between sport management and sport leadership?
10. After your reading of this chapter, can you identify current weaknesses in sport management? Can you use examples from your own experiences to support your answer?
11. What personal qualities do you think someone needs to develop to be a good sport leader?
12. What personal qualities do you think someone needs to develop to be a good sport manager?
13. What are your own development needs in management and leadership? (You might view these as current areas of strength or weakness, but this makes an unnecessary and unhelpful self-judgement. The real point is to discover what you think you have enough of and what you need more of.)
14. To what extent do you think is it possible to succeed at both management and leadership?

OPEN DISCUSSION QUESTIONS

TOPIC A: SHARING AND DISCUSSING DEFINITIONS

1. How do you define sport? Why do you define it in that way?
2. Which definition(s) do you think is more widespread or useful? Why?

3. What definition of sport do you suggest could include all perspectives? Or why do you think this is not possible?
4. How does your definition differ from the definitions outlined here?

TOPIC B: YOUR EXPERIENCES OF MANAGEMENT AND LEADERSHIP IN SPORT AND YOUR CURRENT INTENTIONS

1. Think about a sport club or organization you know. How do you see leadership and management linked in practice rather than theory?
2. From your experience, can anyone in a sport organization be involved in leadership and management responsibilities? Why?
3. Where do you place the emphasis on your own role in the next five years – leadership or management? Why?

Case Study 2.1: Choosing Sport Management and Leadership Roles in a Club

FitLab Gym is a luxury health club and gym offering an extensive range of wellness services, including healthcare, fitness and spa services, golf courses, and more. The club has two directors who assume both leadership and management tasks and responsibilities, but these are at a strategic rather than a day-to-day level. Although the emphasis is on leadership as they strive for constant improvement, evaluate programmes, conduct appraisals, and support the settings by regular meetings with the facilities managers, at the same time they retain some management responsibilities, such as managing financial affairs. They focus on quality through implementing the club strategy in practice. The facilities managers are perceived more as managers than leaders, given that they are responsible for the day-to-day tasks at a practical level, such as implementing educational programmes, managing registers, and overseeing invoices. However, they have a leadership role: particularly, they lead staff meetings, work with other professionals, evaluate practice, and motivate their team.

Questions

1. Who do you think is the right person for that club – a leader or a manager? Why?
2. Can the club rely on just one of these two? Why?
3. Do you think the club's size and the numbers of staff and members affect the need for managers or/and a leader? Why?
4. Can you give examples of clubs relying on management or/and leadership?

Suggested Reading

Freeman, W.H. (2015). *Physical Education, Exercise and Sport Science in a Changing Society.* (8th ed.). Burlington, MA: Jones and Bartlett.

Hoye, R., Smith, A.C.T., Nicholson, M. and Stewart, B. (2012). *Sport Management.* (3rd ed.). London: Routledge. https://doi.org/10.4324/9780080964324.

Hylton, K. (Ed.). (2013). *Sports Development: Policy, Process and Practice.* London: Routledge. https://doi.org/10.4324/9780203082829.

Masteralexis, L.P., Barr, C.A. and Hums, M.A. (Eds.). (2012). *Principles and Practice of Sport Management.* (4th ed.). Boston, MA: Jones and Bartlett.

Watt, D.C. (2003). *Sports Management and Administration.* (2nd ed.). London: Psychology Press.

Note

1 https://www.sportandrecreation.org.uk. In April 2024, the membership directory (Divisions page) stated having over 300 members. (Until 2010, it was known as the Central Council of Physical Recreation.)

References

Afolabi, O.A., Obude, O.J., Okediji, A.A. and Ezeh, L.N. (2008). Influence of Gender and Leadership Style on Career Commitment and Job Performance of Subordinates. *Global Journal of Humanities*, 7(1–2), 1–8.

Antonakis, J. (2012). Transformational and Charismatic Leadership. In: Day, D.V. and Antonakis, J. (Eds.). *The Nature of Leadership.* (2nd ed.). Thousand Oaks, CA: Sage. (256–288).

Arnold, R. and Fletcher, D. (2012). A Research Synthesis and Taxonomic Classification of the Organizational Stressors Encountered by Sport Performers. *Journal of Sport and Exercise Psychology*, 34(3), 397–429. https://doi.org/10.1123/jsep.34.3.397.

Banks, S.A. (1983). Sport: Academic Stepchild. *Journal of Popular Culture*, 16(4), 90. https://doi.org/10.1111/j.0022-3840.1983.1604_90.x.

Barker, R.A. (1997). How Can We Train Leaders If We Do Not Know What Leadership Is? *Human Relations*, 50(4), 343–362. https://doi.org/10.1177/001872679705000402.

Beech, J. and Chadwick, S. (2013). Introduction: The Commercialization of Sport. In: Beech, J. and Chadwick, S. (Eds.). *The Business of Sport Management.* (2nd ed.). Harlow: Pearson Education. (3–22).

Bennis, W.G. and Nanus, B. (1997). *Leaders: The Strategies for Taking Charge.* (2nd ed.). New York: Harper Business.

Bertocci, D.I. (2009). *Leadership in Organizations: There Is a Difference between Leaders and Managers.* Plymouth: University Press of America.

Birch, K., George, K. and McLaren, D. (2004). *BIOS Instant Notes in Sport and Exercise Physiology.* London: Taylor and Francis. https://doi.org/10.4324/9780203488249.

Burns, J.M. (2010). *Leadership*. New York: Harper Perennial Modern Classics.

Chalip, L. (1990). Rethinking the Applied Social Sciences of Sport: Observations on the Emerging Debate. *Sociology of Sport Journal*, 7(2), 172–178. https://doi.org/10.1123/ssj.7.2.172.

Chalip, L. (2006). Toward a Distinctive Sport Management Discipline. *Journal of Sport Management*, 20(1), 1–21. https://doi.org/10.1123/jsm.20.1.1.

Champoux, J. (2010). *Organisational Behaviour: Integrating Individuals, Group, and Organisations*. (4th ed.). London: Taylor and Francis. https://doi.org/10.4324/9780203872918.

Chelladurai, P. (1994). Sport Management. Defining the Field. *European Journal for Sport Management*, 1(1), 7–21.

Chelladurai, P. (2014). *Managing Organizations for Sport and Physical Activity: A Systems Perspective*. (4th ed.). New York: Routledge. https://doi.org/10.4324/9781315213286.

Chernushenko, D., Kamp, A. and Stubbs, D. (2001). *Sustainable Sport Management: Running an Environmentally, Socially and Economically Responsible Organization*. Nairobi: United Nations Environment Programme. https://wedocs.unep.org/20.500.11822/30231.

Coakley, J. (2009). *Sports in Society: Issues and Controversies*. (10th ed.). New York: McGraw-Hill.

Collins, M., Institute of Leisure and Amenity Management, and Sports Council. (1995). *Sport Development Locally and Regionally:* Reading, UK: Institute of Leisure & Amenity Management (ILAM).

Conger, J.A. (1992). *Learning to Lead: The Art of Transforming Managers into Leaders* San Francisco, CA: Jossey-Bass.

Crow, G.M., Matthews, L.J. and McCleary, L.E. (1996). *Leadership: A Relevant and Realistic Role for Principals*. Princeton, NJ: Routledge.

Cunningham, G.B. (2013). Theory and Theory Development in Sport Management. *Sport Management Review*, 16(1), 1–4. https://doi.org/10.1016/j.smr.2012.01.006.

Daft, R.L. (2022). *The Leadership Experience*. (8th ed.). Boston, MA: Cengage Learning.

DeSensi, J.T., Kelley, D.R., Blanton, M.D. and Beitel, P.A. (1990). Sport Management Curricular Evaluation and Needs Assessment: A Multifaceted Approach. *Journal of Sport Management*, 4(1), 31–58. https://doi.org/10.1123/jsm.4.1.31.

Doherty, A. (2013). Investing in Sport Management: The Value of Good Theory. *Sport Management Review*, 16(1), 5–11. https://doi.org/10.1016/j.smr.2011.12.006.

Drath, W.H. and Palus, C.J. (1994). *Making Common Sense: Leadership as Meaning-Making in a Community of Practice*. Greensboro, NC: Center for Creative Leadership.

Elvin, I.T. (1993). *Sport and Physical Recreation*. (2nd ed.). Harlow: Longman.

Ensley, M.D., Pearson, A. and Pearce, C.L. (2003). Top Management Team Process, Shared Leadership, and New Venture Performance: A Theoretical Model and Research Agenda. *Human Resource Management Review*, 13(2), 329–346. https://doi.org/10.1016/S1053-4822(03)00020-2.

Fink, J.S. (2013). Theory Development in Sport Management: My Experience and Other Considerations. *Sport Management Review*, 16(1), 17–21. https://doi.org/10.1016/j.smr.2011.12.005.

Gillentine, A. and Crow, R.B. (Eds.). (2005). Foundations of Sport Management. Morgantown, WV: Fitness Information Technology, Inc.

Goethals, G.R., Sorenson, G.J. and Burns, J.M. (2004). *Encyclopedia of Leadership*. (4 Vols.). London: Sage.

Grint, K. (2005). Problems, Problems, Problems: The Social Construction of 'Leadership'. *Human Relations*, 58(11), 1467–1494. https://doi.org/10.1177/0018726705061314.

Hackman, J.R. and Wageman, R. (2007). Asking the Right Questions about Leadership: Discussion and Conclusions. *American Psychologist*, 62(1), 43–47. https://doi.org/10.1037/0003-066X.62.1.43.

Hernon, P. (2010). The Next Managerial Leadership: Continuation of a Research Agenda. In: Katsirikou, A. and Skiadas, C.H. (Eds.). *Qualitative and Quantitative Methods in Libraries: Theory and Applications*. World Scientific Publishing. (27–36). https://doi.org/10.1142/9789814299701_0004.

Hofstede, G., Neuijen, B., Ohayv, D.D. and Sanders, G. (1990). Measuring Organizational Cultures: A Qualitative and Quantitative Study across Twenty Cases. *Administrative Science Quarterly*, 35(2), 286–316. https://doi.org/10.2307/2393392.

Houlihan, B. and White, A. (2002). *The Politics of Sports Development: Development of Sport or Development through Sport?* London: Routledge. https://doi.org/10.4324/9780203478547.

Hoye, R., Smith, A.C.T., Nicholson, M. and Stewart, B. (2012). *Sport Management: Principles and Applications*. (3rd ed.). London: Routledge. https://doi.org/10.4324/9780080964324

Ireland, R.D. and Hitt, M.A. (1999). Achieving and Maintaining Strategic Competitiveness in the 21st Century: The Role of Strategic Leadership. *Academy of Management Perspectives*, 13(1), 43–57. https://doi.org/10.5465/ame.1999.1567311.

Irwin, R.L. and Ryan, T.D. (2013). Get Real Using Engagement with Practice to Advance Theory Transfer and Production. *Sport Management Review*, 16(1), 12–16. https://doi.org/10.1016/j.smr.2011.12.007.

Kotter, J.P. (1999). *John P. Kotter on What Leaders Really Do*. Boston, MA: Harvard Business Review Press.

Kurland, N.B., Michaud, K., Best, M., Wohldmann, E., Cox, H.M., Pontikis, K. and Vasishth, A. (2010). Overcoming Silos: The Role of an Interdisciplinary Course in Shaping Sustainability Network. *Academy of Management Learning & Education. Special Issue on Sustainability*, 9(3), 457–476. https://doi.org/10.5465/amle.9.3.zqr457.

Lussier, R.N. and Achua, C.F. (2010). *Leadership: Theory, Application, and Skill Development*. (4th ed.). London: Cengage Learning.

Lussier, R.N. and Kimball, D.C. (2009). *Applied Sport Management Skills*. Champaign, IL: Human Kinetics.

Maccoby, M. (2000). Understanding the Difference between Management and Leadership. *Research Technology Management*, 43(1), 57–59. https://www.jstor.org/stable/24132373.

McKenna, P.J. and Maister, D.H. (2002). *First among Equals: How to Manage a Group of Professionals*. New York: Simon and Schuster.

McMahon, T.F. (2004). *Ethical Leadership through Transforming Justice*. Lanham, MD: University Press of America.

Megheirkouni, M. (2017a). Leadership Styles and Organizational Learning in UK For-Profit and Non-Profit Sports Organizations. *International Journal of Organizational Analysis*, 25(4), 596–612. https://doi.org/10.1108/IJOA-07-2016-1042.

Megheirkouni, M. (2017b). Leadership Competencies: Qualitative Insight into Non-Profit Sports Organisations. *International Journal of Public Leadership*, 13(3), 166–181. https://doi.org/10.1108/IJPL-11-2016-0047.

Megheirkouni, M. (2018a). Leadership in Large-Scale Events: An Insight on Leadership Styles and Decision-Making Styles. *Event Management: An International Journal*, 22(5), 785–801. https://doi.org/10.3727/152599518X15299559876162.

Megheirkouni, M. (2018b). Mixed Methods in Sport Leadership Research: A Review of Sport Management Practices. *Choregia*, 14(1), 1–20. https://openurl.ebsco.com/EPDB%3Agcd%3A2%3A14153890/detailv2?sid=ebsco%3Aplink%3Ascholar&id=ebsco%3Agcd%3A129500054&crl=c.

Megheirkouni, M., Amarachi, A. and Shehu, J. (2018). Transformational and Transactional Leadership and Skills Approach: Insight on Stadium Management. *International Journal of Public Leadership*, 14(4), 245–259. https://doi.org/10.1108/IJPL-06-2018-0029.

Megheirkouni, M. and Roomi, M. (2017). Women's Leadership Development Programmes in a Sports Setting: Factors Influencing the Transformational Learning Experience of Female Managers. *European Journal of Training and Development*, 41(5), 467–484. https://doi.org/10.1108/EJTD-12-2016-0085.

Nadler, L. and Nadler, Z. (Eds.). (1990). *The Handbook of Human Resource Development*. (2nd ed.). New York: John Wiley and Sons.

Nicholls, A.R. and Callard, J. (2012). *Focused for Rugby*. Champaign, IL: Human Kinetics.

Northouse, P.G. (2021). *Leadership: Theory and Practice*. (9th ed.). London: Sage.

Pearce, C.L. and Conger, J.A. (Eds.). (2003). *Shared Leadership: Reframing the Hows and Whys of Leadership*. Thousand Oaks, CA: Sage.

Phipps, K.A. and Burbach, M.E. (2010). Strategic Leadership in the Nonprofit Sector: Opportunities for Research. *Journal of Behavioral and Applied Management*, 11(2), 137–154.

Pitts, B.G. and Stotlar, D.K. (2007). *Fundamentals of Sport Marketing* (3rd edn.). Morgantown, WV: Fitness Information Technology.

Rost, J. (1998). Leadership and Management. In: Hickman, G.R. (Ed.). *Leading Organizations: Perspectives for a New Era*. London: Sage. (97–114).

Saxena, S. and Awasthi, P. (2010). *Leadership*. Delhi: PHI Learning Pvt. Ltd.

Siedentop, D. (1994). *Sport Education: Quality PE through Positions Sport Experiences*. Champaign, IL: Human Kinetics.

Solansky, S.T. (2008). Leadership Style and Team Processes in Self-managed Teams. *Journal of Leadership & Organizational Studies*, 14(4), 332–341. https://doi.org/10.1177/1548051808315549.

Talavera-Gonzales, C., Lacia, G.C., Dizon-Poquiz, M.L., Bulanadi, S.G. and Fernando-Callo, L. (2008). *Mapeh in Action III. Worktext in Music, Arts, Physical Education and Health for Third Year High School*. Manila: Rex Book Store.

Vroom, V.H. and Jago, A.G. (2007). The Role of the Situation in Leadership. *American Psychologist*, 62(1), 17–24. https://doi.org/10.1037/0003-066x.62.1.17.

Weinberg, R.S. and Gould, D. (2007). *Foundations of Sport and Exercise Psychology*. (4th ed.). Champaign, IL: Human Kinetics.

Yukl, G. (2013). *Leadership in Organizations*. (8th ed.). New York: Pearson.

Zanger, B.R. and Groves, D.L. (1994). Industrialization of Sport. *Visions in Leisure and Business*, 13(3), Article 5. Available at: https://scholarworks.bgsu.edu/visions/vol13/iss3/5.

Part II

SPORT LEADERSHIP IN CONTEXT

3

LEADERSHIP **IN** DIFFERENT SETTINGS

Learning Outcomes

After reading this chapter, you will be able to:

- Define the leadership differences across settings
- Define leadership similarities across settings
- Understand the nature of the leadership required across settings

INTRODUCTION

This chapter discusses the notion of leadership across three sport settings: the non-profit, for-profit, and public sectors. It gives the reader an opportunity to understand that leadership is equally important across these sport sectors. We address the similarities and differences in leadership across these settings. We use the terms 'setting' and 'sector' somewhat interchangeably, where the emphasis is towards more or less granularity.

LEADERSHIP IN PUBLIC SETTINGS

Leadership research on public organizations began as early as the 1940s. Two leading reviews on the history of public-setting leadership are Van Wart (2003) and Vogel and Masal (2015). Van Wart reviewed previous literature on this topic covering some 60 years; explained the continuing debates in the leadership literature; and compared this with the public-setting (administrative) leadership literature. A tricky point for readers new to this area – and coming from different cultural backgrounds – is determining where the boundaries of 'public' (compared with other settings) might be, and that 'administration' may mean different things: management or management support, or government and related agencies. It is with the latter sense that we use 'public' here. Vogel and Masal mapped literature on public leadership to identify emerging approaches to provide directions for future research. However, that research is beyond the scope of this book.

DOI: 10.4324/9780429290442-5

WHY PUBLIC SETTINGS NEED LEADERSHIP

Implementation of public policy is one of the enduring challenges government faces, thus several scholars confirm that leadership matters in policy effectiveness (Nettles and Herrington, 2007; Raines, 2005; Ingraham et al, 2003). The need for leadership and management of human resources is a critical need for most public organizations because the major portion of costs are for staff salaries and rewards. Responsive public organizations are often considered those that recognize that the vital element for successful and effective organizations is individuals. Thus, not only focus on job demands or organizational environment is important but also individuals' requirements. This is well illustrated by Boyatzis's (2008) framework that highlights performance. Boyatzis argues that the area of overlap or integration between one or more of the three elements – job demand, individual needs, and organizational environment – needs to be maximal for outstanding organizational performance. This might be why public organizations are rapidly recognizing that the art of leadership is the basis for grasping and responding to the requirements of their internal and external environments.

Although leadership may be perceived as one of the 'fashionable' (often intended to be uncomplimentary) and helpful ways for complicated cases in public-setting organizations, there is indeed a need, more recently and very prominently, for investing in this phenomenon in the long term to improve resources and build human and social capitals. Specifically, financial crises and economic recessions have greatly affected all forms (e.g. defined by economic sector) and all levels (macro, meso, micro: broadly speaking, large, medium, small) of economic activity, locally, internationally, multinationally, and globally. In turn, the required restructuring of political, economic, sociological, technological, legal, and environmental systems and responses (cf. PESTLE analysis as a management tool) has been the concern of most countries for limiting negative outcomes. This has created development and implementation challenges for all governments, regardless of their centralization or otherwise.

THE NATURE OF LEADERSHIP IN PUBLIC SETTINGS

We touch upon some of the misgivings associated with the absence of leadership from the public sector after the economic challenges facing most countries around the globe (e.g. financial crisis, economic recession, disease, civil war, natural disaster), which puts most governments under pressure due to existing public policy and decisions taken, or to be taken, to overcome the surrounding challenges.

Dominant models of leadership, including the charismatic model, the visionary models, and transformational models, have mainly been based on the US context. So, it is plausible to name these models 'American models of leadership' (e.g. Conger, 1989; Bass, 1985; Bennis and Nanus, 1985; House, 1976). The main aim of these models has been to change the internal environment of organizations, particularly, during crises and challenges. However, Alimo-Metcalfe and Alban-Metcalfe (2010) criticize these models because they mainly:

- cover the US context
- focus on distant leaders (i.e. hierarchically distant)
- ignore females
- ignore black populations
- ignore informal leadership positions.

Based on Alimo-Metcalfe and Alban-Metcalfe criticisms, we add three additional points. These models also mainly:

- ignore the sensitivities of the national and regional cultures, particularly non-western cultures
- ignore that the applicability of US or western-centred leadership theory is contested in many countries, and increasingly in academic discourse
- ignore the institutional system of each country and its influence on public-setting organizations.

In line with Alimo-Metcalfe and Alban-Metcalfe's argument, the academic community must question the extent to which ideas, findings, and perceptions from US models of leadership can be generalized to other contexts or even be effective in other contexts. Although such questions are not new, they remain important when examining and discussing leadership.

More generally, the OECD (2001) suggests a set of perceptions that can guide further work on leadership in public settings:

- To develop a focus on the future rather than the past
- That the majority of leaders are made, not born
- To adopt many approaches: there is no one best way because the underlying qualities and processes are essentially the same
- That leadership is needed across all levels of organizational structure and not just at the strategic level
- That leadership is mainly about building strong relationships
- To turn the focus towards results.

In addition to previous perceptions of public-setting leadership, OECD (2001) argues that the boundary of public-setting leadership is based on the following roles:

- delivering results
- challenging assumptions
- being flexible to learn from outside
- understanding the influence of the surrounding environment
- being strategic
- developing personal ideas for change
- being creative in the methods of the work.

Furthermore, to accomplish its required role effectively, public-setting leadership needs to take various requirements into consideration. For example, adopting leadership behaviours, competencies, and capabilities is connected with the requirements of the internal and external environments of each organization. However, there is no single, widely accepted model or framework that can be built on.

Yukl, in 1994 (see Yukl, 2013), proposed an integrating conceptual framework based on the assumption that determining performance for individuals, groups, or even the whole organization is connected with leader traits, behaviours, power, the influence process and tactics, and skills. But this framework was criticized by other researchers because it ignored the influence of contextual factors. For example, Heifetz's (1994) model was useful for understanding challenges surrounding leadership. Heifetz made a distinction between challenges that are adaptive, technical, and mixed.

Similarly, Grint (2005) highlighted the interaction between context and leadership and claimed that effective leaders shape the contextual elements and help constitute the context because leaders have a main role in making sense of the context. This approach proposes that leaders are fundamental to sense-making of the context. Thus, how to define a situation and how to frame it for others tend to be the cornerstone of leadership (Hartley, 2002). Furthermore, although leadership is perceived as the critical factor in determining organizational failure or success, the environmental, macro-economic, political, and business influences should be seriously considered because of their impact on organizational performance (Goodwin, 2006; Hartley, 2002). In this regard, Storey (2016) presents a public-setting leadership framework based on four factors: context, perceived leadership need, behavioural and capabilities requirements, and development methods. Storey widens the framework to include outcomes to make it an integrating framework. The author also includes unit performance and internal and external stakeholder evaluations.

Although attempts to present integrating frameworks in the literature continue, Hartley and Benington (2010) argue that the lack of satisfaction with the current frameworks is the main weakness because they fail to integrate theories of leadership. As a result, Hartley and Benington presented what is called the Warwick Six C Leadership Framework. This framework is utilized to examine six different dimensions of leadership, but it does not differ from the previous frameworks in terms of weaknesses. Specifically, Heartly and Benington's framework does not explain phenomena as theories do, and thus the major focus of this framework is on interpreting aspects of leadership.

LEADERSHIP IN FOR-PROFIT SETTINGS

Leadership in for-profit setting has been a dynamic topic in the leadership literature for the last 25 years. Leaders in for-profit settings, like their counterparts in non-profit and public settings, are sometimes promoted into action in the environments in which they already work. However, hopes of organizational survival resting on leaders' efforts in crisis situations make them a primary necessity for companies more than those in public-setting and non-profit settings. In this regard, Abou-Bakr (2013) states that the mechanisms used in public settings in some circumstances fall short during crises, and even need other for-profit actors to step in and provide support. (Although we should note that public-sector actors may need to step in and support for-profit ones.) The following sections address the nature and importance of leadership in for-profit settings and specifically sport settings.

THE NATURE OF LEADERSHIP IN FOR-PROFIT SETTINGS

Not surprisingly, the potential influences of the purpose and strategy of companies and organizations in for-profit settings on the type and role of leadership are likely to be powerful. This is especially the case of leadership because it is typically seen as a way of exerting influence (DuBrin, 2012). Overall, such debate is supported by several studies (e.g. Goldsmith et al, 2010; Baruch and Altman, 2002; Bartlett and Ghoshal, 1997). Specifically several factors, such as business type (Hayes et al, 2000; Northouse, 2021; Blake and McCanse, 1991; Vroom and Jago, 1988), size (Mabey and Finch-Lees, 2008), setting type (Brundrett, 2001; Storey et al, 1997; Avolio and Bass, 1988), and competencies required (Bolden et al, 2003), help to shape the nature of leadership in a company. These factors are discussed here.

We suggest that an understanding of the leadership required in a for-profit setting can be achieved by understanding the nature of the leadership development used in that for-profit setting. According to Mabey and Finch-Lees (2008), it has been established that there is a tendency for subsidiaries of a multinational corporation to adopt the parent company's leadership practices in macro-leadership practices, while the parent allows their subsidiaries greater autonomy in the form of local leadership and practices. It is argued that a company choosing an international strategy has impacts on the concepts of leadership practised in other locales. This is well illustrated by Adler and Ghadar (1991), who distinguished between four types of companies or organizations:

1. **Domestic**: companies or organizations with a 'home' nation and with a centralized structure
2. **International**: companies or organizations that seek to extend their product to an international market and with a centralized structure
3. **Multinational**: companies or organizations that mostly have a centralized hub, but with international affiliates that take various degrees of responsibility and autonomy
4. **Global**: companies and organizations that are mostly characterized by a mix of control from the parent (head office) and from local centres in each country.

According to this stance, business strategy is perceived as one of the fundamental characteristics of leadership in the for-profit setting. As noted in the Alder's division of companies or organizations, business strategy is related to the types of companies or organizations. Goldsmith et al (2010) argue that business leaders are responsible for formulating the type of strategy required and ensuring its effectiveness in practice. This also entails that sport leaders working globally in different business environments and cultures should not only implement change but also become flexible in today's business environment to ensure their success and effectiveness (Kreitner and Cassidy, 2012). For example, some sporting goods companies, such as Sports Direct, have branches in Europe. Such businesses require awareness of the importance of flexibility for most business and training strategies to ensure their implementation, but this does not occur without flexible business leaders to complete their required roles effectively. Similarly, sport team manager vacancies are currently becoming globally available jobs. Specifically, Hayes et al (2000) argue that different leaders working in different contexts may require developing different sets of idiosyncratic competencies to respond to the requirements of their immediate circumstances. For example, although most football managers have very varied skills as a result of working in different football leagues in Europe, working in different football leagues may require flexible leadership behaviours in context to be appropriate to the requirements of each team, league, or even country.

Company size is argued to somehow related to various aspects of organizational functioning and environmental characteristics (Kulkarni and Osicki, 2010; Camison-Zornoza et al, 2004). Company size is mostly investigated in terms of the application of human resource management practices across three types of companies: small, medium, and large, acting as a significant variable in explaining leadership practices. The nature of leadership in companies of different size is investigated by several researchers (e.g. Tell, 2012; Fuller-Love, 2006; Gray and Mabey, 2005; Wong et al, 2000). Some studies emphasize the influence of company size on the nature of leadership because the number of people contributes to shaping the concept of the leader's role and responsibilities. It was found that owners and top managers of small companies are aware of the organizational need, and this may suggest that leadership behaviour can differ because of two factors: the small number of employees and awareness of the whole company. In line with this argument, Westhead and Storey (1997) and Curran et al (1996) had earlier suggested that small companies mostly depend on informal leadership activities because this type of company prefers survival over short-term planning. Research evidence shows that small companies use more workplace innovation than those using formal management practices because leaders/managers in small companies are influenced by managerial fads – i.e. temporarily popular or promoted processes – which is not seen in large organizations (Bartram, 2005). Small companies may be unaware of or ignore how some leadership theory is being used, as it may be obscured by presentation of processes (e.g. 'top 7 things to do' approaches). This is likely caused by the difficulty of applying theories of leadership in smaller contexts, while this tends to be different for large companies because the organizational structure and large number of people make job descriptions very clear for all individuals (Megheirkouni, 2016b).

Similarly, several studies emphasize the importance of business setting type as a contextual factor influencing receptivity for different types of leadership approaches (Tamkin et al, 2006; Brundrett, 2001; Blandford and Squire, 2000; Daresh and Male, 2000; Storey et al, 1997; Avolio and Bass, 1988). The effects of organizational characteristics upon types of leadership (transformational/transactional) and power demonstrated by supervisors might illustrate the reason why leaders/managers in for-profit settings have more freedom in dealing with their subordinates than their counterparts in other settings. Research evidence reveals that for-profit settings have more reward, legitimate and coercive powers than public settings. This may give managers more space in a company to go beyond what a job demands, a company requires, or individuals need for issues such as increasing creativity and innovation.

Other studies have presented a range of different leadership models and competency frameworks currently used amongst for-profit and public-setting companies. For instance, Bolden et al (2003) found that each company in each setting has its own leadership competency framework that fits its purposes. Similar findings for setting characteristics, such as budget, structure, strategy choice, or location, were suggested by Storey et al (1997) who analysed the processes and methods used to develop leaders in eight matched companies from two different countries. Their findings revealed some differences that conform to national stereotypes. Storey and colleagues noted that the differences amongst these companies were caused by the setting in which they are located rather than their context characteristics. This may highlight the relationship between setting type and the adoption of specific behaviours and capabilities in leadership that meet the needs of each setting. Notably, although sport management literature does not contain much empirical evidence on the nature of the required leadership in sport business, sport leadership in for-profit settings is also likely to have sensitivities in terms of models, frameworks, and practices.

Arguably, the characteristics of for-profit setting shape not only the nature of leadership but may contribute to the effectiveness of the space granted to managers' freedom in the for-profit setting, if we are to compare this freedom with the non-profit and public settings. This carries for positive impacts on individuals, jobs, and organizational performance, and thus effectiveness.

WHY FOR-PROFIT SPORT SETTINGS NEED LEADERSHIP

To understand why for-profit sport organizations need leaders, we should ask what makes sport companies successful. Most for-profit companies have spent thousands – to millions – of pounds to improve their leaders' and managers' skills to provide a high-quality service to customers, to improve productivity, and thus company performance. The classical attention towards management and its development reflects the importance of this phenomenon in the business world, regardless of the business type. In line with this interest, we note today that most for-profit setting companies determine that profitability is widely affected by leadership and effective investments in future leadership programmes. Overall, the concept of leadership has been addressed in for-profit settings from different perspectives. However, although such debate is still comparatively rare in sport management literature, leadership literature contains rich data, debate, and information on leadership in for-profit settings which enable us to discuss and evaluate the importance of this phenomenon.

The importance of leadership in for-profit settings can be noted through the application of leadership development programmes. Leaders see developing leadership competencies in for-profit settings as investment rather than expense. This illustrates the essential need for professional leaders to successfully manage or lead resources which at the highest levels are valued in billions of pounds (e.g. football players, sporting goods industries). In this regard, leadership contributes to either a company's success or its failure in the business world.

LEADERSHIP IN NON-PROFIT SETTINGS

Although the non-profit sector is perceived as very rapidly growing, we cannot generalize about what the non-profit sector is, what it does, or how it does it. The types of non-profit setting organizations – sport bodies, universities, health care, and others – vary significantly in scope and scale. An example is grassroots organizations ranging from formal ones with billion-pound foundations, hundreds of employees, thousands to millions of members, and significant assets (physical or otherwise) to informal ones with no employees, no paying members, and no assets (very much ad hoc operationally speaking). This disparity has implications for the nature of (external) laws applicable and internal policies and rules adopted and implemented across these types of non-profit setting organizations.

THE NATURE OF LEADERSHIP IN NON-PROFIT SETTINGS

Different types – considering their scopes and scales, as indicated above – of non-profit setting organizations affect the needs for and of human resources in general and the leadership required in particular. The largest non-profit sport organizations have significantly larger need for leadership skills and competencies to run these organizations effectively, than the smallest, ad hoc ones. Non-profit sport organizations range from small, locally based volunteer-run clubs that have no paid employees, to medium-sized organizations with a mixture of paid staff and volunteers, to global organizations with a mix of paid staff and volunteers (e.g. international governing bodies, National and International Olympic Committees, national voluntary organizations recruiting staff and volunteers for an Olympic Games from around the globe). Notably, a dramatic change in the work of most non-profit organizations has become tangible, given the increasing trend of competitive non-profit organizations in terms of the services offered, roles, tasks, and achievements (Speckbacher, 2003).

Recent research illustrates that strategies at non-profit organizations have become more sophisticated (Brown and Iverson, 2004). In this respect, Taliento and Silverman (2005) argue that leaders in non-profit settings are more entrepreneurial because resources and employee numbers are lower than those in for-profit settings. That may be correct; but it might also be that organization structures and designs simply differ from one non-profit organization to another. For example, departments such as accounting and financial or general relationship management (and others) have an essential role in some but not all non-profit sport settings, and thus leadership roles may differ based on the presence or absence of particular departments. This, in turn, suggests that organization-dependent job descriptions determine leadership roles across non-profit sport organizations.

Arguably, leadership roles have also become more sophisticated across the non-profit sport sector. Frumkin (2002) pointed out that commercialization has an essential role in the profound cultural changes in the workforce of the non-profit/voluntary sector, as a new generation of leaders is entering these increasingly business-like organizations. Herman and Heimovics (2005: 158–159) argued that successful non-profit organizations and successful boards of directors are led by executive leadership who have skills that include:

- facilitating interaction in board relationships
- showing consideration and respect towards board members
- envisioning change and innovation for the organization with the board
- providing useful and helpful information to the board
- initiating and maintaining structure for the board
- promoting board accomplishments and productivity.

And later, Agard (2011) connected the size of non-profit organizations and the exact skills that a leader needs.

Meanwhile, Suarez (2010) outlined four different types of non-profit leaders:

- **Professional administrator**: A leader is 'low non-profit and high management'. Professional administrators have skill sets that are similar to those of social entrepreneurs but lack non-profit ethics. These leaders put business at the top of their priorities and are willing to work in other settings.
- **Social entrepreneur**: A leader is 'high non-profit and high management'. A leader approaches non-profit activity work with a focus on management and innovation, with an interest in costs and finances. A leader has a substantive knowledge but focuses mainly on business and extensive management training. A leader is dedicated to the non-profit setting but with a managerial orientation.
- **Substantive expert**: A leader is 'low non-profit and low management'. Substantive experts are individuals who have much experience or training in specific disciplinary areas, such as coaching or education, but the substantive expert tends to 'discover' management rather than seek it out.
- **Non-profit lifer**: A leader is 'high non-profit and low management'. A leader tends to view the non-profit setting as a distinctive type of organization, but with no alternative in other settings. Leaders who are non-profit lifers recognize a social problem that requires a solution, but they are less interested in management. Non-profit lifers, therefore, work their way up to the top management over time before building management expertise.

More recently, empirical research on leadership competencies in the non-profit sport setting by Megheirkouni (2017a) reveals that there are four meta-competencies not only needed for effective organizational leadership but also work best with different sport leadership positions. These meta-competencies are: understanding the whole sport organization, communication, general management relationships, and change.

Arguably, leaders need specific skills if they work within departments such as finance, human resources, marketing, and others in non-profit sport organizations that contain perhaps thousands of employees and members, with annual budgets in the millions of pounds, just as we would expect at the top of such departments in large for-profit companies. However, this leaves open questions about what skills leaders might have – or need – at the top of non-profit organizations. The skills required for managers in non-profit sport organizations may be the same as their counterparts in for-profit companies, so as to run departments such as finance, marketing department, human resources, etc.

Notably, non-profit sport settings may also deliver new community projects with volunteering schemes and receive small grants to support projects, which require not only skills but also different types of leaders, such as servant leadership (Chapter 9), as non-profit settings vary in scope and scale of community support.

WHY NON-PROFIT SPORT SETTINGS NEED LEADERSHIP

Despite the voluntary nature of non-profit setting organizations, the development of these organizations at the national and international levels increased the need for leadership to accomplish the roles required successfully. Undoubtedly, non-profit sport organizations are increasingly becoming confronted with more pressures and challenges that are similar to the ones surrounding for-profit and public sport organizations. This was evident in some writings on the similarities and differences between non-profit, public, and non-profit organizations (e.g. Sims and Quatro, 2010; Immordino, 2009; Keehley, and Abercrombie, 2008). The increase of pressures and challenges surrounding non-profit sport organizations may justify the interest in non-profit settings for sport leadership. Grint (2005) notes that the central role of leadership is to define and make sense of context. Specifically, the non-profit leadership of change is not just a matter of rational decision-making. In this sense, Pfeffer (1981: 4) claims that the importance of leaders is to provide "explanations, rationalizations and legitimations for activities undertaken in organizations". This has become evident in relation to non-profit sport organizations.

Some researchers have formulated objectives, or challenges of non-profit organizations, at a high level of abstraction. For example, Storey (2016) suggests three types of behaviours and capabilities for leadership: big picture sense-making that refers to scanning the internal and external environment of non-profit organizations, inter-organizational representation that refers to the ability to lead with influence through the ability to communicate vision and strategy with others; and delivering change refers to the ability to foster the change culture in an organization, which might be part of the central challenges for leadership in non-profit sport organizations, regardless of the size. This is perceived as a response to governmental policy directives and economic and social pressures, given the scope and scale of change in non-profit sport organizations.

Notably, leadership needs might be different based on the characteristics of one organization or even the type of setting that reflects the need for specific skills to complete the role required. Mole (2003) argues that capacity building is often setting and even organization specific, for example, a gymnastics federation has allocated one million Euros to contract with a professional coach for four years to minimize the injury average among gymnasts in championships. Specifically, mistakes or safety concerns may be remedied through the coach's intervention: so, a coach stands on the mat during release moves and dismounts to prevent gymnasts from falling off the rings, horizontal bar, or uneven parallel bars as part of a risk assessment. The capability to prevent injury may be increased by intervention, and thus the coach has an essential leadership role not only in achieving better results but also in minimizing the injury average among gymnasts.

For examples of leadership roles – established and evolving – in upper level UK sport organizations, the reader may turn to their active development programmes, board memberships, news items, job adverts, and top-level organizational development plans: the national body, UK Sport (https://www.uksport.gov.uk/), and the four regional bodies, Sport England (https://www.sportengland.org/), Sport Northern Ireland (http://www.sportni.net/), sportscotland – spòrsalba (https://sportscotland.org.uk/), and Sport Wales – Chwaraeon Cymru (https://www.sport.wales/). Note though that the funding and staffing of the regional bodies varies considerably, as does the geographical connectedness of each region.

LEADERSHIP AND SETTING REQUIREMENTS

Leadership is essential for sport organizations, regardless of the type of sport setting (Megheirkouni, 2018). Perhaps the best way to understand the nature of leadership across public, for-profit, and non-profit settings is what Cohen (2001) termed 'functional matching', meaning that the three settings are each able to serve the general population in different ways. However, although this chapter addresses why leadership is important across settings, the impact of 'setting requirements' on the form of the leadership cannot be overlooked (Megheirkouni, 2017b). Motivation, which is important for all sport organizations, is perceived differently across all settings. For example, employees working for non-profit sport organizations are motivated by the desire to serve others (see Chapter 9, 'Servant Leadership') and work–life balance, while employees at for-profit companies are more motivated by earning a living, salary (in scale), rewards, length of annual leave, promotion, and security. Similarly, employees in the public sector are more motivated by earning a living, rewards, promotion, and security. But this does not mean that all public, for-profit, and non-profit sport organizations can regularly stimulate their staff, and this increases the burdens on leaders. Bear in mind, motivational differences/similarities have implications on the type of leadership and the behaviours and capabilities required. This is because different staff or volunteers have different requirements, which in turn need different leadership behaviours and capabilities to facilitate or meet these requirements.

Let us look at setting requirements in a different way. Both the public and non-profit sectors are increasingly responding to political desires to adopt for-profit sector leadership practices as a means of increasing effectiveness and efficiency in many countries. Indeed, Mabey and Finch-Lees state that,

> the parentage of this so-called new public management (NPM) lies in the field of institutional economics with its emphasis on user choice, transparency and incentives and in the rise of business type managerialism incorporating ideas of professional management, the freedom to manage and a focus on outputs.

(2008: 189)

This indicates a direction of travel for approaches to leadership development in the public sport sector will increasingly emulate the for-profit sport sector – and we add, including the non-profit sport sector, as neoliberal trends of decentralization and privatization underpin part of the transformation of this sector. This justifies adopting leadership development methods and activities widely across settings (e.g. Megheirkouni, 2016a, b), or at least being aware that this is happening, regardless of whether one might consider it a 'good thing'.

SUMMARY

This chapter has discussed the role of leadership in three different sport settings: public, for-profit, and non-profit. This enables the reader to define leadership across settings and identify the similarities and differences in leadership between these settings. Although leadership is essential for all sport settings, the impact of 'setting requirements' on the form of the leadership must be taken into account. Each setting has its own characteristics that may need sport leaders with specific behaviours and capabilities. In addition, what works in one setting does not necessarily work in others. Therefore, sport leaders who work across settings may be able to better explain why they may find some difficulties in transferring their experience from one setting to another. In addition, how a country's institutional system shapes public, for-profit, and non-profit sport setting strategies and policies is a key reason for differences and similarities between these settings in terms of human resource management practices, sport company or organization size, and organizational structure, and thus leadership practices.

GENERAL QUESTIONS

1. What are the characteristics of leadership in public sport organizations?
2. What are the characteristics of leadership in for-profit sport organizations, regardless of their type: domestic, international, multinational, or global?
3. What are the characteristics of leadership in non-profit sport organizations at national and international levels?
4. What are the leadership similarities across public, for-profit, and non-profit sport organizations?
5. What are the leadership differences across public, for-profit, and non-profit sport organizations?
6a. How would you decide the extent to which leaders from each sport setting might be able to work in either of the other two settings? Firstly, what criteria do you consider make an effective leader in each setting?
6b. Then to extend your understanding, secondly: for each of the combinations, apply the criteria and determine your results. *Note*: A person may move in either direction between two settings, and there are three pairings of settings. Thus, there are six directionally paired combinations.

OPEN DISCUSSION QUESTIONS

TOPIC A: LEADERSHIP IN FOR-PROFIT SPORT ORGANIZATIONS

In the text, 'company' has been used for for-profit organizations. You may want to check whether you agree that 'company' as a general term is a good fit.

1. Define with your colleagues 'for-profit sport organizations'. Identify three examples of domestic, international, multinational, and global organizations.
2. Discuss reasons that make leadership so important in for-profit sport organizations. Identify three you rate as the most important. Why have you chosen these three?
3. Discuss reasons why or why not sport leaders from the other two types of organizations can work successfully at for-profit sport organizations.
4. To what extent can for-profit organization sport leaders work globally with the same effectiveness as at the national level?

TOPIC B: LEADERSHIP IN NON-PROFIT SPORT ORGANIZATIONS

1. Define with your colleagues 'non-profit sport organizations'. Identify three local, national, international, and global examples.
2. Discuss with your colleagues three reasons that make leadership important for non-profit sport organizations.
3. For what reasons do some sport leaders demonstrate ability to work effectively in different types of organizations, while others cannot?
4. Can you give an example of what you believe makes a successful leader in a non-profit sport setting and support your answer with evidence?

Case Study 3.1: Public Setting Cuts without Damaging Performance

UK Sport is one of several UK government organizations that have succeeded in cutting their administrative costs, without hitting service delivery. Research carried out by the Department for Culture, Media and Sport to understand the operating costs of distributing funding revealed that UK Sport was the most efficient of all the statutory funders appraised. Specifically, it is noted that only four administration staff at UK Sport are required to handle 1500 customers, while previously 20 administration staff had struggled to handle 350 customers.

What is the secret behind this success?

Sharing the leadership role was the common behaviour in this process within a 'bottom up' system. This was evident through the use of a 'system thinking' approach, acting as a means to optimize how business processes operate, working together with suppliers, and for the benefit of the customers, based on the management philosophy of Edwards Deming. Moreover, improving services by empowering people or evaluating what they do was a result of adopting a new type of technology that relies on automating routine tasks. These were positively reflected in performance.

Questions

1. How did UK Sport exceed the challenge of cutting their administrative costs without influencing service delivery?
2. What changes were made to maintain performance?

Source: Adapted from Chassels, D. *The Guardian*. [online]. November 2, 2012. Full text available at: https://www.theguardian.com/public-leaders-network/2012/nov/02/uk-sport-public-sector-admin-costs

Note: The in-source link for Edwards Deming no longer exists. If you're interested, use this instead: https://deming.org/explore/fourteen-points/.

Case Study 3.2: Working across Sport Settings

Use the three 'statements' covering people in leadership in the public, for-profit, and non-profit sport sectors to support your answers to the questions beneath them.

Statement 1: John is a retired chief executive who spent 35 years in the for-profit sector. John has recently signed a 12-month contract with one of the sport federations in the Middle East as a chief executive. John believes he can transfer his leadership experience and knowledge in the sporting goods industry to his new non-profit sport organization setting. He says, "All sport organizations have their own strategy, vision, organizational structure, HR, culture…, but what I did not know was that the government takes a part in leadership decisions here, as it is the only sponsor of non-profit sport organizations".

Statement 2: Sali and George are former marketing assistant managers in the for-profit sport sector. They have worked in several sport companies and groups around the world, such as Sports Direct, Sky Sport, Adidas, Reebok, and Red Bull. Sali has recently moved to a non-profit sport setting and is currently working as a business development advisor at one of the European football associations. Sali is doing well and has not felt any difference between her previous work in marketing in the for-profit sport company and this current role at the non-profit sport organization. Similarly, George has found a new role in a non-profit sport organization. He is currently working as a marketing consultant at the Olympic Council of Asia. However, George has found significant differences between the work in for-profit and non-profit sport settings. Indeed, he feels his current task has not changed very much from previous roles in the for-profit sport sector since 1997. He said, "I am fully conscious that I have not perfectly adapted myself to existing conditions".

Statement 3: In 2001, Chris Grant (OBE) co-founded 14A, which offers management consultancy. Because of his good background in organizational development and group dynamics, his roles and responsibilities have covered chairing boards in some businesses such as the UK Chip and PIN programme as well as designing and delivering interventions for many organizations and companies, including the BBC and Renault UK. He has also been CEO of Sported, a charity using sport leisure and activities for community development to improving the lives of young people. Chris has also occupied several managerial positions in the nonprofit sport sector as a volunteer, such as deputy chair of International Inspiration, a lead facilitator on UK Sport's elite coach programme, and a board member in the Youth Sport Trust. He has been on the Sport England Board and has served as the chair of judges of the BT Sport Industry Awards. He is now Chair of the British Basketball Federation.

Questions

1. What are the similarities between the above cases? Explain, why?
2. What are the differences between the above cases? Explain, why?
3. How might you illustrate that CEOs or managers with different experiences and skills in one setting achieve the same outcomes in other sport settings?
4. How might you illustrate that CEOs or managers with similar experiences and skills in one setting achieve different outcomes in other sport settings?
5. Do you think that the environment in which a sport organization operates can affect its CEO's or managers' success? Why?
6. Can you give examples of CEOs or managers who are successful working in different sport settings?

Source: Based on (statements 1 and 2) fictionalized, real-world stories and (statement 3) 14A (n.d.) 'Chris Grant'. 14aconversations.com. [Online]. Available at: https://www.14aconversations.com/chris-grant; Basketball England. (n.d.) 'Chris Grant OBE appointed as Chair of the British Basketball Federation'. Basketball England. [online]. Available at: https://www.basketballengland.co.uk/news/2022/chris-grant-obe-appointed-as-chair-of-the-british-basketball-federation/; and tshego. (2017). 'Chris Grant: View from the Chair'. Sport Industry Group. [online]. 08 October 2017. Available at: https://www.sportindustry.biz/news-categories/features/chris-grant-view-chair/.

Suggested Reading

Beech, J. and Chadwick, S. (Eds.). (2013). *The Business of Sport Management*. (2nd ed.). Harlow: Pearson Education.

Laine, A. and Vehmas, H. (Eds.). (2017). *The Private Sport Sector in Europe*. London: Springer International. https://doi.org/10.1007/978-3-319-61310-9.

Megheirkouni, M. (2017). Leadership Styles and Organizational Learning in UK For-Profit and Non-Profit Sports Organizations. *International Journal of Organizational Analysis*, 25(4), 596–612. https://doi.org/10.1108/IJOA-07-2016-1042.

Megheirkouni, M. (2018). Insights on Practicing of Servant Leadership in the Events Sector. *Sport, Business and Management*, 8(2), 134–152. https://doi.org/10.1108/SBM-01-2017-0001.

O'Reilly, N. and Brunette, M.K. (2013). *Public-Private Partnerships in Physical Activity and Sport*. Leeds: Human Kinetics.

Robinson, L. (2003). *Managing Public Sport and Leisure Services*. London: Routledge. https://doi.org/10.4324/9780203646557.

Robinson, L. and Palmer, D. (Eds.). (2010). *Managing Voluntary Sport Organizations*. London: Routledge. https://doi.org/10.4324/9780203881354.

Watt, D.C. (2003). *Sports Management and Administration*. (2nd ed.). London: Psychology Press.

References

Abou-Bakr, A. (2013). *Managing Disasters through Public–Private Partnerships*. Washington, DC: Georgetown University Press. JSTOR: https://www.jstor.org/stable/j.ctt4cg8rg.

Adler, N. and Ghadar, F. (1990). Strategic Human Resource Management: A Global Perspective. In: Pieper, R. (Ed.). *Human Resource Management: An International Comparison*. Boston, MA: De Gruyter. (235–260). https://doi.org/10.1515/9783110869101.235.

Agard, K.A. (Ed.). (2011). *Leadership in Nonprofit Organizations: A Reference Handbook* (2 Vols.). Sage. https://doi.org/10.4135/9781412979320.

Alimo-Metcalfe, B. and Alban-Metcalfe, J. (2010). Leadership in Public Sector Organisations. In: Storey, J. (Ed). (2016). *Leadership in Organizations: Current Issues and Key Trends*. (2nd ed.). London: Routledge. (173–202).

Avolio, B.J. and Bass, B.M. (1988). Transformational Leadership, Charisma, and Beyond. In: Hunt, J.G., Baliga, B.R., Dachler, H.P. and Schriesheim, C.A. (Eds.). (1988). *Emerging Leadership Vistas*. Lexington, MA: Lexington Books. (29–50).

Bartlett, C.A. and Ghoshal, S. (1997). The Myth of the Generic Manager: New Personal Competencies for New Management Roles. *California Management Review*, 40(1), 92–104. https://doi.org/10.2307/41165924.

Bartram, T. (2005). Small Companies, Big Ideas: The Adoption of Human Resource Management in Australian Small Firms. *Asia Practice Journal of Human Resources*, 43(1), 137–154. https://doi.org/10.1177/1038411105050311.

Baruch, Y. and Altman, Y. (2002). Expatriation and Repatriation in MNCs: A Taxonomy. *Human Resource Management*, 41(2), 239–59. https://doi.org/10.1002/hrm.10034.

Bass, B.M. (1985). *Leadership and Performance beyond Expectations*. New York: Free Press.

Bennis, W.G. and Nanus, B. (1985). *Leaders: The Strategies for Taking Charge*. New York: Harper and Row.

Blake, R.R. and McCanse, A.A. (1991). *Leadership Dilemmas: Grid Solutions*. Houston, TX: Gulf Publishing.

Blandford, S. and Squire, L. (2000). An Evaluation of the Teacher Training Agency Head-teacher Leadership and Management Programme (HEADLAMP). *Educational Management & Administration*, 28(1), 21–32.

Bolden, R., Gosling, J., Marturano, A. and Dennison, P. (2003). *A Review of Leadership Theory and Competency Frameworks*. Technical Report. Centre for Leadership Studies, University of Exeter. Available at: https://ore.exeter.ac.uk/repository/handle/10036/17494.

Boyatzis, R.E. (2008). Competencies in the 21st Century. *Journal of Management Development*, 27(1), 5–12. https://doi.org/10.1108/02621710810840730.

Brown, W.A. and Iverson, J.O. (2004). Exploring Strategy and Board Structure in Nonprofit Organizations. *Nonprofit and Voluntary Sector Quarterly*, 33(3), 377–400. https://doi.org/10.1177/0899764004265428.

Brundrett, M. (2001). The Development of School Leadership Preparation Programmes in England and the USA: A Comparative Analysis. *Educational Management and Administration*, 29(2), 229–245. https://doi.org/10.1177/0263211X010292007.

Camison-Zornoza, C., Lapiedra-Alcami, R., Segarra-Cipres, M. and Boronat-Navarro, M. (2004). A Meta-Analysis of Innovation and Organizational Size. *Organization Studies*, 25(3), 331–361. https://doi.org/10.1177/0170840604040039.

Cohen, S.D. (2001). A Strategic Framework for Devolving Responsibility and Functions from Government to the Private Sector. *Public Administration Review*, 61(4), 432–440.

Conger, J.A. (1989). *The Charismatic Leader: Behind the Mystique of Exceptional Leadership*. San Francisco, CA: Jossey-Bass.

Curran, J., Blackburn, R., Kitching, J. and North, J. (1996). *Establishing Small Firms' Training Practices, Needs, Difficulties and Use of Industry Training Organisations*. Project Report. DfEE Research Studies 17. London: HMSO. Available at: https://eprints.kingston.ac.uk/id/eprint/3884.

Daresh, J. and Male, T. (2000). Crossing the Border into Leadership: Experience of Newly Appointed British Head Teachers and American Principals. *Educational Management Administration Leadership*, 28(1), 89–101. https://doi.org/10.1177/0263211X000281013.

DuBrin, A.J. (2012). *Leadership: Research Findings, Practice, and Skills.* (7th ed.). Mason, OH: Cengage Learning.

Frumkin, P. (2002). *On Being Non-Profit: A Conceptual and Policy Primer*. Cambridge, MA: Harvard University Press.

Fuller-Love, N. (2006). Management Development in Small Companies. *International Journal of Management Reviews*, 8(3), 175–190. https://doi.org/10.1111/j.1468-2370.2006.00125.x.

Goldsmith, M., Baldoni, J. and McArthur, S. (2010). *The AMA Handbook of Leadership*. New York: American Management Association. JSTOR: https://www.jstor.org/stable/j.ctt1d2dq3q.

Goodwin, N. (2006). *Leadership in Health Care: A European Perspective*. London: Routledge.

Gray, C. and Mabey, C. (2005). Management Development: Key Differences between Small and Large Business in Europe. *International Small Business Journal*, 23(5), 467–485. https://doi.org/10.1177/0266242605055908.

Grint, K. (2005). Problems, Problems, Problems: The Social Construction of 'Leadership'. *Human Relations*, 58(11), 1467–1494. https://doi.org/10.1177/0018726705061314.

Hartley, J. (2002). Leading Communities: Capabilities and Cultures. *Leadership and Organizational Development Journal*, 23(8), 419–429. https://doi.org/10.1108/01437730210449311.

Hartley, J. and Benington, J. (2010). *Leadership for Healthcare*. Bristol: The Policy Press.

Hayes, J., Rose-Quirie, A. and Allinson, C.W. (2000). Senior Managers' Perceptions of the Competencies They Require for Effective Performance: Implications for Training and Development. *Personnel Review*, 29(1), 92–105. https://doi.org/10.1108/00483480010295835.

Heifetz, R.A. (1994). *Leadership Without Easy Answers*. Cambridge, MA: Harvard University Press.

Herman, R.D. and Heimovics, D. (2005). Executive Leadership. In: Herman, R.D. (Ed.). *The Jossey-Bass Handbook of Nonprofit Leadership and Management*. (2nd ed.). San Francisco, CA: Jossey-Bass, 153–170.

House, R.J. (1976). A 1976 Theory of Charismatic Leadership. In: Hunt, J.G. and Larson, L.L. (Eds.). (1977). *Leadership: The Cutting Edge*. Carbondale: Southern Illinois University Press, 189–207. ERIC: https://eric.ed.gov/?id=ED133827.

Immordino, K.M. (2009). *Organizational Assessment and Improvement in the Public Sector*. New York: CRC Press.

Ingraham, P.W., Joyce, P.G. and Donahue, A.K. (2003). *Government Performance: Why Management Matters*. Baltimore, MD: Johns Hopkins University Press.

Keehley, P. and Abercrombie, N.N. (2008). *Benchmarking in the Public and Nonprofit Sectors: Best Practices for Achieving Performance Breakthroughs*. (2nd edn.). San Francisco, CA: John Wiley and Sons.

Kreitner, R. and Cassidy, C. (2012). *Management*. (12th ed.). Mason, OH: South-Western, Cengage Learning.

Kulkarni, M. and Osicki, M. (2010). Recruitment in a Global Workplace. In: Lundby, K. and Jolton, J. (Eds.). *Going Global: Practical Applications and Recommendations for HR and OD Professionals in the Global Workplace*. London: John Wiley and Sons. (111–142).

Mabey, C. and Finch-Lees, T.F. (2008). *Management and Leadership Development*. London: Sage.

Megheirkouni, M. (2016a). Leadership Behaviours and Capabilities in Syria: An Exploratory Qualitative Approach. *Journal of Management Development*, 35(5), 636–662. https://doi.org/10.1108/JMD-02-2015-0022.

Megheirkouni, M. (2016b). Leadership Development Methods and Activities: Content, Purposes, and Implementation. *Journal of Management Development*, 35(2), 237–260. https://doi.org/10.1108/JMD-09-2015-0125.

Megheirkouni, M. (2017a). Leadership Competencies: Qualitative Insight into Non-Profit Sport Organisations. *International Journal of Public Leadership*, 13(3), 166–181. https://doi.org/10.1108/IJPL-11-2016-0047.

Megheirkouni, M. (2017b). Leadership Styles and Organizational Learning in UK For-Profit and Non-Profit Sports Organizations. *International Journal of Organizational Analysis*, 25(4), 596–612. https://doi.org/10.1108/IJOA-07-2016-1042.

Megheirkouni, M. (2018). Self-Leadership Strategies and Career Success: Insight on Sport Organizations. *Sport, Business and Management: An International Journal*, 8(4), 393–409. https://doi.org/10.1108/sbm-02-2018-0006.

Mole, G. (2003). Can Leadership Be Taught? In: Storey, J. (Ed.). *Leadership in Organizations: Current Issues and Key Trends*. London: Psychology Press. (127–139).

Nettles, S.M. and Herrington, C. (2007). Revisiting the Importance of the Direct Effects of School Leadership on Student Achievement: The Implications for School Improvement Policy. *Peabody Journal of Education*, 82(4), 724–736. https://doi.org/10.1080/01619560701603239.

Northouse, P.G. (2021). *Leadership: Theory and Practice*. (9th ed.). London: Sage.

OECD. (2001). *Public Sector Leadership for the 21st Century*. Paris: OECD Publishing. https://doi.org/10.1787/9789264195035-en.

Pfeffer, J. (1981). Management as Symbolic Action: The Creation and Maintenance of Organizational Paradigms. *Research in Organizational Behaviour*, 3(1), 1–52.

Raines, S.S. and Prakash, A. (2000). Leadership Matters: Policy Entrepreneurship in Corporate Environmental Policy Making. *Administration and Society*, 37(1), 1–22. https://doi.org/10.1177/0095399704272594.

Sims, R.R. and Quatro, S.A. (Eds.). (2015). *Leadership: Succeeding in the Private, Public, and Not-for-Profit Sectors*. London: Routledge. https://doi.org/10.4324/9781315702919.

Speckbacher, G. (2003). The Economics of Performance Management in Nonprofit Organizations. *Nonprofit Management and Leadership*, 13(3), 267–81. https://doi.org/10.1002/nml.15.

Storey, J. (2016). Changing Theories of Leadership and Leadership Development. In: Storey, J. (Ed.). (2016). *Leadership in Organizations: Current Issues and Key Trends*. (3rd ed.). Abingdon: Routledge. (17–42). https://doi.org/10.4324/9781315695792.

Storey, J., Edwards, P. and Sisson, K. (1997). *Managers in the Making: Careers, Development and Control in Corporate Britain and Japan*. London: Sage. https://doi.org/10.4135/9781446280249.

Suarez, D.F. (2010). Street Credentials and Management Backgrounds: Careers of Non-Profit Executives in an Evolving Sector. *Non-Profit and Voluntary Sector Quarterly*, 39(4), 696–716. https://doi.org/10.1177/0899764009350370.

Taliento, L. and Silverman, L. (2005). A Corporate Executive's Short Guide to Leading Nonprofits. *Strategy & Leadership*, 33(2), 5–10.

Tamkin, P., Mabey, C. and Beech, D. (2006). *The Comparative Capability of UK Managers*. Skills for Business Research Report 17. Brighton: Institute of Employment Studies. Available at: https://www.employment-studies.co.uk/resource/comparative-capability-uk-managers.

Tell, J. (2012). Managerial Strategies in Small, Fast-Growing Manufacturing Companies. *Journal of Management Development*, 31(7), 700–710. https://doi.org/10.1108/02621711211243890.

Van Wart, M. (2003). Public-Sector Leadership Theory: An Assessment. *Public Administration Review*, 63(2), 214–228. https://doi.org/10.1111/1540-6210.00281.

Vogel, R. and Masal, D. (2015). Public Leadership: A Review of the Literature and Framework for Future Research. *Public Management Review*, 17(8), 1165–1189. https://doi.org/10.1080/14719037.2014.895031.

Vroom, V.H. and Jago, A.G. (1988). *The New Leadership: Managing Participation in Organizations*. Englewood Cliffs, NJ: Prentice-Hall.

Westhead, P. and Storey, D.J. (1997). *Training Provision and Development of Small and Medium-Sized Enterprises*. Research Report No. 26. London: DFEE Publications. ERIC: https://eric.ed.gov/?id=ED419936.

Wong, C., Marshall, J.N., Alderman, N. and Thwaites, A. (2000). Management Training in Small and Medium-Sized Enterprises: Methodological and Conceptual Issues. *The International Journal of Human Resource Management*, 8(1), 44–65. https://doi.org/10.1080/09585199700000040.

Yukl, G. (2013). *Leadership in Organizations*. (8th ed.). New York: Pearson.

Part III

LEADERSHIP THEORIES AND APPROACHES

4 TRAIT THEORIES

Learning Outcomes

After reading this chapter, you will be able to:

- Define the trait theories of leadership
- Identify the weaknesses of trait theories
- Identify the strengths of trait theories
- Draw concepts around trait theories through using examples from different sport settings
- Evaluate the application of trait theories in sport settings

INTRODUCTION

Trait theory was popularized after World War II. It was preceded by what was called the genetic theory of leadership, which was utilized for interpreting historical events. For instance, a son of a king rises to the throne after his father's death because it was believed that leadership was genetically transferred from the king to the son; in pre-gene-science times this would have been described as 'heredity'. The genetic theory was (or appeared) successful for explaining how leadership is inherited from parents, but specifically the father. However, this theory failed to explain why some individuals rose to some power and leadership positions after the era of industrial revolution. In turn, trait theory focused on the universal traits of leaders. In other words, trait theory emphasized that leaders possess exceptional qualities and implies that leaders are born rather than made (Bernard, 1926). This theory attempts to explain leadership through some set of personality characteristics accompanied with success. Accordingly, this suggests that if leaders possess superior qualities that differentiate them from their followers, it may be possible to identify such qualities (Bass and Stogdill, 1990). The bulk of leadership traits research attempted to establish are the personal characteristics of leaders which distinguish them from followers. This was the era of the so-called 'great man' theory (Van Seters and Field, 1990). However, it may be argued that distinguishing leaders and non-leaders tends to be limited in most research done on leadership in organizations. It is noted that although some studies have examined this, most such studies often fail to provide a clear picture of what distinguishes leaders from non-leaders.

DOI: 10.4324/9780429290442-7

TRAIT THEORY

The search for distinguishing traits has led to numerous studies that considered the following to be the common characteristics of leaders: physical characteristics, intelligence and ability, personality, task-related characteristics, social characteristics, and social background (cf. Bass and Stogdill, 1990). In 1948, Stogdill examined more than 124 studies based on the trait approach. In this analysis, he identified a set of leadership traits that help understand how individuals become leaders, including general intelligence, responsibility, insight, self-confidence, sociability, alertness, initiative, and persistence. However, he reported that traits which leaders do have must vary according to the organizational situation. Another survey of 163 traits studies was conducted by Stogdill between 1948 and 1970, who identified several traits found in the first survey, along with an additional set of traits, including tolerance, independence, and aggressiveness. The second survey was clearer and revealed that personality and contextual factors were the two major determinants of leadership.

Another review conducted by Kirkpatrick and Locke reported a set of traits that distinguish leaders from followers. Their literature review suggested a set of traits characteristics, some of which were also reported by Stogdill, including drive, motivation, honesty, integrity, ambition, self-confidence, which they called the 'right stuff' concept (see Kirkpatrick and Locke., 1991: 49). The findings of their study suggested that leaders do need to have this 'right stuff', and they reported that the traits of drive, motivation, honesty, integrity, ambition, self-confidence were present in leaders regardless of their demographic characteristics (e.g. gender, ethnicity, race, age). Arguably, leadership literature about trait theories has reported a wide set of traits. For example, Figure 4.1 presents some of the traits and their respective clusters that were uncovered by traits research over the last five decades. However, some of these traits are considered more important and central to the above list of traits, including self-confidence, intelligence, and sociality.

SELF-CONFIDENCE

Self-confidence is about having a positive attitude about one's competencies and skills. This trait is related to self-efficacy, which refers to the "belief in one's capabilities to organize and execute the courses of action required to produce given attainments" (Bandura, 1997: 3). Leaders displaying certainty in their ability to complete the roles required reinforce confidence among their followers and create commitment between followers and leaders (e.g. Kouzes and Posner, 1993). Although self-confidence is not a substitute for sport training, athletes with this trait can deploy their existing skills for achieving the goal required (Feltz, 1988).

José Mourinho is a good example of a self-confident leader. After Chelsea won the Premier League title in 2005, Mourinho's management was considered second to none, and this was evident in his self-confidence, which was reflected back onto his teams through his charisma. In this regard, player Frank Lampard (Press Association, 2013) said,

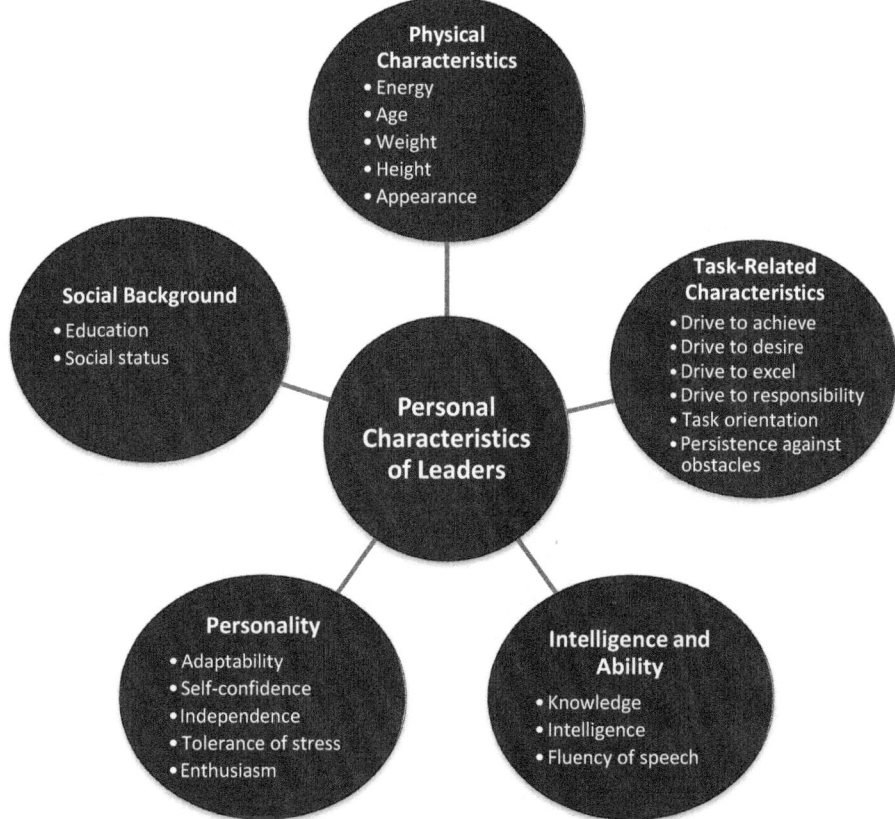

Figure 4.1 Personal characteristics of leaders.
Source: Adapted from Bass, B. (1990). *Bass and Stogdill's Handbook of Leadership: Theory, Research, and Management Applications*. (3rd ed.). New York: Simon and Schuster, 1990. (80–81); and Kirkpatrick, S.A. and Locke, E.A. (1991). Leadership: Do Traits Matter? *Academy of Management Perspectives*, 5(2), 48–60.

He might rub people up the wrong way. [But] as a manager, he's brilliant with his team, tactically, he's brilliant with individuals and I think he's brilliant with the press. I know it creates a storm, but he does protect his players.

SOCIABILITY

Sociability is another important trait for leaders. Sociability refers to a leader's preference to seek out social relationships (Stogdill, 1974). This trait includes such characteristics as being outgoing, friendly, tactful, and diplomatic. This means that social leaders create a cooperative relationship with others, and this is why sociability is linked to transformational leadership (cf. Bass and Riggio, 2005), discussed in Chapter 8. One good example of this trait in sport is Jacques Rogge who, at the 2002 Winter Olympics in Salt Lake City, became the first International Olympic Committee president to stay in the Olympic Village rather than in a hotel for closer contact with the athletes and to be available for their needs.

INTELLIGENCE

Intelligence refers to the cognitive ability to think critically and is linked to job performance, acting as the best predictor (Le et al, 2007). According to their analysis, Lord, Foti, and De Vader (1984) found that intelligence was the only trait that is perceived as a critical trait all leaders must have. This is reinforced by studies that link between intelligence and the traits of effective leaders (House and Aditya, 1997). This brings us to the question of what makes an athlete a champion. No doubt, such factors as training (Bompa, 2000), motivation (Hemery, 1986), tactics (Jobson et al, 1990), a diet plan (Kleiner and Greenwood-Robinson, 2013), and psychological success factors represented by the issues of high level commitment, short- and long-term purposes, level of focus, and pre- and in-competition strategies (Orlick and Partington, 1998), all tend to be essential; but intelligent managers or leaders seem to be the core for international sport competitions in the short and long terms (e.g. Thomas et al, 1986). This trait, therefore, is a vital trait for sport managers and leaders who drive their team and organization to be successful at the national and international sport champions.

THE BIG FIVE MODEL OF PERSONALITY

Earlier attempts to understand our personality traits have led to significant progress in the field of leadership literature, thus identifying five unique factors to help understand our personality. These factors combine to make the Big Five model of personality, namely: neuroticism, extraversion, openness, agreeableness, and conscientiousness. See Table 4.1 for details.

Table 4.1 The Big Five Model of Personality

Factor	*Includes traits such as…*
Neuroticism	anxious, depressed, calm, emotional instability vs relaxed, and insecure
Extraversion	friendly, outgoing, enthusiastic, shy, serious, sociable, and assertive
Openness	creative, informed, and curious
Agreeableness	trusting, flexible, accepting, open to non-traditional values vs conforming
Conscientiousness	reliable, dependable, organized, controlled, lax, careless, and responsible

Source: Adapted from Costa and McCrae (1992, 2008); McCrae and Costa (1996); Goldberg (1993).

Judge et al (2002) tested how the Big Five factors provided the base for leadership traits. They utilized the PsychInfo database between 1887 and 1999, for information on leadership and personality. Their investigation included information on personality, neuroticism, agreeableness, conscientiousness, extroversion, and openness. The reliability of personality factors illustrates that different leadership traits and each of the five personality factors were correlated. Judge et al (2002: 773–774) summarize these factors as follows:

- *Extraversion* emerged as the most consistent correlate of leadership. Not only was it the strongest correlate of leadership in the combined analysis, but it also displayed a non-zero effect in all analyses.
- *Conscientiousness and Openness* were the strongest and most consistent correlates of leadership. Conscientiousness displayed the second strongest correlation with leadership, and it was, in the multivariate analysis (by using N-weighted correlations), the strongest predictor of leadership in two of the three regressions. Conscientiousness was more strongly related to leader emergence than to leadership effectiveness; the organizing activities of conscientious individuals (e.g. note taking, facilitating processes) may allow such individuals to quickly emerge as leaders.
- *Openness* is the most controversial and least understood correlate. One of the problems is that, with a few exceptions, such as creativity and sociopolitical attitudes, openness has not been related to many applied criteria. Openness to experience does appear to be related to leadership. In business settings, it, along with extraversion, was the strongest dispositional correlate of leadership.
- *Agreeableness* was the least relevant correlate of leadership. However, this overall result is masked somewhat by differences in criteria and settings. For agreeableness, Judge and colleagues suggested two situations in which agreeableness was related to leadership. The first appeared when the criterion was effectiveness. The second was with student samples. Because agreeable individuals tend to be passive and compliant, it makes sense that they would be less likely to emerge as leaders. This was found to be particularly true in studies (business, government, or military disciplines) where the nature of agreeable individuals may be most likely to show itself.
- *Neuroticism* was the weakest correlate and was the most negatively related to leaders' emergence and leadership effectiveness.

In general, the findings revealed that there is a strong relationship between the five factors and leadership. In other words, these findings support the belief that effective leaders seem to have personality traits accompanied with their effectiveness (Northouse, 2021; Silverthorne, 2001). The Big Five factors are useful in predicting many behaviours in the sport management discipline, including how well managers and leaders in all positions behave in sport mega events, and international and national sport as champions and in competitions. Although research in the literature of the sport management and leadership discipline is still small, learning from other experience and utilizing research from other research disciplines seem to be useful in understanding the differences and similarities.

EMOTIONAL INTELLIGENCE

The concept of emotional intelligence has been utilized for assessing the impact of traits on leadership. In fact, it is difficult to define emotional intelligence precisely, but one of the common descriptions is the ability to perceive emotions; to access and generate emotions so as to assist thought; to understand emotions and emotional knowledge; and to reflectively regulate emotions so as to promote emotional and intellectual growth (Mayer and Salovey, 1997).

Some researchers suggest five major characteristics to define emotional intelligence:

1. knowing our own emotions
2. managing our own emotions
3. motivating ourselves
4. recognizing others' emotions
5. helping others to handle their emotions.

It is noted that the available literature on the concept of emotional intelligence has included several debates over measurement approaches. Though there are several ways to do so, three tend to be most widely adopted in leadership literature. The first approach is the ability model developed by Peter Salovey and John Mayer and focuses on the individual's abilities to process emotion status and utilize it in controlling the social environment. For example, the Mayer–Salovey–Caruso Emotional Intelligence test (MSCEIT) measures EI as a set of mental abilities (Mayer et al, 2000).

A second approach is the trait model developed by Konstantin Petrides and Adrian Furnham that involves self-description. This test asks questions that help assess particular statements relevant to our abilities (Petrides and Furnham, 2001). This approach is similar to the traditional personality test and measures emotional self-awareness in a test called the EQ-i through "I'm in touch with my emotions". It should be noted that this approach has been criticized as to whether we can reliably self-report our own emotional self-awareness.

Finally, a third approach is the mixed model, which reflects a combination of abilities and trait emotional intelligence. For example, Goleman (2020, 1998) suggests that an integrated concept of emotional, social, and cognitive intelligence offers more than a convenient framework for describing human dispositions. It is seen as a theoretical structure for the organization of personality and linking it to a theory of action and job performance. These three clusters of competencies form the basis for differentiating outstanding from average performers in different contexts (e.g. Megheirkouni, 2017; Boyatzis, 2008, 1982; Spencer and Spencer, 1993; Goleman et al, 2002; Goleman, 1998; Luthans et al, 1988; Kotter, 1982), namely:

1. **Cognitive competencies**: which include systems thinking and pattern recognition.
2. **Emotional intelligence competencies**: which include self-awareness; and self-management competencies, such as emotional self-awareness and emotional self-control.
3. **Social intelligence competencies**: which include social awareness and relationship management competencies, such as empathy and teamwork.

EVALUATION OF TRAIT THEORIES

These theories are characterized by strengths as they give us an assessment of whether the traits we have (and understand) are the best traits for effective leadership. Contradictory research findings on trait theory have formed the scientific basis that points to the important role of these theories in most topics related to the concept of leadership. This theorical approach can be called the parent of the concept of leadership in the 21st century.

Trait theories were criticized for several weaknesses. For instance, they fail to delimit a specific set of leadership traits. Importantly, although some studies have made efforts over the last century, all attempts have been ambiguous. Additionally, the interest in this area by different researchers has provided many trait lists, which entails the possibility that such lists may become endless, and makes the matter more complicated, rather than complex and nuanced, as most research attempts to provide a trait list rather investigating these traits. Another weakness of these theories is that they fail to address contextual variables. Stogdill (1948) points out that each individual and each situation have to be considered separately to better understand both leaders and leadership. In other words, leaders who possess a set of traits that qualify them to be leaders in one situation, culture, setting, or country, may not be suitable in another. This, consequently, may explain why cross-cultural leadership studies have failed to generalize or even suggest a global set of leadership traits without taking contextual factors into account. An additional weakness of these theories is that they confine themselves to men, because it was highly unusual for a female to be a leader even if she had exceptional traits to enable her to be a leader. This is mostly evident in some cultures that are characterized by their high power distance, such as in the Arab world.

TRAIT THEORIES AND SPORT LEADERSHIP RESEARCH

After reviewing and discussing trait theories of leadership, it should be noted that although the personality traits of leadership stem from the earliest leadership debates, contemporary leadership research still relies on the role of personality and traits in the demonstration of leadership in general and sport leadership in particular. Although the trait approach in sport management is still weak in comparison to many research disciplines, such as healthcare education, learning from these disciplines and other fields is necessary. According to Soucie (1994), most leadership research in sport contexts was in coaching and most of the leadership and management studies in sport organizations outside coaching were doctoral theses published between 1969 and 1989. Additionally, Scott (2014) states that most empirical leadership studies in sport contexts since the mid-1990s examine middle and top sport leadership positions, but the predominant leadership studies in the last several years are still within the US intercollegiate athlete setting.

We now move on to review the findings of traits research in sport contexts to classify the predominant literature on trait theories in sport. In this regard, Branch (1990) examines athletic director and selected assistant perceptions of leader behaviour to determine whether their perceptions contributed significantly to the prediction of intercollegiate organizational effectiveness. The findings indicate that there is a strong connection between effective athletic organizations and leaders who are more predisposed to goal and task accomplishment than developing good interpersonal relationships with their subordinates. Another area of research emanating from the personality traits research on leadership attempts to identify leadership competencies and abilities for sport managers and leaders. Some researchers go further to identify specific competencies and characteristics that best work with sport managers and leaders. For example, some studies emphasize that sport managers and leaders need technical skills for using equipment related to sport activities and organizational tasks; human skills including the ability to communicate, social relationship skills; cognitive skills including strategic thinking, risk management, and problem solving; personal skills including assertiveness, negotiation, and perception; and conjoined skills including the ability to balance between the needs of technical, personal, and human skills towards the goal required (Zeigler and Bowie, 1983).

In line with this discussion, some studies address the importance of traits and personality characteristics for effective sport leadership. For example, some researchers explore the relationship between emotional intelligence and sport leadership (Chan and Mallett, 2009); the influence of self-confidence and anxiety on the behaviour of sport managers (Kenow and Williams, 1992), and the ability of sport manager to enhance the possibilities for sociability so as to encourage people to attend sport matches (Melnick, 1993); while others go further to identify models and frameworks of traits and personality competencies. It should be noted that although there are many studies that suggest some personality traits in the area of sport management (e.g. Chan and Mallett, 2011; Glenn and Horn, 1993; Smoll and Smith, 1989) and the area of leadership (e.g. Goleman, 1998; Boyatzis, 1982), there is no agreement in the literature on a specific personality trait framework or model that can be generalized to other settings, contexts, or cultures.

Overall, it can be concluded that adopting and generalizing specific personality traits to all sport leaders at all leadership positions seem to be ineffective. According to Cox (2011), some sport cases demonstrate that leaders are more effective with particular personalities than others. This, accordingly, confirms the need for further research on the quality of traits and personality competencies of leaders in different sports, contexts, or cultures. This would help in understanding how and why specific personality traits work better in specific sports, contexts, or cultures than others.

EVALUATION

Overall, this chapter highlights the weaknesses and strengths of trait theories of leadership. In term of strengths of trait theory, it is noted that it gives leaders a sign of whether the traits they do have are suitable traits for leadership or not. In addition, contradictory 20th-century research on leadership trait theory have established the basis of most topics on the characteristics of leadership. On the other hand, these theories have been criticized because they lack a defined set of leadership traits. Moreover, they fail to address the contextual variables, because each individual and each situation has to be considered separately to better understand both leaders and leadership. Lastly, it is often linked to men rather than women, because women who have leadership roles may be culturally expected to exhibit masculine traits to be effective leaders.

SUMMARY

This chapter highlights the importance of trait theory, deriving initially from hereditary acquisition. This gave researchers the opportunity to search for identifying traits that distinguish leaders from non-leaders from the 1920s, although leading to varying sets of traits. However, some traits were or are considered central, like intelligence, sociability, and self-confidence. Additionally, a usable relationship between effective leaders and the Big Five characteristics has been found.

GENERAL QUESTIONS

1. What do you think about effective sport leaders? And why?
2. What major characteristics do you think they need?
3. Can you suggest additional sport leadership characteristics that you think are vital at international and national sport levels?
4. Is there a relationship between neuroticism and effective sport leaders? Why?
5. Is there a relationship between extraversion and effective sport leaders? Why?
6. Is there a relationship between openness and effective sport leaders? Why?
7. Is there a relationship between agreeableness and effective sport leaders? Why?
8. Is there a relationship between conscientiousness and effective sport leaders? Why?

SELF-ASSESSMENT 4.1: PERSONALITY TRAITS

Identify the appropriate characteristic (a)–(e) for the five statements.

(a) Neuroticism (b) Extraversion (c) Openness
(d) Agreeableness (e) Conscientiousness

Statements

1. The person tends to experience frequent obsessive thoughts before championships, particularly when things go wrong. They also tend to be worried and depressed by the results.
2. The person is social and assertive inside and outside the organization, and also seeks to create a positive environment to enhance performance at all levels: e.g. athletes, coaches, volunteers, employees.
3. The person tends to demonstrate flexibility in all matters they discuss, accepts advice and exchanges opinions on complex problems facing their sport organization with those in different positions of responsibility.

4. The person is creative in nature, emphasizes differentiation in the organization, and encourages sharing leadership knowledge between members, but their curiosity pushes them to understand the entire organization.
5. The person's activities are well organized and dependable. They have a sense of responsibility towards others. Their actions tend to be guided by rules, laws, and moral principles.

Suggested Reading

House, R.J. and Howell, J.M. (1992). Personality and Charismatic Leadership. *The Leadership Quarterly*, 3(2), 81–108. https://doi.org/10.1016/1048-9843(92)90028-E.

Kirkpatick, S.A. and Locke, E.A. (1991). Leadership: Do Traits Matter? *Academy of Management Perspectives*, 5(2), 48–60. https://doi.org/10.5465/ame.1991.4274679.

Megheirkouni, M. (2017). Leadership Competencies: Qualitative Insight into Non-Profit Sport Organisations. *International Journal of Public Leadership*, 13(3), 166–181. https://doi.org/10.1108/IJPL-11-2016-0047.

Tsiotsou, R. (2012). Developing a Scale for Measuring the Personality of Sport Teams. *Journal of Services Marketing*, 26(4), 238–252. https://doi.org/10.1108/08876041211237541.

References

Bandura, A. (1997). *Self-Efficacy: The Exercise of Control*. New York: W.H. Freeman.

Bass, B.M. and Stogdill, R.M. (1990). *Bass and Stogdill's Handbook of Leadership: Theory, Research, and Managerial Applications*. (3rd edn.). New York: Simon and Schuster.

Bass, B.M. and Riggio, R.E. (2005). *Transformational Leadership*. (2nd ed.). New York: Psychology Press. https://doi.org/10.4324/9781410617095.

Bernard, L.L. (1926). *An Introduction to Social Psychology*. New York: Holt.

Bompa, T.O. (2000). *Total Training for Young Champions*. Leeds: Human Kinetics.

Boyatzis, R.E. (1982). *The Competent Manager: A Model for Effective Performance*. New York: Wiley and Sons.

Boyatzis, R.E. (2008). Competencies in the 21st Century. *Journal of Management Development*, 27(1), 5–12. https://doi.org/10.1108/02621710810840730.

Branch, D. (1990). Athletic Director Leader Behaviour as a Predictor of Intercollegiate Athletic Organizational Effectiveness. *Journal of Sport Management*, 4(2), 161–173. https://doi.org/10.1123/jsm.4.2.161.

Chan, J.T. and Mallett, C.J. (2009). How Developing Emotional Intelligence Can Promote Effective Sports Leadership. 4th Annual 'Evolution of the Athlete' Coach Education Conference, November 2–3, Brisbane, Australia.

Chan, J.T. and Mallett, C.J. (2011). The Value of Emotional Intelligence for High-Performance Coaching. *International Journal of Sport Science and Coaching*, 6(3), 315–328. https://doi.org/10.1260/1747-9541.6.3.315.

Costa, P.T. and McCrae, R.R. (1992). *Revised NEO Personality Inventory (NEO-PI-R) and NEO Five-Factor (NEO-FFI) Inventory Professional Manual*. Odessa, FL: Psychological Assessment Resources.

Costa, P.T. and McCrae, R.R. (2008). The Revised NEO Personality Inventory (NEO-PI-R). In: Boyle, G., Matthews, G. and Saklofske, D. (Eds.). *The SAGE Handbook of Personality Theory and Assessment*. (Vol. 2, Chapter 2). London: Sage. (179–198). https://doi.org/10.4135/9781849200479.n9.

Cox, R.H. (2011). *Sport Psychology: Concepts and Applications*. (7th ed.). Boston, MA: McGraw-Hill.

Feltz, D.L. (1988). Self-Confidence and Sports Performance. *Exercise and Sport Sciences Reviews*, 16(1), 423–457.

Glenn, S.D. and Horn, T.S. (1993). Psychological and Personal Predictors of Leadership Behaviour in Female Soccer Athletes. *Journal of Applied Sport Psychology*, 5(1), 17–34. https://doi.org/10.1080/10413209308411302.

Goldberg, L.R. (1993). The Structure of Phenotypic Personality Traits. *American Psychologist*, 48(1), 26–34. https://doi.org/10.1037/0003-066X.48.1.26.

Goleman, D. (1998). *Working with Emotional Intelligence*. New York: Bantam Books.

Goleman, D. (2020). *Emotional Intelligence: Why It Can Matter More Than IQ*. (25th Anniversary ed.). London. Bloomsbury.

Goleman, D., Boyatzis, R.E. and McKee, A. (2002). *Primal Leadership: Realizing the Power of Emotional Intelligence*. Boston, MA: Harvard Business School Press.

Hemery, D. (1986). *The Pursuit of Sporting Excellence*. London: Collins.

House, R.J. and Aditya, R.N. (1997). The Social Scientific Study of Leadership: Quo Vadis? *Journal of Management*, 23(3), 409–473. https://doi.org/10.1177/014920639702300306.

Jobson, G.L., Whidden, T. and Loory, A. (1990). *Championship Tactics: How Anyone Can Sail Faster, Smarter, and Win Races*. London: St. Martin's Press.

Judge, T.A., Bono, J.E., Ilies, R. and Gerhardt, M.W. (2002). Personality and Leadership: A Qualitative and Quantitative Review. *Journal of Applied Psychology*, 87(4), 765–780. https://doi.org/10.1037/0021-9010.87.4.765.

Kenow, L.J. and Williams, J.M. (1992). Relationship between Anxiety, Self-confidence, and Evaluation of Coaching Behaviours. *The Sport Psychologist*, 6(4), 344–357. https://doi.org/10.1123/tsp.6.4.344.

Kirkpatrick, S.A. and Locke, E.A. (1991). Leadership: Do Traits Matter? *Academy of Management Perspectives*, 5(2), 48–60. https://doi.org/10.5465/ame.1991.4274679.

Kleiner, S.M. and Greenwood-Robinson, M. (2013). *Power Eating*. (4th ed.). London: Human Kinetics.

Kotter, J.P. (1982), *The General Managers*. New York: Free Press.

Kouzes, J.M. and Posner, B.Z. (1993). *Credibility: How Leaders Gain and Lose It, Why People Demand It*. San Francisco, CA: Jossey-Bass.

Le, H., Oh, I.-S., Shaffer, J. and Schmidt, F. (2007). Implications of Methodological Advances for the Practice of Personnel Selection: How Practitioners Benefit from Meta-Analysis. *Academy of Management Perspectives*, 21(3), 6–15. https://doi.org/10.5465/amp.2007.26421233.

Lord, R.G., Foti, R.J. and De Vader, C.L. (1984). A Test of Leadership Categorization Theory: Internal Structure, Information Processing, and Leadership Perceptions. *Organisational Behaviour and Human Performance*, 34(3), 343–378. https://doi.org/10.1016/0030-5073(84)90043-6.

Luthans, F., Hodgetts, R.M. and Rosenkrantz, S.A. (1988). *Real Managers*. Cambridge, MA: Ballinger Press.

Mayer, J.D. and Salovey, P. (1997). What Is Emotional Intelligence? In: Salovey, P. and Sluyter, D. (Eds.). (1997). *Emotional Development and Emotional Intelligence: Implications for Educators*. New York: Basic Books. (3–31).

Mayer, J.D., Salovey, P. and Caruso, D.R. (2000). Models of Emotional Intelligence. In: Sternberg, R.J. (Ed.). *Handbook of Intelligence*. Cambridge: Cambridge University Press. (396–420). https://doi.org/10.1017/CBO9780511807947.019.

McCrae, R.R. and Costa, P.T. (1996). Toward a New Generation of Personality Theories: Theoretical Contexts for the Five-Factor Model. In: Wiggins, J.S. (Ed.). *The Five-Factor Model of Personality: Theoretical Perspectives*. New York: Guilford Press. (51–87).

Megheirkouni, M. (2017). Leadership Competencies: Qualitative Insight into Non-Profit Sport Organisations. *International Journal of Public Leadership*, 13(3), 166–181. https://doi.org/10.1108/IJPL-11-2016-0047.

Melnick, M.J. (1993). Searching for Sociability in the Stands: A Theory of Sports Spectating. *Journal of Sport Management*, 7(1), 44–60. https://doi.org/10.1123/jsm.7.1.44.

Northouse, P.G. (2021). *Leadership: Theory and Practice*. (9th ed.). London: Sage.

Orlick, T. and Partington, J. (1998). Mental Links to Excellence. *The Sport Psychologist*, 2(2), 105–130. https://doi.org/10.1123/tsp.2.2.105.

Petrides, K.V. and Furnham, A. (2001). Trait Emotional Intelligence: Psychometric Investigation with Reference to Established Trait Taxonomies. *European Journal of Personality*, 15(6), 425–448. https://doi.org/10.1002/per.416.

Press Association. (2013). Interview. Chelsea's Frank Lampard Says Jose Mourinho's Management Is Second to None. *The Guardian*. [online]. 20 May 2013 14:26 BST. Available at: https://www.theguardian.com/football/2013/may/20/frank-lampard-josemourinho-sport.

Scott, D. (2014). *Contemporary Leadership in Sport Organizations*. Leeds, UK: Human Kinetics.

Silverthorne, C. (2001). Leadership Effectiveness and Personality: A Cross-Cultural Evaluation. *Personality and Individual Differences*, 30(2), 303–309. https://doi.org/10.1016/S0191-8869(00)00047-7.

Smoll, F.L. and Smith, R.E. (1989). Leadership Behaviours in Sport: A Theoretical Model and Research Paradigm. *Journal of Applied Social Psychology*, 19(8), 1522–1551. https://doi.org/10.1111/j.1559-1816.1989.tb01462.x.

Soucie, D. (1994). Effective Managerial Leadership in Sport Organizations. *Journal of Sport Management*, 8(1), 1–13. https://doi.org/10.1123/jsm.8.1.1.

Spencer Jr., L.M. and Spencer, S.M. (1993). *Competence at Work: Models for Superior Performance*. New York: John Wiley and Sons.

Stogdill, R.M. (1948). Personal Factors Associated with Leadership: A Survey of the Literature. *Journal of Psychology*, 25(1), 35–71. https://doi.org/10.1080/00223980.1948.9917362.

Stogdill, R.M. (1974). *Handbook of Leadership: A Survey of Theory and Research*. New York: Free Press.

Thomas, J.R., French, K.E. and Humphries, C.A. (1986). Knowledge Development and Sport Skill Performance – Directions for Motor Behaviour Research. *Journal of Sport Psychology*, 8(4), 259–272. https://doi.org/10.1123/jsp.8.4.259.

Van Seters, D.A. and Field, R.H.G. (1990). The Evolution of Leadership Theory. *Journal of Organizational Change Management*, 3(3), 29–45. https://doi.org/10.1108/09534819010142139.

Zeigler, E.F. and Bowie, G.W. (1983). *Management Competency Development in Sport and Physical Education*. Philadelphia, PA: Lea and Febiger.

5 BEHAVIOURAL THEORIES

Learning Outcomes

After reading this chapter, you will be able to:

- Distinguish between autocratic and democratic leadership
- Distinguish between different initiating structures and considerations
- Distinguish between different employee orientations and job orientations
- Distinguish between five leadership styles: impoverished management, authority compliance, country-club management, middle of the road, and team leadership
- Identify the key strengths and weaknesses of behaviour theories of leadership

INTRODUCTION

The next stage of evolving leadership theory concerned behaviour-based theories of leadership, distinguishing the behaviours of effective and ineffective leaders. This approach began in the 1940s to find the 'best' leadership style that works in all situations. However, most attempts did not achieve finding the best behaviour (Miner, 2003). The four major schools of research in leadership behaviour theory are the University of Iowa, the Ohio State University, the University of Michigan, and the Management/Leadership Grid theory.

RESEARCH FROM THE UNIVERSITY OF IOWA

The early research on leadership behaviour was conducted by Kurt Lewin and associates at the University of Iowa (Lewin and Lippet, 1938; Lewin, 1939; Lewin et al, 1939). These studies concentrated on two major leadership behaviours:

1. **Autocratic leadership behaviour**: This tends to centralize authority, where leaders prefer making decisions and solving problems on their own, expect subordinates to implement what they have been told, and control rewards.
2. **Democratic leadership behaviour**: This tends to delegate authority to others and encourage participants, also relying on subordinates' knowledge to complete tasks. This behaviour is characterized by a high sharing of information.

DOI: 10.4324/9780429290442-8

Table 5.1 Democratic and Autocratic Behaviours

Democratic behaviour is worse in the following situations	*Democratic behaviour is better in the following situations*	*Autocratic behaviour is worse in the following situations*	*Autocratic behaviour is better in the following situations*
• The purpose is to reinforce the correct performance of team members. • It is not sensitive to individuals' needs for achievement and fulfilment. • In organizational crisis.	• When it is supported by higher authority. • Members are well-educated and support the final objectives. • Leaders have usable skills for communication with their followers. • Time is afforded for trust to develop. • Effectiveness is the aim of an organization. • When increasing organizational commitment and job satisfaction.	• There are strikes. • There is low job satisfaction. • There is low organizational commitment. • The purpose is to improve performance. • When managing modern organizations.	• In organizational crisis. • When increasing productivity of people's performance in a highly structured network. • Working closely together is related to communication difficulties. • Leaders have more knowledge than followers.

Source: Adapted from Bass, B.M. and Bass, R. (2008). *The Bass Handbook of Leadership: Theory, Research, and Managerial Applications*. (4th ed.). London: Simon and Schuster.

The democratic and autocratic behaviours of leadership are perceived as two ends of a continuum. Leaders' behaviours tend towards either autocratic or democratic in their approach (see Table 5.1), rather than being a random collection of behaviours.

RESEARCH FROM THE OHIO STATE UNIVERSITY

These leadership studies were conducted from the mid-1940s to mid-1950s. They utilized the Leader Behaviour Description Questionnaire (LBDQ), comprising 150 questions on defined behaviours, and covered nearly 2000 leaders (Hemphill and Coons, 1957). The responses were provided by employees and reflected a clear picture of their leaders' behaviours. The results showed two major categories of leaders' behaviours:

1. **Initiating structure**: This category covers task orientation, including directing jobs, defining roles and responsibilities, and providing structure and schedules for tasks.
2. **Consideration**: This category covers relationship orientation, including listening to subordinates and their problems, ideas, and suggestions, and building trust between leaders and their subordinates based on mutual respect.

These behaviours are independent, giving four, low and/or high pairs. Research indicates that each these four leadership styles is effective in some particular situation. However, other studies indicate that being high on both initiating structure and consideration is most effective (e.g. Nystrom, 1978; Larson et al, 1976).

RESEARCH FROM THE UNIVERSITY OF MICHIGAN

The University of Michigan research explored leadership behaviour by comparing the behaviours of effective and ineffective managers in small groups, e.g. Rensis Likert (1961, 1979). Researchers there identified two leadership styles (Bowers and Seashore, 1966):

1. **Employee-orientation**: This style refers to the behaviour of leaders who approach their subordinates as having human needs. In addition to supporting human needs, this style attempts to reduce the level of conflict through supporting and reinforcing constructive interaction between subordinates. The leader behaviour in this style includes communicating with subordinates to listen to their problems and to build trust and respect.
2. **Job-orientation**: This style refers to the behaviour of leaders who focus on subordinates to accomplish job tasks. This leadership style behaviour seeks to direct subordinates according to their roles, functions, responsibilities, and purposes.

COMPARING THE RESEARCH MODELS FROM THE OHIO STATE UNIVERSITY AND THE UNIVERSITY OF MICHIGAN

In terms of description, the University of Michigan employee-orientation style is similar to the Ohio State University consideration style. The University of Michigan job-orientation style is similar to the Ohio State University initiating structure style.

However, although noting that the two research programmes were conducted at the same time and both adopted the term 'leadership behaviour', their models are distinct:

1. The Ohio State University research conceptualized consideration and initiating structure as independent styles, a two-dimensional model with four leadership styles.

2. The University of Michigan research conceptualized employee-orientation and job-orientation as distinct styles in opposition to one another.

Although the behaviours in both models have strong research support and have been utilized in many past studies (Bass, 1990), it was noted that there is no 'best' style that fits most situations, and certainly not all. The need for further research and for a new theory continued.

LEADERSHIP GRID THEORY

Robert Blake and Jane Mouton at the University of Texas developed the Managerial Grid® in the 1960s, updated it in 1978 and 1985, and in 1991 renamed it the Management Grid® (Blake and McCanse, 1991; Blake and Mouton, 1964, 1978, 1985). This theory is still under investigation and attempts to explain how leaders – as the theory is now extended from managers – can achieve their longer-term organizational aims and objectives (Sui Pheng and Lee, 1997).

Managerial Grid theory, based on the Ohio State University and the University of Michigan studies, modelled leadership styles on two axes: concern for production and concern for people (Blake and Mouton, 1964). Five styles were identified:

1. **Impoverished Style**: This style indicates low concern for both production and people and little leader contact with subordinates. This suggests that impoverished-style leaders exert little effort to remain in their positions.
2. **Country-Club Style**: This style indicates low concern for production and high concern for people. These leaders focus on people's impressions and feelings by meeting subordinates' social and personal needs. This suggests country-club style leader behaviour is cooperative, comfortable, helpful, friendly, easy-going, and tolerant.
3. **Middle-of-the-Road Style**: This style indicates an intermediate concern for both production and people. These leaders balance production and people concerns through using interpersonal relationships and meeting job requirements.
4. **Authority-Compliance Style**: This style indicates high concern for production and low concern for people. These leaders focus on getting the task done, and people are perceived as machines.
5. **Team Style**: This style indicates high concern for both production and people. This suggests that leaders promote a high level of performance and employee satisfaction in order to accomplish results, and this style tends to be the most effective style for all situations (D'Innocenzo et al, 2021). Various researchers have conducted extensive empirical research to determine if high concern for production and people, the 'high-high leader', is the most effective leadership style. For example, Blake and Mouton's (1982) study revealed that the company that adopted their Grid Organizational Development programme to help a manager become a team leader increased profits four times more than the company that did not utilize this programme. Their findings supported their claims that the high-high style (team leadership) results in both high employee performance and high satisfaction.

EVALUATION

The first contribution of leadership behaviour theories is that they made a clear shift in the debate from traits to behaviours. This helped leadership research expand efforts that focus on what leaders do and how they do it. A second contribution is that organizations need both production and people leadership styles and that leaders are more effective when they make a balance between production and people orientations. The third contribution of leadership behaviour theories supports the manager-as-leader notion. Middle management is often called the real leaders of any organization because losing the CEO is not a problem, but if we lose someone in the middle management a real problem occurs as it is difficult to find someone, particularly quickly, to fill the same role (Megheirkouni et al, 2018).

Although leadership behaviour theories make contributions, there are several weaknesses. First, behaviour theories fail to provide a leadership style that can best fit all situations. Leaders utilizing an apparently 'ideal' behaviour may be successful in some, but not all, situations. For example, when a football team manager works in the Spanish football league and after a few years, moves to work within the Chinese football league, the use of the same behaviour in both cultures tends to be questionable if they intend to be a successful manager. Second, behaviour theories cannot be measured scientifically. There are still controversies amongst behaviourists regarding the limitations of each research method.

SUMMARY

The behavioural theories of leadership focus on leaders' actions rather than their personal characteristics. Four research schools have developed such theories: the University of Iowa, the University of Michigan, the Ohio State University, and Leadership Grid theory. The University of Iowa research focuses on two primary behaviours: autocratic leadership behaviour and democratic leadership behaviour. The Ohio State University research is based around the Leader Behaviour Description Questionnaire, that identified two leadership behaviours: initiating structure and consideration. The University of Michigan research identified two, similar leadership behaviours: employee-orientation and job-orientation. Based on the latter two, Blake and Mouton developed the Leadership Grid, which focused on concern for production and concern for people, identifying five leadership behaviours: impoverished, authority compliance, country club, middle of the road, and team. Although behavioural theories are criticized, they still have some strengths in current leadership research.

GENERAL QUESTIONS

1. What are the differences between behavioural theories of leadership and trait theories of leadership?
2. What are the University of Iowa leadership styles?
3. Why might subordinates under a democratic leader perform better than subordinates under an autocratic leader in the leader's absence?

4. What are the University of Michigan leadership styles?
5. What are the Ohio State University leadership styles?
6. What are the Leadership Grid styles?
7. What connections are there between the different models?
8. What leadership style do you prefer? List your reasons?
9. Does it make sense to you that using one leadership style cannot be successful in all situations? Explain advantages and disadvantages of this approach?
10. What how does the type of leader – task-oriented or people-oriented – relate to successful results? Why?

SELF-ASSESSMENT 5.1: THE OHIO STATE UNIVERSITY LEADERSHIP STYLE

Match the two leadership styles – (A) initiating structure and (B) consideration – to the four behaviours with leadership style?

1. The new football manager influences the team to implement the manager's plans and tactics during the match.
2. The sales manager at a hockey club makes regular reports and generalizes them to all sales divisions to create a big picture about sales quota.
3. The chairman of the committee organizing the next Olympic Games shares ideas and suggestions with their subordinates and respects all responses and ideas from the subordinates.
4. The leader trusts their subordinates and meets their needs.

SELF-ASSESSMENT 5.2: UNIVERSITY OF MICHIGAN LEADERSHIP STYLE

Match the two leadership styles
    (A) employee-orientation and (B) job-orientation – to the three behaviours with leadership style?

1. A rugby club manager asks players to complete the roles required by their positions.
2. The head of a gymnastic federation communicates with the first-team players, listens to their problem and supports their needs in and out of competitions.
3. A basketball team manager consults the technical director and medical staff about a decision.

SELF-ASSESSMENT 5.3: THE LEADERSHIP GRID

Match the five leadership styles to the five statements?

    (a) Authority compliance (b) Impoverished (c) Country club
    (d) Team management (e) Middle of the road

Statements

1. A basketball team has high morale, and players enjoy their matches. The match results are low. The team manager is liked by players.
2. A national football team is satisfied with their team managers, and teamwork is average. The match results are average compared to those of other national teams.
3. A hockey team do not like their manager, and their team relationship is low. The match results are high at all levels.
4. A gymnastics team does not do the tasks required in championships, and their idea of teamwork is weak because they do not like their team manager.
5. Athletes show high morale due to their great relationship with the team manager, and this translates into high performance.

Suggested Reading

Gastil, J. (1994). A Meta-Analytic Review of the Productivity and Satisfaction of Democratic and Autocratic Leadership. *Small Group Research*, 25(3), 384–410. https://doi.org/10.1177/1046496494253003.

Harms, P.D., Wood, D., Landay, K., Lester, P.B. and Vogelgesang Lester, G (2018). Autocratic Leaders and Authoritarian Followers Revisited: A Review and Agenda for the Future. *The Leadership Quarterly*, 29(1), 105–122. https://doi.org/10.1016/j.leaqua.2017.12.007.

Luthar, H.K. (1996). Gender Differences in Evaluation of Performance and Leadership Ability: Autocratic vs. Democratic Managers. *Sex Roles*, 35(5), 337–361. https://doi.org/10.1007/BF01664773.

Megheirkouni, M. (2019). Power Bases and Job Satisfaction in Sports Organizations. *Journal of Global Sport Management*, 4(3), 271–290. https://doi.org/10.1080/24704067.2018.1442238.

References

Bass, B.M. (1990). *Bass and Stogdill's Handbook of Leadership: Theory, Research, and Managerial Applications*. (3rd ed.). New York: Free Press.

Bass, B.M and Bass, R. (2008). *The Bass Handbook of Leadership: Theory, Research, and Managerial Applications*. (4th ed.). London: Simon and Schuster.

Blake, R.R. and McCanse, A.A. (1991). *Leadership Dilemmas: Grid Solutions*. Houston, TX: Gulf Publishing.

Blake, R.R. and Mouton, J.S. (1964). *The Managerial Grid*. Houston, TX: Gulf Publishing.

Blake, R.R. and Mouton, J.S. (1978). *The New Managerial Grid*. Houston, TX: Gulf Publishing.

Blake, R.R. and Mouton, J.S. (1982). A Comparative Analysis of Situationalism and 9,9 Management by Principle. *Organizational Dynamics*, 10(4), 20–43. https://doi.org/10.1016/0090-2616(82)90027-4.

Blake, R.R. and Mouton, J.S. (1985). *The Managerial Grid III*. Houston, TX: Gulf Publishing.

Bowers, D.G. and Seashore, S.E. (1966). Predicting Organizational Effectiveness with a Four-Factor Theory of Leadership. *Administrative Science Quarterly*, 11(2), 238–263. https://doi.org/10.2307/2391247.

D'Innocenzo, L., Kukenberger, M., Farro, A.C. and Griffith, J.A. (2021). Shared Leadership Performance Relationship Trajectories as a Function of Team Interventions and Members' Collective Personalities. *The Leadership Quarterly*, 32(5), 101499. https://doi.org/10.1016/j.leaqua.2021.101499.

Hemphill, J.K. and Coons, A.E. (1957). Development of the Leader Behaviour Description Questionnaire. In: Stogdill, R.M. and Coons, A.E. (Eds.). *Leader Behaviour: Its Description and Measurement*. Columbus: Ohio State University, Bureau of Business Research. (6–38).

Larson, L.L., Hunt, J.G. and Osborn, R.N. (1976). The Great Hi-Hi Leader Behavior Myth: A Lesson from Occam's Razor. *Academy of Management Journal*, 19(4), 628–641. JSTOR: https://www.jstor.org/stable/255796.

Lewin, K. (1939). Field Theory and Experiment in Social Psychology: Concepts and Methods. *American Journal of Sociology*, 44(6), 868–896. https://doi.org/10.1086/218177.

Lewin, K. and Lippet, R. (1938). An Experimental Approach to the Study of Autocracy and Democracy: A Preliminary Note. *Sociometry*, 1(3–4), 292–300. https://doi.org/10.2307/2785585.

Lewin, K., Lippett, R. and White, R.K. (1939). Patterns of Aggressive Behaviour in Experimentally Created 'Social Climates'. *Journal of Social Psychology*, 10(2), 271–301. https://doi.org/10.1080/00224545.1939.9713366.

Likert, R. (1961). *New Patterns of Management*. New York: McGraw-Hill.

Likert, R. (1979). From Production- and Employee-Centeredness to Systems 1–4. *Journal of Management*, 5(2), 147–156. https://doi.org/10.1177/014920637900500205.

Megheirkouni, M., Amaugo, A. and Jallo, S. (2018). Transformational and Transactional Leadership and Skills Approach: Insights on Stadium Management. *International Journal of Public Leadership*, 14(4), 245–259. https://doi.org/10.1108/IJPL-06-2018-0029.

Miner, J.B. (2003). The Rated Importance, Scientific Validity, and Practical Usefulness of Organizational Behaviour Theories. *Academy of Management Learning and Education*, 2(3), 250–268. https://doi.org/10.5465/amle.2003.10932132.

Nystrom, P.C. (1978). Managers and the Hi-Hi Leader Myth. *Academy of Management Journal*, 21(2), 325–331. JSTOR: https://www.jstor.org/stable/255767.

Sui Pheng, L. and Lee, B. (1997). 'Managerial Grid' and Zhuge Liang's 'Art of Management': Integration for Effective Project Management. *Management Decision*, 35(5), 382–392. https://doi.org/10.1108/00251749710173751.

6
SITUATIONAL AND CONTINGENCY THEORIES

Learning Outcomes

After reading this chapter, you will be able to:

- Discuss the major difference between behavioural and contingency leadership theories
- Identify the styles and variables of the contingency model
- Identify the styles and variables of the path–goal leadership model
- Identify and discuss the Vroom–Yetton–Jago Contingency styles and the contingency variables
- Discuss the major similarities and differences between the behavioural and contingency leadership theories
- Compare and contrast the major differences among the four contingency leadership models.

INTRODUCTION

Situational leadership focuses on leadership in situations. The major assumptions of the situational theory are that each situation requires a specific kind of leadership and that effective leaders should have the ability to adapt to all situations in order to meet their requirements. Situational leadership is also called 'contingency' because these theories can tell us the extent to which each leadership style matches a specific situation or contingency, which helps us to understand the level of leaders' performance (Gibson et al, 2012; Gupta, 2005; Northouse, 2018).

SITUATIONAL THEORIES

Although leaders may have the ability to change their behaviour to best fit the different requirements of subordinates, it is noted that they do have a dominant or favourable (to them) behaviour. According to Fiedler's (1967) model, three behaviours can reflect the dominant or (self-)favourable behaviours of a leader. These three behaviours, in order of importance, are:

1. **Leader–Member Relations**: This behaviour refers to the extent to which the relation between subordinates and their leader is based on trust, confidence, respect, and loyalty. In other words, if subordinates neither trust and respect, nor have little loyalty and confidence in their leader, leader–member relations are perceived as a weak relation.

DOI: 10.4324/9780429290442-9

2. **Task Structure**: This behaviour reflects the extent to which tasks are structured. This helps in understanding how leaders might have more control and influence when tasks are structured. When tasks are well-defined, implementing rules and relying on routine would lead to achieving the results desired. In contrast, when tasks are ill-defined, there are no rules and guidance, innovation and creativity are more dominant, and tasks are considered at a low level of structure. Thus, when jobs are unstructured, the situation is perceived as less favourable to the leader and vice versa.

3. **Position Power**: This behaviour refers to the extent to which leaders use their authority to control subordinates. With high position power, leaders use their authority to assign tasks, reward, punish, fire, and promote. When leaders have high power, the situation is considered as more favourable to the leader. But with low position power, little authority is used over subordinates and leaders cannot assign tasks, reward, punish, fire, or promote. When leaders have low power, the situation is considered as less favourable. (You may find Chapter 2 useful in this discussion.)

HERSEY AND BLANCHARD'S SITUATIONAL THEORY

One of the best-known models applying situational leadership to understand leadership effectiveness is Situational Leadership II (SLII) by Hersey and Blanchard (1982). This theory focuses on utilizing the characteristics of subordinates as a part of the situation to understand leadership effectiveness. Their theory can be divided into two aspects comprising: first, four leadership styles: delegating, supporting, coaching, and directing; and second, the development level of subordinates at three levels: high, moderate, or low (Blanchard et al, 1985).

The four leadership styles are matched with the development levels of subordinates in Figure 6.1.

HERSEY AND BLANCHARD LEADERSHIP STYLES

Hersey and Blanchard relied on the Ohio State University research (Chapter 5) to develop four leadership styles available to leaders.

1. **Delegating Style**: (also called low-supportive–low-directive style) This style reflects low concern for tasks and relationships. Leaders in this style provide little direction or personal support to subordinates because this style lets subordinates take responsibility for getting the job done, regardless of the way the leader might see as suitable.

2. **Supporting Style**: (also called participating or high-supportive–low-directive style) This style is characterized by high relationship and low task behaviour. The leader in this style shares ideas with subordinates, encourages participation, ideas, and suggestions, and facilitates decision-making.

3. **Coaching Style**: (also called selling or high-supportive and high-directive style) This style reflects a high concern for both tasks and relationships. The leader in this style focuses on goals achievement and meeting the requirements of subordinates. However, although leaders in this style involve

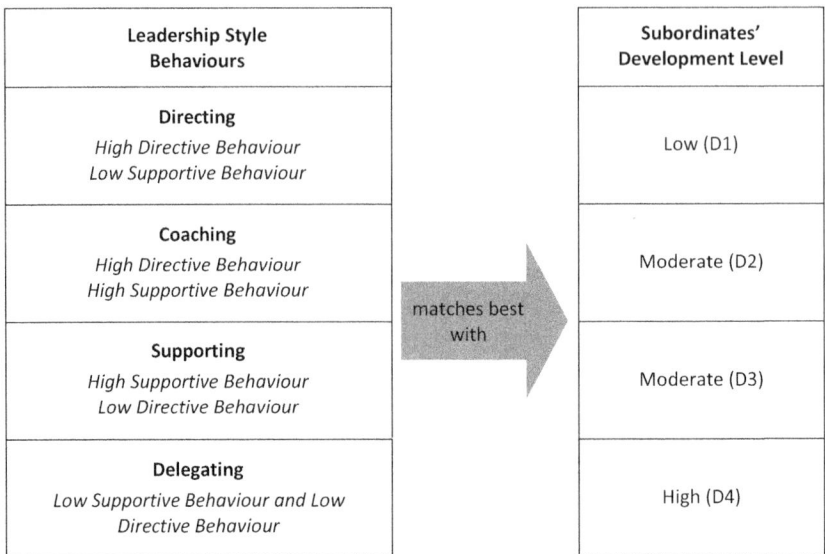

Figure 6.1 Hersey and Blanchard's Situational Theory.

Source: Adapted from Blanchard, K.H., Zigarmi, D. and Nelson, R.B., Situational Leadership® after 25 Years: A Retrospective, *Journal of Leadership Studies*, 1(1), 21–36.

themselves with subordinates by soliciting subordinate input, the leader is still required to make the final decision.

4. **Directing Style**: (also called telling or low-supportive and high-directive style) This style reflects a high concern for tasks and a low concern for people and relationships. Leaders in this style provide specific instruction for subordinates through giving directions and establishing the methods of evaluation required to do so. They closely supervise accomplishing tasks and setting timelines. However, this style devotes little time for utilizing supportive behaviour.

THE DEVELOPMENT LEVEL OF SUBORDINATES

The development level of subordinates is the second part of Hersey and Blanchard's Situational Theory. The essence of this level reflects the extent to which leaders can diagnose a subordinate's development and adopt a style that is appropriate for the development level.

- **Low Category (D1)**: In this category, subordinates are low in the competencies required. Leaders in this category attempt to direct their subordinates to complete the tasks required through telling them what to do, and how to do it.
- **Moderate Category (D2, D3)**: (D2) A coaching leadership style appears to be effective and successful when subordinates lack the education level and the experience required for their job, and demonstrate an ability to learn

and change, but lost their motivation for the job; and **(D3)** Leaders with a supporting leadership style, tend to be more effective when subordinates have the education level and knowledge, but they do not demonstrate confidence to complete the tasks required by themselves. So, leaders assign tasks for subordinates rather than instruct them what to do and how tasks may be performed.

- **High Category (D4)**: Delegating leadership style tends to be more effective when subordinates have a very strong educational background, experience, knowledge, and development to take responsibility and confidence to complete the tasks and jobs required for their own task behaviour.

EVALUATION OF SITUATIONAL LEADERSHIP THEORIES

Even though many training and development programmes have adopted situational leadership theories, these theories have failed to provide an ideal approach without deficiencies (see Fernandez and Vecchio, 1997). The first criticism of situational leadership is that it overemphasizes the situation and thus ignores other equally important factors in the emergence of a particular leader, such as their traits and behaviours. This assumes that supporters of situational leadership theories believe that situation is the only variable that may affect the process and quality of leadership decision-making and problem-solving. However, leadership decision-making and problem-solving may also be affected by other personal and contextual variables, including demographic characteristics. Another criticism of situational leadership theories is pointed at their focus on the leadership ability of an individual leader and motivation in a given situation through four levels, while in fact the extent of the effectiveness of leaders' ability and motivation in a particular situation can be the same in another situation in a different setting. In a similar vein, the Situational Leadership II model has changed from the readiness levels to the developmental levels: D1 high commitment but low competence; D2 low commitment and low competence; D3 moderate competency but low commitment; and D4 high commitment and high competence. Accordingly, this model fails to explain why and how commitment is accompanied with competence in these styles (Northouse, 2018).

Despite the deficiencies of these theories, they contribute to understanding leadership. Firstly, situational leadership theories are vital in leadership training and development because leadership development programmes are mainly designed based on specific needs to target specific skills (Hersey and Blanchard, 1993). Situational leadership theories, therefore, allow instructors to focus more on specific leadership skills and competencies to meet participants' needs. Situational leadership theories are characterized by the leader's awareness of the opportunities suitable to develop subordinates' skills rather than assuming their weakness in skill. Moreover, these theories stress flexible and adaptive behaviour and how subordinates should be treated (Yukl, 2013). This is evident when sport teams' managers work abroad with athletes from different cultures and backgrounds who have different behaviours and needs. Using four styles separately assumes that adopting one leadership style in this circumstance tends to be unsuccessful. Leaders who shift their leadership style based on the situation are likely to be more effective than those who adopt only one leadership style for different situations. Furthermore, situational leadership theories are characterized by their clarity as these theories are easily understood and applied (Northouse, 2018). For example, these theories help leaders shift their leadership style as appropriate for every situation to achieve the results desired in a given situation. The principles of these theories can evidently be applied in different contexts, including sport unions, organizations, federations, associations, committees, clubs, and centres.

PATH–GOAL THEORY

The path–goal theory is another contingency theory of leadership. It was developed by Robert House based on Evans' work in 1970 (House, 1971; Evans, 1970a, b). The major responsibility of leaders according to the path–goal theory is to increase motivation among their subordinates in order to achieve personal and organizational goals. Moreover, the theory is derived from expectancy theory, so subordinates expect that the leader will increase their motivation by ensuring one or more of: (1) that they are able to complete their task; (2) that their efforts do have positive results; or (3) that there is a link between the payoffs and doing their tasks (see Figure 6.2).

According to the path–goal theory, leaders support subordinates to reach their goals by choosing the appropriate style that meets not only the subordinates' needs, but also the situation in which subordinates are working. This would guide subordinates on their way to reach goals (the tasks required) (Northouse, 2018).

SITUATIONAL FACTORS

The path–goal theory is divided into two parts, as follows:

a. **Personal Characteristics**
   Personal characteristics determine how a leader's behaviour is translated by subordinates in a given assignment. The three dominant characteristics in this part are:

   i.   **Need for commitment**: The subordinates' dominant needs and their personal characteristics may influence their commitment and satisfaction by a particular leadership style.
   ii. **Locus of control**: The extent to which a subordinate perceives the internal and external environment. Locus of control is divided into internal and external. With an internal locus of control, subordinates believe that their behaviours control their daily actions. With an external locus of control, subordinates believe that their daily actions are controlled by other forces.
   iii. **Ability**: The extent to which ability is employed to complete and perform the tasks required. This entails that when an individual has low ability to perform the role, or the task required, supportive leadership style might be more effective, but when an individual has the ability required to perform the task, supportive leadership style might be unnecessary.

Figure 6.2 Path–Goal Leadership Style.

Source: Adapted from House, R.J. (1971). A Path-Goal Theory of Leader Effectiveness. *Administrative Science Quarterly*, 16(2), 321–329.

b. Task Environment

Task environment refers to the extent to which a leader's behaviour can influence subordinates' motivation. The three dominant characteristics in this part are:

i. **Task structure**: The extent to which the job description is clear and to which tasks are defined to subordinates.

ii. **Formal authority**: The level of power utilized by leaders to influence subordinates' behaviour. This includes implementing organizational policies and rules that can constrain most subordinates' behaviours.

iii. **Work group**: The features that characterize a group, such as experience, training, education level, and the quality of social relationships among a group. Satisfaction is derived from the group and supportive leader behaviour might be unnecessary.

LEADERSHIP BEHAVIOURS

Based on the path–goal model, situational factors determine the appropriate leader behaviour. The early behaviours in this model included the directive and supportive leadership behaviours. The achievement-oriented and participative leadership behaviours were added to the model to make four dominant leadership behaviours (House and Mitchell, 1974). These four behaviours are illustrated as follows:

1. **Supportive leadership**: This behaviour is characterized by being friendly and showing concern for subordinates' welfare. Supportive leadership behaviour

is similar to consideration or people-oriented leadership. Supportive leadership behaviour is recommended when subordinates have an internal locus of control, their ability is high, task structure is simple, formal authority is not implemented, organizational rules and policies do not constrain subordinates' behaviours, and job satisfaction is not derived from the work group.

2. **Directive leadership**: This behaviour gives guidance and direction to subordinates by telling them what they are expected to do and how it is to be done, making schedules, and setting performance goals. This behaviour is similar to the initiating structure in Ohio State University research and the directive style (or a low-supportive and high-directive style) in situational leadership. Directive leadership behaviour is appropriate when subordinates have an external locus of control and their ability is low, their task structure is unclear and complex, formal authority is then implemented and organizational rules and policies constrain subordinates' behaviours and job satisfaction is derived from the work group.

3. **Participative leadership**: Leaders with participative leadership behaviour share with subordinates the process of decision-making. The dominant characteristic of this behaviour is that leaders accept opinions, suggestions, and exchange ideas with subordinates. Participative leadership behaviour is appropriate when subordinates are qualified and active, have an internal locus of control, their ability is high, task structure is complex, regardless of whether or not the nature of the authority is implemented and organizational rules and policies constrain subordinates, whether job satisfaction is derived from the work group or not.

4. **Achievement-oriented leadership**: This behaviour is characterized by a leader who challenges subordinates to strive for higher standards of performance, stresses learning and development for how to achieve the desired results, and shows confidence in subordinates. Achievement-oriented leadership is appropriate when subordinates have an external locus of control, their ability is high, task structure is clear and simple, formal authority is implemented and organizational rules and policies constrain subordinates' behaviours, regardless of whether job satisfaction is derived from the work group or not.

EVALUATION OF THE PATH–GOAL THEORY

There are several limitations to the path–goal theory, such as the noted lack of research that supports the proposition of this theory. Some studies have focused on a part of this theory and ignored others (e.g. Schriesheim et al, 2006). For example, even though empirical research studies have found an initial relationship between the directive style and subordinate satisfaction, other empirical research studies have failed to confirm such a relationship. Moreover, most research studies have paid more attention to leadership directive and supportive styles, with little attention paid to leadership participative and achievement-oriented styles. Consequently, path–goal theory remains tentative due to the lack of a collective picture of this theory and its assumptions (Schriesheim and Neider, 1996; Podsakoff et al, 1996).

Additionally, this theory fails to explain to what extent leadership behaviour motivates subordinates. It seems to be a hard task knowing how to simultaneously integrate the different characteristics of subordinates with the different characteristics of tasks to define an appropriate leadership behaviour that best matches some situation. Path–goal theory does not describe how a leader uses several behaviours to help subordinates to success and improve processes in the organization (Northouse, 2018). Another criticism of the path–goal theory is that it treats leadership, as Northouse (2018) wrote, as 'a one-way event'. The theory suggests that leaders' role is to provide coaching, supporting, delegating, and directing their subordinates. In this regard, the main problem is that subordinates may become more dependent on their leader to complete the tasks required, which places more responsibility on leaders and fails to consider subordinates' own abilities; they remain or become passive subordinates.

Despite the deficiencies of the path–goal theory, it contributes positively to leadership theory. First, the path–goal theory makes a positive contribution as a guide for understanding several leadership behaviours and their implications for subordinate performance, job performance, and organization performance. In other words, this theory not only provides four styles: directive, supportive, participative, and achievement-oriented, but also expands the attention of prior studies with their classical focus on task-oriented and relationship-oriented behaviour (Jermier, 1996). Moreover, this theory was one of the early situational/contingency theories to illustrate the characteristics of subordinates and the leaders' task and ability to influence subordinates' performance and satisfaction.

Path–goal theory has another positive contribution in that it focuses on the motivation principles of expectancy theory. Northouse (2018: 123) says, "no other leadership approach deals directly with motivation in this way". Consequently, the path–goal theory requires leaders to continuously challenge themselves to improve the payoffs to subordinates and motivate subordinates to increase their performance. Path–goal theory makes leaders aware of such enquiries that focus on and address issues of motivation. Another contribution of the path–goal theory is that it provides a practical framework for understanding leadership. This theory helps leaders to keep in mind that reaching and completing the objectives required occurs through guiding and coaching subordinates. As such, leaders help subordinates to overcome the obstacles and move along the path to achieve a goal.

VROOM–YETTON–JAGO CONTINGENCY MODEL

Another contingency model of leadership is provided by Victor Vroom and Philip Yetton (Vroom and Yetton, 1973). They developed a decision-making leadership contingency model. They built their analysis on three major factors of a leader's decision. First, the 'level of acceptance' refers to the extent to which the decision made is acceptable among subordinates. Second, the 'quality of decision' refers to the degree to which the decision made affects the subordinates' performance. Third, there is the self-explanatory 'time used to make a decision'.

Vroom and Yetton suggested five leadership decision styles:

1. **Autocratic (or Decide style)**: The leader is the only person who solves problems based on their personal experience and the available information they receive from subordinates and others, but they decide solutions alone.
2. **Consult individually style**: The problem is discussed with relevant subordinates, but individually. However, the leader makes the final decision, regardless of the influence of those individuals.
3. **Consult collectively style**: The problem is discussed with relevant subordinates, but as a group. However, the leader makes the final decision, regardless of the influence of teams.
4. **Facilitate style**: The problem is discussed with relevant subordinates as a team in a meeting. The leader and subordinates exchange, evaluate ideas to attempt or reach team consensus on a solution.
5. **Delegate style**: The leader delegates the problem and permits the team to make the decision within prescribed potentials and limits.

The Vroom–Yetton leadership model suggests seven decision rules to guide leaders to identify the appropriate style of leadership for each situation. These rules are:

1. **The information rule**: the quality of decision is required, and the leader lacks the personal experience and available information.
2. **The trust (or goal congruence) rule**: The quality of the decision is required, and subordinates have different goals from those of the organization.
3. **The unstructured problem rule**: The quality of the decision is required, the leader lacks the personal experience and available information, and the problem is unstructured.
4. **The acceptance rule**: Acceptance of the decision by the subordinates is required for the implementation of the decision, the autocratic decision made by the leader would not receive acceptance.
5. **The conflict rule**: Acceptance of the decision by the subordinates is required for the implementation of the decision, an autocratic decision is likely to be unaccepted, and subordinates seem to be in conflict.
6. **The fairness rule**: The quality of the decision does not matter, but its acceptance by subordinates is important, and is not assured by autocratic decision-making.
7. **The acceptance-priority rule**: Acceptance of the decision is required by subordinates, but not assured through an autocratic decision, and the goals of subordinates and the organization are convergent, or even congruent.

CONTINGENCY VARIABLES AND THE APPLICATION OF THE MODEL

The use of one of the appropriate decision styles is based on a set of contingency variables: decision significance, importance of commitment, leader expertise, likelihood commitment, group support, group expertise, and team competence. The leader diagnoses the situation in terms of the seven contingency variables (revised to 12 variables in Vroom and Jago, 1988), that help to select the appropriate decision-making style.

According to those variables' values, the leader follows the decision structure matrices to select one of the five decision-making styles (discussed earlier). The matrix for the time-driven model is used in making an effective decision as quickly as possible, and development-driven model is used for developing the decision-making skills of others. The contingency variables are listed at the top of the matrices, revised from seven to 12 variables (see the previous sections). The leader enters the matrix at the left side, at Problem Statement, and considers the situational questions or variables in sequence from left to right, answering high (H) or low (L) to each one and avoiding crossing any horizontal lines.

THE CHARACTERISTICS OF TIME-DRIVEN AND DEVELOPMENT-DRIVEN MODELS

Selecting the time-driven model or development-driven model is based on whether the situation is driven by one of two scenarios: the importance of time to complete a given task, or the importance of the development of subordinates.

1. **Time-Driven**: This model focuses on the effective decision with minimum cost and time saving, so it is described as a short-term horizon.
2. **Development-Driven**: This model focuses on the effective decision with maximum development of subordinates due to the importance of development and is worth the cost, so it is described as a long-term horizon because the notion of development refers to learning about the growth of the individual but is not related to a specific present or future job.

THE VROOM–JAGO REVISED CONTINGENCY MODEL

The Vroom–Yetton Contingency Model was revised by Vroom and Jago who retained the five decision-making styles suggested by Vroom and Yetton, but added additional contingency variables and extended it to 12 variables (Vroom and Jago, 1988). The computer application model (first published on CD-ROM in 2007) combines the time-driven and development-driven models into one model that includes the revised 12 questions/variables. Vroom and Jago argue that, in the revised model, each of the five decision styles can be successful in given situations and leaders are expected to evaluate the situation that they are experiencing based on the 12 contingency variables:

1. **Quality requirement**: To what extent the quality of the decision is important.
2. **Commitment requirement**: To what extent the subordinate's commitment to the decision is important.
3. **Leader information**: To what extent the information/knowledge of the leader seems to be sufficient for making a high-quality decision.
4. **Problem structure**: To what extent the problem is well structured.
5. **Commitment probability**: If the leader makes the decision autocratically, do subordinates show a high level of commitment or a low level of commitment towards the taken decision?

6. **Goal congruence**: To what extent subordinates support the final objectives and goals of their organization or even team with regard to this particular decision.
7. **Subordinate conflict**: To what extent conflict is seen among subordinates over preferred solutions.
8. **Subordinate information**: To what extent the information/knowledge of the subordinates seems to be sufficient for making a high-quality decision.
9. **Time constraint**: To what extent time limits the ability of a leader to involve subordinates in decision-making.
10. **Geographical dispersion**: Whether costs to bring geographically dispersed subordinates together are justified.
11. **Motivation time**: To what extent can the time it takes to make a given decision be minimized.
12. **Motivation development**: To what extent a leader can maximize the opportunities given to the subordinates for training and development.

EVALUATION OF THE VROOM–YETTON–JAGO CONTINGENCY MODEL

There are several limitations to this model. Decisions are treated as discrete events that occur at a single point in time. However, decision-making, in reality, seems to be a multiprocess of procedures that occur with different people in different contexts, settings or even times in order to reach the final decision. This is well illustrated by Grint's (2005) model that assumes three types of authority, three types of problems, and the technique utilized for decision-making. Furthermore, adopting one of the five leadership styles suggested in the model requires well-skilled leaders to achieve the role required. However, the nature of the required skills for each leadership style is still unknown and is not illustrated in the proposed model. Another weakness is that the Vroom–Yetton model is not conceptually clear. More specifically, there is a distinction between autocratic (decide style), consult individually style, consult collectively style, facilitate style, and delegate style, but the model fails to give clear evidence of the distinctions between the styles of each situation.

Despite the deficiencies of the Vroom–Yetton–Jago Contingency Model, it has strong points. Indeed, this model remains influential, underpinning later decision-making theory. Moreover, the model provides a balance between the short-term time-driven model and the long-term development-driven model. Also, this model has had a significant role in developing the expectancy theory of motivation based on the idea that motivational strength is determined by perceived reasons for success.

SUMMARY

Situational (contingency) leadership helps us understand why some leaders are successful in particular situations, while they fail in others. Situational theories focus on leadership in situations and suggest that leaders are effective in particular situations. The Situational Leadership II model relied on the Ohio State

University research to develop four leadership styles: delegating style, supporting style, coaching style, and directing style. According to Hersey and Blanchard's Situational Theory, leaders are effective when they are able to adopt these four leadership styles and exhibit the appropriate style that best fits each situation.

The path–goal theory is derived from the expectancy approach, where subordinates expect that the leader increases their motivation by three actions: leaders ensure that subordinates can complete their task; their efforts do have positive outcomes, and payoffs are linked to their efforts. The key principle of the path–goal theory is that a leader supports subordinates to reach their goals by choosing the appropriate leadership style (i.e. supportive, directive, participative, or achievement-oriented) that meets not only subordinates' needs, but also the needs of the situation in which subordinates are working.

GENERAL QUESTIONS

1. What is the difference between contingency theory and contingency model?
2. Consider Fiedler's theory. To what extent do you think sport leaders implement these styles in real life? Illustrate your answers with evidence.
3. If you compare Fiedler's contingency model with the path–goal theory, what are the common similarities and differences? Which one do you prefer? Why?
4. Consider Hersey and Blanchard's Situational Theory II. To what extent do you think sport leaders implement these styles in real life? Illustrate your answers with evidence.
5. If you were a sport team manager, how do you assess the development level of your players? Do you think it is possible to shift your leadership style to suit the development level of your player if you are a sport manager or the leader of the national sport federation?
6. What are the two divisions of the path–goal theory?
7. Can you identify the variables of contingency leadership common to all of the leadership theories?
8. Can you explain how the economics of the international sport organizations relate to contingency leadership theory?
9. What are the personal characteristics of the path–goal theory?
10. What are the task-environment factors of the path–goal theory?
11. What are the leadership behaviours of the path–goal theory?
12. What are the common weaknesses and strengths of the path–goal theory?
13. What is the primary difference between the Vroom–Yetton contingency leadership model and Vroom–Jago contingency leadership model?
14. What are the characteristics of time-driven and development-driven models?
15. What are the common weaknesses and strengths of the Vroom–Yetton–Jago Contingency Model?

OPEN DISCUSSION QUESTIONS

1. Identify the contingency leadership model you prefer to adopt in your current sport job or setting and illustrate the reasons.
2. Identify the contingency leadership model you now would have preferred to adopt in your previous sport job or setting and illustrate the reasons.
3. Identify the difference or similarity in the contingency leadership model between your current and previous sport job or setting. Discuss and compare your answers with your colleagues.
4. Can you describe these decisions as time-driven or development-driven? Discuss and compare your answers with your colleagues.
5. Evaluate your colleagues' styles in class by identifying the common characteristics they show. Write a list of these characteristics to compare with what you read in the discussion questions.
6. Discuss and compare your analysis with your colleagues.

Questions for Case Study 6.1

1. What styles of leadership are the sport' leaders utilizing in their role?
2. Can you illustrate their sport leadership level?
3. Can you list the points of strength and weakness for each of Mike, Keith, David, and Anita's leadership?
4. If you were Anita, what would you recommend to the designers and participants of the Women Leadership Development Programme? Why?

Case Study 6.1: For-Profit and Non-Profit Sectors: Sports Direct and UK Sport

Note to students: The ten situations in the following paragraphs might also help you to determine your leadership style – by looking at other peoples' – based on the Situational Leadership II model.

Case Study 6.1: (A) Sports Direct

1. Sports Direct (Frasers Group Plc) is a British retailing group, founded in 1982 by Mike Ashley. The company is the UK's largest sporting goods retailer, operates over 500 stores worldwide, and employs about 2000 staff. It consists of ten areas and each area has its own manager.
2. With several decades in the sport retail business with Sports Direct, Mike is a British businessman whose experience and skills have been used for formulating the vision and strategy of the Sports Direct Group. For that reason, he is invaluable to the Group.
3. Mike is chief executive. He was the sole owner until the Group's listing in March 2007. His experience helped him not only to extend his business, but also to develop the Group. (*Note:* Mike resigned as chief executive from Frasers Group in May 2022.)

4. Prior to joining the team at Sports Direct International plc as chairman of the Nomination Committee (non-executive chairman), Dr Keith Hellawell spent several decades years in public sector management. He has been a non-executive director of Mortice plc, a Singapore-based facilities management company and a director of the Super-League rugby team Huddersfield Giants. He was non-executive chairman of Goldshield Group plc, a marketing-led pharmaceutical and consumer health company, from May 2006 to its sale in December 2009. He has held a number of other non-executive board positions in private companies, including vehicle manufacturing and IT. He also runs his own management and training consultancy company.

5. David Forsey works as a chief executive. He has been in the business world for several decades, which has helped him to acquire significant knowledge and experience of the sport retail business. Generally, Dave has overall responsibility for the daily management of the Group.

6. David was able to post further positive results in April 2012. He announced that sales for the first three months of the year had increased 13.2 per cent to £267.6 million. He courted some controversy with comments he made regarding Dick's Sporting Goods after signing a deal with JJB Sport. He wants to compete on price, but without any indication of how much he will cut prices.

Source: Adapted and updated from from Goodley, S. (2016). From Peter Sutcliffe to Drugs Policy: The Career of Keith Hellawell. *The Guardian*. [online]. 5 September 2016. Available at: https://www.theguardian.com/business/2016/sep/05/from-sutcliffe-to-drugs-policy-the-career-of-keith-hellawell.

Case Study 6.1: (B) UK Sport

7. Dr Anita White has wide ranging experience of sport: as a physical education teacher and lecturer. She previously served on the board of International Development through Sport for seven years. Anita was commissioned to conduct an independent evaluation, reporting on the progress of the Women Leadership Development Programme in UK sports in each year of the programme. Interim reports were presented to the management team.

8. Anita said that the outcome of the programme was twofold: to develop women's leadership by providing an exemplar of how to do so; and to provide training, networking, mentoring, and international experience.

9. The programme was designed to develop 15 selected women leaders in UK sport organizations. This programme was supported by UK Sport, the British Olympic Foundation and the Central Council of Physical Recreation, being managed by UK Sport. Most participants within the programme had some doubts about whether the programme could meet their different needs, and maintain momentum during the three-year programme.

10. Anita recognized that the participants were very experienced, and the programme would not achieve the results required unless the content of the programme met the participants' needs after analysing the primary feedback regarding their weaknesses.

Source: Adapted and updated from: UK Sport. (2016). 'Women in Leadership Programme launched'. News, UK Sport. [online]. 31 August 2006. Available at: www.uksport.gov.uk; Megheirkouni, M. and Roomi, M. (2017). Women's Leadership Development Programmes in a Sports Setting: Factors Influencing the Transformational Learning Experience of Female Managers. *European Journal of Training and Development*, 41(5), 467–484. https://doi.org/10.1108/EJTD-12-2016-0085); and Women in Sport. (n.d.) 'History'. Women in Sport. [online]. Available at: https://womeninsport.org/why-we-exist/history/.

SELF-ASSESSMENT 6.1: HERSEY AND BLANCHARD LEADERSHIP STYLES

For each of the following four scenarios, identify the style utilized and decide on the appropriate leadership style based on the Hersey and Blanchard Leadership model.

1. After appointing the committee organizing an Olympic Games, the chairperson notes that all committee members have very good experience and qualifications to complete their roles effectively.
2. After the old manager leaves a company, a manager from the operations department is selected to lead the footwear operational department as a footwear merchandising manager. The new manager has the same experience and educational level as other employees, but everyone has specific experience based on the job role, so the new manager attempts to share decision-making and problem-solving with their subordinates.
3. One of the best international rugby managers is selected to choose a new national team to compete at the national and international levels over the next decade. The manager has a very strong background and achievement as a player and a coach, but the young players have no rugby experience at international level.
4. During the opening ceremony, the director of the Olympic Games opening ceremony provides very specific notes, feedback, and comments to all participants in the ceremony. They provide valuable comments to achieve the results desired. However, they do not look friendly or easy-going to anyone because they are serious about work, besides being very clever.

SELF-ASSESSMENT 6.2. PATH–GOAL LEADERSHIP THEORY

Determine which of these four styles applies to each of the following four scenarios.

(a) directive; (b) supportive; (c) participative; (d) achievement-oriented

1. Boxers in the national team come to training late without any excuse. They neither commit to the diet system nor the weight range for each boxer. The team manager decides to make theoretical plans and practical changes, and to listen to their needs to place the team on the right track.
2. The chairman of an Olympic Games host city shares decision-making with subordinates. Most subordinates are qualified and show a high level of ability to exchange ideas.
3. The manager of the operations department in a sporting goods company challenges the employees by asking them to do more complex tasks after they finish the first task successfully. The manager uses their position power and the organizational rules and policy to do so.
4. The new task for the chairperson is to correct the organization's track and review the strategic plan after the failure of the previous leader. None of the subordinates are able to work without clear instructions. The deadline to complete building the stadium is soon. Individuals may do different tasks, but it is unclear what. Problems are unanticipated.

SELF-ASSESSMENT 6.3: WHAT IS YOUR CURRENT DECISION STYLE?

STAGE 1: HOW WOULD YOU RESPOND IN DIFFERENT SCENARIOS?

There are 12 scenarios below, each with four options (a, b, c, d). For each question, decide for yourself which one of the four options most closely matches what you would do in this scenario, and circle the appropriate letter in the grid.

Note to students: You might think you would do something different, but determining an overall style based on close-enough matches for a variety of scenarios does work.

When you have answered all 12 scenarios, add up the number of circled answers for each column and put the number in the Totals row.

STAGE 2: WHAT ARE YOUR DECISION STYLES?

Then compare how your choices range across the four styles, using the four style descriptions placed after question 12. They are placed there so that you can focus on the scenarios and give your instinctive answers.

Answer each scenario quickly, as this is more likely to give the response you would use in a real-world situation – rather than the one you might wish you'd given with time to step back and think about it.

You may use one style more often than the other three or find that you mix styles.

Note to students: Remember that this looks at your current style and is non-judgemental. You may find this helpful in thinking about how much your style works for you, and what you might see as a development opportunity.

Scenario	Your response			
1.	a	b	c	d
2.	a	b	c	d
3.	a	b	c	d
4.	a	b	c	d
5.	a	b	c	d
6.	a	b	c	d
7.	a	b	c	d
8.	a	b	c	d
9.	a	b	c	d
10.	a	b	c	d
11.	a	b	c	d
12.	a	b	c	d
Totals				

Scenarios

1. Your group members preparing for a specific paragraph in the opening ceremony is working well. The need for direction and supervision is diminishing.

   a. Stop directing or supervising performance unless there are mistakes.
   b. Reduce the gap between them by getting to know their personality, without ignoring the performance required.
   c. Extend the tasks of group members to make the work environment more attractive and avoid misunderstanding.
   d. Make sure that the tasks required are going well, but supervise them closely.

2. The governing body of swimming adopts its new annual strategy regarding preparing teams for local and international competitions, and recommends all specialists to implement it strictly, but the first national team manager does not commit to it.

   a. The federation manager is strict, but you leave things to the manager as they are achieving satisfying results with the national team.
   b. Warn the manager about ignoring the federation's strategy and appoint a supervisor to work closely with the team.
   c. Use diplomacy and give some flexibility regarding the adopted strategy.
   d. Understand their attitude, but make sure they commit to the federation's policy and rules.

3. The Ministry of Sport holds regular meetings every month with the heads of sport governing bodies, but their calendar for this year fills with external training sessions and championships. The minister of sport suggests

making a change to the dates of monthly meetings to fit their calendar and schedules. Some individuals are satisfied by this suggestion.

   a. Give the right to all heads of sport governing bodies to decide the new schedules.
   b. Adopt the new schedule for every month, and generalize it to all participants, but invite questions.
   c. Ask for new ideas and suggestions to discuss at the next meeting and select the schedule together.
   d. Decide all schedules and generalize them, without accepting any change or discussion.

4. Your club borrows a player to improve its team's defence, but after two matches in the league, the new player fails to provide the performance and role required, and the team still has weaknesses in defence.

   a. Give them more time and an opportunity to adapt to the new team and encourage them.
   b. Tell the player that this is not their mistake, but rather it is the responsibility of the whole team.
   c. Remove them from the team line-up and give other players from the young team this opportunity.
   d. Inform them that they must work hard in training; tell them not to hesitate to see you about any problem.

5. One of our Olympic boxing team won two Olympic gold medals in the last two Olympic Games but failed to win any of the three medals in world and regional boxing championships this year. The boxing federation discovers that they have personal problems with their partner.

   a. Inform the boxer to focus only on training, oversee their training, and closely work on their problem.
   b. Inform the boxer that their problems may affect their future. Be supportive and encourage them.
   c. Discuss the problem with the boxer. Give them a long break to relax and solve their own personal problem without pressure from training or championships to come back stronger.
   d. Discuss the problem and solution with the boxer and supervise them closely.

6. The National Olympic Committee is fighting against doping in sport to protect the integrity of sport and the health of athletes. The committee regularly conducts unannounced doping tests. They have decided to conduct this test after the last national championship when they found that 7 of 33 athletes had relied on doping for competition.

   a. Ask the athletes to test but ignore what happened because the event was a national championship.
   b. Invite the athletes to a seminar about the risks of doping to athletes and advise them to be ready for doping tests happening at any time.

    c. Punish the athletes and expel them from the sport.

    d. Discuss why the athletes used doping and provide a doping specialist to support their training.

7. Your beach volleyball team is playing very well and the performance of two players is identical in terms of tactics and skills; but in the last match, a conflict between the two players became known to the fans.

    a. Tell both players that their conflict will influence team reputation. Encourage them to search for a resolution which satisfies both of them and make sure that this is done.

    b. Leave this conflict to the players to solve.

    c. Tell the players how to resolve their conflict and closely supervise them.

    d. Discuss their conflict and help them find a solution together.

8. David works in a packaging department in the sport goods industry. His role is to check the product before stamping it, but completing his role is mainly based on direction and encouragement. He claims that he must have a day off to attend his son's match at school. When he does this, some colleagues feel angry about doing his job.

    a. Inform him about the problem, and support and help him come up with solutions for maintaining his job.

    b. Inform him that this behaviour creates problems for others, and he that should resolve the problem by himself.

    c. Tell him that he should complete the role required of him. Closely watch his behaviours.

    d. Tell him to complete his task and oversee closely the outcome.

9. Sara is the manager of the women's national basketball team. She suggests establishing schools for creating future talent at low cost with a high outcome. The idea is supported by all members of the basketball federation. She asks to take this responsibility in addition to her current role with the national team.

    a. Support her efforts and ideas but tell her that you want to set some rules and she must agree with them to start the project.

    b. Approve Sara's ideas and let her start this project by herself.

    c. Appoint a committee to evaluate the project progress and closely work on her activities.

    d. Oversee Sara's activities regularly, to help direct and support the project.

10. The National Olympic Committee appoints one of the best national coaches, who has a strong record of achievements over the last 20 years, to write the annual report of the national sport's achievements at the international level. Although he has a strong academic background in management, this is the first time he must do such a task.

    a. Encourage and give him direction in this task with detailed guidance.

    b. Supervise his task and closely check his progress.

    c. Transfer this task to someone else who has previous experience with such reports.

    d. Give him ideas of how to complete the task and let him complete it his way.

11. Pierre is an area manager of sport goods. His stores have the highest sales. The company adopts an international strategy and is very strict regarding its organizational culture, but Pierre does not commit to these issues.

    a. Give him direction and closely oversee to implement the company policy and its rules.

    b. Discuss with him his mistakes and give him examples in the next meeting in order to show a high level of performance without any mistakes.

    c. Tell Pierre that he is doing well and let him do what he sees suitable.

    d. Warn him and tell him that no excuse is accepted next time.

12. The chief of the federation decides to invite a psychological specialist to prepare the national team for the Olympic Games. However, the national team members insist on playing a role in any decision made by the specialist. The specialist emphasizes the need for implementing scientific theories and academic knowledge to prepare the team well.

    a. Inform the team members they should cooperate with the specialist; determine the manner of cooperation.

    b. Encourage the team members to learn from the specialist for the future; closely evaluate their performance.

    c. The job description is strictly implemented; the specialist has the right to do whatever they deem suitable.

    d. Remind the team members of the importance of the specialist role; let them work collectively to reduce weaknesses.

Your Results

Note to students: Resist any temptation to look at these before you've made your choice for all the scenarios!

    a. Autocratic (Decide) Leadership Style: Leaders in this style make the decision autocratically. Leaders tell subordinates how to implement a decision and closely oversee to ensure that subordinates are implementing what they have been told to do.

    b. Consult Leadership Style (Consult collectively and individually styles). Leaders in these styles make discussion with subordinates in a supportive way before making a decision. Leaders in these styles tell subordinates how to implement a decision and closely follow up to ensure that subordinates are implementing what they have been told to do, providing support and encouragement to this process.

    c. Delegate Leadership Style: Leaders in this style give the team the opportunity to make a decision and permit the team to make the decision within prescribed potentials and limits. However, leaders do not tell subordinates what to do, or even facilitate the team within the process of implementing a decision.

d. Facilitated Leadership Style: Leaders in this style discuss cases with relevant subordinates as a team. The leader exchanges ideas with the subordinates and discusses and evaluates ideas and suggestions to reach consensus on a solution.

Suggested Reading

Blanchard, K.H., Zigarmi, D. and Nelson, R.B. (1993). Situational Leadership® after 25 Years: A Retrospective. *Journal of Leadership Studies*, 1(1), 21–36. https://doi.org/10.1177/107179199300100104.

Fernandez, C.F. and Vecchio, R.P. (1997). Situational Leadership Theory Revisited: A Test of an Across-Jobs Perspective. *The Leadership Quarterly*, 8(1), 67–84. https://doi.org/10.1016/S1048-9843(97)90031-X.

Graeff, C.L. (1997). Evolution of Situational Leadership Theory: A Critical Review. *The Leadership Quarterly*, 8(2), 153–170. https://doi.org/10.1016/S1048-9843(97)90014-X.

Thompson, G. and Vecchio, R.P. (2009). Situational Leadership Theory: A Test of Three Versions. *The Leadership Quarterly*, 20(5), 837–848. https://doi.org/10.1016/j.leaqua.2009.06.014.

References

Blanchard, K.H., Zigarmi, D. and Nelson, R.B. (1993). Situational Leadership® after 25 Years: A Retrospective. *Journal of Leadership Studies*, 1(1), 21–36. https://doi.org/10.1177/107179199300100104.

Blanchard, K.H., Zigarmi, P. and Zigarmi, D. (1985). *Leadership and the One Minute Manager*. New York: Blanchard Management Corporation.

Evans, M.G. (1970a). The Effects of Supervisory Behaviour on the Path-Goal Relationship. *Organizational Behaviour and Human Performance*, 5(3), 277–298. https://doi.org/10.1016/0030-5073(70)90021-8.

Evans, M.G. (1970b). Leadership and Motivation: A Core Concept. *Academy of Management Journal*, 13(1), 91–102. JSTOR: https://www.jstor.org/stable/254928.

Fernandez, C.F. and Vecchio, R.P. (1997). Situational Leadership Theory Revisited: A Test of an Across-Jobs Perspective. *The Leadership Quarterly*, 8(1), 67–84. https://doi.org/10.1016/S1048-9843(97)90031-X.

Fiedler, F.E. (1967). *A Theory of Leadership Effectiveness*. New York: McGraw-Hill.

Gibson, J.L., Ivancevich, J.M., Donnelly, J.H. and Konopaske, R. (2012). *Organizations: Behaviour, Structure, Processes*. (14th ed.). New York: McGraw-Hill.

Grint, K. (2005). Problems, Problems, Problems: The Social Construction of 'Leadership'. *Human Relations*, 58(11), 1467–1494. https://doi.org/10.1177/0018726705061314.

Gupta, A. (2005). Leadership in a Fast-Paced World: An Interview with Ken Blanchard. *Mid-American Journal of Business*, 20(1), 7–10.

Hersey, P. and Blanchard, K.H. (1982). *Management of Organization Behaviour: Utilizing Human Resources*. (4th ed.). Englewood Cliffs, NJ: Prentice-Hall.

Hersey, P. and Blanchard, K.H. (1993). *Management of Organizational Behaviour: Utilizing Human Resources.* (6th ed.). Englewood Cliffs, NJ: Prentice Hall.

House, R.J. (1971). A Path-Goal Theory of Leader Effectiveness. *Administrative Science Quarterly*, 16(2), 321–329. https://doi.org/10.2307/2391905.

House, R.J. and Mitchell, T.R. (1974). Path-Goal Theory of Leadership. *Journal of Contemporary Business*, 3(3), 81–97.

Jermier, J.M. (1996). The Path–Goal Theory of Leadership: A Subtextual Analysis. *The Leadership Quarterly*, 7(3), 311–316. https://doi.org/10.1016/S1048-9843(96)90022-3.

Northouse, P.G. (2018). *Leadership: Theory and Practice.* (8th ed.). London: Sage.

Podsakoff, P.M., Mackenzie, S.B and Bommer, W.H. (1996). Meta-Analysis for the Relationships between Kerr and Jemier's Substitutes for Leadership and Employee Job Attitudes, Role Perceptions, Performance. *Journal of Applied Psychology*, 81(4), 380–399. https://doi.org/10.1037/0021-9010.81.4.380.

Schriesheim, C.A., Castro, S.L., Zhou, X. and DeChurch, L.A. (2006). An Investigation of Path-Goal and Transformational Leadership Theory Predictions at the Individual Level of Analysis. *The Leadership Quarterly*, 17(3), 21–38. https://doi.org/10.1016/j.leaqua.2005.10.008.

Schriesheim, C.A. and Neider, L.L. (1996). Path–Goal Leadership Theory: The Long and Winding Road. *The Leadership Quarterly*, 7(3), 317–321. https://doi.org/10.1016/S1048-9843(96)90023-5.

Vroom, V.H. and Jago, A.G. (1988). Managing Participation: A Critical Dimension of Leadership. *Journal of Management Development*, 7(5), 32–42. https://doi.org/10.1108/eb051689.

Vroom, V.H. and Yetton, P.W. (1973). *Leadership and Decision-Making.* Pittsburgh, PA: University of Pittsburgh Press. https://doi.org/10.2307/j.ctt6wrc8r.

Yukl, G. (2013). *Leadership in Organizations.* (8th ed.). New York: Pearson.

7

LEADER–MEMBER EXCHANGE THEORY

Learning Outcomes

After reading this chapter, you will be able to:

- Discuss the major stages of the development of LMX theory
- Distinguish the differences between vertical dyadic linkage theory, LMX, partnership building, and system and network
- Identify the weaknesses and strengths of this theory
- Compare the similarities and differences between LMX theory and the trait, behaviour, and contingency theories

INTRODUCTION

Within the broad area of leadership theories, leader–member exchange (LMX) theory has evolved into one of the more interesting approaches. It conceptualizes leadership as a process and focuses on the linkages between leaders and subordinates. Unlike trait theories, behavioural theories, situational leadership, and the path–goal theory that seek to explain leadership as a function of personal characteristics, behaviours, and skills of leaders, features of particular situations, or an interaction between all of these factors, LMX is unique in making the dyadic relationship between leaders and subordinates the primary aim of the leadership process. This chapter discusses the four stages in the development of LMX, and evaluates this theory.

Most early theories focused only on leaders and ignored the importance of subordinates. Leadership literature, however, draws a strong link between the effectiveness of leaders and the relationship between a leader and subordinates (see Figure 7.1). This relationship is then called dyadic, to refer to the paired relationship (dyad) between a leader and each subordinate individually. Several studies conducted with Olympic athletes and coaches confirmed the influence of the athlete–coach relationship on the athlete's development both as a performer and as a person (Jowett, 2003; Jowett and Cockerill, 2003). Similarly, empirical evidence in stadium management shows that the quality of the leader–member relationship affects job satisfaction, performance, and commitment of staff operating in stadiums and arenas hosting sport mega-events (Megheirkouni, 2017).

DOI: 10.4324/9780429290442-10

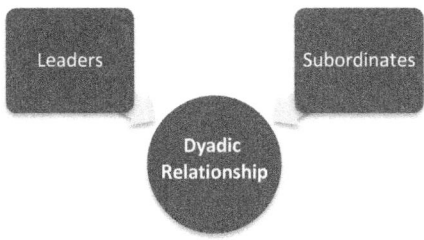

Figure 7.1 Leadership dimensions.

Source: Adapted from Graen, G.B. and Uhl-Bien, M. (1995). Relationship-Based Approach to Leadership: Development of Leader-Member Exchange (LMX) Theory of Leadership over 25 Years: Applying a Multi-Level Multi-Domain Perspective. *The Leadership Quarterly*, 6(2), 219–247.

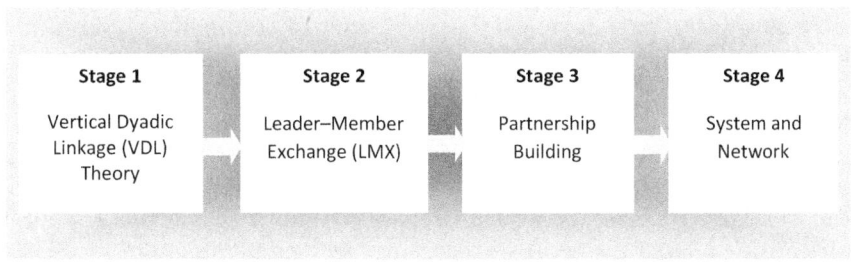

Figure 7.2 Stages in the development of LMX theory.

Source: Adapted from from Graen, G.B. and Uhl-Bien, M. (1995). Relationship-Based Approach to Leadership: Development of Leader-Member Exchange (LMX) Theory of Leadership over 25 Years: Applying a Multi-Level Multi-Domain Perspective. *The Leadership Quarterly*, 6(2), 219–247.

Thus, this theory is best utilized to explain the reasons behind behaviour change of each subordinate (member).

Research on this theory can be divided into early and recent research. The early dyadic theory of leadership was introduced in 1975 (Dansereau et al, 1975; Graen and Cashman, 1975; Graen, 1976), and has been steadily revised (see Figure 7.2).

VERTICAL DYADIC LINKAGE THEORY

The first stage is called the vertical dyad linkage theory (VDL) and is rooted in the individualized leadership approach. A leader's relationship with the work unit as a whole is viewed as a series of vertical dyads. This theory emphasizes the importance of the dyad formed by a leader with each subordinate. It is worth mentioning that the nature of exchanges between the leader and each subordinate helps to determine the form of each dyadic relationship. Some athletes may describe their relationship with their coach as being a high-quality relationship.

This type of relationship will positively reflect in performance at all levels. For example, Coe (1996) argues that when the coach and the athlete are in an ideal harmony, great results can be achieved.

One of the great examples of the individualized relationship in sport is the case of Frederick Carlton (Carl) Lewis. His talent was discovered and coached by his father over his track and field athletic career, in which he won 9 gold and 1 silver Olympic medals and ten World Championships medals including 8 gold. Previous research by Jowett and Cockerill (2003) revealed that the role of feelings of closeness, thoughts of co-orientation, as well as complementary roles and tasks, marked the athletic relationships of the Olympic medallists. Specifically, this study confirmed that the impact of the athlete–coach relationship on the success achieved is evident in former athletes' narratives and recollections. Another example is the role of a high-quality relationship between coach Xiuli Wang and skater Clara Hughes in winning a gold medal (Speed Skating Women's 5,000 m, Turin 2006 Winter Olympics).

Some studies have revealed that the leader–subordinate relationship may link individually with many subordinates, or only a few subordinates, but not all subordinates in the work unit (in-group). In this regard, the nature of exchanges between the leader and subordinates in the work unit (in-group) help to determine the form of this dyadic relationship. However, this relationship is not necessarily homogeneous. Specifically, effective coach–athlete relationships may not be similarly reported by athletes regarding the same coach. Some athletes reported their relationship with the coach as a low-quality relationship. Coaches in this situation are perceived as being of low quality regarding the effectiveness of their leadership behaviours. For example, previous research by Gould et al (1999) revealed that lack of trust, support, communication, and respect among coaches and athletes who operated at the highest level of sport affected athletes' preparation for the 1996 Olympic Games in Atlanta.

The similarities and differences in personal characteristics and the way of thinking of both leaders and subordinates play a fundamental role in determining the nature of the relationship between the two parties, and thus expand their role responsibilities to be a part of either the in-group or the out-group. This depends likely on how they use their similar characteristics, motivations, and visions in developing their relationship further. According to (Northouse, 2021), the *in-group* is based on extra-role, while the *out-group* is based on defined role. Thus, subordinates can be a part of the in-group or out-group based on how effectively they work with the leader and vice versa. In-group subordinates, those who attempt to develop close relationships with the leader, are committed, loyal, and extremely interested in doing activities that exceed the role defined based on the job description in the organizational work unit. The leader, in turn, meets the subordinates' work and efforts with rewards. Additionally, in-group subordinates receive better attention, influence, support, empowerment, and encouragement from the leader. Out-group subordinates, those who do not attempt to develop constructive relationships with their leader, are extremely interested in doing only the roles defined based on the job description. The leader, in turn, often uses formal authority and implements strict behaviour.

LEADER–MEMBER EXCHANGE THEORY

The second stage is called LMX theory and focuses on the relationship and its outcomes. Later studies and investigations of VDL suggested a shift in the focus from VDL to LMX theory because of the existence of different relationships between in-groups and out-groups (Liden et al, 1993). The studies evaluating characteristics of the LMX relationship explored such issues as interactive communications, communication frequency, value agreement, and subordinate loyalty (e.g. Kacmar et al, 2003; Yrle et al, 2002; Fairhurst, 1993; Graen and Scandura, 1987; Markham et al, 2010). Additionally, studies also analysed the implications of the LMX exchange differences on individual and/or organizational effectiveness, including issues such as job satisfaction, job commitment, job climate, job performance, and job empowerment (e.g. Hoye, 2004; Bang, 2011; Lam et al, 2007; Liden et al, 2000; Megheirkouni, 2017; Sparrowe et al, 2006). These studies found that leaders seek to establish an in-group exchange environment with subordinates who have the same personal characteristics as the leader and who score high on the achievement orientation. Overall, the relationships between a leader and each subordinate are not all perceived as equal, which ultimately results in the difference in the quality of LMX relationships. Specifically, high-quality LMX relationships lead to positive outcomes for leaders, subordinates, work units, and the whole organization. Subordinates receive more attention, reward, influence, support, empowerment, and they are active in decision-making; leaders benefit from task completion and role fulfillments; and organizations ultimately benefit from the general productivity of in-group members. Conversely, in low-quality LMX relationships, subordinates fulfill only the role required by their job descriptions, receive less support, attention, influence, empowerment, and leaders often use autocratic behaviours (Yammarino, 2002; Kinicki and Vecchio, 1994).

PARTNERSHIP BUILDING

In the third stage, the debate moves beyond in-group and out-group to focus on effective leadership process through the development of effective leadership relationship. The gist of this stage is that a leader builds a special relationship with each subordinate individually. Specifically, the emphasis is based on developing high-quality relationships with all subordinates rather than a few subordinates to promote the feeling that each individual member is an active part of the in-group. Thereby, this shift in focus takes the theory to an examination of leadership as a partnership (leadership making) (Graen and Uhl-Bien, 1995). It is worth mentioning that leadership-making research initiated two types of debate: the first is around the VDL assumption that leaders develop a high-quality relationship with a few subordinates; the second is what happens if leaders are trained to offer the opportunity to develop a high-quality relationship with all their subordinates. The leadership-making model significantly supports the second type of debate because it proved its effectiveness in terms of improving the productivity of those subordinates who accepted the offer by their leaders. Current research supports this argument (e.g. Ford and Seers, 2006;

Schyns et al, 2005). Graen and Uhl-Bien (1991) suggest that the leadership-making process develops progressively and describe it as a life cycle. In this life cycle, the relationship-building process between leaders and subordinates occurs within three stages.

THE THREE-LEVEL MODEL IN DEVELOPING LMX

LEVEL 1

In the first level of the process for leadership making, leaders and subordinates first come together as strangers, estimating each others' behaviours, personality, and requirements to understand and adopt appropriate behaviours to establish exchange relationships. However, each relationship is based on a more formal basis, in essence negotiation. Within this initial stage, the relationship between a leader and subordinates is defined by the prescribed organizational roles. Overall, a leader provides subordinates with specific tasks to complete. In turn, it is expected that each subordinate will complete the specific tasks based on the job descriptions. Although leaders make requests based on their leadership positions across the organizational structure and subordinates comply because of their formal obligation and motivation (Northouse, 2021), the impression management by subordinates, i.e. how individuals influence others, can influence how leaders perceive them. Feedback seeking is a proactive behaviour that helps to create the impression that subordinates pay attention to, and are concerned about, the quality of their tasks (Crant, 2000). In this regard, two types of motives are used in the literature to measure feedback seeking. The first is performance-related motives that refer to the extent to which subordinates attempt to collect information from the leader to improve their performance. The second is impression management motives that refer to the extent to which each subordinate influences how the leader perceives them (Lam et al, 2007). In contrast, the LMX literature suggests that the ingratiation tactic, i.e. conformity, rendering favours and making people feel comfortable and positive about themselves, is positively associated with LMX quality, and thus leaders' attributions of motives are required. This is because when leaders attribute behaviour to subordinates' feedback seeking, high-quality LMX is achieved. Specifically, this attribution helps explain the effects of subordinates' behaviour on the quality of LMX and ultimately on performance. Empirical research by Megheirkouni (2017) reveals that LMX fully mediated the relationship between job satisfaction and organizational commitment, and between job satisfaction and job performance in sport stadiums.

LEVEL 2

The leader and subordinates at this level become acquainted. The relationship begins with an offer by either the leader or the subordinates in order to improve working relationships through career-oriented social exchange. During this level, they share information on personal and work levels, shaping the roles they can play together. The relationship development between leader and subordinates moves to a new way of relating after the relationship reaches acquaintance (Erdogan et al, 2006). Northouse (2021) calls this relationship development a 'medium quality'. It is worth mentioning that although the relationship development has improved to a medium quality, it is still limited because of being part of an experimental level.

LEVEL 3

The leader and subordinates at this level become part of what is classified as a mature partnership exchange. At this level, the relationship between the leader and subordinates is highly developed, and based on trust, obligation, loyalty, support, and respect. Researchers have confirmed that high-quality exchange between leader and subordinate occurs when the two parties in the exchange relationship share beneficial and valued goals (e.g. Dunegan et al, 2002; Janssen and Van Yperen, 2004; Wang et al, 2005). During this mature partnership, each individual affects and is affected by the other. Therefore, the relationship between leader and subordinates goes beyond the formally defined work contract to become unlimited (Graen and Uhl-Bien, 1995). One implication is that leaders count on subordinates to provide them with partnership assistance when necessary. For example, the leader may ask subordinates to complete some tasks that exceed their job description. In turn, subordinates may rely on the leader to provide them with support and encouragement. this is analogous to transformational leadership that is based on the exchange between leaders and subordinates to achieve the greater good of the team and organization.

SYSTEM AND NETWORK

The final stage extended the debate from LMX relationships as dyads within work groups and independent dyads to include larger systems. The relationships in a leadership network cut across organizational work unit, divisional, functional, and organizational boundaries. It is worth mentioning that the relationships in a leadership network are not limited to leader–subordinate relationships, but rather include the relationships in the leadership network with peers, team-members, and individuals across all levels of the organizational structure. However, it should be noted that to discuss the system and network stage in LMX research, there is a need to shed light on the integration of network debate in leadership. Specifically, Graen (2006: 277) revised and extended Stage 4 in LMX theory by suggesting what he calls the new "LMX-MMX theory of sharing network leadership": MMX for Member–Member Exchange.

Previous studies emphasize the importance of understanding both formal and informal influences on behaviour within small and large networks in an organization when viewing organizations as systems of dyadic 'subassemblies' (Graen and Scandura, 1987; Katz and Kahn, 1978; Uhl-Bien and Graen, 1992, 1993). Based on these studies, Graen (2006: 276) suggested "LMX [as] being vertical and MMX is every direction but vertical" to indicate two types of relationships. Based on previous studies, Uhl-Bien (2006) focused on Relational

Leadership Theory research for a better understanding of the relational dynamics that see leadership as a process by which social systems change through the structuring of roles and relationships; and thus the major focus moves to relational dynamics, rather than a more static state of relational quality with antecedents and outcomes.

EVALUATION OF LMX THEORY

There are several limitations to LMX theory. The lack of equity of the out-group is the common weaknesses of LMX theory in vertical dyad linkage theory (the early stage of LMX theory). Specifically, LMX theory divides organizational work units into two groups: in-group and out-group; but only a few subordinates receive special attention, not all. This makes job equity questionable in the organizations in which leaders adopt this behaviour. In this regard, Scandura (1999) argues that the differentiation between in-group and out-group in the organization has negative impacts on the emergence of organizational justice. Furthermore, although leaders attempt to establish a high-quality relationship with all subordinates, there is no guarantee that all subordinates will accept the offer.

Another criticism is that the research on LMX theory has not comprehensively explored the contextual issues, particularly organizational culture and its impacts on dyadic relationships (Anand et al, 2011). The leading research questionnaires have restricted our exploration of any additional aspects of LMX theory. In this regard, Yukl (2013) argues that qualitative research methods are needed to support and reinforce the evidence on the quality of the relationships. Another example of the lack of research on context and its impact on dyadic relationships is the institutional system or socio-cultural issues. Because sport has become a global phenomenon, we see that football coaches are changing their football teams to work with more than one team over their career. However, although sport globalization research (e.g. Miller et al, 2001) suggests that cultural boundaries are rapidly weakened because of increased exchanges between coaches and athletes around the world, divergent and convergent research regarding the cultural differences is still predominant. In this regard, the quality of coach-athlete relationship may be different from country to country, from team to team, from person to person across cultures because of differences in ways of thinking, particularly if coaches and athletes are from different cultures and ethnic backgrounds. Additionally, although LMX theory has been revised many times, it still has various conceptual gaps that limit its effectiveness. Specifically, the early version of this theory failed to explain how dyadic relationships develop over time, how the different leader–subordinate dyads affect each other, and how inequality in a dyadic relationship affects the general performance of an organizational work unit. Overall, some such differences have been considered in revisions of the theory, but further research is still required to address such conceptual gaps.

Despite the deficiencies of LMX theory, it also has several advantages. First, LMX theory reflects a realistic image of the sport work environment in which we can grasp the gap between in-group and out-group. Furthermore, this theory concentrates on the dyadic relationship between leaders and subordinates, while the other theories and approaches focus on the characteristics of leaders, subordinates, context, or even all of them, as one element of the leadership process (Northouse, 2021). Moreover, LMX theory focuses on the interpersonal relationship aspects of leadership, and thus the high-quality dyadic relationship is linked to the degree to which communication skills between leaders and subordinates are effective. Finally, studies on LMX theory have addressed the issue of how the LMX relationship is related to organizational variables, such as performance, job satisfaction, organizational commitment, organizational citizenship behaviour, innovation, relational demography, and other organizational variables (e.g. Graen and Uhl-Bien, 1995). Taking these strengths into consideration, LMX theory appears to be a promising theory in the sport management and leadership literature which examines the relationship between LMX and sport organizational variables and its implications for general sport performance.

SUMMARY

LMX theory differs from previous theories and approaches in making the dyadic relationship between leaders and subordinates the primary focus of the leadership process. The development of LMX underwent four stages: vertical dyadic linkage theory (VDL), LMX, partnership building, and system and network. In the three-phase model of developing LMX, leader and subordinates in the first level come together as strangers, estimating their behaviours, personality, and requirements to understand and adopt an appropriate behaviour to establish exchange relationships. In the second level, leader and subordinates become acquainted; while leader and subordinates become part of a mature partnership exchange in the third level. The evaluation of LMX reveals that it has several strengths as well as weaknesses.

GENERAL QUESTIONS

1. What are the weaknesses and strengths of LMX theory?
2. How do you describe the relationship between the leader and the subordinate in LMX theory?
3. What are the stages of developing positive LMX theory? Can you explain the process of this development?
4. Do you think that a relationship that is based on trust, obligation, loyalty, support, and respect is productive or not? Why?
5. In what ways have you seen LMX theory implemented in your previous sport management career?
6. How has or will LMX theory contribute to enhancing your personal leadership? Why?
7. How does LMX theory differ from other leadership theories you have studied so far?

OPEN DISCUSSION QUESTIONS

1. Based on LMX theory, how do you describe your relationship with your previous or current leaders? Discuss your experience with colleagues.
2. Based on LMX theory, how do you describe your leaders' relationship with you? Discuss this experience with colleagues.
3. Based on the three-phase process in developing LMX, can you describe your experience at each level? Can you identify the challenges accompanied with this development?
4. After reviewing the four stages of LMX theory, can you explain how LMX theory works?

Case Study 7.1: The Dyadic Relationship in Olympic Settings

The dyadic relationships between Sam, Head of Mission, and all the athletes of the Olympic Mission has implications for the way Sam is perceived. The mission comprises 18 teams and 111 athletes. Sam has had personal relationships with three athletes, including a gold medallist. This is often evident in the Olympic Village, for example, during meals, walking in the Olympic Park, and shopping. However, this does not mean Sam adopts different behaviours with the other athletes; rather Sam views all athletes as heroes, even those who fail to win medals. Sam attempts to reinforce their desire to achieve good results in future competitions, which is the major aim of Sam's National Olympic Committee.

Questions

1. Discuss with your colleagues the dyadic relationships between Sam and Sam's Olympic national teams.
2. Explore to what extent these relationships could impact on how Sam is or will be perceived.

SELF-ASSESSMENT 7.1: YOUR DYADIC RELATIONSHIP

This assessment is based on data collected by Jowett and Cockerill (2003) to examine the dyadic relationships between Olympic athletes and coaches. Review the following statements and see whether they represent your dyadic relationship with a coach or manager you have or have had.

Select Yes or No for each statement.

1. I follow coach's instructions and coach provides me with positive instructions.
2. They have a way to make me work hard – we work together at the pool.
3. They can be very sweet but can also be very hard on us, aggressive, and demanding.
4. I do the best I can and so do they.

5. My coach is very encouraging and pushes me even when I cannot try any harder or do better.
6. I have an inner desire to know that they will support me – and they never let me down.
7. I do not trust my coach entirely because they are at times indecisive.
8. I do not appreciate their efforts because they are hesitant, indecisive, and doubtful. As a result, I do not feel positive about them.
9. They cannot understand me. And as a result, I find training sessions are not consistent with what I feel appropriate and necessary.

SELF-ASSESSMENT 7.2: IN-GROUP AND OUT-GROUP

Determine whether the following seven behaviours are in-group or out-group, say, in a sporting goods company.

1. A manager at operational level gives employees the freedom to solve problems.
2. A manager gives employees specific guidance for how to complete tasks.
3. A manager shows little interest in employees' feedback and their new ideas on how the plan is achieved.
4. A manager is very strict and punishes mistakes.
5. A manager attempts to build interesting job environment by giving employees the opportunity to choose their assignment.
6. A manager imposes their own views and ideas.
7. A manager praises employees' performance and accomplishments.

SELF-ASSESSMENT 7.3: LMX DEVELOPMENT STAGES

Match the following statements with the four stages of in development of LMX theory.

(a) Vertical Dyadic Linkage; (b) Leader–Member Exchange;
(c) Partnership Building; (d) System and Network

1. A gymnastics coach provides guidance, feedback, and consideration to their Olympic players. But this is left to the extent that each player will respond to this initiative, because this has different impacts on players and leads to the creation of in-groups and out-groups. It is noted that only one player rendered an exceptional performance and won a gold medal.
2. In a sporting goods store, the store manager focuses on the quality of each employee relationship through better attention, reward, influence, support, and empowerment. This has positive implications for the store's performance compared to other stores in the area. As a result of this, the store manager benefits from the store's performance, becoming the regional manager.
3. The new football team manager makes a shift from the traditional relationship between a coach–manager and players. They aspire to build positive relationships with all players, rather than a few players. This is evident by

giving players an opportunity for leadership as partners in making and preparing plans and tactics.

4. The initiative of the new president of the volleyball federation begins by creating dyadic relationships in all directions across the organizational structure of the federation to build strong networks that help improve the general performance at all levels: players, leaders, and federation.

Suggested Reading

Case, R. (1998). Leader Member Exchange Theory and Sport: Possible Applications. *Journal of Sport Behavior*, 21(4), 387–395. ProQuest: https://www.proquest.com/docview/215869718.

Graen, G.B. and Uhl-Bien, M. (1995). Relationship-Based Approach to Leadership: Development of Leader-Member Exchange (LMX) Theory of Leadership over 25 Years: Applying a Multi-Level Multi-Domain Perspective. *The Leadership Quarterly*, 6(2), 219–247. https://doi.org/10.1016/1048-9843(95)90036-5.

Megheirkouni, M. (2017). Revisiting Leader-Member Exchange Theory: Insights into Stadia Management. *International Journal of Event and Festival Management*, 8(3), 244–260. https://doi.org/10.1108/IJEFM-03-2017-0022.

Sparrowe, R.T. and Liden, R.C. (1997). Process and Structure in Leader-Member Exchange. *Academy of Management Review*, 22(2), 522–552. https://doi.org/10.5465/amr.1997.9707154068.

References

Anand, S., Hu, J., Liden, R.C. and Vidyarthi, P.R. (2011). Leader-Member Exchange: Recent Research Findings and Prospects for the Future. In: Bryman, A., Collinson, D., Grint, K., Jackson, B. and Uhl-Bien, M. (Eds.). *The Sage Handbook of Leadership*. Thousand Oaks, CA: Sage. (311–325).

Bang, H. (2011). Leader–Member Exchange in Non-Profit Sport Organizations. *Non profit Management and Leadership*, 22(1), 85–105. https://doi.org/10.1002/nml.20042.

Coe, S. and Mason, N. (1996). *The Olympians: A Century of Gold*. London: Pavilion.

Crant, J.M. (2000). Proactive Behaviour in Organizations. *Journal of Management*, 26(3), 435–462. https://doi.org/10.1177/014920630002600304.

Dansereau, F., Graen, G.B. and Haga, W.J. (1975). A Vertical Dyad Linkage Approach to Leadership within Formal Organizations: A Longitudinal Investigation of the Role Making Process. *Organizational Behaviour and Human Performance*, 13(1), 46–78. https://doi.org/10.1016/0030-5073(75)90005-7.

Dunegan, K.J., Uhl-Bien, M. and Duchon, D. (2002). LMX and Subordinate Performance: The Moderating Effects of Task Characteristics. *Journal of Business and Psychology*, 17(2), 275–285. https://doi.org/10.1023/A:1019641700724.

Erdogan, B., Liden, R.C. and Kraimer, M.L. (2006). Justice and Leader-Member Exchange: The Moderating Role of Organizational Culture. *The Academy of Management Journal*, 49(2), 395–406. https://doi.org/10.5465/amj.2006.20786086.

Fairhurst, G.T. (1993). The Leader-Member Exchange Patterns of Women Leaders in the Industry: A Discourse Analysis. *Communication Monograph*, 60(4), 321–351. https://doi.org/10.1080/03637759309376316.

Ford, L.R. and Seers, A. (2006). Relational Leadership and Team Climates: Pitting Differentiation versus Agreement. *The Leadership Quarterly*, 17(3), 258–270. https://doi.org/10.1016/j.leaqua.2006.02.005.

Gould, D., Guinan, D., Greenleaf, C., Medbery, R. and Peterson, K. (1999). Factors Affecting Olympic Performance: Perceptions of Athletes and Coaches from More and Less Successful Teams. *The Sport Psychologist*, 13(4), 371–394. https://doi.org/10.1123/tsp.13.4.371.

Graen, G. (1976). Role Making Process within Complex Organizations. In: Dunnette, M.D. (Ed.). *Handbook of Industrial and Organizational Psychology*. Chicago, IL: Rand McNally. (1201–1245).

Graen, G. and Cashman, J.F. (1975). A Role-Making Model of Leadership in Formal Organizations: A Developmental Approach. In: Hunt, J. and Larson, L.L. (Eds.). *Leadership Frontiers*. Kent, OH: Kent State University Press. (143–166).

Graen, G.B. (2006). Post Simon, March, Weick, and Graen: New Leadership Sharing as a Key to Understanding Organizations. In: Graen, G. and Graen, J.A. (Eds.). *Sharing Network Leadership*. (Vol. 4). Greenwich, CT: Information Age. (269–279). https://doi.org/10.13140/RG.2.1.3057.0002.

Graen, G.B. and Scandura, T.A. (1987). Toward a Psychology of Dyadic Organizing. *Research in Organizational Behavior*, 9, 175–208.

Graen, G.B. and Uhl-Bien, M. (1991). The Transformation of Professionals into Self-Managing and Partially Self-Designing Contributors: Toward a Theory of Leadership Making. *Journal of Management Systems*, 3(3), 33–48. DigitalCommons@University of Nebraska – Lincoln: https://digitalcommons.unl.edu/cgi/viewcontent.cgi?article=1015&context=managementfacpub.

Graen, G.B. and Uhl-Bien, M. (1995). Relationship-Based Approach to Leadership: Development of Leader-Member Exchange (LMX) Theory of Leadership over 25 Years: Applying a Multi-Level Multi-Domain Perspective. *The Leadership Quarterly*, 6(2), 219–247. https://doi.org/10.1016/1048-9843(95)90036-5.

Hoye, R. (2004). Leader-Member Exchanges and Board Performance of Voluntary Sport Organizations. *Nonprofit Management and Leadership*, 15(1), 55–70. https://doi.org/10.1002/nml.53.

Janssen, O. and Van Yperen, N.W. (2004). Employees' Goal Orientations, the Quality of Leader–Member Exchange, and the Outcomes of Job Performance and Job Satisfaction. *Academy of Management Journal*, 47(3), 368–384. JSTOR: https://www.jstor.org/stable/20159587.

Jowett, S. (2003). When the Honeymoon is Over: A Case Study of a Coach-Athlete Relationship in Crisis. *The Sport Psychologist*, 17(4), 444–460. https://doi.org/10.1123/tsp.17.4.444.

Jowett, S. and Cockerill, I.M. (2003). Olympic Medallists' Perspective of the Athlete-Coach Relationship. *Psychology of Sport and Exercise*, 4(4), 313–331. https://doi.org/10.1016/S1469-0292(02)00011-0.

Kacmar, K.M., Witt, L.A., Zivnuska, S. and Gully, S.M. (2003). The Interactive Effect of Leader-Member Exchange and Communication Frequency on Performance

Ratings. *Journal of Applied Psychology*, 88(4), 764–772. https://doi.org/10.1037/0021-9010.88.4.764.

Katz, D. and Kahn, R.L. (1978). *The Social Psychology of Organizations*. (2nd ed.). New York: Wiley & Sons.

Kinicki A.J. and Vecchio, R.P. (1994). Influences on the Quality of Supervisor-Subordinate Relations: The Role of Time Pressure, Organizational Commitment, and Locus of Control. *Journal of Organizational Behaviour*, 15(1), 75–82. https://doi.org/10.1002/job.4030150108.

Lam, W., Huang, X. and Snape, E. (2007). Feedback-Seeking Behaviour and Leader-Member Exchange: Do Supervisor-Attributed Motives Matter? *Academy of Management Journal*, 50(2), 348–363. https://doi.org/10.5465/amj.2007.24634440.

Liden, R.C., Wayne, S.J. and Sparrowe, R.T. (2000). An Examination of the Mediating Role of Psychological Empowerment on the Relations between the Job, Interpersonal Relationships, and Work Outcomes. *Journal of Applied Psychology*, 85(3), 407–416. https://doi.org/10.1037/0021-9010.85.3.407.

Liden, R.C., Wayne, S.J. and Stilwell, D. (1993). A Longitudinal Study on the Early Development of Leader-Member Exchanges. *Journal of Applied Psychology*, 78(4), 662–674. https://doi.org/10.1037/0021-9010.78.4.662.

Markham, S.E., Yammarino, F.J., Murry, W.D. and Palanski, M.E. (2010). Leader–Member Exchange, Shared Values, and Performance: Agreement and Levels of Analysis Do Matter. *The Leadership Quarterly*, 21(3), 469–480. https://doi.org/10.1016/j.leaqua.2010.03.010.

Megheirkouni, M. (2017). Revisiting Leader-Member Exchange Theory: Insights into Stadia Management. *International Journal of Event and Festival Management*, 8(3), 244–260. https://doi.org/10.1108/IJEFM-03-2017-0022.

Miller, T., Lawrence, G., McKay, J. and Rowe, D. (2001). *Globalization and Sport: Playing the World*. London: Sage. https://doi.org/10.4135/9781446218396.

Northouse, P.G. (2021). *Leadership: Theory and Practice*. (9th ed.). London: Sage.

Scandura, T.A. (1999). Rethinking Leader-Member Exchange: An Organisational Justice Perspective. *The Leadership Quarterly*, 10(1), 25–40. https://doi.org/10.1016/S1048-9843(99)80007-1.

Schyns, B., Paul, T., Mohr, G. and Blank, H. (2005). Comparing Antecedents and Consequences of LMX in a German Working Context to Findings in the US. *European Journal of Work and Organizational Psychology*, 14(1), 1–22. https://doi.org/10.1080/13594320444000191.

Sparrowe, R.T., Soetjipto, B.W. and Kraimer, M.L. (2006). Do Leaders' Influence Tactics Relate to Members' Helping Behavior? It Depends on the Quality of the Relationship. *Academy of Management Journal*, 49(6), 1194–1208. https://doi.org/10.5465/amj.2006.23478645.

Uhl-Bien, M (2006). Relational Leadership Theory: Exploring the Social Processes of Leadership and Organizing. *The Leadership Quarterly*, 17(6), 654–676. https://doi.org/10.1016/j.leaqua.2006.10.007.

Uhl-Bien, M. and Graen, G.B. (1992). Leadership-Making in Self-Managing Professional Work Teams: An Empirical Investigation. In: Clark, K.E., Clark, M.B. and Campbell, D.P. (Eds.). *Impact of Leadership*. Greensboro, NC: Center for Creative Leadership. (379–387).

Uhl-Bien, M. and Graen, G.B. (1993). Toward a Contingency Model of Empowerment: Contribution of Self-Management Empowerment and Leadership-Making Empowerment to Uni-Functional and Multi-Functional Professional Work Unit Performance. Paper presented at the Annual Meeting of the Academy of Management, August, 1993, Atlanta, GA.

Wang, H., Law, K.S., Hackett, R.D., Wang, D. and Chen, Z.X. (2005). Leader-Member Exchange as a Mediator of the Relationship between Transformational Leadership and Followers' Performance and Organizational Citizenship Behaviour. *Academy of Management Journal*, 48(3), 420–432. https://doi.org/10.5465/amj.2005.17407908.

Yammarino, F.J. (2002). Individualized Leadership. *Journal of Leadership and Organizational Studies Summer*, 9(1), 90–99. https://doi.org/10.1177/107179190200900107.

Yrle, A.C., Hartman, S. and Galle, W.P. (2002). An Investigation of Relationships between Communication Style and Leader-Member Exchange. *Journal of Communication Management*, 6(3), 257–268. https://doi.org/10.1108/13632540210807099.

Yukl, G. (2013). *Leadership in Organizations, Global Edition*. (7th ed.). London: Pearson.

8 TRANSFORMATIONAL LEADERSHIP

Learning Outcomes

After reading this chapter, you will be able to:

- Understand the components of charismatic leadership
- Distinguish between power and influence in leadership
- Understand the types of leader power
- Understand transformational-transactional leadership factors
- Evaluate the strengths and weaknesses of transformational leadership
- Apply these theories in a sport context

INTRODUCTION

Transformational leadership is one of the dominant approaches to leadership in the current literature. The power of the transformational approach has helped to extend the debates and empirical studies in different research disciplines because this particular approach has dominated not only business and management disciplines but other disciplines such as education, healthcare, and engineering. This kind of leadership represents the process that changes individuals through using an form of influence that encourages subordinates to accomplish or achieve more than what is expected of them regarding the tasks required. As a result, the transformational approach to leadership can be used to influence processes and outcomes from the simple to the complex.

CHARISMATIC LEADERSHIP

In ancient Greek culture, 'charisma' was used to refer to a special gift that certain individuals possess, which enables them to influence others to make them do more than what is expected. It was then and long-since considered something you cannot learn through instruction, and in contemporary terms training sessions, courses, academic degrees, or career development. 'Charisma' first appeared in English as part of theology, and has been discussed for many centuries. The concept and word then entered English again in the writings (in translation in 1930) of Max Weber (1864–1920), the German sociologist, talking about a statesman or military commander (male assumed).

DOI: 10.4324/9780429290442-11

This definition has, since then, been quickly generalized into other contexts, and current usage is now, for example: "a personal magic of leadership arousing special popular loyalty or enthusiasm for a public figure (such as a political leader)" (Merriam-Webster, n.d.).Within many contemporary societies, public figures now include many more cultural figures, such as sport athletes, managers, club owners, pundits, and celebrity fans. Charismatic labels may include 'diva' (which is now heard less often, as it gained a negative connotation) and 'star'; consider expressions such as 'star' quality for someone 'up and coming'. In the following discussion, you will find other points where distinguishing between perceived or supposed personality attributes and actual or expected achievements becomes a critical tool.

COMPONENTS OF CHARISMATIC LEADERSHIP

Understanding charismatic leadership qualities can help subordinates to be strong individuals, and thus 'qualify' them to be in leadership roles. Howell and Shamir (2005) view charisma as residing in the relationship between leaders who exhibit certain personality characteristics and behaviours and subordinates who have, in turn, certain perceptions of and attitudes towards those leaders. The findings of empirical research conducted by Jung and Sosik (2006) to distinguish charismatic leaders and non-charismatic leaders, reveal that managers rated by subordinates as high on charismatic leadership reported higher levels of self-monitoring and self-actualization, and higher motivation to attain social power and self-enhancement values. Additionally, managers rated by superiors as high on charismatic leadership were associated with followers who reported higher levels of extra effort. Jay Conger and Rabindra Kanungo (1987) have identified four stages of personality characteristics and behaviours of charismatic leadership to distinguish between charismatic and non-charismatic leaders.

STAGE 1: ASSESSMENT OF ENVIRONMENT FOR ACHIEVING CHANGE

Charismatic leaders attempt to assess the environmental factors at micro, meso, and macro levels (i.e. small, medium, and large scale) that influence their role and effectiveness in organizations. They are sensitive to both the emotional needs and capabilities of subordinates, and they understand the environmental factors that constrain their effectiveness. An understanding of the environmental challenges and the manner of meeting these challenges is based on realistic assessment of environmental requirements. It is worth noting that leaders may not be considered charismatic otherwise (Conger and Kanungo, 1987).

STAGE 2: ARTICULATING AND COMMUNICATING VISION

Charismatic leaders are often individuals who exhibit disagreement and annoyance with the status quo and go further to revise or change it, in accordance with their vision. However, non-charismatic leaders may be perceived as doing the opposite of what charismatic leaders do in terms of their attitude towards the status quo and their lack of desire to change it. Charismatic leaders are able to articulate their visions by three processes. First, they promote the positive image of their vision of the future in contrast with their negative image of the status quo. Specifically, they present the current situation as unacceptable, and their vision as a clear alternative in terms of effectiveness (Choi, 2006). Second, through expressive modes of action, including verbal and non-verbal, charismatic leaders communicate the convictions behind their own motivation, such as self-confidence and dedication, to give credibility to what they advocate (Yukl, 2013). Third, charismatic leaders express their own motivation to lead by adopting several impression management approaches. This includes the focus on rhetoric by dramatic, symbolic, and metaphoric language, using body language, and other verbal and non-verbal forms (Conger and Kanungo, 1987). It is expected that charismatic leaders may be recognized for, variously, exciting patriot, solidarity, emotional, publicly inspirational, political, and historical oratory (Mio et al, 2005; Sheehan and Sheehan, 2006; Conger et al, 2000). Importantly, oratory is used as a means for delivering a specific message. This assumes that the importance of oratory is not only in the content, but also the style used to deliver content, which is integral to the attribution of charisma.

STAGE 3: BUILDING TRUST AND ADOPTING UNCONVENTIONAL BEHAVIOURS

Building trust with subordinates is an essential need for organizational leadership. Charismatic leaders attempt to adopt unconventional behaviour to transcend the current reality, but they make this appear extraordinary, so that it becomes similar to reverence (Conger and Kanungo, 1987). They demonstrate a concern for subordinates' needs and transform their concern into total dedication and commitment and avoid all forms of selfishness. It is worth mentioning that the relationship between leaders and subordinates should be at a high level of trust. Yukl (2013) claims that integrity is an essential characteristic in building trust relationships, and it is demonstrated through consistency between values and personal actions. Specifically, charismatic leaders possess a set of characteristics that enable them to persist in most challenges and barriers such as high personal risks, incur high costs, and engage in self-sacrifice to achieve a shared vision. When charismatic leaders demonstrate heroic characteristics, this reinforces their capability to attract their subordinates' admiration, and increases the potential of them being trusted (Bromley and Kirschner-Bromley, 2007). It can be stated that the more leaders demonstrate that they are prepared to take high personal risks for achieving the shared vision, the more they are charismatic in the sense of being worthy of trust.

STAGE 4: ADOPTING UNCONVENTIONAL OR EXTRAORDINARY STRATEGIES FOR CHANGE

When leaders demonstrate the capability of transcending the status quo by using unconventional and extraordinary strategies, they are perceived as charismatic. Their past achievements and successes may be a critical factor for the attribution of charisma. Charismatic leaders demonstrate that the conventional processes of the status quo, such as rules, routine, and organizational bureaucracy fail to achieve the wanted vision. In other words, they counter norms, whereas non-charismatic leaders are mostly individuals who conform to current norms (Bromley and Kirschner-Bromley, 2007).

It is worth noting that the strategies by which leaders express expertise are closely related to the power source from which they lead, which helps understand whether leaders are perceived as using negative 'personalized characteristic leadership' or positive 'socialized charismatic leadership' (Howell and Shamir, 2005; Yukl, 2013). Empirical research has shown that personalized charismatic leaders can have detrimental implications on long-term organizational performance, whereas leaders who use socialized behaviour show positive results in improving organizational performance (O'Connor et al, 1995). As expected with positive charismatic leaders, they share power through delegation of authority among subordinates (Yukl, 2013). This gives subordinates an opportunity to be active in the organization and increases their potential to be empowered.

POWER vs INFLUENCE

The terms 'power' and 'influence' are extensively used in leadership literature to refer variously to the leader's role or personality, organizational structure, or environmental issues. Despite the wide use of both terms, understanding the meaning of power and influence tends to be difficult (Hitchner, 1993).

Power refers to the ability to get something done the way you want it (Astley and Pachdeva, 1984; Kaplan, 1964); or the ability to get individuals to do specific tasks you want to be done (Salancik and Pfeffer, 1974). Rahim (1989: 545) defines power as "the ability of one party to change or control the behaviour, attitudes, opinions, objectives, needs, and values of another party". Similarly, Northouse (2016: 10) states that power is the ability to influence others: specifically, he defines it as "the capacity or potential to influence. People have power when they are able to affect others' beliefs, attitudes, and courses of action".

It is worth noting that we do not 'power' something, but we can 'influence' something (Sims, 2002). Power, therefore, is perceived as the 'force' leaders use to get something done in a specific way, whereas influence is perceived as the effect an individual's actions have when exercising power on others and it is noted in others' behavioural response.

TYPES OF LEADER POWER

The early work and the most widely cited research on power derived the notion of power from the framework of dyadic relationships between leader and subordinates. French and Raven (1960) suggested five types of leader power that are available to leaders. These types are divided into two sources of power: position power and personal power. Position power refers to the power derived from a specific role or office across the organizational structure. With position power comes the ability to engage in various behaviours towards subordinates, such as the ability to reward, punish, support, develop, ignore, direct, amongst others.

Personal power refers to the power derived from the leader's specific knowledge or personal characteristics that are seen by subordinates. Both sources of power are differentiated into types, as follows.

POSITION POWER

The three types of position power are derived from a person having formal authority in an organization:

1. **Legitimate**: For example, once a manager has been selected to lead the national team, most (if not always all) players are obligated to implement their guidance regarding, for example, preparation plan, tactic plans, and match schedule prior to the championship. Players accept following this kind of power as it is derived from the manager's legitimate duties to accomplish the organization's goals.
2. **Reward**: This authority helps leaders to access to formal rewards that can be used in different forms based on management level. Overall, leaders can use reward to influence subordinates' behaviour. For example, the leader of a sport-related company may use financial resources to give rewards such as club season tickets to active employees.
3. **Coercive**: Whereas reward is seen as positive, coercive power involves penalizing or punishing others. For example, a netball manager keeps three players on the bench a game as a result of being late to the morning training session. A coach who makes a player sit on the bench because they did not implement the tactics required in the match is also using coercive power.

Note that 'coercive' here does not have a negative or violent meaning; it remains within the boundaries of formal authority. Similarly, 'reward' is within the acknowledge boundaries of organizational authority.

PERSONAL POWER

The two types of personal power are derived from a person having specific knowledge or personal characteristics that are seen by subordinates:

1. **Referent**: This type of power is sourced from the leader's personal characteristics that command subordinates' identification, attention, admiration, commitment, and respect. Referent power is seen when a charismatic relationship exists between the leader and subordinates, so subordinates attempt to identify with the leader: the leader is the reference guide for the subordinates' behaviours.
2. **Expert**: This type of power is derived from the leader's knowledge regarding the work environment. When the leader masters the skills, abilities, and competencies required in the tasks performed by subordinates, the leader is perceived as an expert power. When the head of the national Olympic teams is an Olympic expert, the teams will listen to their recommendations and comments regarding the performance after each competition or match during the Olympic event. It is worth noting that managers may lack

expert power or may have the same expert power of some subordinates. Expert personal power does not automatically transfer between environments. For example, an expert can have high personal power in a motivational visit, but not be able to work in a non-expert environment.

The need for any or all power sources may be equal or varied, and they may have positive or/and negative outcomes on sport organizations in all sectors. For example, empirical research reveals that (a) there are positive relationships between all power sources and job satisfaction; (b) there is no difference between elite and non-elite settings in the importance of power bases (Megheirkouni, 2019).

TRANSFORMATIONAL LEADERSHIP

The phrase 'transformational leadership' was first coined by Downton (1973), but Burns (1978) was the first to conceptualize leadership as either transformational or transactional for getting work done. He linked between the roles of leadership and followership. Bass (1985) expanded the initial version of transformational leadership based on the work of Burns by focusing on subordinates' needs, and extended House's work (House, 1976; House and Howell, 1992) by focusing on the emotional elements and the origins of charisma.

Transformational leadership is defined by Northouse (2016: 186) as "the process whereby a person engages with others and creates a connection that raises the level of motivation and morality in both the leader and the follower". The components of transformational leadership have been identified by previous studies (Bass, 1985; Bycio et al, 1995; Avolio et al, 1995). These components have evolved as a result of the improvement made in both measurement and conceptualization of transformational leadership (Bass and Riggio, 2005). Conceptually, charismatic leadership provides meaning and understanding because subordinates identify with their leaders and emulate them. Additionally, the leader expands the subordinates' use of their capabilities. Moreover, leader provides the followers with the support required. These components can be measured with the Multifactor Leadership Questionnaire (MLQ) (Avolio et al, 1995), and they include:

IDEALIZED INFLUENCE

This is also called charisma. The leader possesses the ability to develop a symbolic power that can help influence subordinates. In other words, leaders are admired, loved, trusted. Subordinates, in turn, identify with their leaders and seek strongly to emulate them, because of the extraordinary capabilities of leaders that help to provide subordinates with a sense of mission. Idealized influence is measured by two major aspects: behaviours, which refers to the way subordinates perceive their leader's behaviours; and attributional elements, which are aspects attributed to the leader by subordinates' perceptions. Bass and Riggio (2005) point out that a sample item that represents idealized influence behaviour factor in the MLQ is the focus on having a collective sense of mission, and a sample item from the idealized influence attributional factor is based on reassuring individuals by confirming the ability to solve problems or overcome challenges.

INSPIRATIONAL MOTIVATION

A transformational leader tends to behave in ways that inspire and motivate subordinates, and communicate expectations to subordinates to be active parts of the shared vision of an organization. The notion of team spirit is enhanced by inspirational motivation. Leaders encourage and support team members to accomplish more for the benefit of all members. This would, in turn, reflect on the organization as a whole. Overall, when leaders demonstrate inspiration, motivation, support, enthusiasm, optimism, and emotion, subordinates will be willing to accomplish more than they would for their own self-interest. For example, although a football team includes several star players, it loses the last three league matches. The manager is unsatisfied because of the team performance. However, the manager continues to be inspiring and to communicate expectations to all players in hope of enhancing the team spirit, because the manager believes that football team's success is a result of collective efforts.

INTELLECTUAL STIMULATION

A transformational leader stimulates subordinates' efforts to be more innovative and creative by raising questions, hypotheses, or ideas, challenging subordinates' values, reframing problems and approaching the status quo in new ways, but without criticizing subordinates' mistakes just because their ideas differ from the leaders'. For example, the head of a swimming federation stimulates not only the board members, but also the clubs, and the sport and leisure coaches and managers to be innovative and creative in ways that help to discover young talents and develop their talents to be effective for future national teams.

INDIVIDUALIZED CONSIDERATION

A transformational leader provides special support to each individual subordinate's needs for achievement, development, and growth. The leader acts as a mentor or coach. Individualized consideration can be seen when new learning opportunities are created in a department or an organization, which require support from a supervisor or line manager. For example, the national boxing team competes in a world championship, but one boxer does not use the technique and tactic required to win the competition and has not even committed to the plans made in the camp. The coach gives specific directives with a high degree of structure to the boxer to improve the performance in future championships and competitions.

TRANSACTIONAL LEADERSHIP

Transactional leadership represents an alternative leadership style alongside transformational leadership. This style is split into three dimensions: contingent reward, active management-by-exception, and passive management-by-exception.

CONTINGENT REWARD

Leaders in this constructive transaction obtain subordinate agreement on what needs to be done and what rewards may be offered in exchange for satisfactory process and goal completion. It is worth noting that although this type of transaction motivates subordinates to achieve a good performance and development, it is not as high as transformational leadership may achieve. An example of contingent reward is the president of a rugby club negotiating with an attacking midfielder player to score and support a Six Nations Cup win to increase their annual salary in the next three seasons.

ACTIVE MANAGEMENT-BY-EXCEPTION

Leaders in this corrective transaction actively monitor subordinates' deviances from rules and standards. Specifically, leaders closely watch the mistakes and errors in their subordinates' assignments and take corrective actions when required. An example of this corrective transaction is a coach who monitors the performance of players in a match and calls them to change their tactic to an alternative plan when needed. Another example is the president of an Olympic Games host city who monitors the work progress in the Olympic Village and quickly contacts the managers of behind-schedule infrastructure construction projects and tells them to avoid any construction delays.

PASSIVE MANAGEMENT-BY-EXCEPTION

Leaders in this corrective transaction prefer to wait passively for deviances, mistakes, and errors of their subordinates to occur and then take corrective action. For example, national rugby team players express their displeasure because of the extensive training sessions in the camp. The coach decides to use the last preparation match to assess the team performance before the world championship. The coach does not provide any feedback or comments, but rather they makes notes and wait for players' mistakes and tactical errors to occur. When they feel they should take a corrective action, they give feedback and revise the team plan in order to improve the result in the second half of the match.

LAISSEZ-FAIRE LEADERSHIP

Laissez-faire leadership is another leadership style. It is also known for its non-leadership approach. The phrase comes from French, roughly 'let it be/happen'; and has long been used in politics and economics.

NON-LEADERSHIP BEHAVIOUR

The leader in this leadership style gives subordinates complete freedom of action, provides them with the materials, but refrains from acting except answering a question when asked, but without giving any feedback or evaluating performance. Laissez-faire style represents the avoidance of leadership: as Northouse

(2010: 192) called it, "a hands-off, let-things-ride approach". The major characteristics of this leadership style can be summarized in the following points:

The leader:

- Makes no decisions.
- Takes no leadership responsibilities.
- Provides no feedback or comments to subordinates.
- Makes no effort to help subordinates satisfy their needs.
- Avoids getting involved when critical issues arise.

An example of laissez-faire leadership is the general manager of a leisure centre who has no long-term strategy for managing staff and running services or even makes little contact with coaches and therapists, because employees (e.g. coaches, therapists) are responsible, experienced, qualified, and conscientious in a way that enables them to accomplish the goals required without the action of the general manager.

EVALUATION OF TRANSFORMATIONAL THEORIES

Transformational leadership theories have several strengths that should be taken into consideration. First, transformational leadership is one of the dominant theories in the literature and is widely investigated in most research disciplines (Lowe et al, 1996; Judge and Piccolo, 2004). Furthermore, it is still promising in young fields, such as sport management and leadership (Megheirkouni et al, 2018).

Second, transformational leadership has 'intuitive appeal' (Northouse, 2021). Transformational sport leaders make sense of a sport network at all levels: organizations, national and international (Wallace and Weese, 1995; Weese, 1995). For example, athletes, fans, club board members, and others recognize the transformational leadership career of football player, coach, and manager Sir Alex Ferguson. Third several leadership models, frameworks, and theories address how leaders use reward systems to accomplish required results. For example, although the heads of national teams have been promised career development after the Olympic Games, they continue to work hard with all team managers to improve annual plans and strategy schedules to improve athletes' performance, not only for the Olympic Games but also other championships and competitions. Specifically, transformational leadership is not only about the exchange of rewards between leaders and subordinates, but also about the attention leaders pay to their subordinates (Avolio, 1999; Bass, 1985).

Ultimately, transformational leadership addresses the notion of leadership as a dyadic process because there is no leadership without both leaders and subordinates. For example, match leadership is not the sole responsibility of a boxing coach, rather it emerges from the interplay between coach and boxer in a match. Consequently, the needs of others are an essence of the transformational leadership. Indeed, subordinates gain a more prominent position in the leadership process because their attributes are instrumental in the evolving transformational process (Bryman, 1992: 176). Moreover, this kind of leadership encourages, motivates, and supports individuals to work for a collective good rather than self-interest (Megheirkouni, 2017). For example, the manager of a national football team encourages all players to avoid self-interest in the FIFA World Football Cup, particularly those who have recently demonstrated selfishness (such as ball-hogging for goal scoring, or forcing difficult or risky passes) in previous matches in hope of gaining recruitment offers from strong football leagues. The manager motivates them to demonstrate the team spirit for the benefit of the whole team. Burns (2003) suggests that transformational leaders attempt to move individuals to higher levels of responsibility. Leaders will thus motivate subordinates (e.g. athletes, staff, teach managers, board members) to transcend their own self-interest for the good of the team, organization, or society.

Although transformational leadership theories have several strengths, there are also several weaknesses. One criticism is that transformational leadership lacks conceptual clarity (Northouse, 2021). Specifically, it is noted that several attributes of transformational leadership overlap with similar components of leadership, such as trust, vision, empowerment, desire to change, motivation, and social awareness. Another concern is that the validity of the MLQ used for measuring transformational leadership has been criticized for two reasons: first, the four components of transformational leadership – idealized influence, inspirational motivation, intellectual stimulation, and individualized consideration – are perceived as highly interconnected components (Tejeda et al, 2001). Second, what unites the four dimensions of transformational leadership compared to transactional leadership and laissez-faire leadership is still unknown (van Knippenberg and Sitkin, 2013), which raises concern regarding validity of transformational leadership and the MLQ.

Additionally, the major concern of transformational leadership has been evidently recognized in training and development sessions. Specifically, transformational leadership may be a personality trait or personal predisposition, and thus difficult to change, rather than a behaviour that can change through learning and development programmes (Bryman, 1992). For example, in the 2014 FIFA World Football Cup in Brazil, Uruguay's striker Luis Suárez was suspended from all football-related activity for four months for biting Italy's defender Giorgio Chiellini. The behaviour of Uruguay's striker might change – be transformed – through training, guidance, or therapy sessions, but this is difficult in a personality trait or personal predisposition.

SUMMARY

Transformational leadership is one of the well-researched approaches in the field of leadership, including sport business and management. This approach focuses on how certain leaders inspire subordinates to complete given tasks. Leaders' personal power is a key characteristic of transformational leaders rather than the position power that comes from organizational leadership authority. One way for better understanding transformational leadership (i.e.

idealized influence, inspirational motivation, intellectual stimulation, and individualized consideration) is to compare this kind of leadership to transactional leadership (i.e. contingent reward, active management-by-exception, and passive management-by-exception), and laissez-faire leadership (non-leadership behaviour). In addition, although transformational leadership has been of great interest to researchers in all fields, including sport business and management, it is still criticized, given that it lacks conceptual clarity, the validity of the MLQ shows highly interconnected components, leaders' personal referent power is difficult to develop or change, and commonalities between transformational leadership, transactional leadership, and laissez-faire leadership factor are still unclear.

GENERAL QUESTIONS

1. Describe charismatic leadership and why it is considered with negative implications. Give examples of four sport leaders that you would consider to be charismatic.
2. What are the components of charismatic leadership?
3. What types of power would be available to the president of a football club? To what extent these types can be effective, successful, and widely implemented in different sport organizations at the national and international levels?
4. How do you define transformational leadership? What are the components of transformational leadership? Give an example of four sport leaders that you would consider to be transformational?
5. How do you define transactional leadership? What are the components of transactional leadership? Give an example of four sport leaders that you would consider to be transactional?
6. Discuss the difference/similarity between transformational and charismatic leadership.
7. Discuss the difference between transformational and transactional leadership.

OPEN DISCUSSION QUESTIONS

1. Discuss with colleagues the difference between leadership and position power. Can you give examples on each one?
2. Discuss with your colleague the difference between power and influence.
3. Give examples of each type from previous sport management events and leagues.
4. Discuss and explain to your colleagues the characteristic of each power type.
5. Give examples on each power type from sport context and try to select your examples answer from international sport bodies.
6. Can you identify the power types that best work in sport context with evidence?

Case Study 8.1: José Mourinho

José Mourinho is one of those extraordinary personalities who have established themselves as internationally recognizable, charismatic icons on the global stage in general and football in particular. So, what is it exactly that makes José such a charismatic model for young managers wishing to develop their personal charisma and leadership effectiveness in the field of football management?

Mourinho has engaged in high personal risk over the league to accomplish the goal required. He has claimed that he is willing to risk "losing everything" in his pursuit of all four trophies with Chelsea from 2004 to 2007. He has the ability to convey a feeling of unshakeable belief in the assured success of a specific event or ventures and build the confidence of the potential of achievements.

Questions

1. What are the major charismatic characteristics of Mourinho?
2. Can you identify additional charismatic characteristics?

SELF-ASSESSMENT 8.1: CHARISMATIC LEADERSHIP

Match the following two leadership styles to the six statements.

(a) Charismatic; (b) Non-charismatic

1. Demonstrating the conventional means of the current situation.
2. Conforming to the rules, routine, and organizational bureaucracy.
3. Preferring not to get involved in high personal risks.
4. Rhetorical art is not a priority.
5. Focusing on the emotional needs and capabilities of subordinates.
6. Demonstrating agreement with the status quo.

SELF-ASSESSMENT 8.2: LEADERSHIP STYLES

Match the three leadership styles to the eight statements.

(a) Transformational; (b) Transactional; (c) Laissez-faire

1. The head of team preparation avoids making decisions regarding future strategies, abdicates responsibilities, and talks about selecting talented players without really doing it.
2. I'd say I prefer seeing how my players' mistakes occur in the match before taking action, because this will help them to understand their mistakes.
3. The president of a tennis federation has been told that one of the young talented players is thinking of retiring. The president does not wait for the player's possible intention to be put into action, but rather uses their position and power to convince the player to stop thinking about this decision.

4. The president of a club promises the basketball star that they will increase their annual salary and compensation if the player works hard to improve the team ranking in the league.
5. Although the gymnastics team has won the Olympic team gold medal, the gymnasts do not continue to demonstrate the same performance as usual. So, the team manager advises each gymnast individually to focus on specific weaknesses.
6. The president of a National Olympic Committee encourages and stimulates staff for creativity and innovation in ways that help to build strong national teams.
7. Although the team is falling to a record low ranking of 122 in the world, the head of the federation, board members, and team manager are still inspiring the team players to enhance and bolster team spirit.
8. Despite the strong competition in the synchronized swimming championship, the coach reassures the team that obstacles will be overcome and they will win the competition. So, the coach is respected and trusted by all swimmers.

Suggested Reading

Bass, B.M. (1999). Two Decades of Research and Development in Transformational Leadership. *European Journal of Work and Organizational Psychology*, 8(1), 9–32. https://doi.org/10.1080/135943299398410.

Bass, B.M. and Riggio, R.E. (2005). *Transformational Leadership*. (2nd ed.). New York: Psychology Press. https://doi.org/10.4324/9781410617095.

Megheirkouni, M. (2017). Leadership Styles and Organizational Learning in UK For-Profit and Non-Profit Sports Organizations. *International Journal of Organizational Analysis*, 25(4), 596–612. https://doi.org/10.1108/IJOA-07-2016-1042.

Megheirkouni, M., Amaugo, A. and Jallo, S. (2018). Transformational and Transactional Leadership and Skills Approach: Insights on Stadium Management. *International Journal of Public Leadership*, 14(4), 245–259. https://doi.org/10.1108/IJPL-06-2018-0029.

Rafferty, A.E. and Griffin, M.A. (2004). Dimensions of Transformational Leadership: Conceptual and Empirical Extensions. *The Leadership Quarterly*, 15(3), 329–354. https://doi.org/10.1016/j.leaqua.2004.02.009.

References

Astley, W.G. and Pachdeva, P.S. (1984). Structural Sources of Intraorganizational Power: A Theoretical Synthesis. *Academy of Management Review*, 9(1), 104–113. https://doi.org/10.2307/258237.

Avolio, B.J. (1999). *Full Leadership Development: Building the Vital Forces in Organizations*. Thousand Oaks, CA: Sage.

Avolio, B.J., Bass, B.M. and Jung, D.I. (1995). *Multifactor Leadership Questionnaire Technical Report*. Redwood City, CA: Mind Garden.

Bass, B.M. (1985). *Leadership and Performance beyond Expectations*. New York: Free Press.

Bass, B.M. and Riggio, R.E. (2005). *Transformational Leadership*. (2nd ed.). Mahwah, NJ: Lawrence Erlbaum. https://doi.org/10.4324/9781410617095.

Bromley, H.R. and Kirschner-Bromley, V.A. (2007). Are You a Transformational Leader? *Physician Executive*, 33(6), 54–57.

Bryman, A. (1992). *Charisma and Leadership in Organizations*. London: Sage.

Burns, J.M. (1978). *Leadership*. New York: Harper and Row.

Burns, J.M. (2003). *Transforming Leadership: A New Pursuit of Happiness*. New York: Atlantic Monthly Press.

Bycio, P., Hackett, R.D. and Allen, J.S. (1995). Further Assessments of Bass's (1985) Conceptualization of Transactional and Transformational Leadership. *Journal of Applied Psychology*, 80(4), 468–478. https://doi.org/10.1037/0021-9010.80.4.468.

Choi, J. (2006). A Motivational Theory of Charismatic Leadership: Envisioning, Empathy, and Empowerment. *Journal of Leadership and Organizational Studies*, 13(1), 24–43. https://doi.org/10.1177/10717919070130010501.

Conger, J. and Kanungo, R.N. (1987). Toward a Behavioral Theory of Charismatic Leadership in Organizational Settings. *Academy of Management Review*, 12(4), 637–647. https://doi.org/10.5465/amr.1987.4306715.

Conger, J.A., Kanungo, R.N. and Menon, S.T. (2000). Charismatic Leadership and Follower Effects. *Journal of Organizational Behaviour*, 21(7), 747–767. https://doi.org/10.1002/1099-1379(200011)21:7<747::AID-JOB46>3.0.CO;2-J.

Downton, J.V. (1973). *Rebel Leadership: Commitment and Charisma in the Revolutionary Process*. New York: Free Press.

French, J.R.P. and Raven, B. (1960). The Bases of Social Power. In: Cartwright, D. and Zander, A. (Eds.). *Group Dynamics: Research and Theory*. (2nd ed.). New York: Harper and Row. (259–269).

Hitchner, E. (1993). Book Review: 'The Power to Get Things Done. Managing with Power: Politics and Influence in Organizations, Jeffrey Pfeffer Boston: Harvard Business School Press, 1992'. *National Productivity Review*, 12(1), 117–122. https://doi.org/10.1002/npr.4040120114.

House, R.J. (1976). A 1976 Theory of Charismatic Leadership. In: Hunt, J.G. and Larson, L. L. (Eds.). (1977). *Leadership: The Cutting Edge*. Carbondale: Southern Illinois University Press. (189–207). ERIC: https://eric.ed.gov/?id=ED133827.

House, R.J. and Howell, J.M. (1992). Personality and Charismatic Leadership. *The Leadership Quarterly*, 3(2), 81–108. https://doi.org/10.1016/1048-9843(92)90028-E.

Howell, J.M. and Shamir, B. (2005). The Role of Followers in the Charismatic Leadership Process: Relationships and Their Consequences. *Academy of Management Review*, 30(1), 96–112. https://doi.org/10.5465/amr.2005.15281435.

Judge, T.A. and Piccolo, R.F. (2004). Transformational and Transactional Leadership: A Meta-Analytic Test of Their Relative Validity. *Journal of Applied Psychology*, 89(5), 755–768. https://doi.org/10.1037/0021-9010.89.5.755.

Jung, D. and Sosik, J.J. (2006). Who Are the Spellbinders? Identifying Personal Attributes of Charismatic Leaders. *Journal of Leadership and Organizational Studies*, 12(4), 12–26. https://doi.org/10.1177/107179190601200402.

Kaplan, A. (1964). Power in Perspective. In: Kahn, R.L. and Boulding, E. (Eds.). *Power and Conflict in Organizations*. London: Tavistock. (11–32).

Lowe, K.B., Kroeck, K.G. and Sivasubramaniam, N. (1996). Effectiveness Correlates of Transformation and Transactional Leadership: A Meta-Analytic Review of the MLQ Literature. *The Leadership Quarterly*, 7(3), 385–425. https://doi.org/10.1016/S1048-9843(96)90027-2.

Megheirkouni, M. (2017). Leadership Styles and Organizational Learning in UK For-Profit and Non-Profit Sports Organizations. *International Journal of Organizational Analysis*, 25(4), 596–612. https://doi.org/10.1108/IJOA-07-2016-1042.

Megheirkouni, M. (2019). Power Bases and Job Satisfaction in Sports Organisations. *Journal of Global Sport Management*, 4(3), 271–290. https://doi.org/10.1080/24704067.2018.1442238.

Megheirkouni, M., Amaugo, A. and Jallo, S. (2018). Transformational and Transactional Leadership and Skills Approach: Insights on Stadium Management. *International Journal of Public Leadership*, 14(4), 245–259. https://doi.org/10.1108/IJPL-06-2018-0029.

Merriam-Webster. (n.d.). 'charisma'. In: Merriam-Webster.com dictionary. Retrieved 20 March, 2024 from: https://www.merriam-webster.com/dictionary/charisma

Mio, J.S., Riggio, R.E., Levin, S.S. and Reese, R.R. (2005). Presidential Leadership and Charisma: The Effects of Metaphor. *The Leadership Quarterly*, 16(2), 287–294. https://doi.org/10.1016/j.leaqua.2005.01.005.

Northouse, P.G. (2010). *Leadership: Theory and Practice*. (5th ed.). London: Sage.

Northouse, P.G. (2016). *Leadership: Theory and Practice*. (7th ed.). London: Sage.

Northouse, P.G. (2021). *Leadership: Theory and Practice*. (9th ed.). London: Sage.

O'Connor, J., Mumford, M.D., Clifton, T.C., Gessner, T.L. and Connelly, M.S. (1995). Charismatic Leaders and Destructiveness: A Historiometric Study. *The Leadership Quarterly*, 6(4), 529–555. https://doi.org/10.1016/1048-9843(95)90026-8.

Rahim, M.A. (1989). Relationships of Leader Power to Compliance and Satisfaction with Supervision: Evidence from a National Sample of Managers. *Journal of Management*, 15(4), 545–557. https://doi.org/10.1177/014920638901500404.

Salancik, G.R. and Pfeffer, J. (1974). The Bases and Use of Power in Organizational Decision Making: The Case of the University. *Administrative Science Quarterly*, 19(4), 453–473. https://doi.org/10.2307/2391803.

Sheehan, J.J. and Sheehan, O.T.O. (2006). The American Presidency: Categorizing and Assessing Leadership Qualities. *Journal of Social Studies Research*, 30(1), 9–14. ERIC: https://eric.ed.gov/?id=EJ832179.

Sims, R.R. (2002). *Managing Organisational Behaviour*. Westport, CA: Greenwood Publishing.

Tejeda, M.J., Scandura, T.A. and Pillai, R. (2001). The MLQ Revisited: Psychometric Properties and Recommendations. *The Leadership Quarterly*, 12(1), 31–52. https://doi.org/10.1016/S1048-9843(01)00063-7.

van Knippenberg, D. and Sitkin, S.B. (2013). A Critical Assessment of Charismatic–Transformational Leadership Research: Back to the Drawing Board? *The Academy of Management Annals*, 7(1), 1–60. https://doi.org/10.1080/19416520.2013.759433.

Wallace, M. and Weese, W.J. (1995). Leadership, Organizational Culture, and Job Satisfaction in Canadian YMCA Organizations. *Journal of Sport Management*, 9(2), 182–193. https://doi.org/10.1123/jsm.9.2.182.

Weese, W.J. (1995). Leadership and Organizational Culture: An Investigation of Big Ten and Mid-American Conference Campus Recreation Administrations. *Journal of Sport Management*, 9(2), 119–134. https://doi.org/10.1123/jsm.9.2.119.

Yukl, G. (2013). *Leadership in Organizations*. (8th ed.) New York: Pearson.

9 SERVANT LEADERSHIP

Learning Outcomes

After reading this chapter, you will be able to:

- Explain the major components of servant leadership
- Identify servant leadership antecedent conditions
- Identify servant leadership behaviours
- Identify servant leadership outcomes
- Explain how servant leadership theory differs from other leadership theories

INTRODUCTION

The words 'servant' and 'leader' are usually thought of as opposites. When these opposites are brought together in a meaningful way, a paradox emerges. Although our traditional beliefs of leadership run counter to how it could be both service and influence, servant leadership is an approach that offers a unique perspective. It has led to creating a quiet revolution in the workplaces of all sectors, and the field of leadership research has witnessed an explosion of interest in, and practice of, servant leadership since 2010 in the sport leadership literature. The study of servant leadership in sport settings remains a popular concept within the practitioner literature.

WHAT IS SERVANT LEADERSHIP?

'Servant' with the meaning 'serve first' was introduced in the early debate on servant leadership by Robert Greenleaf (1970), who is credited with the basic ideas in current scholarship on servant leadership. The main focus of servant leadership is on subordinates' development, because servant leaders see the interests of subordinates as a priority (Hale and Fields, 2007). It is leadership that transcends the leader's self-interest and places the good of subordinates as a priority for achieving their development. We note that servant leadership is here addressed as a behaviour, while some people view it as a trait. Figure 9.1 presents authoritarian leadership and servant leadership as opposite ends of a continuum.

DOI: 10.4324/9780429290442-12

Figure 9.1 Authoritarian leadership and servant leadership styles as a continuum.

CHARACTERISTICS OF SERVANT LEADERSHIP

Greenleaf's original servant leadership writings were reviewed by Spears (2002). This led to Spears identifying ten major characteristics that are central to the development of servant leaders.

LISTENING

Servant leaders should have a deep commitment to listening to others. Listening helps to identify the will of subordinates and help to clarify that will. In other words, servant leaders consider listening as a tool that involves hearing and being receptive to what subordinates have to say. This characteristic helps to reduce the gap between a leader and subordinates through direct communication (eyes and body language) and/or indirect communication (voice and the way of thinking). Listening, therefore, is a fundamental characteristic of the growth of the servant leader. For example, the coach carefully listens to players' needs, and the board members or the president of governing bodies listen to the challenges influencing national coaches preparing the national teams for an Olympic Games.

EMPATHY

Empathy means working and living like subordinates in order to see how they perceive the surrounding environment. Specifically, empathetic servant leaders are able to understand subordinates' point of view, e.g. the way athletes thinking and feel, members' attitudes, and how they perceive sport organizational culture or sport team culture.

HEALING

Servant leaders attempt to help subordinates solve their personal problems. In other words, servant leaders have an opportunity to help subordinates with whom they come in contact to become whole. The purpose of healing is not only to help subordinates become whole, but also for servant leaders to be healed, in what Northouse (2021) calls a 'two-way street'.

AWARENESS

Both general and self-awareness strengthen servant leaders to be acutely attuned and receptive to their values, power, ethics, and other contextual issues.

Specifically, awareness helps us understand ourselves and the impact we have on others, and thus it enables us to view most situations from a more integrated, holistic position. Let's use an example at an international level: to participate in an opening ceremony for an international competition, championship, or sport mega event, the head of the volunteering department in a country located in a cluster, such as the Arab world, should be aware of the sensitivity of issues such as culture, gender, religion, and social habits. Volunteers are often from all parts of a country, so the socio-cultural issues tend to be divergent, possibly greatly so, across cities, areas, or regions. Thus, the servant leader must be aware of this divergence to be able to evaluate and view the differences in the opening ceremony from a more integrated, holistic position.

PERSUASION

A servant leader relies on persuasion for decision-making or problem-solving rather than adopting traditional management means, such as an authoritarian style. Specifically, a servant leader attempts to convince subordinates in specific cases and to avoid any form of authoritarian means, such as coercive compliance (especially in the more negative sense; cf. Chapter 8). This approach helps to highlight the gap between authoritarian leadership and servant leadership (see Figure 9.1). Servant leadership that relies on persuasion demonstrates effective decision-making and solving problem because the outcome is mainly based on consensus within a team, group, or organization.

CONCEPTUALIZATION

Conceptualization means that servant leader makes sense of the surrounding environment from a conceptualizing perspective, taking into consideration that reading the quo status is essential, but that one must think beyond day-to-day realities. A manager focuses on the need to achieve long-term goals, plans, and strategies. For example, the members of the national Olympic teams prepare long-term strategies to make heroes and build strong teams for future competitions based on big-picture sense-making and vision. The level of thinking goes beyond issues such as talents, resources and funding, performance, and sport infrastructure.

FORESIGHT

Foresight refers to the ability of servant leaders to predict the future based on the quo status and prior events. Specifically, a servant leader uses experience and knowledge from previous and current events, such as mistakes, decisions, challenges, and problems, as a base to anticipate what may occur and act according to that understanding. For example, a team manager builds future team plans based on their experience in previous and current champion leagues, perhaps seeking to reinforce the team with new players in particular positions.

STEWARDSHIP

Stewardship refers to considering responsibilities for the leadership role as entrusted to the leader, but not as belonging solely to the leader. A steward takes into consideration a commitment to serving the needs of subordinates or colleagues, on their behalf but not over them, as in the following three examples. Servant leaders may hold sport organizations in trust for a club, management, and players as an interim figure. Referees and their supporting colleagues, who are not their employees, hold the conduct of a match and the reputation of a sport in trust for fans, leagues, and the 'spirit of the game'. (See Chapter 16, 'Responsible Leadership', for further discussion of stewardship.)

COMMITMENT TO THE GROWTH OF PEOPLE

A servant leader emphasizes that individuals have an intrinsic motive beyond their tangible contributions as athletes, coaches, board members, or presidents to sport organizations. Specifically, a servant leader believes that their major responsibility is to use their power to help everyone in sport organizations grow personally and professionally. Spears (2002) states that this can include (but is not limited to) making funds available for developmental purposes, accepting suggestions from everyone, encouraging everyone to take an active part in decision-making and problem-solving, and assisting laid-off athletes, coaches, and others to find other positions.

BUILDING COMMUNITY

A servant leader believes that there is a need to identify all means for building community in the sport environment. The servant leader seeks to reinforce the community culture at all levels of a team, department, organization, or even sport network, to help individuals adopt a sense of collective purpose and general rather than self-interest. This can help individuals to be more effective, e.g. board members may discuss sport issues during informal opportunities in an organization or international competition with people who are not members of formal committee structures. The spirit of such informal opportunities is not, though, that they remove a need for proper accountability, rather than formal, hierarchical meetings do not provide connections with people at all levels in an organization if it is to be perceived as a community.

SERVANT LEADERSHIP FRAMEWORK

Effective servant leaders believe that both the leader and the people they lead have a moral duty towards one another, and thus the common role for all of them is to serve and lead (Smith et al, 2004). Three components of servant leadership are discussed here: antecedent conditions, servant leader behaviours and leadership outcomes, using a framework developed by Northouse (see Northouse, 2021), relying on previous studies (e.g. Liden et al, 2008; Liden et al, 2014).

ANTECEDENT CONDITIONS

Three major antecedent conditions are perceived to influence servant leadership: context and culture, leader attribute, and subordinate receptivity.

CONTEXT AND CULTURE

Servant leadership does not occur in isolation from context or culture (e.g. organizational level, national level, international level). For example, in the opening ceremony of the Olympic Games, operational managers serve the guests from start to end of the ceremony, where the form of serving is more evidently in person. However, in sporting goods companies, the comparison with competition is the primary norm for the purpose of determining who leads the market. Such disparity makes servant leadership different in terms of its application and recognition. Culture (at each level) is another condition that may have an impact on servant leadership. The prevalent way used in the literature to illustrate this influence is Hofstede's dimensions of culture. For example, collectivistic societies (e.g. Confucian Asia) where individualistic sense is low, accept leadership for others, and thus servant leadership tends to be prevalent. However, this does not mean that there is no servant leadership in individualistic societies, but it may present more of a challenge to achieved it.

LEADER ATTRIBUTES

Sport leaders use their own traits and personal characteristics to complete the role required. But the divergence between sport leaders' in their traits and personal characteristics could affect the quality of servant leadership. Divergence in traits and personal characteristics also affects the nature of competencies and capabilities sport leaders have (see e.g. Boyatzis, 1982). For example, particular personal traits or characteristics of football managers who work as volunteers with young players in talent programmes may affect some of these players for better or worse. And some managers have particular leadership competencies that help to encourage these young players to improve their skills. Overall, this kind of debate on leader attributes helps to evaluate the quality of servant leadership in a sport setting.

SUBORDINATE RECEPTIVITY

Leadership literature shows that the subordinate is a vital part of understanding the concept of leadership. In line with this, the importance of subordinate receptivity lies in its role of affecting the quality of servant leadership and its impact on the general performance or results in sport organizations. As we know from the preceding chapters, leadership is a combination of three elements: context (situation, contingencies), leaders, and subordinates. Sport leaders are not able to lead without, for example, athletes, staff, and board members; so, subordinates often play an essential role in terms of determining successes and failures of their leaders (Shankman and Allen, 2008; Collinson, 2011). The literature on servant leadership and subordinates demonstrates contradictory results. For example, research suggests that athletes who perceive their coach to possess servant leader qualities displayed higher intrinsic motivation, were more task-oriented, more satisfied, and performed better than athletes coached by non-servant leaders (Rieke et al, 2008). However, some athletes, staff, board members, and others who do not desire this style of leadership. This is best illustrated by Meuser et al (2011), who found that servant leadership had a negative impact on performance when there is no match between this style and subordinates desire to work with it.

SERVANT LEADER BEHAVIOURS

Servant leadership framework includes seven behaviours that constitute the core of servant leadership. These behaviours are conceptualizing, emotional healing, putting subordinates first, helping subordinates grow and succeed, behaving ethically, empowering, and creating value for the community.

CONCEPTUALIZING

This servant leader behaviour indicates the leader is able to understand the whole sport organization, e.g. policy, rules, strategy, objectives, and problems. This provides a big picture of the servant leader's system thinking awareness through moving 'up-and-out' rather than 'down-and-in'. This capacity helps a servant leader to address problems and find solutions that best fit the final objectives of a sport organization. However, this reaches beyond a single sport organization's border to include volunteering in teams, sport development programmes, or sport mega events. For example, servant leaders in an Olympic Games use conceptualizing to fully understand the cultural differences among volunteers or guests, to assign and schedule volunteers, to educate volunteers about the spirit and mission of the Olympics, and to provide training sessions to volunteers about the Olympic Games on issues such as serving guests, protocols, or venue-specific roles (Robinson et al, 2012).

EMOTIONAL HEALING

This behaviour in a servant leader involves being sensitive to personal problems of others and being willing to address them. A servant leader expresses more commitment to others, shows love, support, and encouragement for their subordinates, and listens carefully to details to find the best course of action (Vargas and Hanlon, 2007). Healing athletes' emotional trauma is an important task of the training cadre before, during, and after competitions. Emotional healing in servant leadership is not dedicated to one person; it may extend to include others, such as a team manager, an assistant manager, medical team, or board members of sport federations.

PUTTING SUBORDINATES FIRST

This behaviour in a servant leader means they perceive help and support for subordinates as a priority. Putting subordinates' interests, concerns, and goals first in servant leadership reflects the noble values of a servant leader because such leaders may make efforts and spend their personal time to assist subordinates. For example, UK Sport in association with the National Olympic Committee ran the Women and Leadership Development Programme (WLDP) for a three-year trial in 2016. (See Case Study 17.1.) The experts and consultants worked as servant leaders, where the support, advice, and help they offered to the participants extended after the programme was finished. Similar programmes now run in various UK higher education institutions.

HELPING SUBORDINATES GROW AND SUCCEED

This behaviour in a servant leader means they evaluate subordinates' goals to help them develop these goals in a good manner. The servant leader invests in subordinates' goals and interests by providing them with the guidance and advice required to accomplish their wishes. One of the best examples of this behaviour in servant leadership is from early-school coaches who have a vital role not only for talent identification, but also mentoring and developing these talents for future competitions. Servant leaders at this stage use several developmental tools that help athletes to grow, e.g. using feedback, adopting a short and long-term strategy, and being willing to help athletes anytime for the sake of their improvements.

BEHAVING ETHICALLY

This behaviour in a servant leader means they hold a set of ethical standards used openly with subordinates. These ethical standards – e.g. non-maleficence, respect for autonomy, honesty, fairness, truthfulness, openness, and justice – include not only the relationship between a servant leader and subordinates, but also the relationships among the subordinates themselves. The servant leader attempts to avoid or overcome all forms of ethical barriers that affect subordinates' success.

EMPOWERING

Empowering in servant leadership means that a servant leader gives more autonomy and power to subordinates to enable them to have an active role in a team or an organization. This includes sharing decision-making and problem-solving. Empowering in servant leadership gives subordinates a space for creativity and innovation because they can think and act independently without pressure.

CREATING VALUE FOR THE COMMUNITY

This behaviour in a servant leader means they are involved locally in activities and practices to encourage a larger number of individuals to take an active part in community service. An example of this behaviour in servant leadership is often seen in underresourced sport clubs or communities when sport celebrities go back to their first club or town to support local people to be able participate in sport, or support people with other important issues. Contributions often extend to encourage the young to train and become sport stars. Overall, those sport celebrities who work as servant leaders create an effect on the short and long-term through the image and value they leave over their contribution.

SERVANT LEADERSHIP OUTCOMES

Servant leadership should also focus on outcomes to produce a positive impact on subordinates. The outcomes of servant leadership include subordinate performance and growth, organizational performance, and societal impact.

SUBORDINATE PERFORMANCE AND GROWTH

Subordinates' performance and growth reflect the level of autonomy and support offered to them to accomplish their personal objectives. According to Greenleaf's multilevel analysis of servant leadership, subordinates begin treating others in the same way their servant leaders treated them (Greenleaf, 1970). In other words, subordinates imitate how their servant leaders empower, support, care, and encourage them; and thus, subordinates may become servant leaders. More specifically, the obligation or agreement between a servant leader and subordinates will have positive outcomes, as a result of the fullness of satisfaction with this type of leadership.

ORGANIZATIONAL PERFORMANCE

We noted in the previous sections that servant leadership has a positive influence on subordinates' performance. Sport leadership literature demonstrates that servant leadership is also a positive attitude towards organizational factors, such as ethical climates, organizational justice, job satisfaction, and trust (Burton and Welty Peachey, 2013; Megheirkouni, 2018; Welty Peachey and Burton, 2017). Research on organizational outcomes is still growing, which is important to substantiate links between servant leadership and organizational performance in sport organizations, picking up on the call for research (e.g. Burton et al, 2017; Megheirkouni, 2018).

SOCIETAL IMPACT

Another outcome of servant leadership is positive impact on society. Research on the societal impact of servant leadership is promising. We noted earlier that a servant leader creates value for the community, and societal impact of servant leadership may be wider than an immediate sport community, including impact across schools, clubs, towns, cities, and beyond.

EVALUATION OF SERVANT LEADERSHIP

Servant leadership theories have weaknesses that should be considered. One criticism is that although servant leadership includes a wide range of personal characteristics, traits, behaviours, and capabilities, there is no agreement among scholars on a specific theoretical framework of servant leadership (Northouse,

2021). Another weakness of servant leadership is the moralistic nature within the leading view of servant leadership. This gives an impression that servant leadership scholars attempt only to investigate the moral quality of servant leadership theory. Another weakness is that the word 'conceptualizing' in the servant leadership framework is vague. Specifically, this word is used in the literature as both a behavioural and a cognitive ability, but there is no research to illuminate such confusion. Moreover, conceptualizing is not necessarily a cognitive ability that works with all leadership styles (Northouse, 2021). Therefore, further research is required on the role of 'conceptualizing' in servant leadership.

Although servant leadership theories have several weaknesses, there are also several strengths. First, servant leadership theory treats influence as a negative factor in leadership process, while all other leadership theories do the opposite. Specifically, servant leaders put subordinates first, and share influence with them. The traditional understanding of influence in leadership means to control and dominate others. However, a servant leader does not incorporate influence in that way but rather gives up control; but note, this is not the same sort of 'give up' as laissez-faire leadership. Second, the Servant Leadership Questionnaire (SLQ), which includes 28 items across seven dimensions of servant leadership, is perceived as unique. The importance of this questionnaire lies in that it measures aspects of leadership that are different from other theories (Liden et al, 2008; Schaubroeck et al, 2011).

SUMMARY

Servant leadership was first described in the early writings of Greenleaf in the 1970s. This approach challenges traditional beliefs about leadership or management and their influence inside organizations, including sport organizations. The essence of the servant leadership approach is to place the good of subordinates as a priority for their development. Ten major characteristics have been identified as central to the development of servant leaders. These characteristics are listening, empathy, healing, awareness, persuasion, conceptualization, foresight, stewardship, commitment to the growth of people, and building community.

This chapter discusses a servant leadership framework with three main components: antecedent conditions, servant leader behaviours, and leadership outcomes. There are three major antecedent conditions perceived to influence servant leadership: context and culture, leader attribute, and subordinate receptivity. There are seven core servant leadership behaviours: conceptualizing, emotional healing, putting subordinates first, helping subordinates grow and succeed, behaving ethically, empowering, and creating value for the community. The three servant leadership outcomes produce a positive impact on subordinates are: subordinate performance and growth, organizational performance, and societal impact.

GENERAL QUESTIONS

1. How do you define servant leadership?
2. How does servant leadership development differ from other leadership theories?

3. What are the major components of servant leadership theory?
4. What are the servant leadership behaviours? Give examples of each one.
5. What are the servant leadership conditions? Give examples of each one.
6. What are the servant leadership outcomes? Give examples of each one.
7. Can you give examples of successful and unsuccessful servant sport leaders from the national and international level? Can you give reasons for this success or failure?
8. Which sports do you think servant leadership works better or worse in?
9. Do you think servant sport leaders are influenced by cultural differences? Give examples.

OPEN DISCUSSION QUESTIONS

TOPIC A: GENERAL EXPERIENCES FROM YOUR SPORTS

1. Discuss with colleagues and give examples of each of the servant leadership characteristics from your sport contexts?
2. Do you think servant leadership is effectively used in sport management? Why?
3. Can you suggest sports in which servant leaders are effective, or ineffective?
4. Can you give examples of unsuccessful servant leaders from your sport? Explain the reasons for the failures and successes of this kind of leadership in different cultures.

TOPIC B: YOUR OWN EXPERIENCES FROM YOUR SPORT INVOLVEMENTS

1. What type of servant leader behaviours did your manager exhibit in your sport?
2. Describe the outcomes of servant leadership in your sport. How did your receptivity influence those outcomes?

Case Study 9.1: Servant Leader Gareth Southgate

In his first tournament as England manager, Gareth Southgate guided England to the 2018 FIFA World Cup and the Nations League semi-finals. Southgate added young players to reduce the average age of the squad. He worked to foster a sense of togetherness within the squad to take to the World Cup in Russia. Southgate insisted that he wanted his players to have strong opinions and believed that listening to them is a vital part of his job. One of the servant behaviours of the England manager was seen after the match with Colombia in the 2018 World Cup. When the Colombian midfielder Mateus Uribe missed his penalty, Southgate, having been in a similar position in the UEFA Euro 96, openly consoled the young midfielder.

Southgate made the decision to name his 2018 World Cup squad early, using awareness and foresight that changes may happen to any finalized squad; particularly, he had been close to such changes when Paul Gascoigne was cut from the finalized Euro 96 squad at the last moment. Southgate explained that it is better to give the players in the finalized squad as much time as possible to get to know each other.

After the England team's failures at successive major tournaments, it achieved positive results under Southgate's stewardship. Southgate's role was crucial in managing and overcoming pressure surrounding his team before each match and supporting the physical and psychological preparation to perform at high level in this and other international football tournaments.

Questions

1. How would you describe the servant of Southgate's leadership? Explain your answer.
2. How would you describe the behaviour of Southgate with Uribe?
3. How would you describe the behaviours of Southgate before the 2018 World Cup?
4. Can you identify other behaviours of the servant leadership of Southgate?
5. What lessons did Southgate learn from Euro 96 and adopt with the 2018 World Cup team?

Source: Based on BBC News. (2018). 'World Cup 2018: Gareth Southgate's compassion praised'. bbc.co.uk. [online]. 4 July 2018. Available at: https://www.bbc.co.uk/news/uk-44715244; BBC Sport. (2018). 'Gareth Southgate says Premier League clubs should give young players a chance'. bbc.co.uk. [online]. 15 July 2018. Available at: https://www.bbc.co.uk/sport/football/44841828; and England Football Learning. (2018). 'Gareth Southgate: my coaching approach'. England Football Learning. [online]. 17 December 2018. Available at: https://learn.englandfootball.com/articles-and-resources/coaching/resources/2022/Gareth-Southgate-my-coaching-approach.

Suggested Reading

Megheirkouni, M. (2018). Insights on Practising of Servant Leadership in the Events Sector. *Sport, Business, and Management*, 8(2), 134–152. https://doi.org/10.1108/SBM-01-2017-0001.

Megheirkouni, M. (2020). Servant Leadership, Trust and Knowledge Management in Sport Organisations. *International Journal of Sport Management and Marketing*, 20(3–4), 211–231. https://doi.org/10.1504/IJSMM.2020.110835.

Megheirkouni, M. (2022). Psychological Contract, Leadership, and Job Satisfaction: An Empirical Investigation into the Non-Profit Sports Sector. *Annals of Leisure Research*, 25(2), 203–226. https://doi.org/10.1080/11745398.2020.1769488.

Welty Peachy, J., Burton, L., Wells, J. and Chung, M.R. (2018). Exploring Servant Leadership and Needs Satisfaction in the Sport for Development and Peace Context. *Journal of Sport Management*, 32(2), 96–108. https://doi.org/10.1123/jsm.2017-0153.

Van Dierendonck, D. (2011). Servant Leadership: A Review and Synthesis. *Journal of Management*, 37(4), 1228–1261. https://doi.org/10.1177/0149206310380462.

References

Boyatzis, R.E. (1982). *The Competent Manager: A Model for Effective Performance.* New York: Wiley and Sons.

Burton, L. and Welty Peachey, J. (2013). The Call for Servant Leadership in Intercollegiate Athletics. *Quest*, 65(3), 354–371. https://doi.org/10.1080/00336297.2013.791870.

Burton, L.J., Welty Peachey, J. and Wells, J.E. (2017). The Role of Servant Leadership in Developing an Ethical Climate in Sport Organizations. *Journal of Sport Management*, 31(3), 229–240. https://doi.org/10.1123/jsm.2016-0047.

Collinson, D. (2011). Critical Leadership Studies. In: Bryman, A., Collinson, D., Grint, K., Jackson, B. and Uhl-Bien, M. (Eds.). (2011). *The SAGE Handbook of Leadership.* London: Sage. (181–194).

Greenleaf, R.K. (1970). *The Servant as Leader.* Westfield, IN: The Greenleaf Center for Servant Leadership.

Hale, J.R. and Fields, D.L. (2007). Exploring Servant Leadership across Cultures: A Study of Followers in Ghana and the USA. *Leadership*, 3(4), 397–417. https://doi.org/10.1177/1742715007082964.

Liden R.C., Panaccio A., Meuser, J.D., Hu, J. and Wayne S.J. (2014). Servant Leadership: Antecedents, Processes, and Outcomes. In: Day, D.V. (Ed.). (2014). *The Oxford Handbook of Leadership and Organizations.* New York: Oxford Academic. (357–379). https://doi.org/10.1093/oxfordhb/9780199755615.013.018.

Liden, R.C., Wayne, S.J., Zhao, H. and Henderson, D. (2008). Servant Leadership: Development of a Multidimensional Measure and Multi-Level Assessment. *The Leadership Quarterly*, 19(2), 161–177. https://doi.org/10.1016/j.leaqua.2008.01.006.

Megheirkouni, M. (2018). Mixed Methods in Sport Leadership Research: A Review of Sport Management Practices. *Choregia*, 14(1), 1–20. EBSCO: https://openurl.ebsco.com/EPDB%3Agcd%3A2%3A14153890/detailv2?sid=ebsco%3Aplink%3Ascholar&id=ebsco%3Agcd%3A129500054&crl=c.

Meuser, J.D, Liden, R.C., Wayne, S.J. and Henderson, D.J. (2011). Is Servant Leadership Always a Good Thing? The Moderating Influence of Servant Leadership Prototype. Paper presented at the Annual Meeting of the Academy of Management, 12–16 August 2011, San Antonio, TX.

Northouse, P.G. (2021). *Leadership: Theory and Practice.* (9th ed.). London: Sage.

Rieke, M., Hammermeister, J. and Chase, M. (2008). Servant Leadership in Sport: A New Paradigm for Effective Coach Behaviour. *International Journal of Sports Science and Coaching*, 3(2), 227–239. https://doi.org/10.1260/174795408785100635.

Robinson, L., Chelladurai, P., Bodet, G. and Downward, P. (2012). *Routledge Handbook of Sport Management.* New York: Routledge.

Schaubroeck, J., Lam, S.S.K. and Peng, A.C. (2011). Cognition-Based and Affect-Based Trust as Mediators of Leader Behaviour Influences on Team Performance. *Journal of Applied Psychology*, 96(4), 863–871. https://doi.org/10.1037/a0022625.

Shankman, M.L. and Allen, S.J. (2008). *Emotionally Intelligent Leadership: A Guide for College Students.* London: John Wiley and Sons.

Smith, B.N., Montagno, R.V. and Kuzmenko, T.N. (2004). Transformational and Servant Leadership: Content and Contextual Comparisons. *Journal of Leadership and Organizational Studies*, 10(4), 80–92. https://doi.org/10.1177/107179190401000406.

Spears, L.C. (2002). Tracing the Past, Present, and Future of Servant-Leadership. In: Spears, L.C. and Lawrence, M. (Eds.). *Focus on Leadership: Servant-Leadership for the 21st Century*. New York: John Wiley and Sons. (1–16).

Vargas, P.A. and Hanlon, J. (2007). Celebrating a Profession: The Servant Leadership Perspective. *The Journal of Research Administration*, 38(1), 45–49. ProQuest: https://www.proquest.com/docview/216592651.

Welty Peachey, J. and Burton, L. (2017). *Servant Leadership in Sport for Development and Peace: A Way Forward*. *Quest*, 69(1), 125–139. https://doi.org/10.1080/00336297.2016.1165123.

10 AUTHENTIC LEADERSHIP

Learning Outcomes

After reading this chapter, you will be able to:

- Define authentic leadership
- Understand its impact on subordinates' attitudes and behaviours
- Understand the components of authentic leadership
- Measure authentic leadership
- Identify the weaknesses and strengths of authentic leadership
- Evaluate how authentic leadership differs from other types of leadership

INTRODUCTION

Upheavals and scandals happen at all levels of sport (organizational, national, and international). These have increased the demand for authentic leadership within the traditional sport press, fan communities, and social media. Age cheating in sport championships and competitions, contract cheating with foreign players (not necessarily by them), embezzlement of club budgets, FIFA scandals, and Olympic Games hosting scandals have all created fears and uncertainties in sport environments and have also affected the prestige of sport leadership and sport bodies. Sport fans, athletes, coaches, and others long for honest leadership they can trust. This is basically because upheavals and scandals in the sport world have negative implications for athletes' commitment, motivation, and career, and the interrelationships between national and international sport governing bodies.

WHAT IS AUTHENTIC LEADERSHIP?

The term 'authenticity' involves owning one's personal experiences, emotions, and thoughts, and refers to needs, wants, preferences, beliefs, processes, and the value captured by self-expression. One of the early definitions of authentic leadership was proposed by Henderson and Hoy (1983: 6) as "the extent to which subordinates perceive their leader to be maximizing the acceptance of organizational and personal responsibility for actions, outcomes, and mistakes; to be non-manipulating of subordinates; and to demonstrate a salience of self over role". Overall, there are many definitions of authentic leadership and no single accepted definition. This might be because each definition has addressed authentic leadership from different perspectives and viewpoints (Northouse, 2021). The leading definitions of authentic leadership take three perspectives: self-based, relational, and developmental.

The self-based perspective of authentic leadership concentrates on what goes on within the leader. Luthans and Avolio (2003) perceive the positive psychological capacities of hope, confidence, optimism, and resiliency, as something that can be nurtured in a leader, and thus these capabilities are neither fixed traits of authentic leader nor copies. In this sense, Luthans and Avolio (2003: 243) propose that authentic leadership emerged from "both positive psychological capacities and a highly developed organizational context, which results in both greater self-awareness and self-regulated positive behaviours on the part of leaders and associates, fostering positive self-development". Kernis (2003: 1) defines authenticity as "the unobstructed operation of one's true, or core, self in one's daily enterprise". He provides an empirically grounded perspective on authenticity, acting as part of a larger theory on 'optimal' self-esteem that is characterized as genuine, true, and stable.

Authentic leadership can be defined from a relational perspective, where subordinates are perceived as active actors within the authentic-leader-follower relationship. This relationship is created by both leaders and subordinates (Klenke, 2005). Ilies et al (2005) argue that the relational aspect has substantial implications for leadership processes, influencing both leaders and subordinates. A relational perspective represents the outcome from both a leader's and their subordinates' reactions. It is a reciprocal process because there are no athletes or sport teams without coaches nor vice versa. Similarly, there are no sport governing bodies without board members and presidents, and in turn, no board members or/and presidents without sport governing bodies.

Finally, authentic leadership can be defined from a developmental perspective. This perspective focuses on the way in which authenticity is developed in leader and subordinates. Avolio and Gardner (2005) view the developmental perspective of authentic leadership as being much more than statically relational because subordinate and leader are shaped in their respective active development. In Shamir and Eilam's (2005) description of this perspective, leaders' life experiences that provide insight into the meaning they attach to life stories, are critical to the development of the authentic leader. Overall, the life story approach is illustrated through critical elements of one's personal history, e.g. family, childhood, culture, school, career, management experiences, and prior leadership roles. Such personal life experiences are stored in memory as personal knowledge (Hoyle et al, 1999). Specifically, the positive roles of family members, teachers, coach, sport fans, or partners may help in the authentic leader's personal growth. Such positive roles are also true for an authentic subordinate.

AUTHENTIC LEADERSHIP IMPACTS ON SUBORDINATES' ATTITUDES AND BEHAVIOURS

By 2011, Gardner et al could report that the previous decade had seen a dramatic increase in academic interest in the topic of authentic leadership in all settings; and this offers us a starting frame for this form of leadership. The debate on the impact an authentic leader on subordinate attitudes and behaviours poses the essence of authentic leadership approach (Cooper et al, 2005). This is evident in special issues of *The Leadership Quarterly* (Vol. 13, Issue 5, 2002 and Vol. 16, Issue 3, 2005), which provide some of the foundation work for the broader theoretical framework relating how authentic leaders influence subordinates' attitudes and behaviours. Avolio et al (2004) developed such a theoretical impact model. This model, which underpins the authentic leadership discussed in the following sections, views the process by which authentic leadership impacts subordinates' attitudes and behaviours (see Figure 10.1).

SUBORDINATE IDENTIFICATION

The importance of personal and social identifications in the leadership process has received much attention by scholars (e.g. Bono and Judge, 2003; Kark and Shamir, 2002; Shamir et al, 2000).

Luthans and Avolio (2003) argue that the major challenge for the authentic leader is to identify subordinates' strengths and link them to a common objective. Specifically, a general perception in leadership literature suggests that leaders not only directly affect the identities of subordinates, but they also have

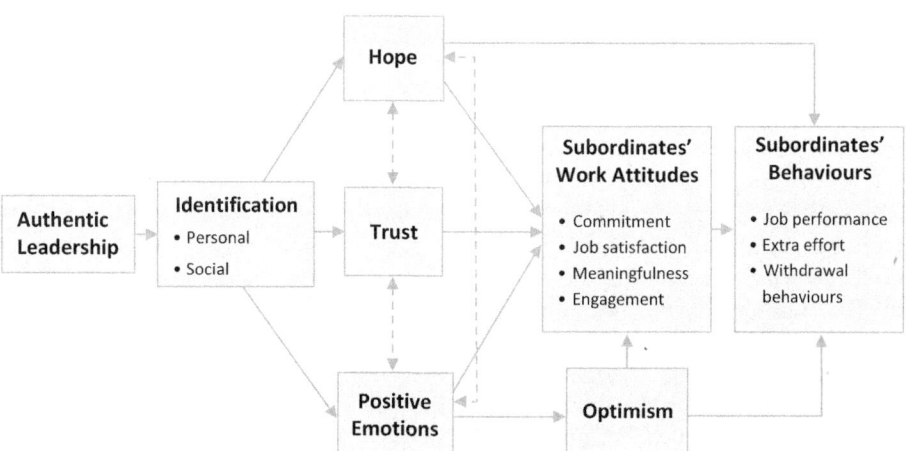

Figure 10.1 How authentic leadership affects follower attitudes and behaviours.

Source: Adapted from Avolio, B.J., Gardner, W.L., Walumbwa, F.O., Luthans, F. and May, D.R. (2004). Unlocking the Mask: A Look at the Process by Which Authentic Leaders Impact Follower Attitudes and Behaviours. *The Leadership Quarterly*, 15(6), 801–823.

impacts on the self-regulatory mechanisms of subordinates, which are central to subordinates' motivation (Day, 2000; Lord and Brown, 2001; Gardner and Avolio, 1998). However, it is also true that the effects of leaders occur indirectly. For example, Lord and Brown (2003) argue that most people's identities are brought to life by activation from current organizational contexts, networking, assignments, and immediate personal experiences. In other words, the effect of leaders occurs through subordinates' self-knowledge or working self-concept, which contains current goals, as being a key self-regulatory structure. Thus, a subordinate brings beliefs about others into their beliefs about themselves, in two forms of identification:

1. **Personal identification**: The process whereby a subordinate's (e.g. athletes, staff, members) belief about a sport leader becomes self-referential or self-defining.
2. **Social identification**: The process whereby a subordinate's belief about a group/team (or sport organizations) becomes self-referential or self-defining.

AUTHENTIC LEADERSHIP AND HOPE

Hope is commonly used in sport. Jensen and Luthans (2006) suggest that hope can be developed at three levels: individual, team, and organization. However, there are many misperceptions about what constitutes hope at athlete, sport team, and sport organizational levels. According to Snyder et al (1991: 287), wherein they presented the psychometric Hope Scale, hope is defined as "a positive motivational state that is based on an interactively derived sense of successful: (1) agency (goal-directed energy) and (2) pathways (planning to meet goals)". Although the notion of hope is fundamental in sport leadership practice, little is known about the processes by which sport leaders (e.g. coaches, senior managers, presidents, heads, chief executives) influence hope in their subordinates (e.g. athletes, staff, employees). At the coaching level, an authentic manager may use hope as a positive psychological element in competitions to support and encourage athletes in difficult situations, such as injury underachievement, where the athlete and others may interpret non-achievement as a deep, personal failure. Avolio et al (2004) propose that authentic leaders offer feedback that accentuates the positive facets of how to navigate challenges, thereby instilling a sense of belief in their team's ability to overcome obstacles and succeed. This emphasis on the 'way-power' aspect – highlighting the feasible pathways to achieve goals – contributes significantly to fostering a sense of hope and efficacy within the team. Another generalized example from the top leadership level that can be employed in a real-world context on hope might be worded thus:

> our Organising Committee for the Olympic Games failed to [rather? *didn't*] win the rights to host the games. Authentic leaders from sport, media, and political settings in our country must pull together and use hope as a means to reduce pressure and increase support for our committee's efforts in future years.

AUTHENTIC LEADERSHIP AND TRUST

Trust, as a very important competency, has attracted considerable attention in leadership literature. Rousseau et al (1998: 395) defined it as a "psychological state comprising the intention to accept vulnerability based upon positive expectations of the intentions or behaviour of another". Gardner et al (2005) linked between authentic leaders who recognize the role of transparency and the notion of 'psychological contract', which refers to the beliefs of athletes, employees, staff, coaches, or board members that are shaped by sport organizations, describing the relation between a leader and subordinates through unwritten rules (e.g. Rousseau, 1995, 1998). For example, when the authentic leader of a sport governing body exemplifies high moral standards, honesty, integrity, dependability, fairness, and ability, their favourable reputation can foster positive expectations among board members, staff, coaches, and athletes, enhancing their levels of trust, and willingness to work with the leader for the benefit of the sport body. Avolio and colleagues state that the transparency of authentic leaders makes the psychological contract between an authentic leader and subordinates a more resilient foundation (Avolio et al, 2004).

AUTHENTIC LEADERSHIP AND POSITIVE EMOTIONS

There is no accepted definition of the phenomenon of emotion in the literature that has consensual conceptualization. However, this example provides a good starting point. Salovey and Mayer (1990: 186) view emotion as "Organized responses, crossing the boundaries of many psychological subsystems, including the physiological, cognitive, motivational and experiential systems". Although many contemporary theories of leadership address the subject of emotion by considering the impact of leaders' styles on subordinates and how subordinates react to their leaders, research on the impact of everyday emotions of athletes, coaches, managers, senior managers, board members, and even leaders of a club, federation, association, or governing bodies is still rare. Overall, emotion is important to authentic leadership because it is perceived as a positive form of leadership which influences athletes, staff, or members' emotional reactions to situations such as poor performance, lack of sport achievements, personal problems of those individuals, or other obstacles. This certainly appears to be true in international and national championships and competitions.

Specifically, Jensen and Luthans (2006) suggest that authentic leadership is positively associated with emotional happiness. Therefore, the authenticity of a leader's emotion expression has direct and indirect influences on subordinates' perception of that leader's beliefs, attitudes, and intentions. In other words, when a coach or manager displays positive emotions, such as hope, empathy, and joy towards their athletes after a championship or competition regardless of their results, this can encourage athletes to do better in future events; similarly, negative emotions can discourage.

OPTIMISM

Optimism as a combination of positive emotion and motivation is a construct that forms part of psychological capital (Luthans and Youssef, 2004). Optimism is defined by Scheier and Carver (1992: 203) as "the tendency to believe that one will generally experience good outcomes in life". Contemporary leadership research suggests there is a strong relationship between authentic leadership and optimism (e.g. Avolio et al, 2004; Gardner and Schermerhorn, 2004; Luthans and Avolio, 2003). Indeed, there is hardly an inspirational coach in most sports, one with a record of great achievements, who does not possess optimism: for example, Aimé Jacquet, France's national team manager in the 1998 FIFA World Cup. His positive attitudes and optimism left a positive influence on his players, leading the French team to winning the cup. This example may indicate why subordinates (e.g. athletes, members, staff) of optimistic authentic leaders (e.g. coaches, managers, presidents) are likely to have positive attitudes and reactions, commitments, satisfaction, and a higher level of performance and achievements.

AUTHENTIC LEADER AND SUBORDINATE DEVELOPMENT

Building on Luthans and Avolio's (2003) initial model of authentic leadership development, Gardner et al (2005) included subordinates in this model (Figure 10.2). Gardner and colleagues incorporated four components of authenticity identified by Kernis (2003): awareness, unbiased processing, action, and rational into self-awareness and self-regulation behaviours.

This model adopts the self-based approach, proposing the roles of leader's and subordinate's personal histories and key trigger events to be antecedents for authentic leadership development. The personal history of the leader may include the influence of family, neighbourhood, community, or school (i.e. the context in which a leader has lived and grown), academic qualifications, career development, and professional experience. Trigger events refer to the dramatic and subtle changes in the individual's circumstances that facilitate transformational change and development of the individual as a result (i.e. not in the more recent sense of negatively triggering). For example, trigger events may arise from the environment surrounding a sport organization that challenges the leader to be more innovative and creative, learning from previous mistakes and daily challenges and problems.

MEASUREMENT OF AUTHENTIC LEADERSHIP

The first scale to measure authentic leadership was developed by Henderson and Hoy (1983). This questionnaire was criticized for lack of validity and generalizable constructs. The most utilized instrument currently used to measure authentic leadership was created by Walumbwa and colleagues (Walumbwa, 2008). The Authentic Leadership Questionnaire (ALQ) includes 16 items used to measure four factors of authentic leadership: self-awareness, internalized moral perspective, balanced processing, and relational transparency. Walumbwa and colleagues validated the factors of the instrument and proposed a positive relationship between authentic leadership and some aspects of organizations.

EVALUATION OF AUTHENTIC LEADERSHIP

Authentic leadership is still in development, and it shows many strengths. First, authentic leadership represents a need for trustworthy leadership in sport

Figure 10.2 A conceptual framework for authentic leader and subordinate development. *Note:* The source contains under 'Subordinate's Performance' the term 'Veritable'. Since meanings and usage may vary across varieties of English, we replace this with 'Verifiable'.

Source: Adapted from Gardner, W.L., Avolio, B.J., Luthans, F., May, D.R. and Walumbwa, F. (2005). Can You See the Real Me? A Self-Based Model of Authentic Leader and Follower Development. *The Leadership Quarterly*, 16(3), 343–372.

organizations and society. For example, authentic leadership provides an essential response to filling the emotional void caused by sport leaders' behaviours, leading to scandals that have increased the gap between sport leaders and, for example, subordinates and fans. Second, authentic leadership can be used as an effective means for those who seek to become authentic leaders (e.g. athletes, coaches, board members), through practice and theory. Additionally, the authentic leadership approach highlights that authentic values can be learnt and developed over time. For example, coaches or team managers in elite and non-elite sports may change their behaviours and values to become more authentic, rather than only to appear so. However, it is not necessary to start their career with authentic values, but their lifetime may help achieve that change. Third, authentic leadership is characterized by the moral dimension that requires sport leaders to do what is good or right for their athletes and society. Authentic coaches, managers, or presidents place their subordinates' needs (e.g. board members, staff, athletes) above their own, which means creating a common good at individual, organizational, and national levels. Importantly, authentic leadership can be measured using the validated ALQ, which gives an opportunity for future research to extend the debate or to apply the authentic leadership approach in other research disciplines. This could provide a fuller understanding of the effective application of this approach.

Although authentic leadership has strengths, there are weaknesses to address. First, the moral component of authentic leadership is not fully explained. That is, the process by which these values influence authentic leadership is still not clear. Second, positive psychological capacities – such as happiness, courage, humour – are used within the components of authentic leadership. However, it is argued that the use of positive psychological capacities in authentic leadership makes it difficult to measure. Particularly, the reasons underlying the inclusion of positive leader capacities in authentic leadership have not been well explained and researched (Einola and Alvesson, 2021). Third, there is a lack of empirical research that: (1) confirms the validity of the components of authentic leadership in sport management literature, and (2) investigates whether it can achieve the goals of sport organizations.

SUMMARY

Leadership failure in the non-profit, for-profit, and public sectors, including the sport aspects, have increased the demand for real and good leaders. Authentic leadership was developed in response to the many scandals and upheavals over the last five decades that continue to damage many national and international organizations. Given that authentic leadership is still in development, its definitions are many and varied, and there is no accepted definition among scholars for this phenomenon. This chapter addressed the impact of authentic leaders on subordinates' attitudes and behaviours, which is the essence of the authentic leadership approach. This chapter addressed the model of authentic leadership development developed by Gardner et al (2005), who importantly, included subordinates. The model incorporates four components of authenticity: awareness, unbiased processing, action, and rational into self-awareness and self-regulation behaviours. This chapter highlighted how authentic leadership is measured, particularly that it is still under development, which suggests the need for developing validated questionnaires to fit future authentic leadership development. This chapter addressed an evaluation of authentic leadership by highlighting the key weaknesses and strengths of this approach.

GENERAL QUESTIONS

1. How does authentic leadership work?
2. How does authentic leadership development differ from other leadership theories?
3. Why is self-regulation important for authentic leadership?
4. Why is trust important for authentic leadership?
5. Why is positive emotion important for authentic leadership?
6. Why is optimism important for authentic leadership?
7. Why is hope important for authentic leadership?

8. Identify five authentic leaders in sport.
9. Discuss the strengths of authentic leadership theory.
10. Discuss the weaknesses of authentic leadership theory.

OPEN DISCUSSION QUESTIONS

1. Define authentic leadership and compare your definition with your colleagues' definitions. Can you identify similarities and differences?
2. Discuss with your colleagues the personality of an authentic leader in your sport.
3. Discuss the process by which authentic leadership impacts subordinates' attitudes and behaviours.

Case Study 10.1: Thailand Cave Rescue

Twelve local boys from a junior association football team and their football coach went for an exploratory trip to a nearby cave, and ended up trapped deep inside the mountain without communication, causing pain to families, friends, local people, and local authorities. Media voiced solidarity with the boys and their coach through broadcasting and publishing breaking news on the rescue process over what turned out to be 19 days. The story began one day, when their training ended, the group decided to cycle into the forested hills that had recently been blanketed in rain. The destination was the Tham Luang Nang Non cave system, the favourite haunt for the boys. Though the group had often ventured as far as 8 km into the cave to write the names of new team members on a cave wall, this time they were trapped for two weeks.

The group found themselves in the cold and dark. They lost all sense of time and fear began to creep in. Though they did not have food for two weeks, drinkable water was available in the form of moisture dripping from the cave walls, a helpful factor for their survival. While local authorities and the world were engrossed in finding solutions to rescue them, the group tried to dig into a cave shelf to create a place where they could stay together and keep warm. In conjunction with the boys' efforts, the coach, who was a former monk, began to teach the boys meditation methods to enable them to stay calm and use as little air as possible, given the lack of oxygen inside the cave. He also told the boys to lie still to conserve their strength. Hope, trust, and positive emotions in the boys were the major factors that helped them overcome stress and fear during an unknowable amount of time. Therefore, the role of the coach was no less important than the role of the rescuers outside the cave.

Questions

1. The coach taught the boys meditation methods to help them stay calm, and use as little air as possible, given the lack of oxygen inside the cave. He also told the boys to lie still to conserve their strength. How was this relevant to his leadership?

2. What are the authentic leadership elements that the coach applied over the two weeks?
3. Can you identify other authentic leadership components not mentioned in the case material above?
4. How did critical events in the cave over two weeks show his leadership role in action?
5. What did you learn from this case? Discuss the answer with colleagues in the group.

Source: Based on BBC News. (2018). 'The full story of Thailand's extraordinary cave rescue'. *bbc.co.uk*. [online]. 14 July 2018. Available at: https://www.bbc.co.uk/news/world-asia-44791998; and Clarke, S., Torpey, P., Scruton, P., Safi, M., Levitt, D., Gutiérrez, P. and Watson, C. (2018). 'Thailand cave rescue: how did the boys get out?'. *The Guardian*. [online]. 9 July 2018 09:31 BST. Available from: https://www.theguardian.com/world/ng-interactive/2018/jul/03/thailand-cave-rescue-where-were-the-boys-found-and-how-can-they-be-rescued.

SELF-ASSESSMENT 10.1: AUTHENTIC LEADERSHIP BEHAVIOURS

Based on what you have done as an authentic leader or what think you would do, use the authentic leadership components described in this chapter to answer the following 12 statements.

Answer either False or True for each statement.

1. Personal identification refers to the process whereby a board member's belief about a sport organization becomes self-referential or self-defining.
2. The authentic chief executive can enhance self-efficacy in a sport organization by supporting the realistic thinking of board members and avoiding emotional reactions.
3. The autocratic behaviour of the authentic leaders is perceived as a positive form of effective leadership, particularly when dealing with complex problems in a sport organization.
4. The transparency of authentic leadership increases the mutual trust between an authentic coach and their athlete.
5. Excessive or unrealistic optimism from an authentic leader has positive outcomes on a sport organization, particularly in crises.
6. Self-awareness in authentic leadership includes three components: internalized, balanced processing, and transparency.
7. Self-regulation of authentic followership includes four components: values, identity, emotions, and motives/goals.
8. An authentic leader puts followers first and helps them grow and succeed.
9. An authentic leader stimulates followers' efforts to be more innovative by raising critical thinking.
10. An authentic leader is characterized by self-observation, self-goal setting, self-reward, self-punishment.

11. The three key personal characteristics of authentic leaders are: authoritarianism, locus of control, and ability.
12. Authentic leaders are born not made because authentic behaviours cannot be developed in leaders.

SELF-ASSESSMENT 10.2: HOW DO YOU DESCRIBE YOUR AUTHENTIC APPROACH TO LEADERSHIP?

You are preparing to submit your application for a new vacancy in the middle management level in an international sport organizations. You have been asked to fill in a personal assessment form describing your authentic behaviours for your application.

Rate the 14 statements carefully. Rate each for whether you would do it or not.

No = 1, Yes = 2.

1. I can make a list of all my hidden weaknesses.
2. I can make a list of all my greatest strengths.
3. I have the power to avoid pressure from others.
4. I listen carefully to the opinions of individuals who disagree with me.
5. I always share my feelings with surrounding individuals.
6. I am interested in letting others know who I am as a person.
7. My moral values affect my choices and actions.
8. I am interested in hearing others' opinions before giving my opinion.
9. I am interested in hearing others' advice before making any decision.
10. I accept criticism and feedback from others that help me understand who I am as a person.
11. I do not impose my opinions and ideas on others.
12. My moral principles guide my leadership behaviours.
13. I admit when I make mistakes.
14. Controversial ideas give me an idea about my attitudes.

To find out your authentic behaviour score, total your numbers from the 14 statements. Your score should be between 14 and 28.

Low = 14–18; Average = 19–22; High = 23–28

The lower your score, the less authentic is your behaviour, and the higher your score, the more authentic is your behaviour. Bear in mind, this is an exercise and may not give a proper assessment of your actual, personal authentic behaviour. If you've given answers just for fun, you won't be surprised by the result!

Suggested Reading

Avolio, B.J. and Gardner, W.L. (2005). Authentic Leadership Development: Getting to the Root of Positive Forms of Leadership. *The Leadership Quarterly*, 16(3), 315–338. https://doi.org/10.1016/j.leaqua.2005.03.001.

Gardner, W.L., Cogliser, C.C., Davis, K.M. and Dickens, M.P. (2011). Authentic Leadership: A Review of the Literature and Research Agenda. *The Leadership Quarterly*, 22(6), 1120–1145. https://doi.org/10.1016/j.leaqua.2011.09.007.

Luthans, F. and Avolio, B.J. (2003). Authentic Leadership: A Positive Developmental Approach. In: Cameron, K.S., Dutton, J.E. and Quinn, R.E. (Eds.). *Positive Organizational Scholarship*. San Francisco, CA: Barrett Koehler. (241–261).

Megheirkouni, M. (2021). Authentic Leadership, Empowerment, and Positive Outcomes: Hearing the Voices of the Events Industry. *Event Management*, 25(5), 445–458. https://doi.org/10.3727/152599519X15506259856615.

Walumbwa, F.O., Avolio, B.J., Gardner, W.L., Wernsing, T.S. and Peterson, S.J. (2008). Authentic Leadership: Development and Validation of a Theory-Based Measure. *Journal of Management*, 34(1), 89–126. https://doi.org/10.1177/0149206307308913.

References

Avolio, B.J. and Gardner, W.L. (2005). Authentic Leadership Development: Getting to the Root of Positive Forms of Leadership. *The Leadership Quarterly,* 16(3), 315–338. https://doi.org/10.1016/j.leaqua.2005.03.001.

Avolio, B.J., Gardner, W.L., Walumbwa, F.O., Luthans, F. and May, D.R. (2004). Unlocking the Mask: A Look at the Process by Which Authentic Leaders Impact Follower Attitudes and Behaviours. *The Leadership Quarterly*, 15(6), 801–823. https://doi.org/10.1016/j.leaqua.2004.09.003.

Avolio, B.J., Luthans, F. and Walumbwa, F.O. (2004). Authentic Leadership: Theory Building for Veritable Sustained Performance. Working paper. Gallup Leadership Institute, University of Nebraska-Lincoln.

Bono, J.E. and Judge, T.A. (2003). Self-Concordance at Work: Toward Understanding the Motivational Effects of Transformational Leaders. *Academy of Management Journal*, 46(5), 554–571. JSTOR: https://www.jstor.org/stable/30040649.

Cooper, C.D., Scandura, T.A. and Schriesheim, C.A. (2005). Looking Forward But Learning from Our Past: Potential Challenges to Developing Authentic Leadership Theory and Authentic Leaders. *The Leadership Quarterly*, 16(3), 475–493. https://doi.org/10.1016/j.leaqua.2005.03.008.

Day, D.V. (2000). Leadership Development: A Review in Context. *The Leadership Quarterly*, 11(4), 581–613. https://doi.org/10.1016/S1048-9843(00)00061-8.

Einola, K. and Alvesson, M. (2021). The Perils of Authentic Leadership Theory. *Leadership*, 17(4), 483–490. https://doi.org/10.1177/17427150211004059.

Gardner, W.L. and Avolio, B.J. (1998). The Charismatic Relationship: A Dramaturgical Perspective. *Academy of Management Review*, 23(1), 32–58. https://doi.org/10.2307/259098.

Gardner, W.L., Avolio, B.J., Luthans, F., May, D.R. and Walumbwa, F. (2005). 'Can You See the Real Me?' A Self-Based Model of Authentic Leader and Follower Development. *The Leadership Quarterly* 16(3), 343–372. https://doi.org/10.1016/j.leaqua.2005.03.003.

Gardner, W.L., Cogliser, C.C., Davis, K.M., and Dickens, M.P. (2011). Authentic Leadership: A Review of the Literature and Research Agenda. *The Leadership Quarterly*, 22(6), 1120–1145. https://doi.org/10.1016/j.leaqua.2011.09.007.

Gardner, W.L. and Schermerhorn Jr., J.R. (2004). Unleashing Individual Potential: Performance Gains through Positive Organizational Behaviour and Authentic Leadership. *Organizational Dynamics*, 33(3), 270–281. https://doi.org/10.1016/j.orgdyn.2004.06.004.

Henderson, J.E. and Hoy, W.K. (1983). Leader Authenticity: The Development and Test of an Operational Measure. *Educational and Psychological Research*, 3(2), 63–75. ERIC: https://eric.ed.gov/?id=ED219408.

Hoyle, R.H., Kernis, M.H., Leary, M.R. and Baldwin, M.W. (1999). *Selfhood: Identity, Esteem, Regulation*. Boulder, CO: Westview Press. https://doi.org/10.4324/9780429305818

Ilies, R., Morgeson, F.P. and Nahrgang, J.D. (2005). Authentic Leadership and Eudaemonic Well-Being: Understanding Leader–Follower Outcomes. *The Leadership Quarterly*, 16(3), 373–394. https://doi.org/10.1016/j.leaqua.2005.03.002.

Jensen, S.M. and Luthans, F. (2006). Relationship between Entrepreneurs' Psychological Capital and Their Authentic Leadership. *Journal of Managerial Issues*, 18(2), 254–273. JSTOR: https://www.jstor.org/stable/40604537.

Kark, R. and Shamir, B. (2002). The Dual Effect of Transformational Leadership: Priming Relational and Collective Selves and Further Effects on Followers. In: Avolio, B.J. and Yammarino F.J. (Eds.). *Transformational and Charismatic Leadership: The Road Ahead*. Oxford: Elsevier. (67–91).

Kernis, M.H. (2003). Toward a Conceptualization of Optimal Self-Esteem. *Psychological Inquiry*, 14(1), 1–26. https://doi.org/10.1207/S15327965PLI1401_01.

Klenke, K. (2005). The Internal Theatre of the Authentic Leader. In: Gardner, W.L., Avolio, B.J. and Walumbwa, F.O. (Eds.). *Authentic Leadership Theory and Practice: Origins, Effects and Development*. Oxford: Elsevier. (155–182).

Lord, R.G. and Brown, D.J. (2001). Leadership, Value, and Subordinate Self-Concepts. *The Leadership Quarterly*, 12(2), 133–152. https://doi.org/10.1016/S1048-9843(01)00072-8.

Lord, R.G. and Brown, D.J. (2003). *Leadership Processes and Follower Self-Identity*. New York: Psychology Press. https://doi.org/10.4324/9781410608864.

Luthans, F. and Avolio, B.J. (2003). Authentic Leadership: A Positive Developmental Approach. In: Cameron, K.S., Dutton, J.E. and Quinn, R.E. (Eds.). *Positive Organizational Scholarship*. San Francisco, CA: Barrett Koehler. (241–261).

Luthans, F. and Youssef, C.M. (2004). Human, Social, and Now Positive Psychological Capital Management: Investing in People for Competitive Advantage. *Organizational Dynamics*, 33(2), 143–160. https://doi.org/10.1016/j.orgdyn.2004.01.003.

Northouse, P.G. (2021). *Leadership: Theory and Practice*. (9th ed.). London: Sage.

Rousseau, D.M. (1995). *Psychological Contracts in Organisations: Understanding Written and Unwritten Agreements*. Newbury Park, CA: Sage. https://doi.org/10.4135/9781452231594.

Rousseau, D.M. (1998). The 'Problem' of the Psychological Contract Considered. *Journal of Organizational Behaviour*, 19(S1), 665–667. https://doi.org/10.1002/(SICI)1099-1379(1998)19:1+%3C665::AID-JOB972%3E3.0.CO;2-X.

Rousseau, D.M., Sitkin, S.B., Burt, R.S. and Camerer, C. (1998). Not So Different after All: A Cross-Discipline View of Trust. *Academy of Management Review*, 23(3), 393–404. https://doi.org/10.5465/amr.1998.926617.

Salovey, P. and Mayer, J.D. 1990. Emotional Intelligence. *Imagination, Cognition and Personality*, 9(3), 185–211. https://doi.org/10.2190/DUGG-P24E-52WK-6CDG.

Scheier, M.F. and Carver, C.S. (1992). Effects of Optimism on Psychological and Physical Well-Being. Theoretical Overview and Empirical Update. *Cognitive Therapy and Research*, 16(2), 201–228. https://doi.org/10.1007/BF01173489.

Shamir, B. and Eilam, G. (2005). 'What's Your Story?': A Life-Stories Approach to Authentic Leadership Development. *The Leadership Quarterly*, 16(3), 395–417. https://doi.org/10.1016/j.leaqua.2005.03.005.

Shamir, B., Zakay, E., Brainin, E. and Popper, M. (2000). Leadership and Social Identification in Military Units: Direct and Indirect Relationships. *Journal of Applied Social Psychology*, 30(3), 612–640. https://doi.org/10.1111/j.1559-1816.2000.tb02499.x.

Snyder, C.R., Irving, L.M. and Anderson, J.R. (1991). The Will and the Ways: Development and Validation of an Individual-Differences Measure of Hope. *Journal of Personality and Social Psychology*, 60(4), 570–585. https://doi.org/10.1037/0022-3514.60.4.570.

Walumbwa, F.O., Avolio, B.J., Gardner, W.L., Wernsing, T.S. and Peterson, S.J. (2008). Authentic Leadership: Development and Validation of a Theory-Based Measure. *Journal of Management*, 34(1), 89–126. https://doi.org/10.1177/0149206307308913.

11 DISTRIBUTED LEADERSHIP

Learning Outcomes

After reading this chapter, you will be able to:

- Define distributed leadership
- Distinguish between different frameworks of distributed leadership
- Identify the major elements of distributed leadership
- Identify the strengths of distributed leadership
- Identify the weaknesses of distributed leadership
- Understand the role of distributed leadership in sport settings

INTRODUCTION

Distributed leadership occurs where the leadership function is distributed through empowerment mechanisms more broadly than autocratic leadership. Here, leadership can be considered as a quality of the entire sport organization. Distributed leadership is based on an understanding of how sport leaders at all organizational levels (e.g. chief executives, presidents, board members, coaches, team managers, department managers) may exercise influence, and how this influence may be perceived within sport organizations as part of completing work.

WHAT IS DISTRIBUTED LEADERSHIP

Distributed leadership has switched focus from behaviours and attributes of leaders to a more systemic perspective (Bolden, 2011). Spillane (2006) states that leadership refers to activities that are designed and understood by certain organizational members to influence the motivation, knowledge, practice of other members. Specifically, Spillane suggests that distributed leadership refers to the collective interactions among leaders, subordinates, and their situation that are paramount. From this perspective, it is argued that:

> Distributed leadership is primarily concerned with the interactions
> and the dynamics of leadership practice rather than a preoccupation

with the formal roles and responsibilities traditionally associated with those 'who lead'.

(Harris, 2013: vii)

Distributed leadership is one of many calls in leadership literature for reframing understanding of leadership through new leadership approaches, such as: 'shared leadership', 'collective leadership', 'collaborative leadership', 'distributive leadership', and 'co-leadership'. These approaches call for a more collective and systemic understanding of leadership as a social process (Barker, 2001). Distributed leadership is described as disciplined and collaborative to counter critics who complain about complex ideas. Harris and Spillane (2008) suggest three reasons for the importance and popularity of distributed leadership:

1. **Collaborative mentality**: The model of the singular, heroic leader has been replaced with (so-called 'post-heroic') leadership that focuses on teams rather than individuals.
2. **Environment requirements**: The work of leadership requires diverse types of expertise and forms of leadership that are flexible enough to meet changing challenges and new demands, and traverse a very different organizational landscape, given the increasingly complex world.
3. **Positive outcome**: Distributed leadership makes a positive difference to organizational outcomes.

Consequently, the question of what is 'distributed leadership' remains unanswered.

ESSENTIAL ELEMENTS OF DISTRIBUTED LEADERSHIP

Various frameworks of distributed leadership have been proposed (Table 11.1). The frameworks suggested by MacBeath et al (2004) and Leithwood et al (2006) focus on school contexts. Those suggested by Gronn (2002) and Spillane (2006) pay attention to the interpersonal dynamics of distributed leadership and the ways in which people can collaborate to achieve shared outcomes in most organizations, including sport organizations.

DISTRIBUTED LEADERSHIP AS NUMERICAL OR ADDITIVE ACTION

Numerical or additive action of distributed leadership refers to the aggregated leadership behaviour of an organization and is dispersed among some, many, or even all of the members of an organization. This sense of distributed leadership means that any members, including players, of a sport organization, union, federation, or association may be leaders at some stage (Wenger, 2000). Arguably, this sense of leadership is contrasted with focused leadership that adopts the idea that only one person in a sport organization is attributed to the status of leader.

Table 11.1 Distributed Leadership Frameworks

Gronn (2002)	Spillane (2006)	Leithwood et al (2006)	MacBeath et al (2004)
Spontaneous collaboration: Groups of individuals with different skills come together to complete particular jobs, then disband.	**Collaborated distribution**: Two or more individuals work together to execute the same leadership routine.	**Planful alignment**: Resources are deliberately distributed to one or more individuals to lead particular tasks.	**Formal distribution**: There are designated roles and responsibilities.
Intuitive working relations: Two or more individuals build close working relations until leadership is manifest in the shared role encompassed by their relationship.	**Collective distribution**: Two or more individuals work separately but interdependently to enact a leadership routine.	**Spontaneous alignment**: Leadership tasks are distributed with little planning, yet the tasks end up with the appropriate people.	**Pragmatic distribution**: Delegation of tasks and responsibilities is mainly ad hoc. **Strategic distribution**: The individuals selected for leadership development contribution are well-chosen.
Institutionalized practice: Formal structures become institutionalized in organizations by design or adaptation to facilitate collaboration between individuals.	**Coordinated distribution**: Two or more individuals work in sequence in order to complete a leadership routine.	**Spontaneous misalignment**: Leadership is distributed in an unplanned way and this leads to an unpredictable outcome. **Anarchic misalignment**: Leaders reject others for particular tasks, resulting from competition between leaders for resources.	**Incremental distribution**: Roles and responsibilities are devolved to demonstrate people's capability to lead. **Opportunistic distribution**: An opportunity is given to individuals willing to take leadership roles and responsibilities. **Cultural distribution**: Leadership practice is perceived as a reflection of habits, traditions, values, and culture.

Source: Based on on Gronn, P. (2002). Distributed Leadership. In: Leithwood, K., Hallinger, P., Furman, G.C., Riley, K., MacBeath, J., Gronn, P. and Mulford, B. (Eds.). *Second International Handbook of Educational Leadership and Administration*. Dordrecht: Springer. (653–696); Spillane, J.P. (2006). *Distributed Leadership*. San Francisco, CA: Jossey-Bass; Leithwood, K., Day, C., Sammons, P., Harris, A. and Hopkins, D. (2006). *Successful School Leadership: What It Is and How It Influences Pupil Learning*. Nottingham: DfES Publications; MacBeath, J., Oduro, G.K.T. and Waterhouse, J. (2004). *Distributed Leadership in Action: A Study of Current Practice in Schools*. Nottingham: National College for School Leadership.

DISTRIBUTED LEADERSHIP AS CONCERTIVE ACTION

Distributed leadership in a numerical/additive sense may be perceived as the sum of its parts, but it could also be understood in a holistic – concertive – sense rather than simply as the aggregation of individual contributions. Gronn (2002) suggests three forms of concertive action: spontaneous collaboration, intuitive working relationships, and institutionalized practices. For Gronn, these three forms of concertive action may be attributed to leadership, and each of them could be considered as a manifestation of 'conjoint agency'. The agents constituting the membership of sport organizations (e.g. board members, committees, directors, departments, coaches, and other stakeholders) act conjointly.

SPONTANEOUS COLLABORATION

Here, leadership practice is stretched over the social and situational contexts of sport organizations to include various organizational areas and different levels pooling their experience, skills, and knowledge for a particular assignment. For example, when athletes who test positive for prohibited recreational drugs for World Athletics Championships are banned, this requires an effective and intensive collaborative effort to cope with this serious problem from the national sport community including, but not limited to, relevant board members, the chief executive, medical staff and coaches at the national athletics organization as well as parliament and government commitment to anti-doping (Houlihan et al, 2019). Additionally, we note that the discovery of new substances in use with apparently doping-relevant effects or old ones with previously unrecognized effects will, and does, provoke spontaneous collaboration, and considerable discussion in media channels.

INTUITIVE WORKING RELATIONS

It refers to a close working relationship between two members (or more) of a sport organization who need each other. A good example of this is the members (e.g. president and deputy president) of an Olympic Games Organizing Committee. The goals, plans, and strategies of the committee's members are manifest in the shared roles and responsibilities encompassed by their partnership. The partners are aware of themselves as co-leaders on the organizing committee.

INSTITUTIONALIZED PRACTICES

Over time, distributed leadership practices may become institutionalized into formal structures by design or adaptation to facilitate collaboration between individuals. Generally, institutional systems differ from country to country, and this has a significant influence on the structures of most organizations, regardless of the type or size of the sector. For example, sporting goods firms operating in global markets may adopt business strategies, policies, or organizational structures and cultures of the parent company. This raises the question as to what extent the third form of concertive action affects the effective use of 'distributed leadership' in the new market.

Notably, the traditional debate on leadership and organizational studies emphasizes that leadership and followership (see Chapter 7, 'Leader-Member Exchange Theory') are related in several ways, which Sims (2002: 221) summarizes in four points:

1. Leaders cannot be successful without subordinates.
2. Leaders, themselves, should be successful subordinates in various roles within an organization.
3. Leaders should understand the importance of subordinates to exhibit their traits and reward them accordingly.
4. Leaders should serve their subordinates rather than one in which subordinates serve leaders.

Leithwood et al (2007) focused on school contexts to draw elements of distributed leadership through understanding what were the tasks or functions of leadership, how leadership was performed and what affected the development of distributed leadership. Specifically, some elaboration and refinement by Leithwood and colleagues on Gronn's (2002) forms of distributed leadership resulted in: planful alignment, spontaneous alignment, spontaneous misalignment, and anarchic misalignment.

- **Planful alignment**: Leadership tasks or functions have been given prior thoughtful consideration by organization members, including figuring out which source of leadership is best to fit each task or function.
- **Spontaneous alignment**: Leadership tasks or functions are distributed with little thought or planning, but the right tasks or functions certainly end up with the right people, which are aligned with the organizational objectives.
- **Spontaneous misalignment**: refers to situations in which the sources of leadership are misaligned with one another which result in an unpredictable outcome. This, in turn, can result in negative implications on both short and long-term organizational performance.
- **Anarchic misalignment**: refers to situations in which leaders actively reject others for particular tasks or functions in the organization, resulting from a highly independently competition between leaders for resources.

Indeed, the need for leadership and followership in sport organizations is essential to achieve the organization's objectives. Scholars have emphasized the role of the situation (or contexts) where leadership is practiced (e.g., Northouse, 2021; Grint, 2005; Yukl, 2013). As we have seen in previous parts of this book, leadership practice, from a distributed perspective, occurs as three discrete organizational components that interact over time: situation (contexts), leaders, and subordinates (see Figure 11.1).

As noted earlier, leadership in an Olympic Games Organizing Committee requires an emphasis on productivity (achievements) and interaction through collaboration. In light of this, Spillane (2006) assumes that distributed leadership is perceived, acting as social interactions of leadership, where leadership role is distributed between several individuals (involving the contributions of multiple actors, not just those in formal managerial roles) in the same committee,

Figure 11.1 The three organizational components that make up leadership practice.

Source: Adapted from Spillane, J.P. (2006). *Distributed Leadership*. San Francisco, CA: Jossey-Bass.

sub-committee, organization, department, and division. Leadership tasks, from a distributed perspective, are shared to achieve a shared outcome.

Three types of distribution have been identified to illustrate the nature of leadership distribution (Spillane, 2006):

1. **Collaborated distribution**: This type means that two or more individuals work together in time and place to execute the same leadership routine.
2. **Collective distribution**: This type means that two or more individuals work separately but interdependently to enact a leadership.
3. **Coordinated distribution**: This type means that two or more individuals work in sequence in order to complete a leadership routine.

Formal networking activity (e.g. formal meetings, observations, training sessions) and informal networking (e.g. lunch time in the work, greeting staff, informal communication with staff) and developmental tools (e.g. 360-degree feedback and observations) are all formal and informal patterns of leadership practice in a sport organization. Situation (context) refers to the routines and tools that constrain leadership practice (Spillane and Coldren, 2011). Overall, this kind of activities can mediate how subordinates practice, shaping social interaction among leaders and subordinates in specific ways. Brooks et al (2007) built on Spillane (2006) who discussed the relationship between leaders, subordinates, and situation, and they stated that leadership practice is a fluid phenomenon that changes from situation to situation and that it evolves over time. This assumes that the form of routines might vary among sport organizations, departments, divisions, committees, or subcommittees due to such factors as organizational culture, national culture, and institutional system.

MacBeath (2005) describes distributed leadership as a developing process and identifies six forms of distributed leadership. Each of these forms not only represents a different way of thinking about leadership, but also exemplifies different processes of distribution. These forms include:

a. **Formal distribution**: Leadership role and responsibility are designed, where activities are structurally delegated.

b. **Pragmatic distribution**: It is characterized by its ad hoc quality, where leadership role and responsibility are divided between different members.

c. **Strategic distribution**: Individuals with particular behaviours, capabilities, and experience are appointed to fulfil certain leadership roles.

d. **Incremental distribution**: It is characterized by pragmatic ad hoc quality and strategic; where a professional development is significantly related to the ability of people to exercise leadership roles they are given.

e. **Opportunistic distribution**: Individuals willingly extend their roles and responsibilities, where there is a natural predisposition to take a lead, organize, determines needs, and make sure that everything is done.

f. **Cultural distribution**: Leadership is intuitive and assumed by members of organizations and shared organically between individuals, where leadership is expressed in activities rather than roles or through individual initiative.

MacBeath (2005) argues that the most appropriate or effective type of distributed leadership depends upon the situation. MacBeath goes further to say that distributed leadership is premised on trust. Far away from natural arguments and discussion among members to adopt one idea eventually, a mutual acceptance may not necessarily occur, which has negative implications for control and authority.

EVALUATION OF DISTRIBUTED LEADERSHIP

One of the strengths of this approach is that it is designed to focus on collaborative work in sport organizations so as to achieve the objectives of the organization. The spirit of collaborative work is the main feature in this approach. In other words, there is no place for ego 'self' in a team or group where collective spirit tends to be the dominant feature in organizational work. Additionally, this approach can help members who have not yet reached a standard to improve their skills and knowledge through learning from others. Undoubtedly, team members are not equal in terms of their experience, knowledge, skills, network, and academic background (van Knippenberg, De Dreu and Homan, 2004). Social constructivists suggest that collaborative learning occurs as connections are made between individual group members' perceptions, ideas, concepts and skills. Moreover, this model helps improve the quality of decision-making through the nature of information, ideas, and suggestions exchanged by team members, regardless of the way in which the decision is made. More importantly, this approach helps individuals 'team members' who proved their effectiveness in an organization to be considered for career development 'team leader'.

Distributed leadership has also weaknesses. First of all, distributed leadership models did not cover all possible leadership skills. Additional skills might be needed, particularly those that focus on leader, subordinates, and situation. A team need to adopt a set of skills that are particularly relevant to its effectiveness (Northouse, 2021). Moreover, the cultural and institutional system such as power distance, traditional hierarchical structures, and gender can be a barrier to the adoption of distributed leadership as those in top management may resist involving or sharing information with subordinates, since autocratic leadership is still dominant in some organizations/contexts. Other barriers to the adoption of models of distributed leadership include the belief that one person holds the decision (e.g. Harris, 2004; Southworth, 2004; Weir, 2010).

SUMMARY

As discussed earlier, there are reasons behind the importance of distributed leadership: its collaborative mentality, its environment requirements, and its positive outcomes. This chapter has addressed distributed leadership as numerical (or additive) action and as concertive action with further details on the three forms of the concertive action: spontaneous collaboration, intuitive working relationships, and institutionalized practices. This chapter has highlighted the elaboration and refinement Leithwood and colleagues made on Gronn's (2002) forms of distributed leadership: planful alignment, spontaneous alignment, spontaneous misalignment, and anarchic misalignment. This chapter has addressed three types of distribution that have been identified to illustrate the nature of leadership distribution: collaborated distribution, collective distribution, and coordinated distribution. Moreover, this chapter has discussed distributed leadership as a developing process and has examined six forms of distributed leadership that include: formal distribution, pragmatic distribution, strategic distribution, incremental distribution, opportunistic distribution, and cultural distribution. The last section of this chapter has presented an evaluation of distributed leadership.

GENERAL QUESTIONS

1. What are the three reasons for the importance and popularity of distributed leadership?
2. Discuss the difference between numerical or additive action and concertive action of distributed leadership.
3. What are the forms of concertive action?
4. Why do sport organizations increasingly use distributed leadership?
5. Can you summarize the relationship between leadership and followership?
6. What are the types of distribution used to illustrate leadership distribution?
7. What are the similarities and differences between formal distribution, pragmatic distribution, strategic distribution, incremental distribution, opportunistic distribution, and cultural distribution?
8. Discuss the tasks or functions of leadership in the following forms of distributed leadership: planful alignment, spontaneous alignment, spontaneous misalignment, and anarchic misalignment.
9. List two situations in sport leadership for which you believe distributed leadership is perceived as essential and two where it is perceived as useless.

OPEN DISCUSSION QUESTIONS

1. Discuss with your colleagues, what kinds of leadership might be needed to complete daily tasks in the organizing committees of sport mega events?

Use your choice of sport mega event, which might or might not be an Olympic Games event.

2. Was there any deliberate attempt to distribute leadership in your chosen event?
3. Was the committee led by more than one leader? Whether yes or no, what is your evaluation of the committee's results?

Case Study 11.1: The Spirit of a Team! – What We Cannot See

Many people consider team sports as good examples of the spirit of effective teamwork and collective performance. We're exhilarated when our favourite teams win and depressed after they lose. When a team wins a championship, we remember all the team players and all the difficult moments our team players experienced during the championship.

Sometimes the truth might be different from what we believe we see. Most of us agree that such factors as player apathy, lack of team cohesion, lack of moral responsibility towards the team, conflicts among players, confusion about roles, lack of trust between players and with the coach, and a failure to implement the team tactics or plans are all fundamental factors influencing team performance. But it may be the case that these factors did not affect the team's success. One of the best examples of this is the New York Yankees Major League Basketball World Series wins in 1977 and 1978 despite the lack of team discipline, fights between players and with coaches, poor communication, and threatened firings. The team won and was the most effective team regarding goal accomplishment.

Questions

1. Can you find examples of sport clubs or organizations with different strategies, internal processes, and objectives that achieve similar results?
2. Can you find examples of sport clubs or organizations with similar strategies, objectives, and internal processes that achieve different results?
3. Is shared leadership essential for team performance? Why?
4. Do individual experience and qualification replace teamwork? Why?
5. Player apathy, lack of team cohesion, conflicts among players and between players and the coach are a few examples of the forms of the relationships between the New York Yankees team. Yet they were successful. So, how did they succeed despite the breakdown of expected team behaviours?
6. Can you give other examples of teams that lacked team cohesion and moral responsibility towards the players and fans, and still won?
7. If you've done questions 5 and 6 on your own, discuss your answers with colleague and compare the similarities and differences.
8. What impacts did these particular basketball games have in the UK and elsewhere?

SELF-ASSESSMENT 11.1: YOUR ATTITUDES TOWARDS DISTRIBUTED LEADERSHIP

Based on what you have done as a team leader, or what you think you would do, use the team situations and attitudes described to answer the following seven statements. Answer 0 for False or 1 for True for each statement.

1. A sport team should keep its members informed almost daily of information that could affect their work.
2. I prefer working through social media or other platforms to complete tasks with board members.
3. I feel somewhat tense while working and communicating with members from other cultures.
4. If I am out of the office for an annual leave, I expect work will be accomplished in my absence.
5. I am confident about leading team members when a team includes experienced staff.
6. I expect that each member has different opinions and suggestions when working on a proposal for hosting international championships.
7. I nearly always prefer rationality when an important task has to be done right.

Total your scores. The result will be between 0 and 7. Higher scores indicate a more favourable attitude towards distributed leadership.

SELF-ASSESSMENT 11.2: DISTRIBUTED LEADERSHIP IN YOUR PRACTICE

Think back to your most recent experience working in a team. Use your sport as an example. Write down your answers to the following seven questions about your role in the team. Particularly, note aspects where distributed leadership played a part.

1. What was your role in the team?
2. What did the team members appreciate about your role?
3. What did you learn from the team members? And what did the team members learn from you?
4. What are the main skills that worked with you in the team?
5. What are the main skills you think they were not appropriate for the team?
6. What were your strengths and weaknesses in the team?
7. Evaluate your answers and write a short report summarizing the whole answer. How do you feel about the answers? Is there improvement you would like to work on?

Suggested Reading

Bolden, R. (2011). Distributed Leadership in Organizations: A Review of Theory and Research. *International Journal of Management Reviews*, 13(3), 251–269. https://doi.org/10.1111/j.1468-2370.2011.00306.x.

Gronn, P. (2002). Distributed Leadership as a Unit of Analysis. *The Leadership Quarterly*, 13(4), 423–451. https://doi.org/10.1016/S1048-9843(02)00120-0.

Harris, A. (2009). *Distributed Leadership: Different Perspectives*. London: Springer. https://doi.org/10.1007/978-1-4020-9737-9.

Jones, R.L. (Ed.). (2006). *The Sports Coach as Educator: Re-Conceptualising Sports Coaching*. London: Routledge.

Lumsden, G., Lumsden, D. and Wiethoff, C. (2009). *Communicating in Groups and Teams: Sharing Leadership*. (5th ed.). London: Cengage Learning.

Megheirkouni, M. (2018). Mixed Methods in Sport Leadership Research: A Review of Sport Management Practices. *Choregia*, 14(1), 1–20. EBSCO: https://openurl.ebsco.com/EPDB%3Agcd%3A2%3A14153890/detailv2?sid=ebsco%3Aplink%3Ascholar&id=ebsco%3Agcd%3A129500054&crl=c.

Pearce, C.L. and Conger, J.A. (Eds.). (2003). *Shared Leadership: Reframing the Hows and Whys of Leadership*. London: Sage. https://doi.org/10.4135/9781452229539.

Pearce, C.L., Conger, J.A. and Locke, E.A. (2008). Shared Leadership Theory. *The Leadership Quarterly*, 19(5), 622–628. https://doi.org/10.1016/j.leaqua.2008.07.005.

Price, M.S. and Weiss, M.R. (2011). Peer Leadership in Sport: Relationships among Personal Characteristics, Leader Behaviours, and Team Outcomes. *Journal of Applied Sport Psychology*, 23(1), 49–64. https://doi.org/10.1080/10413200.2010.520300.

Slater, M.J., Coffee, P., Barker, J.B. and Evans, A.L. (2014). Promoting Shared Meanings in Group Memberships: A Social Identity Approach to Leadership in Sport. *Reflective Practice*, 15(5), 672–685. https://doi.org/10.1080/14623943.2014.944126.

Spillane, J.P. (2006). *Distributed Leadership*. San Francisco, CA: Jossey-Bass. [e-book: 2012].

Spillane, J.P. and Diamond, J.B. (Eds.). (2007). *Distributed Leadership in Practice*. New York: Teachers College Press, Columbia University.

References

Barker, R.A. (2001). The Nature of Leadership. *Human Relations*, 54(4), 469–494. https://doi.org/10.1177/0018726701544004.

Bolden, R. (2011). Distributed Leadership in Organizations: A Review of Theory and Research. *International Journal of Management Reviews*, 13(3), 251–269. https://doi.org/10.1111/j.1468-2370.2011.00306.x.

Brooks, J.S., Jean-Marie, G., Normore, A.H. and Hodgins, D.W. (2007). Distributed Leadership for Social Justice: Exploring How Influence and Equity Are Stretched over an Urban High School. *Journal of School Leadership*, 17(4), 378–408. https://doi.org/10.1177/105268460701700402.

Grint, K. (2005). Problems, Problems, Problems: The Social Construction of 'Leadership'. *Human Relations*, 58(11), 1467–1494. https://doi.org/10.1177/0018726705061314.

Gronn, P.C. (2002). Distributed Leadership. In: Leithwood, K., Hallinger, P., Furman, G.C., Riley, K., MacBeath, J., Gronn, P. and Mulford, B. (Eds.). *Second International Handbook of Educational Leadership and Administration*. Dordrecht: Springer. (653–696). https://doi.org/10.1007/978-94-010-0375-9_23.

Harris, A. (2004). Distributed Leadership and School Improvement: Leading Or Misleading? *Educational Management Administration and Leadership*, 32(1), 11–24. https://doi.org/10.1177/1741143204039297.

Harris, A. (2013). *Distributed Leadership Matters: Perspectives, Practicalities, and Potential.* London: Sage.

Harris, A. and Spillane, J. (2008). Distributed Leadership through the Looking Glass. *Management in Education*, 22(1), 31–34. https://doi.org/10.1177/0892020607085623.

Houlihan, B., Vidar Hanstad, D., Loland, S. and Waddington, I. (2019). The World Anti-Doping Agency at 20: Progress and Challenges. *International Journal of Sport Policy and Politics*, 11(2), 193–201. https://doi.org/10.1080/19406940.2019.1617765.

Leithwood, K., Day, C., Sammons, P., Harris, A. and Hopkins, D. (2006). *Successful School Leadership: What It Is and How It Influences Pupil Learning*. Report. Nottingham: DfES Publications.

Leithwood, K., Day, C., Sammons, P., Harris, A. and Hopkins, D. (2007). The Impact of Leadership on Student Outcomes: How Successful School Leaders Use Transformational and Instructional Strategies to Make a Difference. *Educational Administration Quarterly*, 52(2), 221–258.

MacBeath, J. (2005). Leadership as Distributed: A Matter of Practice. *School Leadership and Management*, 25(4), 349–366. https://doi.org/10.1080/13634230500197165.

MacBeath, J., Oduro, G.K.T. and Waterhouse, J. (2004). *Distributed Leadership in Action: A Study of Current Practice in Schools*. Report. Nottingham: National College for School Leadership. Available at: https://core.ac.uk/download/pdf/4152258.pdf.

Northouse, P.G. (2021). *Leadership: Theory and Practice*. (9th ed.). London: Sage.

Sims, R.R. (2002). *Managing Organizational Behaviour.* Westport, CA: Greenwood Publishing.

Southworth, G. (2004). Overview and Conclusions. In: Coles, M. and Southworth, G. (Eds.). *Developing Leadership: Creating the School of Tomorrow*. Maidenhead: Open University Press. (158–173).

Spillane, J.P. (2006). *Distributed Leadership*. San Francisco, CA: Jossey-Bass. [e-book: 2012].

Spillane, J.P. and Coldren, A.F. (2011). *Diagnosis and Design for School Improvement: Using a Distributed Perspective to Lead and Manage Change*. New York: Teachers College Press.

van Knippenberg, D., De Dreu, C.K.W. and Homan, A.C. (2004). Work Group Diversity and Group Performance: An Integrative Model and Research Agenda. *Journal of Applied Psychology*, 89(6), 1008–1022. https://doi.org/10.1037/0021-9010.89.6.1008.

Weir, T. (2010). Developing Leadership in Global Organizations. In: Lundby, K. and Jolton, J. (Eds.). Going Global: Practical Applications and Recommendations for HR and OD Professionals in the Global Workplace. (2nd ed.). San Francisco, CA: Wiley-Blackwell, (203–230).

Wenger, E. (2000). Communities of Practice and Social Learning Systems. *Organization*, 7(2), 225–246. https://doi.org/10.1177/135050840072002.

Yukl, G. (2013). *Leadership in Organizations*. (8th ed.). New York: Pearson.

12 WOMEN **AND** LEADERSHIP

Learning Outcomes

After reading this chapter, you will be able to:

- Understand gender differences in leadership styles
- Understand gender stereotypes
- Determine how women leaders can be effective
- Define the factors influencing diversity
- Understand women leadership in context
- Evaluate women leadership in sport settings

INTRODUCTION

As the number of women increases in more sport settings and in sport leadership roles, it is important to introduce the reader to theoretical and practical models for thinking about leadership, organization, and gender in sport. Although there is general agreement that women face real barriers to becoming sport leaders across all sport settings, and sport leadership roles that are male-dominated in particular (Megheirkouni, 2014), many studies of women in leadership draw on an 'ethics of care' such as, responsiveness, sensitivity to others, acceptance, collaboration, as major characteristic of the way women lead. However, this does not explain the complex systemic factors that influence the functioning of women within sport organizations. The primary research questions now are: Do women lead differently from men? Are there leadership style differences between women and men? Such questions are often subsumed under a larger question: "Why are women underrepresented in elite sport leadership and other roles at national and international levels?" This chapter addresses gender stereotypes and differences in leadership, women's effectiveness, and factors influencing leadership diversity. Additionally, it addresses sport women in three contexts: coaching, management, and leadership.

Note that in the discussion we use female and male as well as woman and man; however, the research described, unless stated, is about adults in leadership rather than younger people. The gender-related issues do not, however, suddenly appear on reaching 'adulthood'.

DOI: 10.4324/9780429290442-15

GENDER AND LEADERSHIP

As more women are rapidly occupying positions of leadership in politics, management, sport, law, academia, and sport (Klenke, 2011), important questions are raised and accompanied this evolution, including whether women lead with a different style from men. Debate on gender differences in leadership may be perceived as a subset of a larger field of inquiry into male–female differences conducted in across all disciplines. The way gender differences are described gives a sense that these differences are fixed. Klenke concluded that there are either no differences or minor differences between male and female leaders regarding leadership styles. This result can be reached whether leaders used self-rating or were described by subordinates (Klenke, 2004).

GENDER DIFFERENCES AND LEADERSHIP STYLES

Sport leadership is framed as a meritocracy where qualifications, experience, and skills contribute all in being a successful leader (e.g. Coakley, 2021). However, such ideology seems to be imprecise in a world where sport leadership is unbalanced and contains a majority of men at the national and international levels. Overall, liberal feminism, although it has increased sport participation opportunities for females, is problematic, given that it reinforces or naturalizes gender differences (Messner and Musto, 2014).

Researchers have examined gender differences in leadership style and evaluations of male and female leaders. Early research investigating style differences between women and men compared either interpersonal-oriented and task-oriented behaviours or democratic and autocratic behaviours. Eagly and Johnson (1990) revealed in a meta-analysis that women were found to lead in a less interpersonally oriented and more task-oriented way than their male counterparts in organizational contexts. These differences were found only when the behaviour of men and women is regulated by experimental tasks and social settings. The only strong evidence Eagly and Johnson found on gender differences in leadership styles was the tendency for men to adopt a more autocratic or directive style and for women to adopt a more democratic or participative style. Similarly, Echiejile (1995) divided gender-specific leadership styles into masculine leadership that included instrumental traits, agentic qualities, and a more autocratic and task-oriented set of leadership behaviours; and feminine leadership that included expressive traits, communal qualities, and a more interpersonally oriented and participative set of leadership behaviours.

GENDER STEREOTYPES AND LEADERSHIP STYLES

Stereotypes refer to sets of beliefs about characteristics of all individuals in a group. A gender stereotype is a set of beliefs about what it means to be female or male. Gender stereotypes can be analysed with regards to four separate components that people use to differentiate male and female – traits, behaviours, physical characteristics, and occupations. These components are interrelated (Deaux and Lewis, 1984); for, it was claimed, simply knowing that an individual is male implies that person will have some traits (e.g. rational, aggressive, competitive, and powerful) and certain physical characteristics (e.g. increased muscle mass, sexual characteristics, body hair, and deep voice). However, such components might not apply in sport because males and females, although they are different in terms of physical characteristics, e.g. muscle development, can participate in the same sports, such as body building, football, rugby, athletics, boxing, wrestling, and body lifting.

After traits theories and behavioural approaches, the leadership theory and practice was tended towards subordinates' participation and empowerment. The leadership styles preferred and recommended by leading scholars in the field are transformational, charismatic, and visionary behaviours (Bass, 1990; Bass and Riggio, 2005; Bryman, 1992; House and Shamir, 1993). Transformational leadership behaviours have been depicted as a 'feminine' leadership style (Bass et al, 1996; Carless, 1998; Helgesen, 1990; Yammarino et al, 1997). However, a large-scale meta-analysis of the literature was conducted by Eagly et al (1992) to evaluate both male and female leaders who were equated on all leadership behaviours and characteristics. The results revealed that women were devalued compared with men when they led in a 'masculine' way (e.g. using autocratic or directive styles), when they occupied a typically 'masculine' leadership role (e.g. men's gymnastics coaches or managers), and when the evaluators were men. This gives a sense that female leaders experience more effectiveness advantages in 'feminine' leader roles than 'masculine' leader roles.

It may be stated that empirical research supports small differences in both leadership styles and behaviours when female leaders lead in masculine leader roles regardless of being effective or not. Therefore, fully understanding gender stereotypes and differences needs consideration of the contexts in which women work.

WOMEN'S EFFECTIVENESS IN SPORT LEADERSHIP

Leadership effectiveness is perceived as an evaluation process. Women's effectiveness can be evaluated either generally by asking "How effective is the women leader?" or specifically by asking "How well does a woman leader do in a specific role and show specific behaviours and capabilities?". The results of women-in-leadership research in sport settings have addressed these questions and demonstrated that women are perceived significantly less favourably as sport directors because this position is commonly stereotyped as masculine, despite having qualifications similar to those of male candidates; and women are rated slightly less likely to be hired for the position of sport directors (Burton et al, 2009; Burton et al, 2011; Hovden, 2010). Māori women, in New Zealand, face marginalization as women and as ethnic minorities; however, they have been able to leverage performance as one mechanism to obtain leadership roles in sport (Palmer and Masters, 2010). This implies that women need to be evaluated for leadership effectiveness through performance, particularly those who are distinguished through the salience of noticeable characteristics (e.g. physical characteristics).

Viewed broadly, in the literature on women's leadership when comparing the effectiveness of male and female leaders, women are perceived as equally effective leaders, but gender differences arise where women and men are more effective in leadership roles that are seen as congruent with their gender (Eagly et al, 1995). Moreover, women are likely to be perceived as less effective than men particularly when they supervise a higher proportion of male subordinates. In addition, understanding women's effectiveness in leadership is highly affected by context, because women are less effective in military positions than men, but more effective in education, government, and social services. This may not be the case all over the world, given the differences in the institutional systems. In other words, what makes women more effective in particular sectors in one country might be less effective in the same sectors in other countries (Chhokar et al, 2007; House et al, 2004).

Overall, empirical research in all disciplines, including sport leadership, support less difference in leadership effectiveness and styles between women and men, regardless of the sector type. Rich data is available on how women exceed men in the use of contingent reward behaviour and transformational leadership behaviours which are associated with contemporary notions of effective leaders (Northouse, 2021). There is, though, no agreement in the sport leadership literature on whether there is a large gap between women and men in terms of effectiveness, particularly if they are treated equally across all situations and environments.

FACTORS INFLUENCING DIVERSITY

To increase job satisfaction, organizational commitment, and performance, non-profit, for-profit, and state sport organizations have to encourage and take advantage of the potentials of diversity in sport settings. But sport leaders often face a range of challenges at individual, job, and organizational levels that impede diversity in all its forms. Removing obstacles to diversity in sport settings requires, in the first place, the desire for change, particularly in thought; and second a transformation in the organizational culture from exclusionary to inclusionary culture that contributes positively to achieve the sport organization's objectives effectively. This section addresses the four major obstacles that influence diversity in sport settings: prejudice, fundamentalism and ethnocentrism, the glass ceiling, and work environment. The focus of this chapter is on female–male gendered leadership; however, people with other characteristics experience similar obstacles, if in different ways, around the world – race, ethnicity, sexual orientation, non-binary sex or gender, physical attractiveness, social status, economic status, physical or mental health.

PREJUDICE

This is the most prevalent factor influencing diversity in sport organizations. Although most people may be aware of acts of prejudice, this does not necessarily mean they fully understand it. In the most general sense, prejudice refers to a negative, or even pathological, act or belief towards another person or group based on actual or supposed out-group qualities seen as or expected to be different from the in-group. Prejudices – i.e. pre-judgements – tend to be made before actual contact and may come with a continuing unwillingness to reconsider whether the reasons or evidence for the prior judgement hold up. This descriptive approach does not explain why anyone has a prejudice.

Stereotypes and prejudice often lead to discrimination in leadership (Aicher and Sagas, 2009; Burton et al, 2011; Burton and Welty Peachey, 2014; Honeybourne et al, 2000). For instance, men who believe women should not take leadership positions in sport organizations (a prejudice) may harass women who are involved in sports (an act). Often, minority groups within a community are labelled as having certain characteristics or even traits, and this may lead them to being involved in certain sports and away from others. In other words, women may find themselves steered into certain sport leadership positions and far away from others due to other's beliefs about real or supposed traits or characteristics.

In recent years in the UK, highly visible discussions have opened up in public with the public about how prejudices keep women often on the edge of sports: for example, wives and girlfriends who wash team gear but don't play or perhaps even spectate; grid girls, the podium, and champagne (e.g. in Formula 1 Racing), or participation and perhaps funding in junior levels and exclusions from adult or higher competition levels.

FUNDAMENTALISMS AND ETHNOCENTRISM

Although the terms 'fundamentalism' and 'ethnocentrism' have different definitions, they have commonalities, and both affect diversity in sport organizations. The terms are unevenly used and this is widely affected by institutional systems, laws, morality, values, individual knowledge, and personal culture. Fundamentalism can be described as:

> a tendency, a habit of mind, found within religious communities and paradigmatically embodied in certain representative individuals and movements. It manifests itself as a strategy or set of strategies, by which beleaguered believers attempt to preserve their distinctive identity as a people or group.
>
> (Marty and Appleby, 1992: 34)

Jarvie (2013) states that fundamentalism may be viewed in the West as problematic; it is no more so than other forceful ideologies of the 21st century, such as global and domestic free markets extending as widely and as rapidly as possible. Fundamentalism does not imply that ideologies need to be significantly different in their disagreements; many fundamentalist positions are set against others within a belief system. It only takes one difference held between groups of adherents to become a schism.

There are increasing calls for a return to nationalism in many countries, in part related – but certainly not exclusively – to changes in Western societies caused by immigration and terrorism, both of which are contested terms when applied to real situations. Women born in Western countries within religious minorities are likely to find themselves at career risk and under pressure in sport leadership because of this tendency. Ethnocentrism is increasingly evident between people due to nationalisms; i.e. the belief that one's own background and culture are naturally superior to other backgrounds and cultures. The in-group focus, which can also be seen as a positively group-self reinforcing prejudice, develops into a more structured set of fundamentals setting the in-group apart from others. Women leaders in sport organizations that lack ethnic diversity may also find themselves surrounded by a homogeneous culture inside the organization. Removing both fundamentalism and ethnocentrism and replacing them with openness and belief that all groups, cultures, sub-cultures, and belief systems are valued (without implying some kind of universalist approval), may have positive implications for the performance of women leaders and the productivity of their sport organizations.

THE GLASS CEILING, GLASS WALL, AND GLASS CLIFF

The phrase 'the glass ceiling' was coined in a 1978 speech by Marilyn Loden (1946–2022, writer, management consultant, diversity advocate) to talk about obstacles high-achieving women experience in their careers; and a widely cited article in the *Wall Street Journal* by reporters Carol Hymowitz and Timothy D. Schellhardt (1986) is often credited with popularizing the phrase. In the USA, at least, the glass ceiling has been extended to racial or ethnic differences. Morrison and Von Glinow (1990: 200) defined the glass ceiling as describing "a barrier so subtle that it is transparent, yet so strong that it prevents women and minorities from moving up in the management hierarchy". Evidence of the glass ceiling is seen in sport despite the increasing number of women entering operational and middle management in the sport industry (Cunningham, 2003; Smucker et al, 2003; Whiteside and Hardin, 2012).

Second, a concept related to the glass ceiling is what some call the 'glass wall phenomenon', which is an invisible or hidden barrier influencing women's career development in leadership positions in the sport organization. Research has suggested that the glass wall relates to the concept of occupational segregation and refers to lateral barriers that prevent employees from seeking the kinds of jobs that lead to promotions (Browne and Giampetro-Meyer, 2003). For example, a woman seeks to obtain a top-level leadership position in football but she is placed in a human resources position, perceived as 'a feminine role'. Decision-makers may withhold job and career-development opportunities from women.

Third, there is the concept of the 'glass cliff phenomenon'. The glass cliff refers to situations in which women are promoted to leadership positions in unusual situations such as crises, increasing the risk of their failure. Women then become subjected to accountability due to their failure, and are pushed rather than fall off glass cliff (Galloway, 2012; Ryan et al, 2007; Ryan and Haslam, 2007). A woman who has been said to fail then becomes a stereotype for most or all women in the future. For example, a club board dismisses the team manager (male) and then promotes a woman to 'give a woman a chance'. When the dismissal occurs at a critical time in league matches, it is possible that no one will succeed at short notice; but a man might be commiserated with a 'difficult time' and the woman undermined with 'well, that's what you get for promoting a woman'. The prejudicial aspects are, at least, twofold: a tokenistic offer to a woman with an expectation of failure, and a confirmation bias that any woman would fail based on one example.

WORK ENVIRONMENT

The work environment for women in sport leadership positions is more reject-ing, frustrating, cold, with a stressful nature, and unfriendly working environ-ment than it is for men. Offensive language, jokes, gestures, comments, religious harassment, sexual harassment, or potential sexual harassment, often make the work environment uncertain, unpleasant, and sometimes hostile (LaVoi and Dutove, 2012; Miller, 1997; Miller and Schoepfer, 2017). Women leaders in sport organizations can find themselves excluded from internal and external social activities such as meetings, due to multiple forms of harassment that cause feel-ings of anxiety and depression, and often lead to feelings of disappointment and frustration and to self-helping behaviours such as continued efforts to look for another job.

SPORTSWOMEN IN CONTEXT

Context influences what leaders want to, can and must do. At all levels, context shapes the process and form of leadership. The term 'context' can be defined from different perspectives. Cappelli and Sherer (1991) describe context as the surroundings associated with phenomena that help illuminate such phenom-ena. The authors' work shows internal environment as providing context for individual members, and the external environment as providing context for organizations. Johns (2006) argues that context refers to situational opportuni-ties and constraints that affect the occurrence. Klenke (1996: 18) states that "the context of leadership may be private or public, a small or large organisation, an affluent or poor community, or a developed or underdeveloped nation, each with its own distinguishing contextual features". Overall, sport contexts have three major levels which can influence the form and application of leadership. These levels are:

1. The sport rules and laws (e.g. national and international sport organiza-tions, leagues, and championships).
2. The immediate social network (e.g. direct and indirect communication in a federation, association, governing body, union among/between leaders, managers, board members, coaches, and athletes).
3. The culture and institutionalism (e.g. across cultures, national culture and organizational culture, training and development, funding, employment, and membership).

Understanding women's leadership from this perspective enlarges the picture of women's authority in different contexts. Women in three different contexts are discussed here: coaching, management, and leadership.

COACHING

It is not uncommon to see women as coaches in different sports at the national and international levels. Many female coaches leave a positive footprint in sport world such as, but not limited to, Hope Powell, Maureen 'Mo' Marley, Shelley Kerr, though the number of women coaches is not large. However, this success does not take place without challenges and obstacles that should be highlighted when considering women as coaches. Nicole LaVoi in her book *Women in Sports Coaching* raised several issues affecting women in sport coaching such as, lesbian coaches, women coaches of colour, women coaching men (LaVoi, 2016). Lesbian coaches often avoid being open to their sexual orientation fearing how it would impact their career, where few situations demonstrated that lesbian coaches are likely to be fired due to being open about their lesbian identity (Kamphoff and Gill, 2013; Zimmerman, 2013).

In addition, the 'lesbian issue' can be differently perceived over the world. For example, tolerance may be adopted, as a means to ensure not losing those coaches in open and tolerant cultures. Unlike in tolerant cultures, women coaches working abroad must be very careful about displaying their sexual orientation, given its sensitivity in religious countries, because lesbian coaches may not only be fired, but they may also be prosecuted and jailed (or worse). Others argue that the threat of being called a lesbian affects all women. Such environments are likely to have negative effects on individual and collaborative productivity – and lives, given that lesbian coaches, and even lesbian athletes, make efforts and waste time to find ways to hide their sexuality (e.g. Kamphoff, 2010).

An issue to highlight arises for woman coaches of colour. Discrimination occurs when individuals such as club owners, general managers, or board members of sport governing bodies, favour a certain group of women coaches and ignore others due to colour. This may have negative effects for sports in general and athletes and team members in particular. Deploying colour as an obstacle towards women coaches may be practised by those who are in top management, and this often transfers to players. This may be evident through poor relationships between the woman coach and team members. Several players might refuse to apply the coach's plan or tactics to ensure their coach takes greater responsibility for and chance of failure. Or, the team may lose its balance due to some players refusing to play with others from the same ethnic group as the coach.

Also, women coaching men is another issue that must be considered in the coaching world. Unfortunately, the number of women coaching men is still rare, although many coaching positions for women's teams are held by men (Fields, 2008). Kanter (1977) notes that segregation is likely to be seen due to the marginalization of women into less desirable sport leadership. Although increased globalization has changed the face of sport organizations in the 21st century, it is notable that no women coach men in professional team sports (i.e. football, rugby, basketball, hockey, cricket). This marginalization is likely to keep women in less powerful sports. Kamphoff and Gill (2013) argue that a decorated background is an essential need for women intending to coach men in elite sports;

that is, women coaches must have a strong record as elite athletes at Olympic and professional levels or as extremely successful coaches. That implies that a prestigious reputation is the major factor that may influence, or 'permit', women to coach men.

MANAGEMENT

As noted, sexual orientation, ethnic challenges, and marginalization can be seen as key obstacles resulting in the low number of women in sport managerial positions, particularly at middle management level. However, the low number of women at middle management level in sport organizations in the non-profit, for-profit, and state sectors, may differ across cultures, given the differences in the cultural-institutional system of countries (e.g. Megheirkouni, 2014). The low number of women at middle management level in certain major sports can also be caused by lack of participants in these sports. In other words, when women support certain sports and ignore others, this would affect any future opportunity for their career development to managerial or leadership positions in the ignored sports. In addition, though masculinities seem to be essential to middle management roles in sport sectors, being seen as a part of the strong personality of sport managers in the workplace, women who show masculinities are mainly excluded from middle management roles, given that they are seen to be 'bitchy' (specifically, see Shaw and Hoeber, 2003).

LEADERSHIP

There are several major sports in the UK where women are still treated as second-class citizens or almost not recognized, such as boxing. Great effort over the last decade to fill this gap through designing women leadership development programmes has hoped to help women in certain leadership positions improve their leadership skills (Megheirkouni and Roomi, 2017). Still, despite the importance and value of such initiatives, women do not seem to have achieved as much as hoped. Watt (2003) states that women have not been fully represented in the sport as participants, coaches, or leaders. Even in sports such as gymnastics, in which around 80 per cent of the participants are female, the top leadership positions are often held by men. Gendered leadership expectations and stereotypes often favour men. Explicit masculinities are common in the discussions on middle management positions in sport organizations. Specifically, the use of terms such as businessman, chairman, president, often gives an impression that individuals holding the top management positions in sport organizations would necessarily be men (Shaw and Hoeber, 2003).

Overall, it can be stated that the role of women in sport, as in so many other fields, has been complex and uncertain. Although there has been a marked increase in the number of women participating in sport over the last three decades, the value of women's role in middle and top management or as coaches has not obviously increased in the UK, despite support and learning and development initiatives.

EVALUATION OF WOMEN LEADERSHIP

The first criticism concerns the lack of essential complementary research agendas in the global sphere. Specifically, research investigating gender in sport leadership has been conducted in Western contexts, but there is little research elsewhere (Megheirkouni, 2014). As seen above, the debates on the obstacles facing female leaders in sport organizations mostly stem from cultural factors in society. However, such obstacles may not be seen in other societies. Therefore, research findings on gender in sport leadership cannot be generalized to all sport settings across cultures. Consequently, further research on gender in sport leadership from a cross-cultural perspective is needed. Another criticism is that research on gender in sport leadership should be understood and investigated in terms of diversity, given the similarities and differences between issues surrounding women in leadership and issues surrounding minorities. Sport leadership researchers should investigate the impact of the many diversity types noted at the top of this chapter, as well as the interactive impacts between these types, known as intersectionality. A final criticism is related to decreasing the gender gap in sport leadership positions. Northouse (2021) believes that decreasing the leadership gap in the workplace needs a concurrent focus on closing the gender gap at home.

The effects of gender in sport leadership have important implications for a comprehensive understanding of leadership and should be taken into consideration. First, research on gender in sport leadership is productive in shedding light upon the gaps between women and men, including those obstacles that are difficult to see. This may encourage more researchers to explore these invisible obstacles. Second, this is an opportunity to activate leadership development programmes that target women in different leadership positions in sport organizations, to dispel concerns about the ineffectiveness of women in sport leadership roles. Third, understanding the many factors influencing diversity in sport leadership can help researchers to identify the major requirements that help resist inequality between men and women in sport leadership across all organizational levels: operational, middle, and top. Fourth, debates and research on gender in sport leadership affect effective leadership or successful leadership styles, whether gender-specific or general. Importantly, contemporary literature on leadership proves that gender is an essential part of contemporary debates on effective leadership styles in sport settings, even as they have changed over time from the traditional, autocratic management (supposedly 'masculine' styles) to democratic and transformational leadership (supposedly 'feminine' styles). This increases the need to investigate, explore, and develop issues of female leadership that are essential for understanding effective leadership styles in sport settings.

SUMMARY

The increased importance of gender equality, diversity, inclusivity, and representation in leadership roles and debate has driven a growing interest in women and leadership research in all fields, including sport. However, women's roles in sport leadership positions is still perceived as underrepresented. This chapter has addressed gender differences and gender stereotypes in leadership styles and women's effectiveness in sport leadership. This chapter has discussed four major obstacles influencing diversity in sport settings: prejudice; fundamentalism and ethnocentrism; the glass ceiling, glass wall, and glass cliff; and work environment. This chapter has addressed how women experience three contexts: coaching, management, and leadership – and how that experience is often negative.

GENERAL QUESTIONS

1. In what ways do you think that male and female leaders lead differently or similarly?
2. Where do you think female leaders are best able to work? Why?
3. List five reasons for underrepresentation of women in sport leadership
4. Would you prefer to have a male or female leader for your sport organization?
5. Should international sport organizations appoint females in leadership positions from countries that do not support equal rights between men and women? Why?
6. List three sports you think women are best able to lead in?
7. List three sports you think women are not best able to lead in?
8. Are the factors influencing diversity in sport organizations fixed or variable? Why?

OPEN DISCUSSION QUESTIONS

1. List three characteristics of gender stereotypes in sport leadership in your favoured sport.
2. List three gender differences in sport leadership from your experience.
3. Discuss with colleagues whether or not you agree on gender stereotypes or gender differences in sport leadership? Why?
4. Discuss with colleagues the factors that would show that a woman leader was in a hostile work environment.
5. What is the leading factor influencing diversity in your sport organization? To what extent is this affected by countries' characteristics?
6. Do you think organizational culture can lead to a hostile work environment in sport settings? Why?

Case Study 12.1: Women in Sport Leadership

Tracey Crouch, CBE, was Parliamentary under Secretary of State for Sport, Tourism and Heritage in the UK, 2015–2018. She has been Conservative MP for Chatham and Aylesford since 2010. Crouch is, in 2024, only the third woman to become sport minister. Crouch is a strong supporter of women's sport and women in sport. She is a qualified FA coach and an ex-footballer herself, and managed a girl's team in Kent. Crouch's leadership in sport has been evident through her strategy to support sport organization in the UK. She said, "It is vital that our domestic sport bodies and organisations uphold the very highest standards of governance and lead the world in this area".

Questions

1. What factors brought Tracey Crouch into advanced leadership roles?
2. What factors do you think have contributed to her effectiveness?
3. What could sport organizations' policies do to achieve gender equality across all organizational levels, particularly chief executive roles?
4. To what extent do you believe that there may be any relationships between political affiliation and opportunities that women might benefit from to reach top sport leadership positions?

Source: The quotation and more information on other roles are available in Butler, N. (2016). 'Gender Diversity Criteria Included in New UK Sport Governance Code'. www.insidethegames.biz. [online]. 31 October 2016. Available at: https://www.insidethegames.biz/articles/1043214/gender-diversity-criteria-included-in-new-uk-sport-governance-code.

SELF-ASSESSMENT 12.1: WOMEN AND LEADERSHIP

Read the following five statements carefully. Choose False or True for each.

1. Prejudice refers to negative behaviour directed to a certain group, such as gender, race, ethnicity, or any other definable characteristic.
2. Ethnocentrism refers to a tendency found within religious communities. It manifests itself as a strategy by which beleaguered believers attempt to preserve their distinctive identity as a people or group.
3. The glass cliff refers to invisible or hidden barriers found in organizational structures influencing women's career development in leadership positions in sport organizations.
4. Fundamentalism refers to the belief that one's own background and sub-culture are naturally superior to others' backgrounds and sub-cultures.
5. The glass ceiling refers to situations in which women are often promoted to leadership positions in unusual situations, such as crises that increase a risk of their failure.

SELF-ASSESSMENT 12.2: WHO IS YOUR PREFERRED LEADER?

For each of the following seven statements, assign the number 1 (for men) or 2 (for women) that represents your view. We note that structured like this, the self-assessment is binary. This is not a test of whether you personally have particular attitudes or have a particular or even defined view of gender identities. And you can use the questions afterwards to directly address any issues that come up for you.

Total the numbers for all statements. Place the total on the scale below the statements.

The questions following the scale are the important part of this; please do this part before looking ahead.

1. She/He is better able to lead in crises.
2. He/She is better able to provide me with the work experience that I need.
3. She/He is better able to make important decisions under unusual circumstances.
4. He/She listens carefully to my needs.
5. She/He is open to me when I bring up ideas that slow down the work.
6. He/She has high moral standards.
7. She/He has the emotional capacity to comfort us when we work through intense issues.

Male   7   8   9   10   11   12   13   14   **Female**

What issues does this self-assessment raise for you? For example:

a. Did you read any of this part before you finished rating the statements? If you did, the last question (z) is for you.
b. How do you react to the position of your total? If so, do you have any observations – for yourself, at least – about the position?
c. What aspects of your experience may have formed part of your current 'ratings'?
d. Does changing the order of 'she' and 'he' make any statements read differently for you?
e. How did you feel about the question itself?
f. If you found the question problematic, how might you rework it?
z. For those who answered yes to question (a): Why did you look ahead? What effect may looking ahead have on how you answered?

Suggested Reading

Burton, L.J. (2015). Underrepresentation of Women in Sport Leadership: A Review of Research. *Sport Management Review*, 18(2), 155–165. https://doi.org/10.1016/j.smr.2014.02.004.

Elling, A., Hovden, J. and Knoppers, A. (Eds.). (2018). *Gender Diversity in European Sport Governance*. London: Routledge. https://doi.org/10.4324/9781315115061.

Klenke, K. (2017). *Women and Leadership: A Contextual Perspective*. (2nd ed.). Leeds: Emerald. https://doi.org/10.1108/9781787430631.

Lough, N. and Geurin, A.N. (2019). *Routledge Handbook of the Business of Women's Sport*. London: Routledge.

Megheirkouni, M., Thirlwall, A. and Mejheirkouni, A. (2020). Entrepreneurial Leadership in Middle East Sport Businesses: The Impact of Gender Differences in Cultural Values. *Gender in Management: An International Journal*, 35(2), 167–188. https://doi.org/10.1108/GM-01-2019-0006.

O'Connor, K. (2010). *Gender and Women's Leadership: A Reference Handbook.* (Vol. 1). London: Sage. https://doi.org/10.4135/9781412979344.

Rhode, D.L. (2017). *Women and Leadership.* Oxford: Oxford University Press.

Staurowsky, E.J. (Ed.). (2016). *Women and Sport: Continuing a Journey of Liberation and Celebration.* London: Human Kinetics.

Sykes, H. (2016). *The Sexual and Gender Politics of Sport Mega-Events: Roving Colonialism.* London: Routledge.

References

Aicher, T. and Sagas, M. (2009). An Examination of Homologous Reproduction and the Effects of Sexism. *Journal for the Study of Sports and Athletes in Education,* 3(3), 375–386. https://doi.org/10.1179/ssa.2009.3.3.375.

Bass, B.M. (1990). From Transactional to Transformational Leadership: Learning to Share the Vision. *Organizational Dynamics,* 18(3), 19–31. https://doi.org/10.1016/0090-2616(90)90061-S.

Bass, B.M., Avolio, B.J. and Atwater, L. (1996). The Transformational and Transactional Leadership of Men and Women. *Applied Psychology,* 45(1), 5–34. https://doi.org/10.1111/j.1464-0597.1996.tb00847.x.

Bass, B.M. and Riggio, R.E. (2005). *Transformational Leadership.* (2nd ed.). New York: Psychology Press. https://doi.org/10.4324/9781410617095.

Browne, M.N. and Giampetro-Meyer, A. (2003). Many Paths to Justice: The Glass Ceiling, the Looking Glass, and Strategies for Getting to the Other Side. *Hofstra Labor and Employment Law Journal,* 21(1), 61–106. Available at: https://law.hofstra.edu/pdf/labor_vol21no1_giampetro.pdf.

Bryman, A. (1992). *Charisma and Leadership in Organizations.* London: Sage.

Burton, L.J., Barr, C.A., Fink, J.S. and Bruening, J.E. (2009). "Think Athletic Director, Think Masculine?": Examination of the Gender Typing of Managerial Subroles within Athletic Administration Positions. *Sex Roles,* 61(5–6), 416–426. https://doi.org/10.1007/s11199-009-9632-6.

Burton, L.J., Grappendorf, H. and Henderson, A. (2011). Perceptions of Gender in Athletic Administration: Utilizing Role Congruity to Examine (Potential) Prejudice against Women. *Journal of Sport Management,* 25(1), 36–45. https://doi.org/10.1123/jsm.25.1.36.

Burton, L. and Welty Peachey, J. (2014). Ethical Leadership in Intercollegiate Sport: Challenges, Opportunities, Future Directions. *Journal of Intercollegiate Sport,* 7(1), 1–10. https://doi.org/10.1123/jis.2014-0100.

Cappelli, P. and Sherer, P.D. (1991). The Missing Role of Context in OB: The Need for a Meso-Level Approach. *Research in Organizational Behavior,* 13(1), 55–110.

Carless, S.A. (1998). Gender Differences in Transformational Leadership: An Examination of Superior, Leader, and Subordinate Perspectives. *Sex Roles,* 39(11–12), 887–902. https://doi.org/10.1023/A:1018880706172.

Chhokar, J.S., Brodbeck, F.C. and House, R.J. (Eds.). (2007). *Culture and Leadership across the World: The GLOBE Book of In-Depth Studies of 25 Societies.* London: Routledge. https://doi.org/10.4324/9780203936665.

Coakley, J. (2021). *Sports in Society: Issues and Controversies.* (13th ed.). New York: McGraw-Hill.

Cunningham, G.B. (2003). Already Aware of the Glass Ceiling: Race-Related Effects of Perceived Opportunity on the Career Choices of College Athletes. *Journal of African American Studies,* 7(1), 57–71. https://doi.org/10.1007/s12111-003-1003-8.

Deaux, K. and Lewis, L.L. (1984). Structure of Gender Stereotypes: Interrelationships among Components and Gender Label. *Journal of Personality and Social Psychology,* 46(5), 991–1004. https://doi.org/10.1037/0022-3514.46.5.991.

Eagly, A.H. and Johnson, B.T. (1990). Gender and Leadership Style: A Meta-Analysis. *Psychological Bulletin,* 108(2), 233–256. https://doi.org/10.1037/0033-2909.108.2.233.

Eagly, A.H., Karau, S.J. and Makhijani, M.G. (1995). Gender and the Effectiveness of Leaders: A Meta-Analysis. *Psychological Bulletin,* 117(1), 125–145. https://doi.org/10.1037/0033-2909.117.1.125.

Eagly, A.H., Makhijani, M.G. and Klonsky, B.G. (1992). Gender and the Evaluation of Leaders: A Meta-Analysis: Correction to Eagly et al. *Psychological Bulletin,* 112(3), 557–564. https://doi.org/10.1037/h0090375.

Echiejile, I. (1995). We Need Good Managers, Not Gender Stereotypes. *People Management,* 1(24), 19.

Fields, S.K. (2008). Title IX and African American Female Athletes. In: Lomax, M.E. (Ed.). *Sports and the Racial Divide: African American and Latino Experience in an Era of Change.* Jackson: University. Press of Mississippi. (126–145). JSTOR: https://www.jstor.org/stable/j.ctt2tvcq4.

Galloway, B.J. (2012). The Glass Ceiling: Examining the Advancement of Women in the Domain of Athletic Administration. *McNair Scholars Research Journal,* 5(1), 6–24. https://commons.emich.edu/mcnair/vol5/iss1/6.

Helgesen, S. (1990). *The Female Advantage: Women's Ways of Leadership.* New York: Doubleday.

Honeybourne, J., Hill, M. and Moors, H. (2000). *Advanced Physical Education and Sport for A-Level.* (2nd ed.). Cheltenham: Nelson Thornes.

House, R.J., Hanges, P.J., Javidan, M., Dorfman, P.W. and Gupta, V. (Eds.). (2004). *Culture, Leadership, and Organizations: The GLOBE Study of 62 Societies.* London: Sage.

House, R.J. and Shamir, B. (1993). Toward the Integration of Transformational, Charismatic, and Visionary Theories. In: Chemers, M.M. and Ayman, R. (Eds.). *Leadership Theory and Research: Perspectives and Directions.* San Diego, CA: Academic Press. (81–108).

Hovden, J. (2010). Female Top Leaders – Prisoners of Gender? The Gendering of Leadership Discourses in Norwegian Sports Organizations. *International Journal of Sport Policy and Politics,* 2(2), 189–203. https://doi.org/10.1080/19406940.2010.488065.

Hymowitz, C. and Schellhardt, T.D. (1986, March 24). The Glass Ceiling: Why Women Can't Seem to Break the Invisible Barrier That Blocks Them from the Top Jobs. *The Wall Street Journal,* D1, D4–D5.

Jarvie, G. (2013). *Sport, Culture and Society: An Introduction.* (2nd ed.). London: Routledge.

Johns, G. (2006). The Essential Impact of Context on Organizational Behavior. *Academy of Management Review,* 31(2), 386–408. https://doi.org/10.5465/amr.2006.20208687.

Kamphoff, C.S. (2010). Bargaining with Patriarchy: Former Female Coaches Experiences and Their Decision to Leave Collegiate Coaching. *Research Quarterly for Exercise and Sport,* 81(3), 367–379. https://doi.org/10.1080/02701367.2010.10599684.

Kamphoff, C.S. and Gill. D.L. (2013). Discrimination in the Coaching Profession. In: Potrac, P., Gilbert, W. and Denison, J. (Eds.). *Routledge Handbook of Sports Coaching*. New York: Routledge. (52–66). https://doi.org/10.4324/9780203132623.

Kanter, R.M. (1977). *Men and Women of the Corporation*. New York: Basic Books.

Klenke, K. (1996). *Women and Leadership: A Contextual Perspective*. New York: Springer.

Klenke, K. (2004). *Women and Leadership: A Contextual Perspective*. (2nd ed.). New York: Springer.

Klenke, K. (2011). *Women in Leadership: Contextual Dynamics and Boundaries*. Bingley, UK: Emerald.

LaVoi, N.M. (Ed.). (2016). *Women in Sports Coaching*. London: Routledge. https://doi.org/10.4324/9781315734651.

LaVoi, N.M. and Dutove, J.K. (2012). Barriers and Supports for Female Coaches: An Ecological Model. *Sports Coaching Review*, 1(1), 17–37. https://doi.org/10.1080/21640629.2012.695891.

Marty, M.E. and Appleby, R.S. (1992). *The Glory and the Power: The Fundamentalist Challenge to the Modern World*. Boston, MA: Beacon Press.

Megheirkouni, M. (2014). Women-Only Leadership Positions in the Middle East: Exploring Cultural Attitudes towards Syrian Women for Sport Career Development. *Advancing Women in Leadership*, 34(1), 64–78. https://doi.org/10.21423/awlj-v34.a320.

Megheirkouni, M. and Roomi, M. (2017). Women's Leadership Development Programmes in a Sports Setting: Factors Influencing the Transformational Learning Experience of Female Managers. *European Journal of Training and Development*, 41(5), 467–484. https://doi.org/10.1108/EJTD-12-2016-0085.

Messner, M.A. and Musto, M. (2014). For the Sociology of Sport: Where Are the Kids? *Sociology of Sport Journal*, 31(1), 102–122. https://doi.org/10.1123/ssj.2013-0111.

Miller, J.J. and Schoepfer, K.L. (2017). *Legal Aspects of Sports*. (2nd ed.). Burlington, MA: Jones and Bartlett Learning.

Miller, L.K. (1997). *Sport Business Management*. Burlington, MA: Jones and Bartlett Learning.

Morrison, A.M. and Von Glinow, M.A. (1990). Women and Minorities in Management. *American Psychologist*, 45(2), 200–208. https://doi.org/10.1037/0003-066X.45.2.200.

Northouse, P.G. (2021). *Leadership Theory and Practice*. (8th ed.) London: Sage.

Palmer, F.R. and Masters, T.M. (2010). Māori Feminism and Sport Leadership: Exploring Māori Women's Experiences. *Sport Management Review*, 13(4), 331–344. https://doi.org/10.1016/j.smr.2010.06.001.

Ryan, M.K. and Haslam, S.A. (2007). The Glass Cliff: Exploring the Dynamics Surrounding the Appointment of Women to Precarious Leadership Positions. *Academy of Management Review*, 32(2), 549–572. https://doi.org/10.5465/amr.2007.24351856.

Ryan, M.K., Höpfl, H., Haslam, S.A. and Postmes, T. (2007). Reactions to the Glass Cliff: Gender Differences in the Explanations for the Precariousness of Women's Leadership Positions. *Journal of Organizational Change Management*, 20(2), 182–197. https://doi.org/10.1108/09534810710724748.

Shaw, S. and Hoeber, L. (2003). 'A Strong Man Is Direct and a Direct Woman Is a Bitch': Gendered Discourses and Their Influence on Employment Roles in Sport Organizations. *Journal of Sport Management*, 17(4), 347–375. https://doi.org/10.1123/jsm.17.4.347.

Smucker, M.K., Whisenant, W.A. and Pedersen, P.M. (2003). An Investigation of Job Satisfaction and Female Sports Journalists. *Sex Roles*, 49(7–8), 401–407. https://doi.org/10.1023/A:1025120406343.

Watt, D.C. (2003). *Sports Management and Administration*. (2nd ed.). London: Psychology Press.

Whiteside, E. and Hardin, M. (2012). On Being a 'Good Sport' in the Workplace: Women, the Glass Ceiling, and Negotiated Resignation in Sports Information. *International Journal of Sport Communication*, 5(1), 51–68. https://doi.org/10.1123/ijsc.5.1.51.

Yammarino, F.J., Dubinsky, A.J., Comer, L.B. and Jolson, M.A. (1997). Women and Transformational and Contingent Reward Leadership: A Multiple-Levels-of-Analysis Perspective. *Academy of Management Journal*, 40(1), 205–222. JSTOR: https://www.jstor.org/stable/257027.

Zimmerman, B. (Ed.). (2013). *Encyclopedia of Lesbian Histories and Cultures*. New York: Routledge. https://doi.org/10.4324/9780203825532.

CULTURE **AND** LEADERSHIP

INTRODUCTION

The topic of culture is a multifaceted one – that focuses on relevant ideas, insights, and approaches rather than one single, unified theory. Of all the new and pressing challenges that leaders handle daily in sport organizations at national and international levels, one specific challenge stands out: the challenge of leaders to confront diversity issues across a broader stage than ever. An increasingly significant source of diversity in the sport industry is globalization, which requires leaders to be more aware of the socio-cultural environment and develop wider cultural knowledge. This chapter focuses on research that addresses the concept of culture, cultural dimensions, and the major effects of culture on leadership.

WHAT IS CULTURE?

The concept of 'culture' can be defined and understood in many different ways from different perspectives. Herskovits (1955: 305) defined culture as "the human made part of the environment". Hofstede (1980: 25) defined culture as "the collective programming of the mind that distinguishes the members of one group or category of people from another". Northouse (2018: 384) was more specific in defining culture, as he defined it as "the learned beliefs, values, rules, norms, symbols, and traditions that are common to a group of people. It is these shared qualities of a group that make them unique". For the purpose of this book, culture is defined as the shared beliefs, values, rules, norms, habits, and traditions among people due to their direct and indirect connections. These shared components may last for a short or long time and can have direct/indirect and positive/negative impacts.

 DOI: 10.4324/9780429290442-16

There are additional, relevant concepts related to culture to those discussed in Chapter 12. These concepts impact how leaders influence subordinates in sport organizations, and they include: prejudice, fundamentalism, ethnocentrism, multiculturalism, and diversity. It's important to note that these are not truly independent of each other, rather they attempt to pick out different aspects of cultural attitudes and differences and similarities. Unfortunately and circularly, the terms themselves may lead to arguments about what values are 'better'.

- *Fundamentalism* and *Ethnocentrism* refer to the belief that one's own group or sub-culture – this can include gender, race, ethnicity, sexual orientation, religion, or other belief system – is' naturally' superior to other groups and cultures inside and outside sport organizations, having in this view the shared feature that the in-group features are held as distinguishing fundamentals. (See Chapter 12 for a fuller description.)
- *Prejudice* refers to a negative, or even pathological, act or belief towards another person or group based on actual or supposed out-group qualities seen as or expected to be different from the in-group. (Also, see Chapter 12.)
- *Multiculturalism* refers to a general rejection of a cultural assimilation norm, the promotion of equality for racial and ethnic groups, respect for, tolerance of, and celebration of cultural diversity, the facilitation of cultural difference, and an assertion of rights and protections for particular racial and ethnic groups (Bass, 2008). Multiculturalism could refer to supposedly regional cultures, such as African, American, Asian, European, or Middle Eastern, although as labels these are so generic as to render them superficial in contextual practice. In such practice, 'culture' has to be read with care to include many features, such as religion, language, family structure, and awareness of issues relating to, for example, gender and sexual orientation.
- *Diversity* refers to the existence of different cultures, genders, colours, religions, ethnicities, or any other definable characteristics within a group or an organization.

THE LEVELS OF CULTURE

Culture can be analysed at several different levels. The term 'level' refers to the manner in which cultural aspects are visible to the observer. An understanding of these levels can provide the observer with a precise picture of culture through a different lens. Cultural levels often range from very tangible overt manifestations that people can see or feel to more implicit or subtle manifestations. Amongst these layers lie the various beliefs, values, norms, and rules of behaviour that sport leaders and subordinates use as a means of depicting a culture to themselves and others. Schein and Schein (2016) suggest three levels of culture: artefacts, espoused beliefs and values, and basic underlying assumptions.

ARTEFACTS – SEE

This level refers to what an observer would see, hear, and feel when they encounter a new group with an unfamiliar culture. Artefacts in sport environments include the architecture of stadium and arenas, Olympic Villages; the language of athletes, team coaches and managers, and board members; the use of technology to light the Olympic flame, analyse sport performance, officiate, measure time, design sport equipment, and offer spectator viewing; and each country having its official team colours in international sport championships. Observed behaviour in sport organizations (e.g. clubs, associations, unions, federations, sporting goods companies) is an artefact, given that such behaviour made in the organizational processes is a routine. In addition, structural issues in a sport organization (e.g. formal rules, descriptions of how the organization works, an organizational chart) regardless of the sector, are each perceived as an artefact.

Overall, the essence of this level of culture is easy to observe and yet may be very difficult to decipher. For example, when you watch a boring football match in the UEFA Champions League, you may interpret that as relating vaguely to poor teams; but if you have a sport background, you may come to the view that a boring football match means that teams do not have fit stars or lack plans, tactics, or effective implementation. Equally, if you see a very strong football match, you may interpret that to be a sign of some individuals' lack of skills; but your own experience may lead you to the view that such a match means that collective tactics are dominant in the match rather than individual actions. Or, it is evident that one team adopts offensive tactics, while the other uses tactics focusing on defending and then counterattacking. For Schein and Schein (2016), if you want to understand the match quickly, you must ask people who are insiders (people specializing in football, e.g. players, coaches, team managers, sport academics, and even fans) "why do they what they do?" You will then discover artefacts.

ESPOUSED BELIEFS AND VALUES – SAY

This level refers to a set of beliefs and values which form the basis for choosing between alternative sources of action. Group learning may reflect the beliefs and values of those who have influenced that group. Individuals who can influence a group to adopt certain behaviours may later be identified as founders or leaders. For instance, if a football club went bankrupt due to excess transactions in previous seasons, the club president may suggest, "We must increase emotive charity advertising" because of their belief that emotive advertising always increases donations. Other stakeholders in that club, never having experienced this situation, will hear that assertion as a statement of the president's beliefs and values: "They believe that when a club is in trouble, it is important to increase emotive advertising for donations". According to Schein and Schein (2016), what the club president initially proposes, does not have any status other than a value to be debated, challenged, and tested. If the president convinces the club stakeholders to act according to their belief and the solution works, the value of 'emotive advertising for donation' becomes transformed into a shared belief and value, then into a shared assumption. As a result, club stakeholders will ignore everything that happened earlier, when they were not sure about this belief, but still perceive it as a proposal to be debated.

However, beliefs and values that provide meaning to the stakeholders of a sport organization may not be congruent with the beliefs and values related to certain organizational aspects, such as effectiveness or performance. In this case, the espoused values of a sport organization that reflect the desired behaviour, may not be reflected in observed behaviour. This can be evident when the annual report of a sport organization emphasizes and promotes equality and diversity in employment, but its record contradicts what it says. Overall, not all beliefs and values undergo such transformation. Schein and Schein (2016: 19) suggest three situations in which beliefs and values undergo transformation:

1. Beliefs and values that can be empirically tested, where solutions based on these beliefs and values work reliably, will be transformed into assumptions.
2. Certain value domains may not be testable; particularly those which deal with the less controllable elements of the environments or with moral matters. In this regard, consensus through social validation, which means that certain beliefs and values are confirmed only by the shared social experience of a group, is still possible. But it is not automatic.
3. The strategy and goals of the organization are likely to be tested through consensus because the relationship between strategy and performance may be hard to prove.

BASIC UNDERLYING ASSUMPTIONS – BELIEVE

The level that comes closest to characterizing a culture is called basic underlying assumptions, which include predictions about how the sport industry operates as well as cross-situational rules in sport organizations. The main idea of basic underlying assumptions, which are invisible, is that when a solution to a particular problem works frequently, it is often adopted. This means that what was earlier perceived as an assumption, supported only by a value, gradually comes to be treated as a reality. Certain underlying assumptions are perceived as helpful, for instance: "If elite athletes keep training hard for Olympic Games, they might ultimately make tangible progress". However, other underlying assumptions are perceived as unhelpful, for instance:

> If a football team loses three players to red cards and needs to score three goals to achieve a draw in the last two minutes, and the team manager decides to switch from attacking to defending in those minutes, this procedure has no value at all.

There are particular attributes that contribute to a culture's strengths. According to Sathe (1985), the attributes which make cultures stronger are:

- **Thickness**: 'Thick' cultures have a higher number of shared values, beliefs, and ways of working in use by members than 'thin'.
- **Extent of sharing**: The degree to which values, beliefs, and ways of working are widely shared throughout the sport organization.
- **Clarity of ordering**: The degree to which values, beliefs, and ways of working are order in a way which organizational members can understand as reasonable.

Sport organizations with a strong culture, regardless of their sector type, can create a setting in which stakeholders are committed to one another and share an overriding sense of mission. Deal and Kennedy (1982) identify five components of a strong culture and argue that organizational success can be enhanced through the development of a strong culture. These components are:

1. The *orientation of an organization* within the surrounding environment, given its instrumental orientation in shaping the cultures of organizations with survival potential.
2. *Values* which are the essence of organizational culture are the beliefs that members hold for an organization.
3. *Heroes* are personifications of the organization's values who make success attainable and human.
4. *Rites* and *rituals* are ceremonies through which an organization reinforces its values.
5. The *cultural network* is the communication system inside and outside the organization through which cultural values are reinforced.

DIMENSIONS OF CULTURE

Unsurprisingly, identifying and classifying of cultures is the first step towards understanding the relationships and differences between them. A wide number of studies have focused on ways to identify, classify, and analyse culture across a variety of disciplines in the last four decades (Northouse, 2018). Of all these studies, the research of Hofstede (1980, 2001) is perceived as the benchmark for much of the research on cultures and is the most referenced in different disciplines. Five major dimensions of culture were identified by Hofstede: power distance, uncertainty avoidance, individualism–collectivism, masculinity–femininity, and long-term–short-term orientation.

In addition, research on culture and leadership has increased our understanding of the interactions across clusters of cultures and the impact of culture on the kind of leadership (e.g. the required styles, behaviours, and capabilities) and leadership effectiveness. *Culture, Leadership, and Organisations: The GLOBE Study of 62 Societies* by House et al (2004) in this regard provides the strongest findings on culture and leadership. Global research on culture and leadership, initiated by Robert House in the 1990s, is still an active programme. Nine dimensions of culture have been developed by GLOBE researchers based on the work of others (e.g. Hall, 1976; Hofstede, 1980, 2001; Kluckhohn and Strodtbeck, 1961; McClelland, 1961; Triandis, 1982, 1995; Trompenaars and Hampden-Turner, 2020). These cultural dimensions are: power distance, uncertainty avoidance, institutional collectivism, in-group collectivism, gender egalitarianism, assertiveness, future orientation, performance orientation, and humane orientation.

POWER DISTANCE

Power distance helps understand the extent to which societies encourage the idea that power should be unequally distributed. The dimension of power distance refers to the degree to which sport organizations accept social stratification between employees and with managers. In high power distance, interactions and communication between individuals of high and low power tend to be restricted; whereby societies and sport organizations characterized by high levels of power distance are often autocratic, with power and resources held only by particular high-status leaders. In low power distance, individuals expect equality in power; whereby societies and sport organizations characterized by low levels of power distance are often democratic, with power and resources spread out among various individuals or groups.

UNCERTAINTY AVOIDANCE

This is the extent to which members of a society or sport organization rely on established social norms, rituals, and bureaucratic practices to decrease the probability of unpredictable future events that can affect its operation. The dimension of uncertainty avoidance helps understand how societies and sport organizations deal with orderliness, structure, and rules to reduce unpredictability and uncertainty. In high uncertainty avoidance, members feel uncomfortable in ambiguous situations and tend to exhibit a related set of traits and practices. For example, those members have a strong tendency towards formalizing their interactions with others. They formalize policies and procedures, have higher levels of anxiety and energy, are often older sport leaders, and wait before leaving responsibility in the hands of younger managers or leaders. In low uncertainty avoidance, members of a sport organization or society have a higher level of tolerance for uncertainty and ambiguity, and tend to exhibit a different set of traits and practices. They show lower levels of anxiety and energy, are less formal, less concerned with orderliness, and rely on the ideas of others whom they trust rather than contractual arrangements.

INSTITUTIONAL COLLECTIVISM

This is the extent to which organizational and societal institutional practices can support and reward collective distribution of resources and collective action. Institutional collectivism helps understand whether societies or sport organizations are integrated into broader entities. A good example is that we can see most local councils, national governing bodies, associations, unions, ministries, and others involved in hosting an Olympic Games. Therefore, a society or sport organization can be described as institutionally collectivist when institutional practices support collective action and collective distribution of resources.

IN-GROUP COLLECTIVISM

In comparison, this is the extent to which individuals demonstrate pride, loyalty, and cohesiveness in their sport organization, team, circle of close friends, or other such small groups. In-group collectivism reflects the strength of ties, prescribed roles, and respect for authorities within such small groups.

GENDER EGALITARIANISM

This is the extent to which a group, a society or sport organization can reduce the gap between men and women by promoting the equity and equality of genders in all aspects of work or life. Gender egalitarianism is concerned with the level of stereotyping held by a society or sport organization that favours one gender over the other.

ASSERTIVENESS

Assertiveness is the extent to which members in a society or sport organization are allowed to be dominant, confrontational, and aggressive in social relationships. The dimension of assertiveness helps understand how a society or sport organization encourages individuals (e.g. sport managers, leaders, coaches, athletes, and volunteers) to be dominant and tough, as opposed to being soft and tender. For example, when a manager works with subordinates on developing a plan for increasing productivity in their sporting goods company, a manager may show aggressive behaviours such as saying, "what a stupid idea", or a coach may use a harsh tone of voice with team players.

FUTURE ORIENTATION

This is the extent to which members in society or sport organization engage towards future activities. This dimension is often applied to those in top management, given that their positions require working on creating vision, setting future strategies, establishing future agendas and rules, setting timetables, and allocating resources. A good example is the bidding process of hosting sport mega events such as Olympic Games, which normally starts several years beforehand. Future orientation means that the more a society or sport organization engages individuals for those behaviours, the more it can be said to have a future orientation.

PERFORMANCE ORIENTATION

This is the extent to which a society or sport organization supports and rewards individuals to enhance their performance and productivity. Performance orientation means that the more a sport organization rewards individuals for performance improvement, the more a sport organization has performance orientation. For example, some national governing bodies reward their athletes after winning a medal, while other such bodies that reward their athletes regularly whether they win medals or not.

HUMAN ORIENTATION

Finally, this means that a society or sport organization supports and rewards individuals as a result of their sense of responsibility, being fair, honest, friendly, generous, impartial, stable, reliable, firm, caring for satisfaction, and caring about ethics. Human orientation means that the more a society or sport organization encourages and rewards individuals for those traits, the more it can be stated to have human orientation. For example, there are many stories about national and international ethical athletes who have left an imprint on the sport world. Therefore, many businesspeople, media, governments, and national and international sport organizations honour athletes, such as fair-play heroes, because of their ethical behaviours.

EVALUATION OF CULTURE AND LEADERSHIP

Research on culture and leadership theories has various weaknesses to consider. One criticism is that although there are many GLOBE studies, resulting in many findings on the concept of leadership across cultures, there is no single theory on how culture is related to leadership. Additionally, although cultural researchers provide definitions and descriptions of cultural dimensions and leadership, the meanings of certain cultural dimensions, such as power distance, are still somehow vague and difficult to understand.

Another criticism concerns the way in which leadership was conceptualized in the GLOBE studies. There is more focus on what people perceive to be leadership, ignoring a large body of research that focuses on what leaders do. Therefore, there is a need for further research on how leadership functions in different cultures, because this raises the need for developing particular leadership behaviours and capabilities that help the way leaders function (Megheirkouni, 2017). It is worth noting that GLOBE research provides a provocative list of universally desirable leadership attributes. However, it is not easy to identify a universal attribute in isolation from the context in which sport leaders/manager operate (the situational factors influencing leaders). Specifically, the GLOBE studies ignored the attributes that determine effective leaders.

Research on culture and leadership has also several strengths. The present chapter does not present a single, unified theory of leadership, but it presents the major strengths of several studies on culture and leadership. The GLOBE studies discussed here present data collected from up to 62 countries around the world; the study has, however, continued to expand. The results of this project provide a unique opportunity to understand how cultures around the world perceive the notion of leadership. Additionally, the findings from the GLOBE studies are valuable because they were designed based on a well-developed quantitative approach. Although there are many qualitative studies that explore in-depth how people around the world perceive leadership, these studies are limited in scope and generalizability within and across cultures.

Another strength to consider is that Project GLOBE, which provided a broader and more elaborate way of describing dimensions of culture, expanded the five dimensions identified by Hofstede (i.e. power distance, uncertainty avoidance, individualism–collectivism, masculinity–femininity, and long-term–short-term orientation) to include nine dimensions (i.e. uncertainty avoidance, power distance, institutional collectivism, in-group collectivism, gender egalitarianism, assertiveness, future orientation, performance orientation, and human orientation).

Finally, the GLOBE studies are valuable because they provide information about what good or bad leadership styles are. People around the world perceive good or effective leaders differently. For example, in some cultures, transactional leadership is viewed as a good style, while in others transformational leadership may be viewed as better. Similarly, some competencies are viewed as essential needs for effective leadership, such as interpersonal skills, teamwork, communication, but these competencies may not have such importance in other cultures.

SUMMARY

It is obvious that globalization is a common feature of all sport sectors, and no national sport organization can afford to ignore international sport policies, rules, laws, international training activities, or global leadership competencies. This has raised the need for flexible leaders with an awareness and a full understanding of the notion of globalization as well as differences and similarities across cultures, if leaders seek to lead effective and successful change in their sport organizations. The concept of culture can be defined in different ways and understood from different perspectives. Culture has been defined as the shared beliefs, values, rules, norms, habits, and traditions among people due to their direct and indirect connections. These shared components may last for a short or long time and can have direct/indirect and positive/negative impacts.

This chapter has defined concepts relevant to culture. These concepts are: fundamentalism and ethnocentrism, prejudice, multiculturalism, and diversity. This chapter discussed three levels of culture: artefacts, espoused beliefs and values, and basic underlying assumptions and highlighted three particular attributes that contribute to a culture's strength: thickness, extent of sharing, and clarity of ordering, alongside the five components of a strong culture suggested by Deal and Kennedy (1982). Based on several benchmark studies (e.g. Hall, 1976; Hofstede, 1980, 2001; House et al, 2004; Kluckhohn and Strodtbeck, 1961; McClelland, 1961; Triandis, 1982, 1995; Trompenaars and Hampden-Turner, 2020), this chapter discussed the major dimensions of culture: power distance, uncertainty avoidance, institutional collectivism, in-group collectivism, gender egalitarianism, assertiveness, future orientation, performance orientation, and human orientation. This chapter also addressed an evaluation of culture and leadership research.

GENERAL QUESTIONS

1. What is culture?
2. To what extent do national cultures determine the culture of sport organizations?
3. Explain the following terms in your own words: artefacts, espoused beliefs and values, and basic underlying assumptions.
4. How does the notion of diversity vary in sport organizations around the world?
5. Explain the difference between multiculturalism and diversity.
6. Explain the difference between ethnocentrism and prejudice.
7. What insights have Deal and Kennedy provided to widen our understanding of culture in sport organizations?
8. What are the main benefits of understanding culture in sport leadership?
9. Do you agree that we can employ the same organizational culture throughout national sport organizations or across international sport organizations? Why?

OPEN DISCUSSION QUESTIONS

1. Identify the major concepts you think have impacts on how leaders influence subordinates in sport organizations. Why have you selected these ones?
2. Discuss with colleagues the cultural levels and identify three examples from your sport that best represent these levels.
3. What are the attributes that contributes to a culture's strength in your sport organization? Why?
4. Explain the following terms in your own words: power distance, uncertainty avoidance, institutional collectivism, in-group collectivism, gender egalitarianism, assertiveness, future orientation, performance orientation, and human orientation.
5. From your experience, what cultural dimension do you think might not exist in your sport organization? Why?
6. Discuss with your colleagues why it is important for sport managers or leaders to develop their cultural awareness in sport organizations? And, do you think sport managers or leaders who have no experience with staff, members, athletes/players, volunteers, and others different from them are able to adapt to cultural differences in their way of thinking and behaving?

Case Study 13.1: Challenges Facing Sport Business Graduates in Global Jobs

David and Melissa graduated from the sport business course in 2017 and decided to apply for global sport vacancies to enhance their international experience. After they submitted their applications to many organizations in Europe, America, Asia, and the Middle East, their applications were shortlisted for interviews in the same company specialized in managing and organizing sport events in the Middle East based in Dubai. Although there were many experienced candidates who were invited to interviews from the region, David and Melissa fortunately got the jobs. They started their new jobs just one month after the interview outcomes. David and Melissa were appointed in the ceremonies committee, given that they had volunteering experience in the London Olympic Games and the Glasgow Commonwealth Games, where in both time management was important. Although Dubai is a multinational city, David and Melissa began suffering from the differences in their new life, including differences in the way of thinking, habits, culture, and religion, not only inside their work, but also outside it. These differences forced David and Melissa to rethink their work and try to figure out how to overcome the surrounding challenges so as to adapt to cultural barriers, although they have not faced problems affecting their work yet. A few months later, they are appointed to prepare an Arabic championship alongside Arab colleagues. Their concerns became real because the preparation for the Arab championship requires training national volunteers and school students for the opening and closing ceremonies.

One of the challenges facing Melissa is the Arabic language. Arabic is used to communicate between David and Melissa's colleagues, national volunteers, and school students. Two colleagues left their own tasks and stayed with David and Melissa as interpreters, leading to slowing down the preparation for the ceremony for at least four days. Furthermore, this way of communicating with colleagues became a problem, particularly when Melissa was telling male colleagues about some mistakes in their work. If a woman tells 'a man about his mistake' in Arabic culture, this is perceived as impolite behaviour: "It is different in my country", said Melissa.

A challenge that David faces is that all colleagues, volunteers, and some students leave work to pray, which requires the team to take another break after the lunch break, waiting for them to finish praying. The situation is made worse as that Ramadan time is in summer, when all colleagues, volunteers, and students need many breaks during the day; since, during Ramadan, they are fasting, which includes no liquids, and feel thirsty due to the high temperature. David feels depressed all the time because he thinks he will fail to complete the proposed work as scheduled. "I recognized late how Arabic culture and Islamic religion influence all aspects of life", said David.

Questions

1. What do you identify as the first mistake David and Melissa make before they begin their work?
2. How would you describe the challenges that David and Melissa face?
3. What is the cultural dimension that represents the challenge that Melissa faced?
4. What is the cultural dimension that represents the challenge that David faced?
5. How would you describe David's and Melissa's work experience after 12 months?
6. How, if at all, can we overcome cultural challenges facing individuals who are willing to work globally?
7. Are there any links between Melissa's and David's potential cultural misunderstandings and the sport business course they participated in?

Source: Based on anonymized, real-world experiences of various students.

SELF-ASSESSMENT 13.1: CULTURE AND LEADERSHIP

Match the nine following cultural dimensions to the nine statements.

(a) Power Distance; (b) Uncertainty Avoidance; (c) In-group Collectivism; (d) Institutional Collectivism; (e) Gender Egalitarianism; (f) Future Orientation; (g) Human Orientation; (h) Performance Orientation; (i) Assertiveness

1. The extent to which you rely on established social norms and bureaucratic practices to decrease the probability of unpredictable future events.

2. The extent to which sport organizations accept social stratification between employees and with managers.
3. The extent to which employees in a sport organization engage in future activities.
4. The extent to which the sport organization supports and rewards its people because of its sense of responsibility, being honest, fair, kind to others, and generous.
5. The extent to which the sport organization encourages its stakeholders to be dominant and aggressive in social relationships inside and outside the sport organization.
6. The extent to which the sport organization supports giving rewards to enhance its people's performance.
7. The extent to which a sport organization is affected in its operation by the level of stereotyping that favours one gender over the other.
8. The extent to which a board member demonstrates loyalty, commitment, support, and respect to their team members in the same sport organization.
9. The extent to which a sport organization can support collective distribution of resources and collective actions which reflect that it can be integrated into broader entities.

Suggested Reading

Chhokar, J.S., Brodbeck, F.C. and House, R.J. (Eds.). (2007). *Culture and Leadership across the World: The GLOBE Book of In-Depth Studies of 25 Societies.* (2nd ed.). London: Routledge. https://doi.org/10.4324/9780203936665.

Edelman, R. and Wilson, W. (Eds.). (2017). *The Oxford Handbook of Sports History.* Oxford: Oxford University Press. https://doi.org/10.1093/oxfordhb/9780199858910.001.0001.

Frontiera, J. (2010). Leadership and Organizational Culture Transformation in Professional Sport. *Journal of Leadership and Organizational Studies,* 17(1), 71–86. https://doi.org/10.1177/1548051809345253.

Graen, G.B. (2006). In the Eye of the Beholder: Cross-Cultural Lesson in Leadership from Project GLOBE: A Response Viewed from the Third Culture Bonding (TCB) Model of Cross-Cultural Leadership. *Academy of Management Perspectives,* 20(4), 95–101. https://doi.org/10.5465/AMP.2006.23270309.

Hassan, D. and Lusted, J. (Eds.). (2012). *Managing Sport: Social and Cultural Perspectives.* London: Routledge. https://doi.org/10.4324/9780203856574.

House, R.J., Dorfman, P.W., Javidan, M., Hanges, P.J. and de Luque, M.F.S. (2013). *Strategic Leadership across Cultures: The GLOBE Study of The CEO Leadership Behaviour and Effectiveness in 24 Countries.* London: Sage.

House, R.J., Hanges, P.J., Javidan, M., Dorfman, P.W. and Gupta, V. (Eds.). (2004). *Culture, Leadership, and Organizations: The GLOBE Study of 62 Societies.* London: Sage.

Megheirkouni, M. and Weir, D. (2019). Insights into Informal Practices of Sport Leadership in the Middle East: The Impact of Positive and Negative Wasta. *International Journal of Sport Policy and Politics,* 11(4), 639–656. https://doi.org/10.1080/19406940.2019.1634620.

Schein, E.H. and Schein, P.A. (2016). *Organizational Culture and Leadership*. (5th ed.). London: John Wiley and Sons.

References

Bass, S.B. (2008). Multiculturalism, American Style: The Politics of Multiculturalism in the United States. *International Journal of Diversity in Organisations, Communities, and Nations: Annual Review*, 7(6), 133–141.

Deal, T.E. and Kennedy, A.A. (1982). *Corporate Cultures: The Rites and Rituals of Corporate Life*. Boston, MA: Addison-Wesley.

Hall, E.T. (1976). *Beyond Culture*. New York: Doubleday.

Herskovits, M.J. (1955). *Cultural Anthropology*. New York: Knopf.

Hofstede, G. (1980). *Culture's Consequences: International Differences in Work Related Values*. Beverly Hills, CA: Sage.

Hofstede, G. (2001), *Culture's Consequences: Comparing Values, Behaviors, Institutions, and Organizations across Nations*. (2nd ed.). Thousand Oaks, CA: Sage.

House, R.J., Hanges, P.J., Javidan, M., Dorfman, P.W. and Gupta, V. (Eds.). (2004). *Culture, Leadership, and Organizations: The GLOBE Study of 62 Societies*. London: Sage.

Kluckhohn, F.R. and Strodtbeck, F.L. (1961). *Variations in Value Orientations*. Evanston, IL and Elmsford, NY: Row, Peterson.

McClelland, D.C. (1961). *The Achieving Society*. Princeton, NJ: Van Nostrand.

Megheirkouni, M. (2017). Leadership Competencies: Qualitative Insight into Non-Profit Sports Organisations. *International Journal of Public Leadership*, 13(3), 166–181. https://doi.org/10.1108/IJPL-11-2016-0047.

Northouse, P.G. (2018). *Leadership Theory and Practice*. (8th ed.). London: Sage.

Sathe, V. (1985). How to Decipher and Change Corporate Culture. In: Kilmann, R.H., Saxton, M.J. Serpa, R. and Associates (Eds.). *Gaining Control of the Corporate Culture*. San Francisco, CA: Jossey-Bass. (230–261).

Schein, E.H. and Schein, P.A. (2016). *Organizational Culture and Leadership*. (5th ed.). Hoboken, NJ: John Wiley and Sons.

Triandis, H.C. (1982). Dimensions of Cultural Variation as Parameters of Organizational Theories. *International Studies of Management and Organization*, 12(4), 139–169. https://doi.org/10.1080/00208825.1982.11656354.

Triandis, H.C. (1995). *Individualism and Collectivism*. Boulder, CO: Westview Press. [e-book, 2019]. https://doi.org/10.4324/9780429499845.

Trompenaars, F. and Hampden-Turner, C. (2020). *Riding the Waves of Culture: Understanding Diversity in Global Business*. (4th ed.). London: John Murray Press.

14 ETHICAL LEADERSHIP

Learning Outcomes

After reading this chapter, you will be able to:

- Define ethical leadership
- Distinguish between factors determining ethical behaviour
- Understand the nature of ethical value in sport organizations
- Understand the link between value and leader–follower relationships
- Measure ethical leadership
- Evaluate the strengths and weaknesses of ethical leadership

INTRODUCTION

Ethical leadership is an approach to contemporary leadership that runs fundamentally counter to unethical behaviours; and it has widely spread in the sport environment at national and international levels. An early interest people have when appointing someone to a sport leadership position is whether that leader will be ethical; by then, they hope to have established from work and other histories that the person has been ethical; and there will keen interest from beyond the appointing committee regarding how the new leader accomplishes the required roles and goals effectively without use of unethical and illegal actions. Although such up-front ethical leadership may challenge our traditional beliefs about political leadership, it is an approach that offers a unique perspective in the sport world. Many athletes, coaches, national and international governing board members, National Olympic Committees, and top executives have been embroiled in many scandals, involving hundreds of millions of dollars in bribes paid for votes or match-fixing, resulted in public outrage about activities and conduct in the sport world. Ethical behaviours of leaders concern not just isolated, individual matters, but also unwritten 'policies', informal communications, the financial status of clubs, and the environments in which people live: any of these can become embroiled in a sport organization's activities. Ethical practice distinguishes between leaders in sport organizations.

WHAT IS ETHICAL LEADERSHIP?

The term 'ethics' derives from the ancient Greek word 'ethos', meaning custom or character. *The Oxford English Dictionary* (2010) defines ethics as the "moral

DOI: 10.4324/9780429290442-17

principles that govern or influence a person's behaviour". Note that 'ethics' and 'morals' for individual principles are often used interchangeably; 'ethics' may be found used for an external code and morality for non-codified principles; 'ethic' is sometimes used; and then there are 'moral' and 'morality', too. This mixture of usage in both public and academic discussions and different forms of English is so varied that it can create much debate and little clarity, as you may find in the end-of-chapter materials. So, we use 'ethics' and 'ethical' throughout, where possible, though specifically retain 'moral philosophy' and 'moral development' as recognized terms. Ethics is a branch of moral philosophy concerned with principles of right and wrong conduct. Ethics is understood and defined by branches of ethics (Thiroux and Krasemann, 1980), traditionally associated with philosophy. The branches are: meta-ethics, normative ethics, descriptive ethics, and applied ethics; although in practice there are many more-focused branches. As you'll see here, ethical questions can become more difficult as more questions are asked.

- **Meta-ethics**: This explores the meanings of concepts, values, words, properties, and beliefs associated with one's ethics. Meta-ethics raises questions that focus on theoretical meaning and references of ethics propositions such as, what do we mean by bad and wrong or good and right? What is the source of ethics? And can we generalize ethical principles across cultures? An example of this branch of ethics is: sport doping is perceived as an unethical behaviour, and has been taken very seriously by the Court of Arbitration for Sport (CAS) and its Anti-Doping Division. The Olympic Movement governing body, during the Olympic Games, oversees all doping control and testing processes in compliance with the Code regulations. Anti-doping rule violations help shape our thinking in terms of 'right or wrong'. Anti-doping rule violations also increase the sense of responsibility to support National Olympic Committees to educate and encourage their national Olympic athletes to avoid this practice. Coaches and athletes feel comfortable when implementing anti-doping rules in all Olympic teams as the 'right thing to do'.
- **Normative ethics**: This explores how an individual should act ethically. Normative ethics helps determine the guidelines of one's behaviour based on ethical principles. For example, Sport England funds schemes that help grassroots clubs with different projects, covering the costs of delivering projects from training to marketing. It also provides grants from £300 to £10,000 for projects that increase participation and development opportunities. If this funding is spent on irrelevant purposes, such as personal purchases, the question arises: is this action ethical? If not, is the action wrong because it violates the funding policy? Is this action acceptable because the diverted funding did not affect the targeted projects? Would the action be acceptable if the sponsor that provided the funding forgives the use of funding for simple personal purchases?
- **Descriptive ethics**: This helps us understand our attitudes and those of others. It can reveal the values and beliefs that are utilized to determine what the right or good is in a specific situation. An example of this branch is the career path of elite coaches with experience in previous roles that gave them a good understanding of the beliefs and values influencing their

view of right and wrong attitudes in critical situations, leading to wrong and right decisions in final matches.

- **Applied ethics**: This deals with ethical questions that ask about the outcomes in specific, contested practices. An example is: the International Olympic Committee (IOC) launched the Olympic Refuge Foundation, which aims to support displaced young people through sport with their futures and displaced people and athletes gain access to sport (see https://olympics.com/en/olympic-refuge-foundation/). However, the foundation does not support athletes from countries suffering from poverty, economic collapse, corruption, or who flee to other regions in the same country. The question here is whether the foundation's aims are an exercise of ethical principles or a breach of the basic values of the IOC. This example represents the essence of applied ethics, given that it applies ethical theories to a practical problem.

For sport leadership, how leaders behave is one of the fundamental factors that contribute to determining the level of ethical behaviour in a sport organization (Pfleegor and Seifried, 2016). For a comparison of ethical and unethical behaviours, see Table 14.1. Ethical behaviour of leaders directly concerns what leaders do and how they do it. Thus, ethical behaviour affects leadership effectiveness (Veiga, 2004). Chief executives with their board members in a sport governing body make decisions on sometimes apparently simple, often complex, and usually sensitive issues about athletes and employees, on matters such as

Table 14.1 Comparing Ethical and Unethical Leader Behaviours

Ethical Leaders	Unethical Leaders
<ul><li>Are seen as consistently moral in both their personal and professional lives.</li><li>Have a reputation for being fair, principled, honest, and trustworthy.</li><li>Demonstrate a concern for other people' needs and are also seen as approachable.</li><li>Use the tools of the position of leadership to promote ethical conduct at work.</li><li>Set and communicate ethical standards and use rewards and punishments to ensure those standards are followed.</li></ul>	<ul><li>Encourage corruption.</li><li>Demonstrate oppressive, abusive, and manipulative behaviours.</li><li>Condone unethical acts among followers.</li><li>Ignore punishments for followers' transgressions and wrongdoing.</li><li>Promote like-minded individuals who heighten unethical behaviours.</li><li>Engage in unethical behaviour if followers are agreeable to this and/or high in authoritarianism*.</li></ul>

Note: Although current trends might suggest that this is a feature of one political 'wing', we believe history shows that authoritarianism can occur in any ideological position.
Source: Adapted from Brown, M.E. and Mitchell, M.S. (2010). Ethical and Unethical Leadership: Exploring New Avenues for Future Research. *Business Ethics Quarterly*, 20(4), 583–616.

performance, achievement, racism, and sexual harassment. The way in which chief executives and board members respond to the immediate issue and to the potential for similar problems is directed by their ethical development.

FACTORS DETERMINING ETHICAL BEHAVIOUR

Leaders may ignore, avoid, or disregard the connection between sport and values, not just profit, productivity, and performance. That is why it is important that ethical principles should be applied to everything as an umbrella that covers all sport activities in general and leaders in particular (Megheirkouni and Weir, 2019). When assessing the impact of ethical leadership behaviours in the sport world–as distinct from other aspects of leadership–personality traits, moral development, and quality work environment are interrelated and perceived as indicators of impact (Figure 14.1).

PERSONALITY TRAITS

Ethical principles can be thought of as falling within individual needs and personality traits (Litzky et al, 2006). A sport leader with certain personality traits can use power for unethical purposes, such as personal benefit. For example, to gain membership in a sport governing body, some people use their qualifications, experience, achievements, or national and international reputations to gain such membership; while others use their social characteristics, such as sociability, interpersonal skills, tact, and diplomacy; social background, such as educational level; personal characteristics, such as age and appearance; and intelligence and ability, such as fluency of speech, knowledge, intelligence, and judgement to exercise certain forms of pressure and influence, and thus gain other members' approval, votes, or resources. In addition, emotionally unstable sport leaders and those who refuse to take a personal responsibility for their performance or failure in the organization are more likely to adopt unethical behaviours to defend their attitudes or avoid accountability. However, though the characteristics of virtue, integrity, and authenticity are perceived as fundamental to

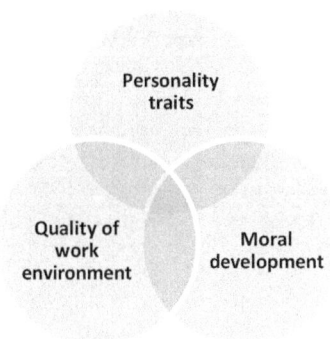

Figure 14.1 Factors influencing ethical behaviour.

ethical leadership (Lawton and Páez, 2015), personality traits are not all related to unethical behaviour of leaders (Walumbwa and Schaubroeck, 2009).

MORAL DEVELOPMENT

The second factor influencing ethical behaviour of sport leaders is moral development. This refers to leaders' choices of what they do in decision-making situations and how they react to these situations (DeSensi and Rosenberg, 2010; Sagas and Wigley, 2014; Sonenshein, 2007). Moral development of individuals in the sport world is widely affected by people (who they are), roles and positions (the nature of responsibilities entrusted to them), and the context in which they operate (Bredemeier and Shields, 1986; Roby, 2014). How people think about ethical issues goes through three levels of moral development as developed by Kohlberg (1984). They are: pre-conventional, conventional, and post-conventional.

a. **Pre-conventional**: Individuals' behaviours at this level are more likely to be motivated by moral principles for what they do and the consequences of their actions. Two different behaviours can be seen at this level. The first behaviour is that the morality of individuals is controlled by law and policy. A good example is: Olympic athletes know that although doping can enhance their performance, it is handled seriously by the Court of Arbitration for Sport and anti-doping rule violations will lead to negative consequences for their sport career. The second behaviour is that the morality of individuals is affected by self-interest. For example, a candidate for membership in a sport's international federation/national governing body might say (or imply), "I'll offer you £50.000, if you give me your vote".

b. **Conventional**: Individuals' behaviours at this level are based on the morality of their action that is likely to be defined by expectations of the surrounding environment. The morality of what individuals do is not subject to legal accountability. There are two different behaviours at this level. The first behaviour is that the moral choices of an individual's action are based on their fit with the expectations of others. For example, take a football coach working on a project funded by a local council to increase participation of young people in football in poor communities. They think twice before making a decision about using the funding for some personal purchases. They say: "I'm not going to spend any money on my personal purchases because that is not what an honest coach does". The second behaviour is that the morality of an individual's action is related to the benefit of the group, a sport team, sport organization, club, city, or country as a whole, which can be also called a 'sense of responsibilities toward our nation or a sense of patriotism'. A good example of this behaviour is when Nelson Mandela, a former president of South Africa, sent a letter in the 2006 bid book to support his country's application to host the 2010 FIFA World Cup. Despite his age, he also joined his country's bid delegation in Zurich to support hosting the finals.

c. **Post-conventional**: Post-conventional moralists develop their own personal moral principles that help guide their actions. But people react variously to this level of morality because they may become intolerant, or fanatical about their own personal moral principles, if they are forced to respect or commit to others' moral principles. Two different behaviours can be seen at this level. The first behaviour at this level is that individuals make moral decisions based on what they believe to be positive or good for the public interest. Moral decisions of different individuals may be contradictory: "your good for society is my bad" and vice versa. When government and local authority announce the success of the bid to host a sport mega event, this is often accompanied with contradictory responses from local people. For example, millions of Brazilians took to the streets in protests against hosting the 2014 FIFA World Cup because of economic conditions, while others demonstrated a supportive response to the successful bid to host the finals, as an opportunity to improve the economic and social aspects of the hosting cities and regions through the investments triggered by staging the event.

QUALITY WORK ENVIRONMENT

The third factor affecting ethical behaviour is the quality work environment. People consider the environment in which sport organizations operate as an important factor influencing how to make ethical or unethical decisions (Malloy and Zakus, 1995). Unethical behaviour occurs more often when there is no sense of ethical responsibility or accountability, no formal guide nor written rules of ethical principles in a sport organization that support people (such as fans, athletes, coaches, board members, chief executives), nor encouragement of a culture of self-assessment of their ethics at internal and external environmental levels. Particularly, when sport stakeholders come from a wide spectrum of society there may be friction over a given code of ethics.

- **External Work Environment**: This level refers to the degree to which political, economic, and social environmental factors can determine whether a person will use ethical or unethical behaviours. The relationship between external work environment and unethical behaviour is well-illustrated through the following three examples: (1) politicizing global sport events through sport boycotts is perceived as an unethical behaviour. When sport organizations in a country choose to boycott some sport events for political reasons, it may result in negative consequences for their athletes (Sarantakes, 2010). (2) It is known that hosting sport mega events often brings economic benefits through the investment in the hosting city or country. But the ways some countries use to win votes remain ethically unacceptable (e.g. Crowther, 2002). (3) The process of relocation or eviction of hundreds of businesses and residents due to preparation for the London 2012 Olympic Games was accompanied with resistance and resentments within the local community (Raco and Tunney, 2010), and this is not the only hosting city or country to do this.
- **Internal Work Environment**: This level refers to the extent to which internal organizational climate (such as racial inequality, gender pay gap,

experiential opportunities, and sexual harassment) can determine whether a person will use ethical or unethical behaviours, as illustrated in the following examples: (1) when the ethics policy and code are not well-defined or are ignored inside a sport organization it is likely to encourage internal stakeholders towards unethical actions. For example, more than 140 women and girls, under the guise of medical treatment, were sexually abused by a former USA women's gymnastics team doctor (Edelman and Pacella, 2019). (2) The continuing pay gap between male and female leaders holding equivalent roles is an unethical practice sport business. (3) Despite being ethically unacceptable, racial inequality remains culturally embedded in most national and international sport organizations, and it occurs, for example, between athletes, coaches, board members, executives, media, and the sport community (Cleland and Cashmore, 2014, 2016), and in any combination. Such unethical behaviour is complex and will take time and effort to address.

- **Exceptional Policy and Rules**: Despite the importance of the ethics policy and code of a sport organization, there are exceptions that forbid policymakers or executives in sport from stopping unethical behaviours in specific situations. Written rules of ethics sometimes cannot protect us from making unfortunate decisions, whether there is an unethical element or not, which cannot be corrected later, in specific situations. For example, FIFA's rules ensure that the referee is the only person who can make decisions within the match, and no one is allowed to influence the referee's decision-making. However, in the case of Diego Maradona's so-called 'hand of God' in the Argentina v England quarter final of the 1986 World Cup, Maradona scored with a handball; but neither the referee nor the linespersons had a view which enabled them to see it was not a legitimate goal. Despite one photographer's capture of the moment – and Maradona's much later admission – the result stood. England, on the other hand, benefitted from a different exception regarding the ball and a goal line, and won the final of the 1966 World Cup.

ETHICAL VALUE IN SPORT ORGANIZATIONS

Of the values that define an organization's culture and strategy at any level, ethical values are considered an essential element for organizational stakeholders, particularly after scandals invading the sport industry, in any sector. In light of contemporary scandals, it appears that a wide number of sport organizations have begun to emphasize the role of ethical principles in developing their culture, strategies, and policies, besides encouraging their stakeholders to think ethically and place ethical principles at the fore when taking actions. For example, the Australian Football League applied a range of strict penalties to the Essendon Football Club because of cheating in the league. The penalties included resigning its CEO, paying a US$2 million fine, removing the team from post-season play and future draft picks, and suspending its coach for a year (Pritchard and Burton, 2014).

Others sport organizations are still reforming their policy to include ethical values as a part of their informal culture, but with slow pace. As noted earlier, the problem of unethical actions is still embedded within a wider culture of abuse seen daily, including racial prejudice and hate-related abuse, which is taking time to address. For example, though sport policies in the UK have witnessed fundamental changes for women's representation in the sport industry, the role of female officials is still based on gender stereotypes (Forbes et al, 2015). And female referees are still significantly under-represented in men's football at the professional level.

To broaden our discussion of ethical values in sport organizations, and as has been noted, a significant difference exists between sport organizations that are setting up or developing a code of ethical conduct and those that continue to employ unethical practices. Specifically, many sport businesses today claim that they are values-based businesses. These claims are shown to be superficial when unethical practices become publicly visible. A good example is the sport gambling market. The 2009 European football betting scandal is perceived as one of the biggest match-fixing scandals to hit Europe. The investigations revealed that roughly 200 fixtures were involved, including national league games in several European countries, three qualifying matches in the UEFA Champions League, and 12 in the UEFA Europa League.

VALUE-BASED LEADER–FOLLOWER RELATIONSHIP

The salience of ethical values in organizations is enhanced through leaders' use of different mechanisms to transmit values. Leader–member relationships that are based on shared values more often shape the organizational climate (Grojean et al, 2004). Personal ethics of sport leaders play a pivotal role in enhancing ethical values in their organization, because a leader can give legitimacy to the followers' values, linking these values to the organizational objectives. Although this culture is rare in the non-profit sport sector, many cases have emerged to reflect the ethical responsibility of some chief executives during financial crises, when they commit to cut their own salaries to support their companies (Murray, 2010).

Perhaps not all people can be leaders; but without followers, there would be no leaders in any sport sector. When followers react positively and learn from the ethical values of their leaders, they will go further towards developing a value-based relationship (Dose, 1999). Although people bring a wide range values, personality traits, beliefs, and habits to sport organizations, these factors integrate with the ethical behaviour of the leader, which contribute to serve a general ethical purpose. A good example is when a national Olympic team represents its home country, with each athlete having their own values, personality traits, and beliefs. In fact, some athletes aim to grab the Olympic titles from other Olympic athletes, others intend to smash new Olympic records, while others promise family to do their best. Similarly, Olympic coaches also have their own values, personality traits, and beliefs. Indeed, the Olympic title represents the 'general ethical purpose' of both coaches and athletes; this is called 'utilitarianism'

(Morgan, 2017), reflecting the shared values, beliefs, and traits directed towards the greatest good for the greatest number.

MEASUREMENT OF ETHICAL LEADERSHIP

Though there are many perspectives and theoretical formulations on ethical leadership, development continues. Few valid questionnaires have been developed to measure ethical leadership. One of these questionnaires is the Perceived Leader Integrity Scale (PLIS) developed by Craig and Gustafson (1998). Thirty-one statements are used to evaluate ethical leadership by measuring the degree to which subordinates are committed to an organization's policy and rules to achieve the greatest good for the greatest number. Sample items are "my supervisor would treat me better if I belonged to a different ethnic group" and "my supervisor would limit my training opportunities to prevent me from advancing". The Ethical Leadership Questionnaire (ELQ) was developed by Yukl et al (2013). Fifteen statements are used to evaluate how ethical leadership is related to leader–member exchange and work performance. Sample items are "my boss is fair and objective when evaluating member performance and providing rewards" and "my boss shows a strong concern for ethical and moral values".

EVALUATION OF ETHICAL LEADERSHIP

Although ethical leadership research in sport is still in the early stages of theoretical development, it has proved its worth in light of the scandals plaguing the sport industry since the 1960s (Morgan, 2017). Ethical leadership research offers empirical evidence and explanations of ethical and unethical behaviours in the sport world, which help leaders correctly understand these practices and cope effectively with similar situations in the future. Second, ethics, as illustrated, is perceived as an indicator of influence which can be intertwined with a wide range of theories and approaches, including, but not limited to, trait approaches through integrity; leader–member exchange through mutual trust, obligation, respect, and loyalty; transformational leadership through creating meaning for followers; and servant leadership through putting followers first. As a result, we can conclude that ethical leadership is one of few approaches that has a life-long potential to develop and grow. Third, despite its importance, ethical leadership skills may not take individuals a long time to learn in a leadership development programme. The reason is likely to be linked to humans' instinctive ability to learn and distinguish between unethical and ethical conduct, even if such conduct may be culturally or personally developed. Our ability to make ethical or unethical actions is highly related to our own motivation rather than the level of our understanding of this conduct.

   This theory has weaknesses. First, although there are many empirical studies on ethics, these studies have not investigated all aspects of ethical leadership. Specific empirical studies are needed to explore and investigate ethical leadership in particular situations in the sport industry, to understand the nature of conflict between ethical leadership actions and exceptional policy and rules.

Second, although there is an increasing interest in ethical behaviour in sport organizations, it is still unknown what factors can affect a leader's actions to change their decisions from unethical to ethical behaviour, and vice versa. For example, when a referee makes unethical decisions, do they also make other such decisions in similar situations in the same match or in other matches.

Contemporary unethical practices in many national and international organizations and various countries have increased the demand for developing ethical policies by decision-makers in most of today's sport organizations. Indeed, ethical leadership was developed in response to citizens' and organizations' unethical practices continually affecting the reputation of many governments.

SUMMARY

This chapter has discussed the meaning of ethical leadership, highlighting and explaining four branches of ethics: meta-ethics, normative ethics, descriptive ethics, and applied ethics. This chapter addressed the factors determining ethical behaviours. The first factor is personality traits that help explain why a sport leader with certain personality traits can use power for unethical purposes, such as personal benefit. The second factor is moral development, which helps explain leaders' choices in decision-making situations, and how they react to these situations. The third factor is the quality work environment that helps understand how environments in which leaders or sport organizations operate, influence ethical or unethical decision-making. This chapter discussed ethical values in sport organizations, and value-based leader–follower relationships with specific examples. As ethical leadership is still under development, measuring it has been discussed, as has an evaluation of the strengths and weaknesses of ethical leadership.

GENERAL QUESTIONS

1. How do you describe ethical leadership?
2. How do you define meta-ethics, normative ethics, descriptive ethics, and applied ethics?
3. How does ethical leadership differ from other leadership theories/approaches?
4. List the factors demonstrating ethical behaviour discussed in the present chapter with examples. Can you suggest other factors? Do your suggested factors differ from the ones explained in the present chapter?
5. Describe the pre-conventional level of moral development and give examples from your favourite sport.
6. Describe the conventional level of moral development and give examples from your favourite sport.
7. Describe the post-conventional level of moral development and give examples from your favourite sport.
8. How do you describe ethical value in the club you support? Why?
9. What are the strengths and weaknesses of ethical leadership?

OPEN DISCUSSION QUESTIONS

The questions may themselves raise ethical issues. Be ethical in how you discuss other people anonymously. Whether you identify yourself is up to you; but if you are willing to name yourself, be aware that people may be able to identify other people you're talking about.

1. Identify three unethical leadership behaviours. Discuss the answer with colleagues in the group. Are there any similar answers?
2. Identify three ethical leadership behaviours. Discuss the answer with colleagues in the group. Are there any similar answers?
3. Discuss with colleagues the branches of ethics and identify three examples that best represent these branches from your sports.
4. Can you recall some decisions you or your leader have to make? Can you describe these decisions in terms of ethical or unethical behaviour? Discuss and compare your answers with your colleagues.
5. Define in your own words the branches of ethics presented in this chapter and give an example of each one from your experience.
6. Discuss factors determining ethical behaviour. Can you give examples of each one from your sport?
7. Can you suggest situations from your sport in which you noted unethical or ethical practices? Discuss your answer with colleagues.
8. Can you identify three ethical leadership behaviours and three unethical behaviours based on your experience?
9. How do you describe your behaviour in unethical sport environments? Why? Can unethical sport environments change your behaviour? Explain your answer.

Case Study 14.1: Salt Lake City 2002 Winter Olympic Games Bid

In 2002, there were serious allegations against the International Olympic Committee (IOC) that some of its members were embroiled in unethical behaviours, involving bribes in many forms to give Salt Lake City, Canada, the 2002 Winter Olympic Games. Two head organizers of Salt Lake City's bid were charged with paying bribes to win votes of some IOC delegates, and bribes were also given to a United States Olympic Committee official to assist in securing Salt Lake City's bid. The leadership of the IOC was under pressure to react decisively to this scandal: to show it was committed collective and proactive action for transparency, accountability, and reform, for this case and future cases. An independent ethics panel investigating Salt Lake City's bid indicated that bid organizers had lavished more than US$1 million in cash, jobs, medical treatment, shopping sprees, scholarships, excessive travel, and 'expensive baubles' to the IOC delegates and their families. The Salt Lake City scandal destabilized the IOC, given its leadership role on the international sport stage. The result of the internal investigation of the IOC recommended that all members involved in this scandal should resign.

Questions

1. How would you describe the behaviour of the two head organizers of Salt Lake City's bid? Explain your answer.
2. Do you think that the IOC was blamed for this scandal? Why?
3. What relationship is there between the Olympic candidature process and ethical principles?
4. Is there a clear ethical dimension to IOC delegates visiting the Candidate Cities? Discuss the answer with colleagues in the group.
5. At the end of the case, the result of the internal investigation of the IOC has recommended that all members who were involved in this scandal should resign. Was this decision enough to maintain the ethical leadership of the IOC?

Source: Adapted from Siddons, L. (1999). 'IOC expels six members in Salt Lake City scandal'. *The Guardian*. [online]. 17 March 1999, 11:00 GMT. Available at: https://www.theguardian.com/sport/1999/mar/17/ioc-expels-members-bribes-scandal; and BBC News. (1999). 'Olympics must ban "gift-giving"'. *bbc.co.uk*. [online]. 1 March 1999, 20:25 GMT. Available at: http://news.bbc.co.uk/1/hi/sport/288650.stm.

Case Study 14.2: Ethics and Morality in the Sport World

Use the following three statements to help you answer the questions.

1. Alexander Dale Oen, a Norwegian swimmer, was well-known in the swimming community as a breaststroke world champion. Alex's death caused by a heart attack left family and friends in a state of shock. Most swimmers expected that Alex would win the 200-metre Olympic breaststroke event if he were still alive. The swimming community paid tribute to Alex's family in different ways. At the London 2012 Olympic Games, the gold medal winner of the 200-metre Olympic breaststroke event, the Hungarian Dániel Gyurta, paid homage to Alex by having a copy made of his gold medal and sending it to Alex's family.
2. One of the most touching stories reflecting a person's moral commitment to their country in international championships and competitions is the story of Tanzanian John Stephen Akhwari at the Mexico 1968 Olympic Games. Despite his knee injury during the race, he ended the marathon race last, some 90 minutes after the penultimate runner. He could have left the race due to his injury, but his moral commitment towards completing the race for Tanzania motivated to finish, regardless of the result.
3. The expression 'one-club man' is often used when a player spends their entire career playing, coaching, and managing in one club. Santiago

Bernabéu played for Real Madrid from 1909 until retiring in 1927. He later worked with the club until 1935, as a director, an assistant manager, and a manager of the first team. He also served as the club's president between 1943 and 1978. During his presidency, he was credited with transforming Real Madrid into one of the world's top football clubs. Given that Bernabéu was one of the most important Spanish men to serve Real Madrid, their current stadium was named in his honour.

Questions

1. How would you describe Gyurta's level of morality of for having a copy made of his gold medal for Alex's family?
2. How would you describe Akhwari's level of morality for insisting on finishing the race despite his injury?
3. How would you describe Bernabéu's level of morality for spending his playing and managerial career at the same club?
4. What are the similarities and differences between Gyurta, Akhwari, and Bernabéu?
5. Can you give other examples of ethics and morality in your sports?

Source: Based on The Guardian (2012). 'Daniel Gyurta to have gold medal made to honour Alexander Dale Oen'. *The Guardian*. [online]. 6 August 2012, 11:06 BST. Available at: https://www.theguardian.com/sport/2012/aug/06/daniel-gyurta-alexander-dale-oen; IOC News. (2020). '"I never thought of stopping": marathon man Akhwari on his epic effort at the '68 Games'. International Olympic Committee. [online]. 20 October 2020. Available at: https://olympics.com/ioc/news/-i-never-thought-of-stopping-marathon-man-akhwari-on-his-epic-effort-at-the-68-games; and Real Madrid. (n.d.). 'Bernabéu: A goal scoring forward'. Real Madrid. [online]. Available at: https://www.realmadrid.com/en-US/the-club/history/football-legends/santiago-bernabeu-de-yeste.

SELF-ASSESSMENT 14.1: ETHICAL LEADERSHIP

How do you describe your ethical behaviour? In the current exercise, you will use a set of statements to describe your actions.

In practice, we recognize that this is not a result you might want to share with other people, regardless of its direction. However, self-knowledge is valuable, here. If you wish to change your ethical practice, you need to know where your practice gaps are, and find ways of asking for help – a development matter – to resist real-world practices you wish to avoid or even challenge.

You might do this exercise in different ways. For example, imagine yourself to be a person who is dedicated to a particular goal. And below we offer this exercise as a form of role play.

Rate how you think you would act for each of the following statements
No = 1 Yes =2

While you – imagining yourself as this person – are working with a local club on a project or a local council for managing local sport events, you are:

1. Falsifying records if it would help your work situation.
2. Withholding information or constructive feedback that affect colleagues' development.
3. Taking sick leave for days, when not sick, and getting paid for it.
4. Using the project or work's funding for personal purchases.
5. Using the work's tools or equipment for personal purposes.
6. Spending a long time on social media, using the work devises, such as computers for chatting.
7. Revealing personal information related to colleagues at work to untrustworthy people.
8. Manipulating reports or submitting false information on your work that does not reflect the actual status.
9. Manipulating personal data to make yourself look better than your colleagues.
10. Parking your car in bays reserved for disabled drivers and cheating the blue badge system.
11. Exaggerating colleagues' mistakes deliberately to make them look bad to the line manager.
12. Treating some of your colleagues better when they belong to your sex, religion, or/and ethnic group.
13. Showing lack of interest in tasks/objectives that don't bring personal recognition.
14. Supporting conflict between colleagues or with managers at work.
15. Putting responsibility on your team in case of failure.
16. Putting your personal interests ahead of the group.
17. Putting your colleagues in risk to protect yourself from accountability.
18. Asking colleagues to cover your absence from work.
19. Taking part in sabotage deliberately inside your organization.
20. Deliberately avoid implementing the work objectives to cause problems for other team members.

Total the results for the 20 statements. Place your rating on the scale:

Ethical 20 ... 25 ... 30 ... 35 ... 40 Unethical

The lower your score is, the more ethical is your behaviour. However, this exercise may not give a precise assessment of your ethical behaviours in real life.

Questions

1. What do you think may happen to you? (this person)
2. What activities might change your life–career path as this person?

Suggested Reading

Bowen, J., Katz, R.S., Mitchell, J.R., Polden, D.J. and Walden, R. (2017). *Sport, Ethics and Leadership*. London: Routledge. https://doi.org/10.4324/9781315184739.

Brown, M.E. and Treviño, L.K. (2006). Ethical Leadership: A Review and Future Directions. *The Leadership Quarterly*, 17(6), 595–616. https://doi.org/10.1016/j.leaqua.2006.10.004.

Burton, L. and Welty Peachey, J. (2014). Ethical Leadership in Intercollegiate Sport: Challenges, Opportunities, Future Directions. *Journal of Intercollegiate Sport*, 7(1), 1–10. https://doi.org/10.1123/jis.2014-0100.

Ciulla, J.B. (Ed.). (2014). *Ethics, the Heart of Leadership*. (3rd ed.). Oxford: ABC-CLIO.

Constandt, B., Parent, M.M. and Willem, A. (2020). Does It Really Matter? A Study on Soccer Fans' Perceptions of Ethical Leadership and Their Role as 'Stakeowners'. *Sport Management Review*, 23(3), 374–386. https://doi.org/10.1016/j.smr.2019.04.003.

Hardman, A.R. and Jones, C. (Eds.). (2010). *The Ethics of Sports Coaching*. London: Routledge.

Marques, J. (2017). *Ethical Leadership: Progress with a Moral Compass*. New York: Routledge. https://doi.org/10.4324/9781315205946.

Shapiro, J.P. and Stefkovich, J.A. (2021). *Ethical Leadership and Decision Making in Education: Applying Theoretical Perspectives to Complex Dilemmas*. (5th ed.). London: Routledge.

Thornton, P., Champion Jr, W.T. and Ruddell, L.S. (2011). *Sports Ethics for Sports Management Professionals*. London: Jones and Bartlett Learning. Available at: https://www.classprofessional.co.uk/public-health-health-sciences/health-fitness-sport/sport-management/sports-ethics-for-sports-management-professionals/.

Westerbeek, H. and Smith, A. (2005). *Business Leadership and the Lessons from Sport*. London: Palgrave Macmillan. https://doi.org/10.1057/9780230524415.

References

Bredemeier, J.B. and Shields, L.D. (1986). Moral Growth among Athletes and Non-Athletes: A Comparative Analysis. *Journal of Genetic Psychology*, 147(1), 7–18. https://doi.org/10.1080/00221325.1986.9914475.

Brown, M.E. and Mitchell, M.S. (2010). Ethical and Unethical Leadership: Exploring New Avenues for Future Research. *Business Ethics Quarterly*, 20(4), 583–616. https://doi.org/10.5840/beq201020439.

Cleland, J. and Cashmore, E. (2014). Fans, Racism and British Football in the Twenty-First Century: The Existence of a 'Colour-Blind' Ideology. *Journal of Ethnic and Migration Studies*, 40(4), 638–654. https://doi.org/10.1080/1369183X.2013.777524.

Cleland, J. and Cashmore, E. (2016). Football Fans' Views of Racism in British Football. *International Review for the Sociology of Sport*, 51(1), 27–43. https://doi.org/10.1177/1012690213506585.

Craig, S.B. and Gustafson, S.B. (1998). Perceived Leader Integrity Scale: An Instrument for Assessing Employee Perceptions of Leader Integrity. *The Leadership Quarterly*, 9(2), 127–145. https://doi.org/10.1016/S1048-9843(98)90001-7.

Crowther, N. (2002). The Salt Lake City Scandals and the Ancient Olympic Games. *The International Journal of the History of Sport*, 19(4), 169–178. https://doi.org/10.1080/714001796.

DeSensi, J.T. and Rosenberg, D. (2010). *Ethics and Morality in Sport Management*. (3rd ed.). Morgantown, WV: Fitness Information Technology.

Dose, J.J. (1999). The Relationship between Work Values Similarity and Team–Member and Leader–Member Exchange Relationships. *Group Dynamics: Theory, Research, and Practice*, 3(1), 20–32. https://doi.org/10.1037/1089-2699.3.1.20.

Edelman, M. and Pacella, J.M. (2019). Vaulted into Victims: Preventing Further Sexual Abuse in US Olympic Sports through Unionization and Improved Governance. *Arizona Law Review*, Paper No. 2018-08-05. 61(463). https://doi.org/10.2139/ssrn.3234438.

Forbes, A., Edwards, L. and Fleming, S. (2015). 'Women Can't Referee': Exploring the Experiences of Female Football Officials within UK Football Culture. *Soccer and Society*, 16(4), 521–539. https://doi.org/10.1080/14660970.2014.882829.

Grojean, M.W., Resick, C.J., Dickson, M.W. and Smith, D.B. (2004). Leaders, Values, and Organizational Climate: Examining Leadership Strategies for Establishing an Organizational Climate Regarding Ethics. *Journal of Business Ethics*, 55(3), 223–241. https://doi.org/10.1007/s10551-004-1275-5.

Kohlberg, L. (1984). *Essays on Moral Development: Vol. 2. The Psychology of Moral Development*. San Francisco, CA: Harper and Row.

Lawton, A. and Páez, I. (2015). Developing a Framework for Ethical Leadership. *Journal of Business Ethics*, 130(3), 639–649. https://doi.org/10.1007/s10551-014-2244-2.

Litzky, B.E., Eddleston, K.A. and Kidder, D.L. (2006). The Good, the Bad, and the Misguided: How Managers Inadvertently Encourage Deviant Behaviours. *Academy of Management Perspectives*, 20(1), 91–103. https://doi.org/10.5465/amp.2006.19873411.

Malloy, D.C. and Zakus, D.H. (1995). Ethical Decision Making in Sport Administration: A Theoretical Inquiry into Substance and Form. *Journal of Sport Management*, 9(1), 36–58. https://doi.org/10.1123/jsm.9.1.36.

Megheirkouni, M and Weir, D. (2019). Insights into Informal Practices of Sport Leadership in the Middle East: The Impact of Positive and Negative Wasta. *International Journal of Sport Policy and Politics*, 11(4), 1–18. https://doi.org/10.1080/19406940.2019.1634620.

Morgan, W.J. (Ed.). (2017). *Ethics in Sport*. (3rd ed.). Champaign, IL: Human Kinetics.

Murray, A.S. (2010). *The Wall Street Journal Essential Guide to Management: Lasting Lessons from the Best Leadership Minds of Our Time*. New York: Harper Business.

Oxford English Dictionary. (2010). 'Ethics'. In: *The Oxford English Dictionary of English*. (3rd ed.). Oxford: Oxford University Press.

Pfleegor, A.G. and Seifried, C.S. (2016). Practical Application of the Etho-Conventional Decision-Making Model. *International Journal of Sport Management*, 17(3), 383–408.

Pritchard, M.P. and Burton, R. (2014). Ethical Failures in Sport Business: Directions for Research. *Sport Marketing Quarterly*, 23(2), 86–99.

Raco, M. and Tunney, E. (2010). Visibilities and Invisibilities in Urban Development: Small Business Communities and the London Olympics 2012. *Urban Studies*, 47(10), 2069–2091. https://doi.org/10.1177/0042098009357351.

Roby, P.P. (2014). Ethical Leadership in College Athletics. *Journal of Intercollegiate Sport*, 7(1), 35–39. https://doi.org/10.1123/jis.2014-0086.

Sagas, M. and Wigley, B.J. (2014). Gray Area Ethical Leadership in the NCAA: The Ethics of Doing the Wrong Things Right. *Journal of Intercollegiate Sport*, 7(1), 40–57. https://doi.org/10.1123/jis.2014-0084.

Sarantakes, N.E. (2010). *Dropping the Torch: Jimmy Carter, the Olympic Boycott, and the Cold War*. Cambridge: Cambridge University Press. https://doi.org/10.1017/CBO9780511761805.

Sonenshein, S. (2007). The Role of Construction, Intuition, and Justification in Responding to Ethical Issues at Work: The Sensemaking-Intuition Model. *Academy of Management Review*, 32(4), 1022–1040. https://doi.org/10.5465/amr.2007.26585677.

Thiroux, J.P. and Krasemann, K.W. (1980). *Ethics: Theory and Practice*. (2nd ed.). Upper Saddle River, NJ: Pearson Prentice Hill.

Veiga, J.F. (2004). Bringing Ethics into the Mainstream: An Introduction to the Special Topic. *Academy of Management Perspectives*, 18(2), 37–38. https://doi.org/10.5465/ame.2004.13837442.

Walumbwa, F.O. and Schaubroeck, J. (2009). Leader Personality Traits and Employee Voice Behavior: Mediating Roles of Ethical Leadership and Work Group Psychological Safety. *Journal of Applied Psychology*, 94(5), 1275. https://doi.org/10.1037/a0015848.

Yukl, G., Mahsud, R., Hassan, S. and Prussia, G.E. (2013). An Improved Measure of Ethical Leadership. *Journal of Leadership and Organizational Studies*, 20(1), 38–48. https://doi.org/10.1177/1548051811429352.

15 SELF-LEADERSHIP

INTRODUCTION

The notion of self-leadership refers to the ability to influence yourself to think and behave in ways that enable you to pursue your goals. To do so, you need to know yourself and ask the following questions: what ideas do I have? where am I going? what are my qualifications, skills knowledge, experience? and how do I link between these qualifications or experience and the objective I want to achieve? Unlike many of the theories discussed in this book, self-leadership is still in a formative development. It needs to be considered more tentatively; it is likely to change as new research on the theory is conducted. This chapter begins by presenting an overview of the definitions of self-leadership. It then discusses the conceptual foundations of self-leadership and addresses self-leadership strategies. This chapter also discusses team self-leadership, while its last section includes an evaluation of self-leadership.

WHAT IS SELF-LEADERSHIP?

The term self-leadership first emerged in management and organization theory in the mid-1980s as an expansion of the term of self-management, which was rooted in clinical self-control theory and inspired by Steven Kerr and John Jermier's notion of substitutes for leadership (Neck and Houghton, 2006). Self-leadership over the past three decades has attracted considerable attention from scholars and researchers representing many disciplines. The term self-leadership

DOI: 10.4324/9780429290442-18

is defined as "the process of influencing oneself" (Manz, 1991: 7), first introduced by Manz (1983), who described self-leadership as:

> a comprehensive self-influence perspective that concerns leading oneself toward the performance of naturally motivating tasks as well as managing oneself to do work that must be done but is not naturally motivating.
>
> (Manz, 1983: 589)

Manz and Sims (1991) later pointed out that the self-leadership concept is distinguished from self-management by "What, Why, and How" questions. Manz described self-management, discussed in the next section, as:

> a self-influence process and set of strategies that primarily address *how* work is performed to help meet standards and objectives that are typically externally set ... [which] relies on extrinsic motivation and to focus on behaviour.
>
> (Manz, 1991: 17)

Additionally, Manz described self-leadership as:

> a self-influence process and a set of strategies that address *what* is to be done (e.g., standards and objectives) and *why* (e.g., strategic analysis) as well as how it is to be done ... [which] relies on intrinsic motivation and focuses on cognitive processes.
>
> (Manz, 1991: 17)

To clarify the distinction between self-leadership and self-management, it can be stated that self-leadership is less driven by external forces whereas self-management processes are dependent on extrinsic incentives (e.g. pay and rewards, career development). However, self-leadership still allows for influences such as the empowering actions of a leader who creates intrinsic reward opportunities as well as external incentives (Stewart et al, 2011).

Neck and Manz (2010) argue that the previous definitions of self-leadership are still general and do not provide the details necessary to enable a better understanding or a more effective execution of the process. Therefore, they defined self-leadership as:

> a comprehensive process of self-influence that involves specific behavioural and cognitive strategies. These strategies are designed to help us address not only *what* we need to do (e.g., determining the standards and objectives) but also *why* (e.g., strategic analysis) and *how* we should do it (e.g., strategic implementation). Therefore, they stress the importance of both intrinsic motivation and effective cognitive processes.
>
> (Neck and Manz, 2010: 37)

FUNDAMENTAL CONCEPTS OF SELF-LEADERSHIP

The term of self-leadership is derived primarily from research and theory in the field of psychology, particularly self-regulation theory, social cognitive theory, self-management, intrinsic motivation theory, and positive psychology (Neck et al, 2017). These theories are related to the theoretical context in which self-leadership takes place.

- *Self-regulation theory* is conceptualized as a personal source of influence (Bandura, 1976) and refers to "the self-generated thoughts, feelings, and actions that are planned and cyclically adapted to the attainment of personal goals" (Zimmerman, 2000: 14). The self-regulation process is similar to the operation of a mechanical thermostat. The thermostat senses temperature variations relative to a given standard and signals appropriate action to reduce the discrepancy. In much the same way, self-regulation theory refers to those processes that enable a sport leader or manager to guide his/her goal-directed activities over time and across changing circumstances. For example, if there is a difference between the managers' actual level of performance and the standard in a sport organization, this proposes that those managers need to adjust their effort and attempt to change their behaviour to improve their performance and reduce this gap. Self-regulatory processes do not always lead to successful performance outcomes and goal fulfilments. Therefore, the term 'self-regulatory failure' has been used to describe certain situations of failure in the self-regulatory process. In this regard, Latham and Locke (1991: 240) suggested that: "although people are natural self-regulators in that goal-directedness is inherent in the life process, they are not innately effective self-regulators".
- *Social cognitive theory* involves a dual-control system of both discrepancy production and discrepancy reduction. The basic assumption is that individuals have control over establishing their own performance objectives. Based on their previous performance experiences, people set goals in ways that create discrepancies, which then results in behaviours and efforts aimed at reducing these discrepancies. When discrepancies are eliminated, higher objectives are set, and the process of discrepancy reduction begins again. Social cognitive theory suggests that three important self-influence processes help motivate individuals to achieve their goals (Neck et al, 2017). The first influence is the triadic reciprocal model of behaviour, which proposes that human behaviour is best explained by the environment that surrounds people, by internal personal factors, and the behaviour itself. The second influence is self-satisfaction. The third influence is self-efficacy, which describes an individual's self-assessment of the required capabilities to complete a specific task (Bandura, 1986). The concept of self-efficacy is of particular importance to self-leadership, given its impact on aspirations, effort, persistence, and through-patterns (Neck and Houghton, 2006); particularly that a major objective of self-leadership strategies is the enhancement of self-efficacy, given that it leads to higher performance levels (Bandura, 1991; Neck and Houghton, 2006; Prussia et al, 1998).

- *Self-management* is a process through which individuals apply a set of specific strategies in an attempt to manage their behaviours in terms of reducing discrepancies from established objectives. Although self-management does not involve any assessment of the objectives themselves, it allows for very little self-influence regarding what is to be done (e.g. standards and objectives) and why (e.g. strategic analysis). Self-management may fall in the middle on a continuum ranging from complete internal influence to complete external influence (Neck et al, 2017).
- *Intrinsic motivation theory* emphasizes the ability of people to harness the natural enthusiasm that they have for certain tasks (Deci, 1975). Self-leadership relies on intrinsic motivation and more self-determination and focuses on cognitive processes. Competence and self-determination tend to be the major mechanisms that drive intrinsic motivation. The role of competence is to exercise and extend one's capabilities, whereas the role for self-determination is to make one feel free from pressures such as contingent rewards (Deci and Ryan, 1985). When people identify the challenges that affect them and work hard to overcome these challenges, this would help increase their feelings of competence and self-determination.
- *Positive psychology* studies positive emotions (such as happiness, gratitude, and fulfilment) and positive character traits (such as character strengths, resilience, and optimism).

SELF-LEADERSHIP STRATEGIES

BEHAVIOUR-FOCUSED STRATEGIES

Behaviour-focused strategies attempt to heighten an individual's self-awareness in order to facilitate behavioural management, especially the behaviours related to necessary but unpleasant tasks (Neck and Houghton, 2006). Behaviour-focused strategies include self-observation, self-goal setting, self-reward, self-punishment, and self-cueing.

- *Self-observation* refers to deliberate attention to specific aspects of one's behaviour. It raises our awareness of when and why we engage in specific behaviours. It is perceived as a necessary first step towards changing or eliminating ineffective and unproductive behaviours (Neck et al, 2017). Behaviours can be assessed on four dimensions: quantity, quality, rate, and originality (Bandura, 1986).
- *Self-goal setting* refers to the process of settings individual goals as a means to increase performance levels. This process is often effective if it is accompanied with self-set rewards (Neck et al, 2017).
- *Self-reward* contributes significantly to energizing the efforts required to accomplish goals. Self-set rewards may be tangible or intangible (Neck and Houghton, 2006). For example, a team manager is proud to have helped his team participate in a a world cup match (intangible); or the team manager might go with family for a private holiday or decide to rent a yacht after the positive results obtained with the team in the tournament (tangible).

- *Self-punishment* (or self-correcting feedback) refers to a positively framed and introspective examination of failures and undesirable behaviours leading to the reshaping of such behaviours (Neck and Houghton, 2006). For example, rugby team players make several mistakes in the final match, and these are directly responsible for them losing the Rugby World Cup. After the tournament, the team manager may criticize the team players through general and specific assessments of the reasons that led to this negative result, so the players make a conscious effort not to repeat these mistakes in the future. Some players may go further and punish themselves by staying in their rooms without communication with the others, and without food or drink for few days.
- *Self-cueing* environmental cues can be used as an effective means of encouraging constructive behaviours and reducing or eliminating destructive ones through the process of self-cues, which can help keep attention and effort focused on goal attainment (Neck and Houghton, 2006; Neck et al, 2017). These cues may be lists, notes, screensavers, and motivational wall posters.

NATURAL REWARD-FOCUSED STRATEGIES

Natural reward strategies aim to create situations in which an individual is motivated or rewarded by inherently enjoyable aspects of the task or activity (Neck et al, 2017; Manz and Sims, 2001). There are two types of natural reward-focused strategies that can help create feelings of competence and self-determination and energize task-related behaviours and performance-enhancing. These types are:

1. **Building more pleasant features**: When individuals work on difficult or boring assignments, they could build more pleasant and enjoyable features that can help them complete their assignments. For example, team players may listen to music during warming up prior the match.
2. **Shaping perceptions**: Individuals here focus on the task's inherently rewarding aspects. For example, board members of several sport governing bodies are attending leadership training sessions. The content of the programme is complex and includes action learning, significantly leading to more pressure on the participants. However, all participants attempt to move their attention away from the unpleasant aspects of the programme and refocus on the benefits of the programme and how good they will feel when it is done.

CONSTRUCTIVE THOUGHT-FOCUSED STRATEGIES

Constructive thought pattern strategies are used to facilitate the formation of constructive thought patterns and habitual ways of thinking that can positively impact performance (Neck et al, 2017; Neck and Manz, 1992). Constructive thought pattern strategies include:

- **Replacing dysfunctional beliefs**: Individuals examine first their thought patterns and replace their dysfunctional irrational beliefs and assumptions with more constructive thought processes.
- **Mental imagery**: It is defined as "those quasi-sensory and quasi-perceptual absence of those stimulus conditions that are known to produce their genuine sensory perceptual counterparts" (Richardson, 1969: 2–3). For example, athletes who envision successful performance of an activity in advance of actual performance are more likely to perform successfully when they are faced with the actual task (Neck and Houghton, 2006).
- **Positive self-talk**: Self-talk refers to what people covertly tell themselves. Individuals need to identify and analyse negative/destructive self-talk and replace it with more positive/ optimistic self-dialogues.

Indeed, self-leadership strategies may be the most appropriate forms of leadership for establishing positive outcomes in sport organizations. In his investigation of the mediator role of self-efficacy between self-leadership strategies and career success, Megheirkouni (2018) found that there is a significant relationship between self-leadership strategies and self-efficacy, and between self-efficacy and career success. Furthermore, self-efficacy was found to fully mediate the relationship between self-leadership and career success. Though self-leadership is still emerging in the field of sport management, its application can reduce the pressure on HR managers and resources.

TEAM SELF-LEADERSHIP

One of the more exciting areas of self-leadership research relates to shared leadership. As was noted in the previous chapter, distributed leadership is primarily concerned with the interactions and the dynamics of leadership practice rather than a preoccupation with the formal roles and responsibilities traditionally associated with those 'who lead'. The term SuperLeadership, which means leading others to lead themselves, was originally published in 1989 (Manz and Sims, 1989). Given the demand for individual empowerment as a means for survival, SuperLeadership might be seen as essential to 21st-century sport organizations in all sectors: for-profit, non-profit, and public sport sectors. The SuperLeader is often contrasted with three other common leadership types: the Strongman, the Transactor, and the Visionary Hero (Manz and Sims, 2001).

1. **Strongman**: This type of leadership focuses on the directive leadership roles and responsibilities. It also means that a leader, who provides answers to problems, assigns goals/objectives, and threatens or intimidates subordinates into a fear-based compliance.
2. **Transactor**: This type of leadership is classic, and it combines some of Strongman leadership and Visionary Hero leadership. It focuses on transactional behaviours and roles such as exchanging relationships with subordinates and contingent reward.
3. **Visionary Hero**: This focuses on transformational behaviours and roles of inspiring and motivating others. This type of leadership is characterized by supporting and energizing others to pursue the vision.

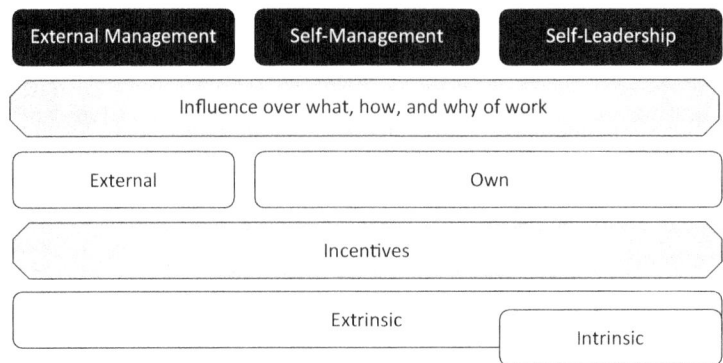

Figure 15.1 External management, self-management, and self-leadership at individual and team levels.

Source: Adapted from from Stewart, G.L., Courtright, S.H. and Manz, C.C. (2011). Self-Leadership: A Multilevel Review. *Journal of Management*, 37(1), 185–222.

Team self-leadership needs to be assessed in a way that is consistent with individual differences. According to Manz (1991, 1992), this depends on the degree that teams give to exercise self-influence regarding 'what' (aims, objectives, criteria), 'why' (values for the aims and objectives), and 'how' (the performance of the work) of work (Figure 15.1).

EVALUATION OF SELF-LEADERSHIP

Self-leadership has several strengths that should be taken into consideration. First, a Revised Self-Leadership Questionnaire (RSLQ) has provided a greater degree of reliability and validity than the initial SLQ. The applications of the RSLQ show that it is an effective means to measure self-leadership with positive potential for facilitating additional empirical self-leadership research in all organizational aspects (Neck and Houghton, 2006). Second, self-leadership can play a fundamental role in preparing athletes psychologically prior, during, and after competitions and tournaments. It can help athletes know how to navigate and manage themselves in a relatively wide variety of circumstances.

Although self-leadership has enjoyed an enduring and expanding popularity based on a strong intuitive appeal, it has a several weaknesses to consider. Firstly, most self-leadership research is still conceptual with relatively few empirical studies examining self-leadership in all organizational aspects. The reason behind this lack of empirical research may be related to the lack of valid self-leadership measurement scale. Specifically, researchers suffered from several psychometric problems in the first Self-Leadership Questionnaire (SLQ). Secondly, self-leadership consists of a broad set of strategies that are based upon other established theories of motivation and self-influence. Therefore, some theorists have questioned whether self-leadership is a unique theory and have suggested that it is a mere repackaging of individual differences already presented by existing psychological constructs such as the personality dimension of conscientiousness (Guzzo, 1998; Markham and Markham, 1995, 1998). Thirdly, self-leadership is introduced to the theorists and scholars as a normative model which focuses on how leadership tasks should be done in sport organizations rather than a descriptive or deductive theory which attempts to explain the basic operation of various phenomena in sport organizations. Fourthly, the intercultural and global aspects of self-leadership have not been fully explored and examined to date nor its influence was surveyed across a wide variety of sport settings and situations. For example, ways of thinking, the way how people live, learn, and grow up, or uncertainty, could be fundamental factors influencing the use of self-leadership across cultures (e.g. Alves et al, 2006; Georgianna, 2005).

SUMMARY

Unlike traditional theories and approaches discussed in this book, self-leadership is one of the newest approaches in the field of leadership and is still in the early stage of its development. As noted earlier, most of the leadership theories and approaches discussed in previous chapters have addressed leadership from a leader or follower perspective, the context, or/and the processes of their interaction. The current chapter, however, has focused on the self-leadership approach that view leadership as the process of influencing oneself in ways that enable that leader to pursue his or her goals. The term of self-leadership first emerged in management and organization theory in the mid-1980s as an expansion of the term of self-management, but it has not attracted considerable attention from scholars and researchers till the last two decades. This chapter has discussed the key fundamental concepts of self-leadership: self-regulation theory, social cognitive theory, self-management, intrinsic motivation theory, and positive psychology. This chapter has also addressed three self-leadership strategies: behaviour-focused strategies, natural reward-focused strategies, constructive thought-focused strategies. In addition, this chapter has discussed team self-leadership and has highlighted the notion of SuperLeader, which is often contrasted with three other common leadership types: the Strongman, the Transactor, and the Visionary Hero. Finally, an evaluation of the strengths and weaknesses of the self-leadership approach was presented.

GENERAL QUESTIONS

1. How do you define self-leadership?
2. Can self-leadership be learned or developed? If yes, how? If no, why?
3. What are the theories that represent the conceptual foundations of self-leadership?
4. What are the self-influence processes that motivate individuals to achieve their goals?
5. Provide examples of the behaviour-focused strategies that you might use to improve your sport performance.
6. Provide examples of the behaviour-focused strategies that you might use to improve your sport performance.

7. Provide examples of the natural reward-focused strategies that you might use to improve your sport performance.
8. Provide examples of the constructive thought pattern strategies that you might use to improve your sport performance.
9. List three weaknesses of the self-leadership theory.
10. List three strengths of the self-leadership theory.

OPEN DISCUSSION QUESTIONS

1. How to define self-management and self-leadership?
2. Discuss with your colleagues the similarities and differences between self-management and self-leadership in your sport.
3. Choose one of the following conceptual foundations of self-leadership: self-regulation theory, social cognitive theory, self-management, intrinsic motivation theory, and positive psychology. Explain what you have chosen with examples from your experience or your sport.
4. What conceptual foundations, you think, are best to represent your self-leadership? Why?
5. How does the term 'SuperLeader' differ from the terms 'Strong-man', 'Transactor', and 'Visionary Hero'? Support your answer with examples.
6. Identify four weaknesses of self-leadership. Discuss the answer with colleagues in the group. Are there any similar answers?
7. Identify four weaknesses of self-leadership. Discuss the answer with colleagues in the group. Are there any similar answers?

Case Study 15.1: Lewis Pugh – The Patron of the Oceans

In attempt to shed light on the phenomenon of ocean pollution and its impact on the marine life in the UK, Lewis Pugh committed to a campaign for a bright future for oceans and the creation of Marine Protected Areas by swimming the length of the Channel from Cornwall to Dover, although ten swimmers had died crossing the Channel. Pugh completed his 330-mile journey in less than 50 days, but not without problems for him and the accompanying team. After 50 days of swimming in the busiest shipping lane in the world, teeming with jellyfish, waves, and predators, particularly sharks, Pugh succeeded in making the impossible possible.

Pugh refused to wear a wet-suit or a dry-suit in the most dangerous swim he had ever attempted the English Channel in an attempt to convince world leaders to do more to protect the environment. He said, "Swimming in a wet-suit or a dry-suit would not send the right message. So, I swim according to Channel Swimming Rules, i.e. in just a Speedo swimming costume".

The first thing came to Pugh's mind when he dived into water was the focus on how to control his body while swimming rather than the thoughts of victory or defeat because "I'd be out the water in seconds", said Pugh.

Given that Pugh swam wearing almost nothing, hypothermia was the most serious problem affecting his life. It required a serious change in his plan, represented by breaking the swim down into two-hour sessions to give his body the time to restore his activity and warm. Pugh was told that he had tendonitis ten days before the end of the journey, and he was advised to rest due to his injury. But he insisted on completing the journey as planned. One of the fundamental reasons for Pugh's success in this challenge as a pioneer swimmer were his capabilities to learn from previous mistakes and of never giving up. According to Pugh, there are five fundamental factors that can help other swimmers successfully swim the length of the Channel from Cornwall to Dover. These factors are: (1) to secure experienced pilots to guide the swimming route; (2) be patient for managing time; (3) train on cold-water swimming; (4) secure inspirational individuals to stay in the boat along the journey; and (5) leave your own doubts once you complete the challenge.

Questions

1. How would you describe the self-leadership of Lewis Pugh? Explain your answer.
2. How would you describe the self-observation, self-goal setting, self-reward, and self-cueing of Lewis Pugh on his Channel journey?
3. Can you identify any components of the natural reward-focused strategies and constructive thought pattern strategies of Lewis?
4. At the end of the case, Lewis Pugh advised other swimmers willing to swim along the Channel to follow five steps. Can we apply the term SuperLeader to Lewis Pugh? Discuss the answer with colleagues in the group. Are there any similar answers?

Source: Based on material from https://www.lewispugh.com/.

SELF-ASSESSMENT 15.1: SELF-LEADERSHIP STRATEGIES

Look through the table of self-leadership strategies. Then answer the questions.

Behaviour-focused strategies	*Natural reward-focused strategies*	*Constructive thought pattern strategies*
• Self-observation • Self-goal setting • Self-reward • Self-punishment • Self-cueing	• Building more pleasant features • Shaping perceptions	• Replacing dysfunctional beliefs • Mental imagery • Positive self-talk

Questions

For each of the following seven scenarios, determine the appropriate self-leadership strategy.

1. A pole vault athlete envisions successful performance of an activity in advance of an actual performance.
2. Seven times a week, a football player could stop and deliberately ask themself questions about what they have accomplished and what they have not, to devise means of changing the unproductive behaviours in order to enhance performance.
3. A gymnastics national team was invited to attend a closed camp for one month before the Olympic Games. All athletes attempted to move their attention away from the boring aspects of the camp and refocus on the benefits of the camp for the Olympic achievements.
4. An organizing committee of the FIFA World Cup might go for a few weeks holiday after hosting the event.
5. A boxer identifies and analyses pessimistic self-talk after losing the title and replaces it with more optimistic self-dialogues when they decide to train for the next championship.
6. Given the pressure on the organizing committee of Olympic Games, they decided to watch a film every day at lunch time.
7. Rugby team players examine their thought patterns and replace them with more constructive thought processes.

Suggested Reading

Manz, C.C. and Sims Jr., H.P. (2001). *The New Superleadership: Leading Others to Lead Themselves*. San Francisco, CA: Berrett-Koehler.

Megheirkouni, M. (2018). Self-Leadership Strategies and Career Success: Insight on Sports Organizations. *Sport, Business and Management: An International Journal*, 8(4), 393–409. https://doi.org/10.1108/sbm-02-2018-0006.

Neck, C.P. and Houghton, J.D. (2006). Two Decades of Self-leadership Theory and Research: Past Developments, Present Trends, and Future Possibilities. *Journal of Managerial Psychology*, 21(4), 270–295. https://doi.org/10.1108/02683940610663097.

Neck, C.P., Manz, C.C. and Houghton, J.D. (2016). *Mastering Self-Leadership: Empowering Yourself for Personal Excellence*. London: Sage.

Neck, C.P., Manz, C.C. and Houghton, J.D. (2019). *Self-Leadership: The Definitive Guide to Personal Excellence*. (2nd ed.). London: Sage.

Stewart, G.L., Courtright, S.H. and Manz, C.C. (2011). Self-Leadership: A Multilevel Review. *Journal of Management*, 37(1), 185–222. https://doi.org/10.1177/0149206310383911.

References

Alves, J.C., Lovelace, K.J., Manz, C.C., Matsypura, D., Toyasaki, F. and Ke, K. (2006). A Cross Cultural Perspective of Self-Leadership. *Journal of Managerial Psychology*, 21(4), 338–59. https://doi.org/10.1108/02683940610663123.

Bandura, A. (1976). Self-Reinforcement: Theoretical and Methodological Considerations. *Behaviorism*, 4(2), 135–155. JSTOR: https://www.jstor.org/stable/27758862.

Bandura, A. (1986). Observational Learning. In: Bandura, A. (Ed.). (1986). *Social Foundations of Thought and Action: A Social Cognitive Theory.* Englewood Cliffs, NJ: Prentice-Hall. (169–195). Short version published as a as chapter. In: Donsbach, W. (Ed.) (2008). *The International Encyclopedia of Communication* Online: John Wiley & Sons. https://doi.org/10.1002/9781405186407.wbieco004.

Bandura, A. (1991). Social Cognitive Theory of Self-Regulation. *Organizational Behavior and Human Decision Processes*, 50(2), 248–287. https://doi.org/10.1016/0749-5978(91)90022-L.

Deci, E.L. (1975). *Intrinsic Motivation.* New York: Plenum Press. https://doi.org/10.1007/978-1-4613-4446-9.

Deci, E.L and Ryan, R.M. (1985). The Support of Autonomy and Control of Behaviour. *Journal of Personality and Social Psychology*, 53(6), 1024–1037. https://doi.org/10.1037/0022-3514.53.6.1024.

Georgianna, S. (2005). *Intercultural Features of Self-Leadership.* Aachen: Shaker-Verlag.

Guzzo, R.A. (1998). Leadership, Self-Management, and Levels of Analysis. In: Dansereau, F. and Yammarino, F.J. (Eds.). *Leadership: The Multiple-Level Approaches: Classical and New Wave.* Stanford, CT: JAI Press. (213–219).

Latham, G.P. and Locke, E.A. (1991). Self-Regulation through Goal Setting. *Organizational Behavior and Human Decision Processes*, 50(2), 212–247. https://doi.org/10.1016/0749-5978(91)90021-K.

Manz, C.C. (1983). *The Art of Self-Leadership: Strategies for Personal Effectiveness in Your Life and Work.* Upper Saddle River, NJ: Prentice Hall.

Manz, C.C. (1991). Leading Employees to be Self-Managing and Beyond: Toward the Establishment of Self-Leadership in Organizations. *Journal of Management Systems*, 3(3), 15–24.

Manz, C.C. (1992). Self-leading Work Teams: Moving Beyond Self-Management Myths. *Human Relations*, 45(11), 1119–1140. https://doi.org/10.1177/001872679204501101.

Manz, C.C. and Sims Jr., H.P. (1989). *SuperLeadership: Leading Others to Lead Themselves.* San Francisco, CA: Berrett-Koehler.

Manz, C.C. and Sims Jr., H.P. (1991). SuperLeadership: Beyond the Myth of Heroic Leadership. *Organizational Dynamics*, 19(4), 18–35. https://doi.org/10.1016/0090-2616(91)90051-A.

Manz, C.C. and Sims Jr., H.P. (2001). *The New Superleadership: Leading Others to Lead Themselves.* San Francisco, CA: Berrett-Koehler.

Markham, S.E. and Markham, I.S. (1995). Self-Management and Self-Leadership Reexamined: A Levels-of-Analysis Perspective. *The Leadership Quarterly*, 6(3), 343–59. https://doi.org/10.1016/1048-9843(95)90013-6.

Markham, S.E. and Markham, I.S. (1998). Self-Management and Self-Leadership Reexamined: A Levels-of-Analysis Perspective. In: Dansereau, F. and Yammarino, F.J. (Eds.). *Leadership: The Multiple-Level Approaches: Classical and New Wave.* Stanford, CT: JAI Press. (193–210).

Megheirkouni, M. (2018). Self-Leadership Strategies and Career Success: Insight on Sports Organizations. *Sport, Business and Management: An International Journal*, 8(4), 393–409. https://doi.org/10.1108/sbm-02-2018-0006.

Neck, C.P. and Houghton, J.D. (2006). Two Decades of Self-Leadership Theory and Research: Past Developments, Present Trends, and Future Possibilities. *Journal of Managerial Psychology*, 21(4), 270–295. https://doi.org/10.1108/02683940610663097.

Neck, C.P. and Manz, C.C. (1992). Thought Self-leadership: The Influence of Self-talk and Mental Imagery on Performance. *Journal of Organizational Behavior*, 13(7), 681–699. https://doi.org/10.1002/job.4030130705.

Neck, C.P. and Manz, C.C. (2009). *Mastering Self-Leadership: Empowering Yourself for Personal Excellence*. (5th ed.). Upper Saddle River, NJ: Prentice Hall.

Neck, C.P., Manz, C.C. and Houghton, J.D. (2017). *Mastering Self-Leadership: Empowering Yourself for Personal Excellence*. London: Sage.

Prussia, G.E., Anderson, J.S. and Manz, C.C. (1998). Self-Leadership and Performance Outcomes: The Mediating Influence of Self-Efficacy. *Journal of Organizational Behavior*, 19(5), 523–538. https://doi.org/10.1002/(SICI)1099-1379(199809)19:5%3C523::AID-JOB860%3E3.0.CO;2-I.

Richardson, A. (1969). *Mental Imagery*. New York: Springer. https://doi.org/10.1007/978-3-662-37817-5.

Stewart, G.L., Courtright, S.H. and Manz, C.C. (2011). Self-Leadership: A Multilevel Review. *Journal of Management*, 37(1), 185–222. https://doi.org/10.1177/0149206310383911.

Zimmerman, B.J. (2000). Attaining Self-Regulation: A Social Cognitive Perspective. In: Boekaerts, M., Pintrich, P.R. and Zeidner, M. (Eds.). *Handbook of Self-Regulation*. San Diego, CA: Academic Press. (13–39). https://doi.org/10.1016/B978-0-12-109890-2.X5027-6.

16 RESPONSIBLE **LEADERSHIP**

Learning Outcomes

After reading this chapter, you will be able to:

- Provide a basic definition of responsible leadership
- Understand responsible leadership quality
- Distinguish responsible leadership roles
- Understand how to measure responsible leadership
- Evaluate responsible leadership

INTRODUCTION

Responsible leadership represents one of the newest topics of leadership research. It focuses on social-relational and ethical phenomena, which occur in social processes of interaction. As the name of this approach implies, responsible leadership refers to the values-based and ethics-driven relationship between leaders and stakeholders inside and outside sport organizations. Like ethical, authentic, and self-leadership, despite the existence of several viewpoints and theoretical formulations on responsible leadership, it is remains in development. The importance of responsible leadership is not limited to calls for responsible behaviours after the increasing number of scandals in the sport world or changes in how the for-profit sport sector operates at the national and international levels. Responsible leadership needs to be considered more tentatively, particularly when we discuss the changes occurring in the form and structure of the non-profit sport sector that enable or force it to become similar to the for-profit sport sector (Megheirkouni, 2017a). As a result, our conceptions of responsible leadership are likely to change after new empirical research on this approach.

WHAT IS RESPONSIBLE LEADERSHIP?

Despite the increasing need for responsible leaders over the last decade, very little research has been published on the theoretical foundations of responsible leadership. There have been many studies on responsible leadership since the 2000s, but these studies have not been theoretically and practically tested in the field of sport leadership. Among leadership scholars at least, there is agreement that research is responding to gaps in leadership theory as well as the practical challenges facing leadership (Pless and Maak, 2011). Pless provides the most frequently referenced definition:

> Responsible leadership can be described as values-based and thorough ethical principles-driven relationship between leaders and stakeholders who are connected through a shared sense of meaning and purpose through which they raise one another to higher levels of motivation and commitment for achieving sustainable values creation and social change.
>
> (Pless, 2007: 438)

Despite the differences, responsible leadership has been described as a mix of all the best of transformational leadership, servant leadership, authentic leadership, charismatic leadership, and ethical leadership, with a specific focus on a wider range of stakeholders: peers, suppliers, board members, customers, employees' direct reports, families, fellow citizens, other stakeholders, and future generations (Maak and Pless, 2006). Whether the definition of responsible leadership can make a claim to combine 'the best' of these things requires discussion, much empirical research, and successful application in practice.

RESPONSIBLE LEADERSHIP QUALITIES

Leadership requires the capability to build effective relationships with a wide range of stakeholders. So far, the definition of responsible leadership suggests two fundamental qualities of the responsible leader: facilitating relational processes – relational intelligence; and leader–stakeholder exchange quality – moral quality.

FACILITATING RELATIONAL PROCESSES – RELATIONAL INTELLIGENCE

As leadership is in essence a relational process, a responsible leader needs to integrate people from different cultures and ethical backgrounds, understand their needs, facilitate formal and informal dialogues, build lasting and trustful relationships, and inspire a shared vision with and between other stakeholders as 'followers' inside and outside the sport organization. For example, the chief executive of the Football Association (FA), for England (mostly) is ultimately accountable for facilitating multiple and complex relational processes with and between the FA Board, the FA Council, and the Football Association's Management Team to produce an effective organization for the greater good of the English football community. Moreover, the FA's chief executive is ultimately accountable for facilitating external relationships. Similarly, there exist the Football Association of Wales, Irish Football Association, and Scottish Football Association.

LEADER–STAKEHOLDER EXCHANGE QUALITY – MORAL QUALITY

Alongside their responsibility for facilitating relational processes, responsible leaders are accountable for the quality of these relationships, which extend across a wide range of stakeholders inside and beyond sport organizations. The relationship quality stems from the reciprocal configurations such as, shared values, mutual responsibility, mutual tolerance, mutual interest, mutual trust, mutual engagement, and mutual concern. For example, the relationships between a UK Olympic gymnastics coach and their gymnasts are based on reciprocal respect, shared values, and mutual trust that serves a common goal, which is currently seen specifically as winning an Olympic medal. When the relationship is not ethically sound, especially given close and intense physical proximity, immediate damage is done to those with less power, and scandal happens (see Chapter 14, 'Ethical Leadership').

Women's participation in organized football, professional and otherwise, has had a very long and difficult journey, which is far from finished. In England it was banned from FA recognition and venues from 1921 to 1970. The FA's own account (The Football Association, n.d.) is interesting for what it does acknowledge; but more interesting for a critical reading of how it presents the story. The story makes an interesting source for comparing with the following responsible leadership roles.

EIGHT RESPONSIBLE LEADERSHIP ROLES

Stakeholder theory conceptualizes the sport organization as individuals, units, or divisions that have different relationships with it, and with different degrees of influence on it. Stakeholder models are likely to differ between for-profit, non-profit, and public sport organizations or between sport events. In general, stakeholders in sport organizations consist of employees, volunteers, managers, coaches, athletes, board members, chief executives, owners, fans, and sponsors (Walters and Tacon, 2013). Stakeholder research in the field of sport business and management is well-established (Friedman et al, 2004); and since Parent (2008), stakeholder leadership theory is emergent in the sport domain. On the broader level, early responsible leadership research focused on the link between responsible and stakeholder leadership, leading to the emerging and developing of a new area of research that emphasizes the roles and responsibilities that leaders have in relation to a wide range of stakeholders (Maak and Pless, 2006; Megheirkouni, 2019; Pless, 2007; Pless and Maak, 2011) (Figure 16.1).

STEWARD

The term 'stewardship' means that a leader holds in trust the wellbeing of the whole sport organization through placing the notion of 'service' ahead of 'control' (see Chapter 9, 'Servant Leadership'). Hernandez (2008: 122) defines stewardship as "the attitudes and behaviours that place the long-term best interests of a group ahead of personal goals that serve an individual's self-interests". The

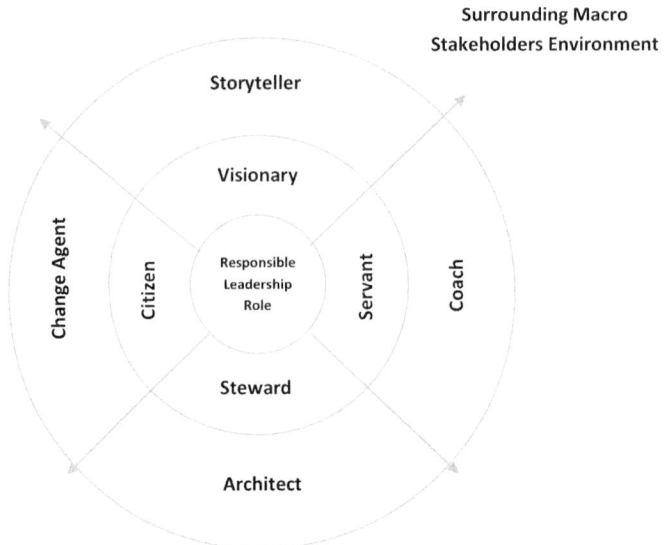

Figure 16.1 Model of responsible leadership roles.

Source: Adapted from Maak, T. and Pless, N.M. (2006). Responsible Leadership in a Stakeholder Society–A Relational Perspective. *Journal of Business Ethics*, 66(1), 99–115.

term stewardship supports the idea that sport leaders are deeply accountable for rather than only to their followers, teams, organizations, and societies, without defining what others should do, without caretaking, or without taking control, as Block puts it:

> Stewardship is defined as the choice to preside over the orderly distribution of power. This means giving people at the bottom and the boundaries of the organisation choice over how to serve a customer, a citizen, a community.
>
> (Block, 2013: xxiv)

Thus, if we link the notion of stewardship to both resources and social values in sport projects, a responsible sport leader would introduce themself as a custodian of social and sport values and resources. In this sense, responsible leaders as steward are those who have a sense of responsibility to work for the common good. Also, responsible the leader-as-steward plays an effective role in dealing with conflicts between stakeholders and guide them to assess when different opinions need to be respected, and when these differences are wrong (Donaldson, 1996). For example, some international organizations offer grants of over £1 million for sport development projects. The scale makes risk management crucial and visible for the success of such projects. When the responsible leader of a project thinks as a steward and guides their stakeholders in assessing their conflicts, for example, on establishing a project plan, organizing human resources, and managing finance, this will reduce the risk of failure.

CITIZEN

The term of organizational citizenship is applied when leaders fulfil their responsibilities towards a restricted group of stakeholders. Contemporary leadership is not responsibility-free. For better understanding of its effectiveness, we need to look at what goals can a leader achieve and the contents of such goals. We can think of responsible leaders as effective citizens when they succeed in changing the attitudes and behaviours of stakeholders for the common good, foster a sense of belonging to the organization in which they operate, demonstrate an ethical commitment, and seek to promote the culture of commitment. Therefore, the responsible leader-as-citizen are supportive in nature, treat all stakeholders equally, and exercise wisdom in their actions.

Responsible leaders-as-citizens can evolve from followership position in sport organization. The internal legal order of sport organizations can support members into citizenship leadership roles, but it is not guaranteed that they will display responsible behaviours in leadership. For example, for health reasons, the president of an international sport governing body needs a 12-month break from work. The internal legal order of the organization states that one of the vice-presidents must occupy the president position. Vice-presidents may rotate or be replaced if unsuccessful.

VISIONARY

Vision is a key leadership behaviour. The term 'vision' in leadership refers to an ideal, desired, and long-term future that a leader seeks to create in a sport organization. Visionary leadership is about how to attract and inspire followers as stakeholders to pursue and achieve shared purposes beyond expectations inside and outside the sport organization (Goethals et al, 2004). A responsible vision is said to be one reason that provides ethical actions for achieving desired future outcomes such as sustainable benefits. Although the idea of visionary leadership, in early leadership research, is connected with charismatic, transformational leadership, and ideological leadership, developing a vision in organizations is also an important part of responsible leadership (Maak and Pless, 2006). As noted earlier in this chapter, responsible leadership quality is determined through the capability of leaders to facilitate ethical principle-driven relationship with, for example, such as reciprocal respect and mutual trust, which stem from developing or creating shared vision between sport leaders and stakeholders that aims to achieve sustainable values and desired future outcomes.

SERVANT

Servant leadership emphasizes that leaders go beyond their own self-interest and focus on the concerns of their followers and support them build their personal capabilities. Moral responsibility of servant leaders towards their followers (Walumbwa et al, 2010) and stakeholders (Ehrhart, 2004) is the most important principle that distinguishes the servant leadership from other leadership behaviours. Despite the differences, servant leadership and responsible leadership both focus on the idea that leadership must be mainly about moral responsibilities towards the people surrounding the leader inside and outside organization (followers or stakeholders) (Pless and Maak, 2011).

Responsible leaders-as-servants, in this sense, include ethical, spiritual, humanistic, scientific, aesthetic values seen inside and outside sport organizations. Thinking as servant stems from the sense of responsibility towards all stakeholders and the right actions that a sport leader takes for creating sustainable values and social change. Thus, as you might expect, the underlying and visible motivation of the responsible leader is based both on how to serve stakeholders inside or outside their sport organization and on how to respond to stakeholders' needs.

COACH

Leadership coaching and coaching by leaders significant – and somewhat overlapping – leadership development methods used for developing leaders and managers, individually and collectively, at all management levels. Specifically, the leader-as-coach is a potentially powerful means to enhance learning experience for effective outcomes in all sport sectors. Leaders-as-coaches may bring together board members and other senior managers in collaborative leadership assignments to transfer a broader level of leadership knowledge and expertise regarding current and future strategy and trends, identifying current challenges surrounding leadership while exploring new possibilities, ensuring accountability, sustaining leadership and management development, and support for achieving purposes (Ting and Hart, 2004). Other levels may be similarly coached by an appropriately senior organizational leader figure. According to Frankovelgia and Riddle (2010), the effective role of the leader–coach can be determined through six principles. According to these principles, the leader–coach is able to:

1. **Create an Effective Learning Environment**: The leader–coach must create a positive learning environment to achieve the purposes of learning, whether directly inside the organization or elsewhere. The learner will feel comfortable and safe when making mistakes, taking risks, making complex decisions, and launching initiatives; and this would help promote learning from actions. At a minimum, the leader–coach must clarify that what is happening between the coach and the learner during training sessions must remain confidential. In other words, any information used outside the coaching purpose will affect the learning purposes, the willing to learn, and thus the learner's progress.

2. **Ensure the Learner's Ownership**: The learner is responsible for driving the process of learning, the content, and the purpose of the coaching method. Learners know best about their strengths and weaknesses. The purposes and contents of training sessions and coaching programmes are affected by the organization's goals and strategies and may differ between public, for-profit, and non-profit sport sectors (cf. Megheirkouni, 2017b).

3. **Facilitate and Collaborate**: Sustainable development is affected by the degree to which leadership coaching undergoes continuous improvements

inside and outside sport organizations. The content of internal and external coaching programmes can be assisted by partners, experts, experienced leaders, and academics. The importance lies in the critical contributions they may offer through reflecting, inquiring, giving feedback, content advising, and evaluating outcomes from other perspectives. Bear in mind that the primary responsibility for the internal leader–coach is to focus on developing particular leadership capabilities with specific training strategy led by an HR department, in larger organizations, implemented to serve the sport organization in the shorter term, particularly noting that the internal leader–coach and HR managers are the only people who make the ultimate decision about the course of action. In contrast, the key responsibility for the external leader–coach is to develop learners based on their needs, given that learners make the decision about the coaching course purposes and contents.

4. **Advocate Self-Awareness**: A prerequisite for developing leadership learning is to identify the learner's weaknesses and strengths, and be attentive to the learner's own learning and leadership needs (Antonacopoulou and Bento, 2003). So, self-awareness for the learner is the base of leadership development. The leader–coach needs to be a role model for reflective awareness. To do so, the leader–coach needs to adapt their own part of interactions by modifying thoughts, priorities, leadership and learning styles, and the way they influencing others in conjunction with a set of leadership development standards and a learner's current state. This places the leader–coach in a position that enables them, with growing experience, to analyse, assess, and predict results of their interactions with the learner, to reach the required outcomes.

5. **Promote Sustainable Experiential Learning**: According to Kolb (2014: 41), "learning is the process whereby knowledge is created through the transformation of experience". Learning from experience refers to all forms of formal and informal action learning in which the individual leader can transform most his or her acquired experiences and place them within a broader conceptual context. Learning from experience or action learning is one fundamental and effective leadership development method (Megheirkouni, 2016). However, the notion of experiential learning by itself does not make it inherently sustainable. Learners on their way to be leaders to be provided with and take for themselves regular opportunities for reflection on what they have done and what others have and are doing. A coach can play a significant role in this by providing methods for continuing professional and personal development, and may provide long-term support that is periodic if not frequent.

6. **Model What You Coach**: The leader–coach must show their emotional intelligence competencies in, for example, social awareness and self-awareness, emotional self-awareness, self-management, emotional self-control, adaptability, achievement orientation, positive outlook, and empathy (Boyatzis, 2011) and also employ these competencies in the learning process, particularly when the leader–coach applies 360-degree feedback or any kinds

of assessments for developmental purposes. The leader–coach must consistently exhibit flexibility, innovation, and openness in coaching methods. For example, the leader–coach can help a learner to explore, without explaining, ask the right question rather than provide the right answer, and provide alternative solutions rather than pushing a specific solution.

STORYTELLER

Storytelling is a typical activity used in many formal and informal leadership development programmes, knowledge-sharing conferences, and workshops. It gives learners an opportunity to get exposure to the experiences of other organizations and leaders in the sport industry (Megheirkouni and Roomi, 2017). Although the use of storytelling activities may differ between developmental programmes, training sessions, forums, conferences, and workshops, all of them include questions and dialogue sessions after storytelling activities. The interaction between a storyteller and participants can help create a 'creativity lab' to solve problems, create innovative ideas, and share experience, particularly when responsible storytellers are professional coaches, chief executives, or presidents of national or international sport organizations, whom learners would not otherwise meet.

A responsible leader-as-storyteller in sport organizations has the task of transporting core values and creating a sense of responsibility, using particular tales and previous events that inspire internal and external stakeholders to achieve sustainable social benefits or changes. Storytellers are responsible for their story choices as the intention is to influence stakeholders: storytellers, including in sport leadership roles, thus have a moral responsibility towards others.

ARCHITECT

A key responsibility of the leader-as-architect is to transform the sport organization's inputs into outputs. But the success of such a task is affected by the degree to which a leader understands three key factors (Bernstein et al, 2014), as follows:

- *Organizational Strategy*: To make sport organizations successful, responsible leaders must act as strategic architects and set the right strategic direction at national and international levels; those at local level may need to keep an eye on trends in national and even international events. It is also important to ensure that the strategy can be implemented, while acting as facilitators and translators of the proposed strategy leading to a powerful and compelling statement for the entire organization.
- *Shaping Organizational Identity*: The idea of the responsible sport leader-as-architect is about their capability to articulate, cultivate, and facilitate a work environment in which equality, diversity, and inclusivity are a priority and well-respected. For example, many responsible leaders today create a zero-tolerance policy for discrimination or harassment behaviours in their sport organizations to enable followers to contribute to their highest

potential, particularly in job performance and achievements. Policy is, however, not enough – responsible, visible commitment is required; and policy for the sake of legal compliance is open to failure.

- *Management Systems and Processes*: The leader-as-architect must ensure that management systems and processes in the sport organization are designed in a way that supports all management levels to serve the organization's objectives. Systems are always, in the end, about people. So, it is also important that a leader accounts for launching their own initiatives to deal effectively with organizational structure (e.g. power, coordination, and control), organizational culture (e.g. norms, values, and beliefs distinguishing the organization from other ones), people (e.g. volunteers, members, sponsors, paid employees, athletes, coaches), and critical tasks (e.g. preventing or overcoming resistance, health and safety, or managing crises).

CHANGE AGENT

The term 'change agent' refers to the individual or group that is responsible for leading or implementing change in the sport organization. These changes can include, but are not limited to, change in organizational strategy, process, policy, structure, culture, human resource development, or technology. Inevitably, changing one of these can have significant, and unforeseen, impacts on the others. Although change agents may have formal lines of authority, such as chief executives, board members, and middle managers, change rarely occurs within the sport industry without proper consultations with external experts with sufficient professional experience and employees to reduce resistance to change and discover the in-situ experience that others may not see. Institutional factors, such as sport sector and organization size, will affect everything from strategy to implementation. Change, by its very nature, needs qualified, skilled, and experienced individuals to effectively implement it. The capability of the responsible change agent is will be a critical element for successful change. In fact, becoming a change agent requires a set of abilities that enable the responsible leader to accomplish the intended outcome (Table 16.1).

As an effective change agent, the responsible leader not only has to adopt the idea of the need for meaningful change in the sport organization in the long term, but they must also build sustainable relationships with stakeholders. These relationships should be based on mutual trust and respect through ongoing sense-making activities, and on sustaining commitment in the organization by keeping momentum in times when external change causes uncertainty, insecurity, and disorientation, beside creating a clear vision to overcome challenges (Maak and Pless, 2006).

A good example of a change agent organization is the International Olympic Academy Participants Association (IOAPA). As an association of Olympic education, it fosters an international and multicultural Olympic fellowship of IOA past participants, providing tools and resources to facilitate Olympic education and support Olympism worldwide. The IOAPA aims to promote the cause of Olympism. Members serve as implementers and change agents by, for

Table 16.1 Key Abilities of Responsible Agents

Big picture sense-making	Leading change	Relational management and social awareness
• Able to understand the entire organization • Able to solve problems • Able to make decision • Able to think critically • Able to think creatively	• Able to communicate • Able to coach • Able to advise • Able to develop change • Able to negotiate • Able to create transformational change	• Able to build trust • Able to inspire others • Able to manage conflicts • Able to mobilize stakeholders • Able to recognize/ understand emotional information about stakeholders

Source: Adapted from Megheirkouni, M. (2017). Leadership Competencies: Qualitative Insight into Non-Profit Sport Organisations. *International Journal of Public Leadership*, 13(3), 166–181.

example, spreading Olympism, consultancies to IOAPA, organising IOAPA sessions at which Members of IOAPA may share practical experience with respect to the task of spreading Olympism, and rekindle enthusiasm for that task, through personal contact with other Members of IOAPA, and facilitating the exchange of Olympic information with members of the association (IOAPA, 2019, Article 3). In many cases, it is hard to distinguish between the IOAPA and its members and the International Olympic Committee and its members because promoting Olympism around the world provides members of the IOAPA with exceptional opportunities to exercise their leadership abilities.

MEASURING RESPONSIBLE LEADERSHIP

Few valid questionnaires have been developed to measure this approach; so, the theory-to-empirical result-back to theory gaps may explain why responsible leadership is still under development. The Socially Responsible Leadership Scale (SRLS) was the first scale used to assess concepts associated with responsible leadership. It was originally designed by Tyree (1998) to assess college students' leadership participation. The SRLS is a 103-item instrument that measures values associated with leadership development. Although this scale included Confirmatory Factor Analysis (CFA) along with other tests to establish the validity and reliability of scales, it was criticized because of its large number of items. Thus, the second revision of the SRLS developed by Dugan (2006) reduced the number of items to 68. The SRLS-R2 was used to examine college students' capacities for socially responsible leadership. The SRLS-R2 used CFA along with other tests to establish the validity and reliability of scales with some degree of transferability across other contexts.

Another empirical scale that extended our understanding of Discursive Responsible Leadership was developed by Voegtlin (2011). It concludes that responsible leadership is based on the ideal of discourse ethics that goes beyond the dyadic leader–follower relationship to include all stakeholders. The scale of Discursive Responsible Leadership validated a one-dimensional construct with high internal consistency, as well as discriminant and predictive validity. Sample items are "My direct supervisor demonstrates awareness of the relevant stakeholder claims" and "My direct supervisor weighs different stakeholder claims before making a decision".

Given that responsible leadership is still in the formative stages of development, establishing a new instrument of responsible leadership will be necessary to fit the evolution of this approach in future research. Further research on responsible leadership in the sport context may predict new empirical scales to assess responsible leadership not only in the for-profit sport sector, but in non-profit and public sport sectors as well.

EVALUATION OF RESPONSIBLE LEADERSHIP

As noted earlier, although responsible leadership is one of the newest topics of leadership research, it has several strengths. First, this approach fulfils the need for responsible leadership and responsible leaders because of the scandals of many sport leaders and organizations in recent years. Responsible leadership approach helps build and sustain benefit to stakeholders inside and outside sport organizations.

Second, like transformational, servant, and authentic leadership, responsible leadership includes moral values and relational qualities. The idea of responsible leadership is that a leader builds sustainable relationships and copes with the complex problems surrounding leadership in uncertain and interconnected contexts, using moral and relational qualities (Pless and Maak, 2011).

Third, responsible leadership attributes are not related to certain people or reserved for a hierarchical few. Any stakeholder inside or outside the sport organization can learn to be a responsible leader, and there is an additional empirical support for the importance of developing competencies used for building sustainable stakeholder relations (Pless and Schneider, 2005; Pless et al, 2011).

Although responsible leadership approach has many strengths, it also has weaknesses.

First, the responsible leadership approach is an underdeveloped topics in leadership. As noted earlier, little research has been published on the theoretical formulations of responsible leadership. Further, responsible leadership research has been largely conceptualized and tested in the for-profit sector, with fewer in in the non-profit sport sector (Megheirkouni, 2019) or public sport sector. Until more empirical studies have been conducted to explore, understand, and examine the responsible leadership approach in public, for-profit, and non-profit sport sectors, theoretical formulations about the process of this approach, particularly in the sport sector, are more likely to remain open to change.

Second, the current measurement instruments may or may not be valid to measure this construct in future sport research, despite the evidence of the present measurements' validity. Researchers need to establish measurements of this form of evolving leadership leading to a generally accepted theory in the future.

Third, although the number of studies on this approach has been increasing since the 2000s, these studies have not explored positive and negative outcomes for stakeholders in much detail, and particularly in sport settings.

SUMMARY

Responsible leadership is still in development, and various questions still need to be addressed in this theory. Despite the increasing need for responsible leadership behaviours in in contemporary sport settings, little research has been published on the theoretical foundations of responsible sport leadership. This chapter has discussed the meaning of responsible leadership and addressed two qualities of responsible leaders: facilitating relational processes (relational intelligence) and leader–stakeholder exchange quality (moral quality). Eight responsible leadership roles were discussed: steward, citizen, visionary, servant, coach, storyteller, architect, and change agent. The need for valid responsible leadership measurement instruments in sport has been noted. This chapter has also discussed key strengths and weaknesses of this approach.

GENERAL QUESTIONS

1. Identify the different and similar facets between the definitions of responsible leadership on one hand, and transformational, servant, and authentic leadership definitions, on the other.
2. To what extent can responsible leadership replace other leadership styles? Why?
3. To what extent can responsible leadership work effectively in all sport sectors? Why?
4. Provide examples of responsible leadership as a coach from your sport/s.
5. Provide examples of responsible leadership as a visionary from your sport/s.
6. Provide examples of responsible leadership as a servant from your sport/s.
7. Provide examples of responsible leadership as a citizen from your sport/s.
8. Provide examples of responsible leadership as a steward from your sport/s.
9. Provide examples of responsible leadership as a storyteller from your sport/s.
10. Provide examples of responsible leadership as an architect from your sport/s.
11. Provide examples of responsible leadership as a change agent from your sport/s.
12. List two weaknesses of the responsible leadership approach from your sport/s.
13. List two strengths of the responsible leadership approach from your sport/s.

OPEN DISCUSSION QUESTIONS

1. Describe the responsible leader in two words and compare your words with your colleagues' answers. Can you identify similarities and differences?
2. Discuss with your colleagues the qualities a responsible leader needs.
3. What roles of responsible leadership, do you think, most represent your leadership? Explain why.
4. Choose one of the responsible leadership roles and explain what you have chosen with examples from your experience or your sport.
5. Identify with your colleagues six key abilities of responsible agents in sport sectors. Can these abilities differ between the for-profit, non-profit, and public sport sectors? Why?

Case Study 16.1: Sebastian Coe

Sebastian Coe, often referred to as Lord Coe or Seb Coe, is a former track and field athlete and British politician. Coe set eight world records in middle-distance track events in 1979, and the 800 metres in 1981. He was one of the Britons to dominate middle-distance racing through the 1980s. Coe won four Olympic medals, including the 1,500 metres gold medal at the Olympic Games in 1980 and 1984. Coe became a work as a member of parliament for the Conservative Party from 1992 to 1997, following his retirement from athletics and became a Life Peer in 2000. Coe has occupied several sport leadership positions since the 2000s.

Lord Coe was elected twice as a vice-president of the International Association of Athletics Federations (IAAF) between 2007 and 2015. He has been president of the IAAF since 2015. Because of the leaking of the IAAF's doping files related to the Russia doping scandal under his presidency, Coe promised to tackle corruption and doping scandals. His planned reforms of athletics' world governing body received overwhelming backing (95 per cent) from member countries.

Coe was appointed the chairman of the London Organising Committee for the Olympic Games. The 2012 Summer Olympic Games was perceived as the most successful games of modern times and the then Prime Minister David Cameron thanked Lord Coe, for "lifting our hearts". This was due to the role Coe had played since the bidding stage to host the games, using his diplomatic, strategic, and cognitive skills, relational management and social competencies, and sport background and experience, as one of the greatest British athletes.

Following the successful Olympic Games in London, Coe was appointed chairman of the British Olympic Association in 2012. Cameron said that Coe would play a critical role after the 2012 games through inspiring young Britons to take up sport as well as preparing Team GB for future events. During his presidency, Team GB continued their success and the UK finished second in the Rio 2016 Olympic Games medal table.

Coe was appointed a member of the Tokyo 2020 Olympic Games Coordination Commission.

Questions

1. How would you describe the responsible leadership of Sebastian Coe? Explain your answer.
2. Because of his success in the 2012 Olympic Games, Lord Coe was thanked for 'lifting British hearts'. What does this mean for responsible leaders?
3. How would you describe the responsible leadership roles of Coe during his presidency of the IAAF?
4. Can you identify other responsible roles of Sebastian Coe?
5. Can we describe Coe's membership of the Tokyo 2020 Olympic Games Coordination Commission representing the Association of National Olympic Committees as an 'ethical principles-driven relationship' between leaders (Coe) and stakeholders (Olympic community)? Discuss this with colleagues.

Source: Based on International Olympic Committee. (n.d.). 'Lord Sebastian COE'. International Olympic Committee. [online]. Available at: https://olympics.com/ioc/lord-sebastian-coe; Team GB. (n.d.). 'Seb Coe'. Team GB. [online]. Available at: https://www.teamgb.com/athlete/seb-coe/y2puymX4czKjiuB07Xrqk; and UK Parliament. (n.d.). 'Lord Coe'. UK Parliament. [online]. Available at: https://members.parliament.uk/member/783/career.

SELF-ASSESSMENT 16.1: RESPONSIBLE LEADERSHIP ROLES

Match the following eight roles of responsible leadership to the eight statements.

(a) Visionary; (b) Steward; (c) Servant; (d) Citizen;
(e) Storyteller; (f) Coach; (g) Architect; (h) Change Agent.

1. David, as a football manager, understands himself as a custodian of social, moral, and environmental values in the team. He works on protecting what he is entrusted with.
2. Despite of the conflicts among players, confusion about roles, lack of trust between players, Lorraine has not only demonstrated she has an ethical obligation to the team, but also has succeeded in changing the attitudes and behaviours of all players for the common good and promoting the culture of commitment before the 2024 Olympic Games.
3. Although the club has had financial problems in the last four seasons, the new chief executive was able to gain the trust of investors and sponsors once she published the club's five-year plan and future actions to avoid past mistakes.
4. Simon and Charlotte, as former Olympic coaches, become social activists in sports. They believe in serving others in the field of sport. Given the sense of responsibility towards society, they take part in most development projects funded by Sport England. One of their activities is to work with less-experienced coaches to improve their abilities to become successful

coaches who can create a sustainable benefit and social change within the communities in which they live.

5. Ali is a chief executive of one of the leading firms organizing sport events in the Middle East. Given that he worked as a designer of leadership development programmes across the three sport sectors, Ali insists on bringing as many employees and managers together as he can in regular sessions to discuss current and future trends for the firm. He believes such sessions represent a golden opportunity to transfer leadership knowledge.

6. Most national governing bodies in the UK encourage their members to attend national and international conferences in sport leadership. Such conferences represent an opportunity to listen to speakers who are professional coaches and chief executives of international sport organizations.

7. Since Sara was elected as a head of one of the local authorities in the UK, she has begun work on monitoring racist incidents and discrimination in sport in cooperation with many sport governing bodies to create a healthy sport environment in which equality, diversity, and inclusivity are well-respected.

8. Because of the growing number of counterfeit items and products of poor quality of sporting goods, chief executive officers of some leading sporting goods manufacturers have begun making significant changes to their strategies for their brand protection, to help protect genuine goods and detect counterfeits in cooperation with many governments around the world.

Suggested Reading

Dugan, J.P. (2006). Involvement and Leadership: A Descriptive Analysis of Socially Responsible Leadership. *Journal of College Student Development*, 47(3), 335–343. https://doi.org/10.1353/csd.2006.0028.

Haski-Leventhal, D. (2021). *Strategic Corporate Social Responsibility: A Holistic Approach to Responsible and Sustainable Business*. (2nd ed.). London: Sage.

Maak, T. (2007). Responsible Leadership, Stakeholder Engagement, and the Emergence of Social Capital. *Journal of Business Ethics*, 74(4), 329–343. https://doi.org/10.1007/s10551-007-9510-5.

Maak, T. and Pless, N.M. (2006). Responsible Leadership in a Stakeholder Society–A Relational Perspective. *Journal of Business Ethics*, 66(1), 99–115. https://doi.org/10.1007/s10551-006-9047-z.

Megheirkouni, M. (2019). Responsible Leadership as a Mediator between Emotional Intelligence and Team Outcomes in Sport Organizations. *International Journal of Sport Management*, 20(1), 87–107.

Megheirkouni, M. Naylor, M. and Oshimi, D. (2022). Responsible Leadership as an Approach to Facilitate Olympic Work Engagement via Learning Organization. *Event Management*, 26(5), 993–1006. https://doi.org/10.3727/152599522X16419948390826.

Miska, C. and Mendenhall, M.E. (2018). Responsible Leadership: A Mapping of Extant Research and Future Directions. *Journal of Business Ethics*, 148(1), 117–134. https://doi.org/10.1007/s10551-015-2999-0.

Pless, N.M. (2007). Understanding Responsible Leadership: Role Identity and Motivational Drivers. *Journal of Business Ethics*, 74(4), 437–456. https://doi.org/10.1007/s10551-007-9518-x.

Pless, N. and Maak, T. (Eds.). (2021). *Responsible Leadership*. (2nd ed.). London: Routledge. https://doi.org/10.4324/b22741.

Voegtlin, C., Patzer, M. and Scherer, A.G. (2012). Responsible Leadership in Global Business: A New Approach to Leadership and Its Multi-Level Outcomes. *Journal of Business Ethics*, 105(1), 1–16. https://doi.org/10.1007/s10551-011-0952-4.

References

Antonacopoulou, E.P. and Bento, R. (2003). Methods of 'Learning Leadership': Taught and Experiential. In: Storey, J. (Ed.). *Leadership in Organizations: Current Issues in Leadership and Management Development*. Oxford: Blackwell. (81–102).

Bernstein, E., Raffaelli, R. and Margolis, J. (2014). *Leader-as-Architect: Alignment*. Harvard Business School Background Note, 415-039, October 2014. Available at: https://www.hbs.edu/faculty/Pages/item.aspx?num=48193.

Block, P. (2013). *Stewardship: Choosing Service over Self-Interest*. (2nd ed.). San Francisco, CA: Berrett-Koehler.

Boyatzis, R.E. (2011). Managerial and Leadership Competencies: A Behavioural Approach to Emotional, Social and Cognitive Intelligence. *Vision: The Journal of Business Perspective*, 15(2), 91–100. https://doi.org/10.1177/097226291101500202.

Donaldson, T. (1996). Values in Tension: Ethics Away from Home. *Harvard Business Review*, 74(5), 48–56. https://hbsp.harvard.edu/product/96502-PDF-ENG.

Dugan, J.P. (2006). *SRLS-Rev 2: The Second Revision of SRLS*. College Park, MD: National Clearinghouse for Leadership Programs.

Ehrhart, M.G. (2004). Leadership and Procedural Justice Climate as Antecedents of Unit-level Organizational Citizenship Behaviour. *Personnel Psychology*, 57(1), 61–94. https://doi.org/10.1111/j.1744-6570.2004.tb02484.x.

Football Association, The. (n.d.) 'The story of women's football in England'. *thefa.com* [online]. Available at: https://www.thefa.com/womens-girls-football/heritage/kicking-down-barriers.

Frankovelgia, C.C. and Riddle, D.D. (2010). Leadership Coaching. In: Van Velsor, E., McCauley, C. and Ruderman, M.N. (Eds.). *The Center for Creative Leadership Handbook of Leadership Development*. (3rd ed.). San Francisco, CA; Greensboro, NC: Jossey-Bass; Center for Creative Leadership. (125–146).

Friedman, M.T., Parent, M.M. and Mason, D.S. (2004). Building a Framework for Issues Management in Sport through Stakeholder Theory. *European Sport Management Quarterly*, 4(3), 170–190. https://doi.org/10.1080/16184740408737475.

Goethals, G.R., Sorenson, G.J. and Burns, J.M. (2004). *Encyclopedia of Leadership*. (4 Vols.). London: Sage.

Hernandez, M. (2008). Promoting Stewardship Behaviour in Organizations: A Leadership Model. *Journal of Business Ethics*, 80(1), 121–128. https://doi.org/10.1007/s10551-007-9440-2.

International Olympic Academy Participants Association (IOAPA). (2019). *Statutes*. Available at: https://ioapa.org/organization/statutes/.

Kolb, D.A. (2014). *Experiential Learning: Experience as the Source of Learning and Development*. (2nd ed.). Upper Saddle River, NJ: Pearson Education.

Maak, T. and Pless, N.M. (2006). Responsible Leadership in a Stakeholder Society: A Relational Perspective. *Journal of Business Ethics*, 66(1), 99–115. https://doi.org/10.1007/s10551-006-9047-z.

Megheirkouni, M. (2016). Leadership Development Methods and Activities: Content, Purposes, and Implementation. *Journal of Management Development*, 35(2), 237–260. https://doi.org/10.1108/JMD-09-2015-0125.

Megheirkouni, M. (2017a). Leadership Competencies: Qualitative Insight into Non-Profit Sport Organisations. *International Journal of Public Leadership*, 13(3), 166–181. https://doi.org/10.1108/IJPL-11-2016-0047/.

Megheirkouni, M. (2017b). Leadership Styles and Organizational Learning in UK For-Profit and Non-Profit Sports Organizations. *International Journal of Organizational Analysis*, 25(4), 596–612. https://doi.org/10.1108/IJOA-07-2016-1042.

Megheirkouni, M. (2019). Responsible Leadership as a Mediator between Emotional Intelligence and Team Outcomes in Sport Organizations. *International Journal of Sport Management*, 20(1), 87–107.

Megheirkouni, M. and Roomi, M.A. (2017). Women's Leadership Development in Sport Settings: Factors Influencing the Transformational Learning Experience of Female Managers. *European Journal of Training and Development*, 41(5), 467–484. https://doi.org/10.1108/EJTD-12-2016-0085.

Parent, M.M. (2008). Evolution and Issue Patterns for Major-Sport-Event Organizing Committees and Their Stakeholders. *Journal of Sport Management*, 22(2), 135–164. https://doi.org/10.1123/jsm.22.2.135.

Pless, N.M. (2007). Understanding Responsible Leadership: Role Identity and Motivational Drivers. *Journal of Business Ethics*, 74(4), 437–456. https://doi.org/10.1007/s10551-007-9518-x.

Pless, N.M. and Maak, T. (2011). Responsible Leadership: Pathways to the Future. *Journal of Business Ethics*, 98(S1), 3–13. https://doi.org/10.1007/s10551-011-1114-4.

Pless, N.M., Maak, T. and Stahl, G.K. (2011). Developing Responsible Global Leaders through International Service-Learning Programs: The Ulysses Experience. *Academy of Management Learning and Education*, 10(2), 237–260. https://doi.org/10.5465/amle.10.2.zqr237.

Pless, N.M. and Schneider, R. (2005). Towards Developing Responsible Global Leaders. The Ulysses Experience. In: Pless, N.M. and Maak, T. (Eds.). *Responsible Leadership*. London: Routledge. (213–226). https://doi.org/10.4324/9780203002247.

Ting, S. and Hart, E.W. (2004). Formal Coaching. In: McCauley, C.D. and Van Velsor, E. (Eds.). *The Center for Creative Leadership Handbook of Leadership Development*. (2nd ed.). San Francisco, CA; Greensboro, NC: Jossey-Bass; Center for Creative Leadership. (116–150).

Tyree, T.M. (1998). Designing an Instrument to Measure the Socially Responsible Leadership Using the Social Change Model of Leadership Development. University of Maryland, College Park ProQuest Dissertations Publishing. 9836493. ProQuest: https://www.proquest.com/openview/453448079f40bda554f326e40f4cd460/1.

Voegtlin, C. (2011). Development of a Scale Measuring Discursive Responsible Leadership. *Journal of Business Ethics*, 98(S1), 57–73. https://doi.org/10.1007/s10551-011-1020-9.

Walters, G. and Tacon, R. (2013). Stakeholder Engagement in European Football. In: Paramio-Salcines, J.L., Babiak, K. and Walters. G. (Eds.). *Routledge Handbook of Sport and Corporate Social Responsibility*. London: Routledge. (236–248).

Walumbwa, F.O., Hartnell, C.A. and Oke, A. (2010). Servant Leadership, Procedural Justice Climate, Service Climate, Employee Attitudes, and Organizational Citizenship Behaviour: A Cross-Level Investigation. *Journal of Applied Psychology*, 95(3), 517–529. https://doi.org/10.1037/a0018867.

Part IV

SPORT LEADERSHIP DEVELOPMENT

17 LEARNING AND DEVELOPMENT

Learning Outcomes

After reading this chapter, you will be able to:

- Define concepts about learning and development
- Determine the differences and similarities between learning theories and approaches
- Identify perceived needs for leadership learning and development
- Explain and distinguish between leadership development methods and activities
- Evaluate the outcome of leadership learning development

INTRODUCTION

Learning lies at the heart of any sport organization regardless of its sector or geographical location. If the word 'learning' is used in its widest sense, learning occurs when people are aware of the potential to learn and willing to share that learning. Individuals, through learning, can acquire skills and knowledge, and thus build the experience that enables them to complete required tasks or roles effectively. Learning enables individuals and sport organizations to fulfil personal goals and organizational objectives. Learning can be a tangible or intangible process. This chapter defines the concepts of training, education, and development and introduces the leading theories and approaches on learning. Perceived needs for leadership learning and development are discussed, followed by leading leadership development methods and activities. Leadership learning and development is evaluated.

EDUCATION, TRAINING, AND DEVELOPMENT

Broadly, Nadler, and Nadler (1990) gathered the notions of education, training, and development together: education is learning as preparation not related to a specific current or future job; training is learning related to a current job; and development is learning for growth and not related to a specific current or future job.

EDUCATION

Education is perceived as a means to legitimate pedagogical action. Education enables young people and adults to understand the environment in which they live and the ideal way to contribute to it. It involves learning about laws, policies, culture, and skills that are key for personal development and communication (Manpower Services Commission, 1981). Unlike training, education is considerably broader in its scope. For the sport context here, there are several programmes at undergraduate and postgraduate levels which specialize in sport-orientated topics: human resource management in sport, sport management, sport leadership and sport business. Students learn from these topics and may go for further research. As a result, theoretical knowledge, theories, approaches, case studies, and assessments enable students to become qualified and have a strong base for any sport leadership positions at national and international levels.

TRAINING

Training refers to the planning process of acquiring and developing particular behaviours, capabilities, knowledge, and attitudes through instructional activities for better performance in current work, and thus to satisfy the needs of the organization, regardless of its sector type (Taylor et al, 2015; Wilson, 2005). In other words, training is essentially about making learning happen in a sport organization, and it can target all individuals (e.g. athletes, employees, board members, volunteers, coaches, and leaders) in sport organizations at national and international levels. Training can be divided into two types: formal training that refers to planned courses with a specific aim and objectives that target specific managers or leaders in specific roles in sport organizations and can be delivered either in classrooms or actions in both off-job and on-job training. Informal training, on the other hand, refers to ad hoc, situational, training that occurs in action, but without specific or pre-arranged aims or objectives.

In the sport business environment, learning occurs naturally as a by-product of everyday experience (action learning), but in the case of large-scale sport events, such as Olympic Games, everyday experience may be imprecise, given the nature of this kind of event, with exceptions such as volunteers and staff who prepare, for example, for the Opening Ceremony of an Olympic Games. Cities often host an Olympic Games just once or with a significant gap between each hosting: for example, London in 1908, 1948, and 2012, one of the few to host the Games three times. That implies that the training of leaders and managers for better performance in large-scale sport events may occur over many years and in many stages, through which those managers and leaders learn and build their experience, so as to make their selection to lead or manage the National Organising Committee well-considered (see the next section on development). Thus, the notion of training must be understood and carefully used because leader and manager training does not occur through immediate action learning in case of large-scale sport events.

DEVELOPMENT

One of the primary reasons that sport organizations invest or support development of volunteers, employees, board members, managers, and leaders is to enhance and protect their human capital (Day, 2000). Development can have general or specific scopes. In its most general sense, development is defined as "the modification of the biosphere and the application of the human, financial, living and non-living resources to satisfy man's need and improve the quality of human life" (IUCN, 1980, para 1.4). But the notion of development can also be more precise, as it can refer to the growth of an individual's or group's ability through learning, using development programmes including elements of planned study and experience, and supported by coaches, experts, and consultants. From a large-scale organizational perspective, when investing in development, the emphasis typically can be on: (1) individual-based knowledge, behaviours, and capabilities associated with formal sport leadership responsibilities and roles, regardless of whether the role is at the national or international level; and (2) building networked relationships among individuals inside the sport organization and outside its boundaries that will enhance cooperation, experience, and resource exchanges, and thus create organizational value.

LEARNING THEORIES AND APPROACHES

Various theories and approaches make a useful contribution in sport leadership development research and practice. However, each presents only a partial insight into individuals' learning. That implies that there is a need for a variety of perspectives to appreciate sport leadership development as a field of practice. Having mentioned the need to have a variety of perspectives of learning, we begin by highlighting selected theories that help us understand learning and how it is practised.

BEHAVIOURISM

The key ideas and theories of what is known as behaviourism go back to the theoretical development in the first half of the 20th century. Behaviourism developed as a response to psychoanalytic theories, which behaviourists held were unmeasurable and thus not open to scientific investigation. Some psychologists' question about what we can actually see and measure was answered with: behaviour. The behaviourist idea is that learning comes about as a response to a stimulus. Behavioural psychologists such as Ivan Pavlov (1849–1936), Edward Thorndike (1874–1949), Clark L. Hull (1884–1952) and B.F. Skinner (1904–2001) assumed a specific, machine-like response of people to a specific stimulus that is reinforced by feedback: correct responses receive positive reward, incorrect responses receive negative punishment.

Undoubtedly, behaviourism as a learning theory has a resonance with leadership development initiatives (Allen, 2007). Specifically, when we design or implement leadership development programmes in sport settings, state, for-profit, and non-profit, for developing specific sport leadership skills for a particular role and position, this proposes that sport managers and leaders can be trained to the specification of functions and roles until successful. But to do so, assessment of the perceived needs is required. This occurs through identifying gaps that can help achieve objectives in the sport organization.

Regarding assessment, behaviourist thinking in learning relies on the role of reinforcement as feedback. However, feedback does not necessarily lead sport managers and leaders to practice new skills or even transfer what they have already learnt into practice. This is due to internal and external factors in sport organizations, such as organizational thinking, pressure, culture, managers' or leaders' characteristics, and differences in leadership behaviours. However, some experienced (and inexperienced) sport managers and leaders may not accept any feedback from others, as this feedback is often interpreted as criticism (VandeWalle, 2004). Two possible ways of reinforcing learning in general and via feedback in particular, are through the formal use of feedback for developmental and assessment purposes and the use of experts as mentors who can provide corrective feedback to managers and leaders, and thus enable them to learn from their mistakes.

COGNITIVISM

The development of the cognitive approach was a reaction against the dominance of behaviourism. Unlike behaviourism, cognitive psychology focuses on the internal aspects of learning. Cognitivism explains learning in terms of memory and associated cognitive processes. Specifically, proponents of cognitivism posit that learning is like information processing in a computer game (a modern version of the metaphor) where inputs are registered through the senses, then processed in some way prior to storage in memory, to be recalled as required when dealing with particular situations. This could occur through, for example, simulation-style game play such as Electronic Arts' *FIFA 16*, released in 2015, notable as the first in their series to include women, for skills such as choices in acceleration, aggression, composure, tactical awareness, ball control, standing tackle, sliding tackle, crossing, curve, dribbling, and balance. In other words, learning, according to cognitivists, is viewed as the acquisition of knowledge and the development of decision-making or problem-solving skills which can then inform action taken in new tasks and situations (Derry, 1996; Borthick et al, 2003). The term 'schema' is used to explain how information is organized as knowledge which can be activated as necessary (Sadler-Smith, 2006). In this way, football managers can build their cognitive schema to organize information in a variety of ways, and thus decision-making schema represent decisions according to situations. For example, how does a football team manager deal with a situation when a red card is issued against three players in the team, or when the main goalkeeper is injured in the first ten minutes of the final match of a FIFA World Cup.

Of course, sport managers or leaders can choose particular ways of thinking, given that they are more connected to certain features of the surrounding environment than others. This, in turn, can tell them what they are (more) interested in, and what they are (more) motivated to do. Psychologists have developed tests that help managers and leaders in all fields measure how to gather,

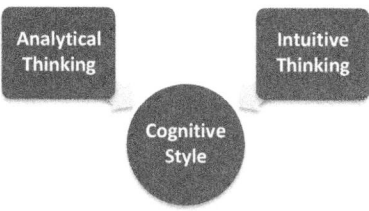

Figure 17.1 Components of cognitive style.

Source: Adapted fromAllinson, C.W. and Hayes, J. (1996). The Cognitive Style Index: A Measure of Intuition Analysis for Organisational Research. *Journal of Management Studies*, 33(1), 119–135.

process, and evaluate information. Many dimensions of cognitive style have been highlighted in the literature (e.g. Armstrong, 1999; Coffield et al, 2004; Nickerson et al, 1985; Ornstein, 1977). Allinson and Hayes (1996) argue that these dimensions essentially refer to the rational and intuitive sides of the individual. In keeping with established terminology these modes of cognition are labelled 'analytic' and 'intuitive', respectively (Figure 17.1). Allinson and Hayes (1996) developed one of the most well-known tests, Cognitive Style Index (CSI) for use in organizational contexts.

For example, analytic thinking by elite team managers and coaches, or even the sport governing bodies, will result in structured decision-making after an Olympic Games based on systematic review of the poor team results and their causes, which is followed by systematic steps to find appropriate solutions. A step-by-step approach is preferred, rather than grand gestures, such as dismissing the entire team structure and 'going back to the drawing board'. In contrast, intuitive thinking by elite team managers and coaches during the critical period of a World Cup final may result in more open steps towards decision-making processes based on sharing ideas to reach creative and innovative solutions for achieving the best possible results. Additionally, sport managers and leaders may use holistic information processing that takes place through the interaction of both thinking styles. Of course, these thinking styles are as vital when things go well – to discover, evaluate, maintain, develop, and modify what has worked.

SOCIAL LEARNING

Social learning extends the notion of reinforcement and was founded in 1977 by Albert Bandura (1925–2021), who developed the contemporary form of social learning theory. While behaviourism is concerned with stimulus–response and cognitivism is concerned with the individual's processing of information, social learning is about learning by observation of other people's behaviour. Social learning theory sees human behaviour as a reciprocal interaction between three factors: cognition, behaviour, and environment (Bandura, 1978; Lajoie and Azevedo, 2006). Bandura (1978) suggests that environment influences behaviours, and individuals partly produce the environment condition by their behaviour, contributing to creating the social milieu which arises in their transactions every day. Social learning, therefore, as a social activity, is concerned with understanding how social influence can change individuals' feelings, thoughts, attitudes, and actions through the interaction between the person and others. Charbonneau et al (2001) addressed leadership development in a social learning model. They found that adolescents tend to mirror behaviours displayed by their parents and thus display such behaviours with their peers. Overall, social learning has implications for leadership and its development in sport settings. Sport managers and leaders can make use of the mistakes and successes of other managers and leaders through observation and interpretation. This way of learning is widely implemented in the business world, being considered an effective and economic activity for most organizations.

SITUATED LEARNING

The concept of situated learning has evolved from the field of education. Lave and Wenger (1991) developed situated learning theory to explain how learning takes place within a social framework of participation. Individuals participate in communities as 'naive' learners about practice; then, interaction and communication with experienced and skilled individuals leads to moving towards another level of learning called 'legitimate peripheral participation'. Gradually, a person will embrace the required knowledge and skills to move towards full participation in communities of practice. The locus of learning is 'action-in-context'. This debate takes us to Social Learning Theory, where learning occurs through observations and interpretation. However, it is also correct that face-to-face interactions or communications and social network (daily actions) have positive implications for excellence learning (Sadler-Smith, 2006). For example, students and individuals in training sessions and MBA courses in sport directorship/leadership learn from open discussion of case studies and telling stories about leadership practices based on real events or situations of particular sport organizations. Similarly, sandwich placements (a block of 'on-site' learning within a course) enable learners to learn not only from observations but also from everyday actions in particular situations in the workplace.

EXPERIENTIAL LEARNING

Sport management and leadership development as a process of 'learning-from-experience' is based on the precept that learning does not take place through short-term or long-term courses in classrooms, but rather, in its general sense, does take place when individuals are engaged in formal or informal daily activities, in both their work and personal lives. The idea of experience in learning can be traced back to the American educationalist John Dewey (1859–1952), who focused on experiential education in 1938. His view was based on the concept that "there is an intimate and necessary relation between the processes of actual experience and education" (Dewey, 1938/1997: 7). Another writer that focused on experiential learning is the humanist psychotherapist Carl Rogers (1902–1987), whose works focused on the personal involvement and personal experience of individuals as the main influence on their learning activities. The four

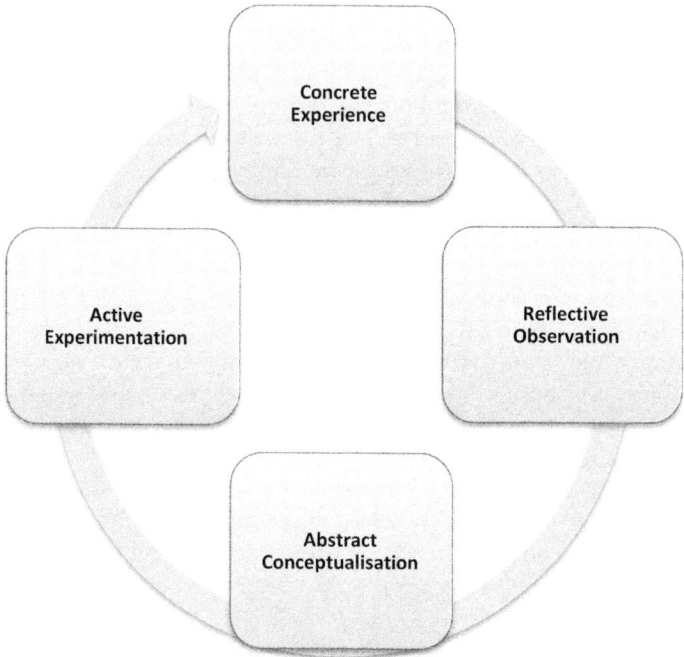

Figure 17.2 Kolb's experiential learning cycle.
Source: Adapted from Kolb, D.A. (1984). *Experiential Learning: Experience as the Source of Learning and Development.* London: FT Press.

main principles of Roger's experiential learning are: (1) the personal involvement of the learner, (2) the learner-initiated activity of the active learner, (3) the self-assessment and self-evaluation processes of the learner, and (4) the pervasive effects on the learner of the learning event (Rogers, 1969). One of the most well-known and influential models in human resource development and leadership and management learning and development is rooted in the work of David Kolb, whose model views learning as "the process whereby knowledge is created through the transformation of experience" (Kolb, 1984: 41), shown in Figure 17.2.

Kolb's experiential learning cycle involves a four-stage cycle of concrete experience, reflective observation, abstract conceptualization, and active experimentation. The cycle provides an explanation of how learning occurs. The concrete experience stage emphasizes feeling as opposed to thinking, where learning occurs through personal involvement with people in daily situations. Reflective observation focuses on learners understanding the ideas and situations through observation, and learning occurs from effectively reflecting on what learners see. Abstract conceptualization emphasizes thinking and use of logic and is concerned with building general theories. Active experimentation focuses on dynamically influencing people and changing situations into tangible results. It emphasizes practical applications as opposed to feeling and logic.

A good example of how experiential learning can be applied in sport settings is learning from coaching courses that aim to improve coaching skills and knowledge in most sports. The participants in these courses are likely to go round the learning cycle several times, using several methods used in courses such as self-assessment, reading, learning theoretical tactics, watching matches, making and presenting notes and comments on particular situations in matches, receiving feedback, and analysing and reflecting on their practice in real situations. Whether by repetition or variation, participants' journeys around the learning cycle enable them to reinforce and extend what they have learnt. Participants can use the self-assessment Learning Style Inventory (LSI) to enable them to identify their preferred learning style within the different stages in the cycle. Kolb first developed the LSI in 1971, which is now in version 4 as the Kolb Learning Style Inventory (KLSI) (Kolb and Kolb, 2013).

Learning style refers to the way in which individuals adapt to learn. Unsurprisingly, different people have different learning needs and learn in different ways. This requires input from consultants, experts, and designers of sport leadership and management development programmes to take into account learning styles because this has positive and negative implications for learners. People can learn better and more quickly when teaching techniques used in leadership development programmes match their preferred learning styles. However, this does not mean that using only a preferred style is good for learning, as it can create dependency on a style.

Kolb's experiential learning cycle was the base for the work of Peter Honey and Alan Mumford (Honey and Mumford, 1989), who designed their own Learning Styles Questionnaire (LSQ) to identify individuals' learning styles as 'activist', 'reflector', 'theorist', and 'pragmatist'. They explain these styles as follows:

- **Activists** learn best from doing everything without any planning and involving themselves in new experiences. Activists are known as open-minded, 'try anything once', being 'thrown into things', resisting repetition, and resisting passive activities.
- **Reflectors** learn best from observing and reflecting. They are effective at collecting information, analysing what happens and why, through looking at issues from different perspectives. Reflector individuals in any leadership and management positions in sport organizations are likely to need more time than others to make a decision or solve a problem. Reflectors are known as being cautious, and good listeners and observers.
- **Theorists** are good at building a theory on the basis of analysis and understanding ideas and conceptions, thus integrating different pieces of information about situations and problems. Theorists' strengths lie in building concepts for why things occur. They may learn from a theory, a model, or a framework, linking theory with actions based on logic, and resisting ambiguous and unstructured activities.
- **Pragmatists** are those who like to use what they have learnt and work out whether they can apply it in real situations. They tend to plan how to transfer what they have learnt into practice. They are pragmatic, showing interest only in information they can use in practice. They are practical individuals and learn best when there is an obvious link between the subject matter and real situations.

TRANSFER OF LEARNING AND DEVELOPMENT

Here, we consider the link between learning and development and performance. The purpose of manager and leader learning and development (individually or collectively) in sport organizations is to acquire required behaviours and capabilities that enable them to improve their performance, but may also enable them to develop and grow in their career. This link encourages creating and establishing focused training initiatives and programmes based on a systematic learning and development programme cycle to support individuals, jobs, and organizations. However, learning and development initiatives based on such cycles may not necessarily be most appropriate to meet the needs of sport organizations, given the dynamic changes in sport environments at the national and international levels. Additionally, the application of such learning and development initiatives may not be applicable to all sport organizations in all contexts without modification (e.g. Torrington et al, 2014).

For a better understanding of the transfer process of learning and development in current sport environments, there is a need to describe the potential application of learning and development initiatives within a systematic learning and development programme cycle (outlined in Figure 17.3).

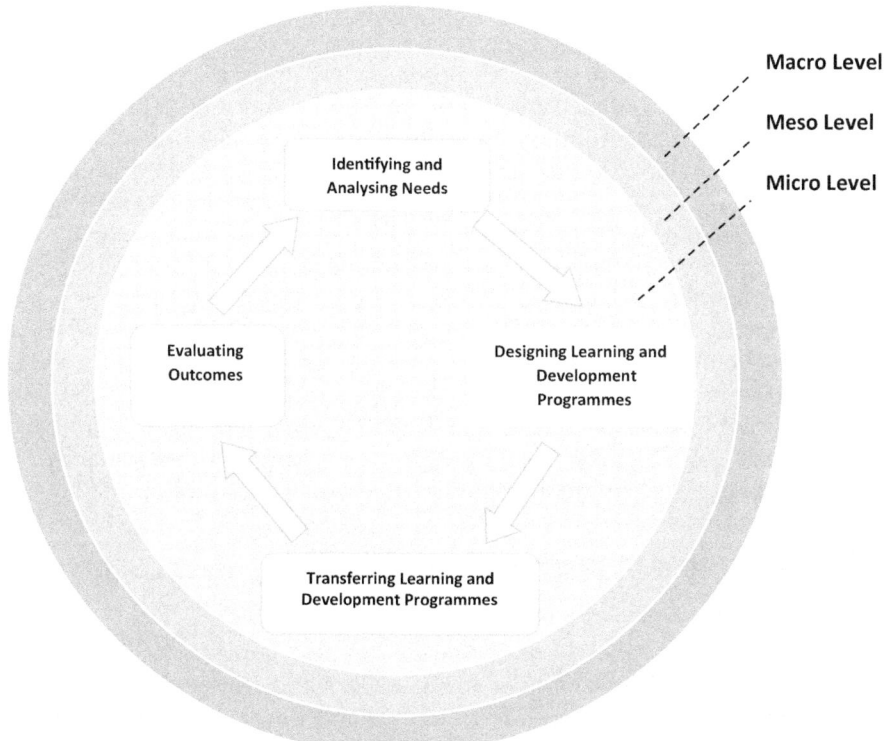

Figure 17.3 Systematic learning and development programme cycle.

IDENTIFYING AND ANALYSING LEARNING AND DEVELOPMENT NEEDS

Learning and development need to be based on a full understanding of what should be done and how and why it should be done. The purpose of learning and development activities is defined by identifying and analysing learning and development needs. The concept of identifying and analysing learning and development needs can be conducted at multiple levels (McGehee and Thayer, 1961). These levels are:

- The *Organizational level* refers to learning and development needs by identifying and analysing where learning and development should be utilized in the sport organization.
- The *Job level* refers to learning and development needs by analysing information about a particular role or task in order to identify the leadership behaviour and capabilities required to carry out the task, role, or job correctly.
- The *Individual level* refers to learning and development needs by analysing and identifying the learning and development needs of each individual employee to help them perform effectively.

Learning or development needs analysis is often defined as the process of identifying the learning weaknesses resulting from the difference between what it is and what it should be. However, we note that 'weakness' suggests a deficit model of development, rather than a positive view of improvement. The learning and development needed to fill the gap can be specified. The focus is on developing existing or adopting new behaviours and capabilities to deal with internal and external challenges. The general strategy of sport organizations and the event industry indicate the types of behaviours and capabilities needed, who should be targeted (operational, middle, or top level), how many people will be involved, and how long learning and development processes will need. Qualitative and quantitative data are valuable to gather views of all people in sport organizations and the event industry on what they need to learn. However, some people who are interviewed may not be able to put what they want into context. Therefore, the interview questions must target specific situations in the workplace, thus enabling people to give detail on the work, its strengths and weaknesses (or challenges), and what should be done to improve performance at all levels. This may give a summative picture of learning and development needs.

DESIGNING AND IMPLEMENTING LEARNING AND DEVELOPMENT PROGRAMMES

The fundamental considerations in the design and implementation of learning and development programmes for managers and leaders in sport organizations and the event industry are to understand how people learn and how the internal and external environments influence the learning and development process. According to Megheirkouni (2016), leadership development methods and activities can be designed not only to target different purposes, but also to be implemented in different ways (formal or informal learning). Many factors determine the design of learning and development programmes such as, but not limited to, cost, development strategy, organization size, and management level. Specifically, such factors can determine whether a learning and development programme takes place in a structured and intentional way. A good example of formal learning is the Women and Leadership Development Programme that was designed to target women in middle management in several sport organizations in the UK, where learning took place in training rooms and classrooms (Megheirkouni and Roomi, 2017).

TRANSFERRING LEARNING AND DEVELOPMENT

The transfer of learning and development involves the application of the lessons learnt in classrooms and training sessions into different settings. This is one of the major concerns for sport organizations and the event industry today, because sport managers and leaders are expected to make a real impact on subordinates, sport organizations, and event industry in terms of performance, effectiveness, and productivity, among other things. Transfer of learning and development can be conducted at the individual, job, and organizational levels. This is widely affected by development and organizational strategies. For example, strategy might target only the individual level, and then the focus will be on people in the organization. It is worth noting that organizational needs mean the transfer of learning and development at several levels, not only, for example, to people at the top or middle levels, but also the transmission of learning and development to others in the organization (Dixon, 2000). Positive transfer occurs when learning that has taken place on one task helps in the learning of another. For instance, learning to drive one type of Formula 1 racing car helps in learning to drive another because the systems on a Formula 1 car work in essentially the same way as others.

Yip and Wilson (2010) proposed three levels for transfer of learning and development:

1. **Organizational level**: Learning and development can be transferred from what learners have learnt in the classroom, training sessions, or experience by codifying the learning as a means to transform general practice.
2. **Group level**: Learning and development can be transferred to other people in sport organizations and the event industry when learners share what they have learnt in classrooms and training sessions with others, and the team or group reflects collectively on what has been shared.
3. **Individual level**: Learning and development can be transferred when the learner abstracts the outcomes of the application of leadership principles through enhancing knowledge in multiple settings.

EVALUATING THE OUTCOMES

Determining whether the action of the sport leader is attributable to particular learning and development initiatives or whether it is a function of other unknown variables is not easy. Simply knowing how to analyse, identify, design, and transfer learning and development needs is not enough. There is also an essential need to evaluate what has been done because this gives a big picture of strengths and weaknesses. If the evaluation reveals that the outcome of learning and development did not achieve the required results, there will be a need to return to the different steps of the learning and development cycle and make necessary revisions. Goldstein (1993: 181) defined evaluation as "the systematic collection of descriptive and judgemental information necessary to make effective decisions related to the selection, adoption, value, and modification of various instructional activities". Nonetheless, evaluation is problematic perhaps because it is perceived as being difficult to do well. When the aim is to achieve greater precision, we might need to employ the validation techniques to measure accurately whether specific learning objectives and required outcomes have been completely achieved (Newby, 1992). According to Sadler-Smith (2006), learning and development should meet internal and external validation criteria:

- *Internal validity* is concerned with whether learning and development has met the objectives that were set.
- *External validity* is concerned with whether the objectives and outcome of learning and development are realistically based on an accurate understanding of the learning needs.

LEADERSHIP DEVELOPMENT METHODS AND ACTIVITIES

This section addresses leadership development methods and activities in sport business, with more focus on the sport event industry for two reasons: First, the idea of sport leadership development methods and activities in sport business organizations is still open despite some attempts (Megheirkouni and Roomi, 2017). Second, we believe that an understanding of leadership development methods and activities in the context of sport events can give a wider picture of the perceived needs of leadership and its development from different perspectives other than the context of a sport organization.

Sport events have become increasingly popular vehicles for economic, social, cultural, political, and environmental benefits for host cities or countries over the last 40 years. Specifically, the organizing committees of sport events attempt to present these events as beneficial to gain new facilities, investments, and regeneration to the hosting country or city in the short and long terms (e.g. Talavera et al, 2019). Leadership and management in the sport and event industries deal with a multitude of partners and other stakeholders. These stakeholders, including individuals, groups/teams, and organizations, regardless of sector type, may affect or be affected by the event itself or the environment surrounding the event. Stakeholders who have a variety of needs due to their involvement in the sport events expect certain returns from those who are in authority (Parent, 2008).

Clearly, working with all stakeholders in sport events, such as Olympic Games, needs different leadership behaviours and capabilities to ensure completing the required tasks and roles effectively in that event (e.g. Kaplan, 2005).

Thus, it might be argued that a successful sport event is greatly affected by leadership and management (Parent and Séguin, 2008; Megheirkouni, 2018). Therefore, a variety of leadership development methods and activities should be seriously considered to meet leadership and management needs.

For better understanding leadership and management development in the sport and event industries, we must not disregard the nature of sport events, such as size, type, structure of organizing committees, and human resources used for the event, so as to help us understand the importance of learning and development for the organizing committees and sub-committees of large-scale sport events. As described by Day:

> Leadership development can be through as an integration strategy by helping people understand how to relate to others, coordinate their efforts, build commitments, and develop extended social networks, by applying self-understanding to social and organisational imperatives.
>
> (Marquardt, Day, 2000: 586)

BEST PRACTICES

As there is currently relatively little research in leadership development in the sport and event industries, a brief examination of leadership development methods and activities in the leadership literature is presented here. Comprehensive reviews of leadership development methods and activities have been provided by several studies (e.g. Conger, 1992; Cacioppe, 1998; Conger and Benjamin, 1999; Fulmer et al, 2000; Hartley and Hinksman, 2003; Hernez-Broome and Hughes, 2004). Leadership development methods and activities have also been derived from the extant research informed especially by reviews and meta-analyses (e.g. Collins, 2001; Day, 2000). According to these and other reviews and meta-analyses, the leading leadership development methods and activities that have been consistently accepted in the literature include 360-degree feedback, coaching, job assignments, action learning, job rotation, and networking (Megheirkouni, 2016), described in the following sections.

Within leadership development methods feedback is an important element of most learning processes, acting as a significant instructional design in training and development programmes (Goldstein and Ford, 2001) and an important element during instructional delivery by increasing learning and improving its transfer (Schoenfeldt, 1996).

360-DEGREE FEEDBACK

This specifically feedback-orientated method is based on collecting views about an individual's behaviour and the influence such behaviour has from people of all kinds around the individual, like a leader, colleagues, team members, and external stakeholders. An important assumption of 360-degree feedback is that performance differs in different contexts and leader behaviour also differs with different constituencies. Feedback processes via multiple sources serves to identify some of the differences these multiple sources have in observing different aspects of an individual's performance. Megheirkouni (2016) argues that 360-degree feedback helps leaders to understand the whole organization. It is important to realize that the use of 360-degree feedback by the leaders of large-scale sport events, to collect data about all committees before, during, and after a particular event, requires considering the purpose of using 360-degree feedback. Empirical research conducted by Jhun et al (2012) revealed that managers who initially performed poorly showed more performance improvement than those whose initial performance was good. Besides, a significant improvement of performance was also revealed when the purpose of an upward feedback method changed from developmental to administrative purposes on performance. That implies that the 360-degree feedback method can be used in sport business and event management for developmental and assessment purposes.

NETWORKING

Networking is one of the activities and methods classified within experiential learning. Networking refers to a supportive system in which information and services can be shared among people and groups, and its benefits can be reviewed by relationships, opportunities, and resources (Lawson, 2008). Ibarra (1995) emphasizes the importance of networking and its role in accomplishing tasks and developing personally and professionally. Three types of networking are suggested by Ibarra. First, task networks that help accomplish tasks and facilitate exchange of resources. Second, career networks that are related to self-development because of their role in facilitating the leader information about career progress by offering career advice, mentoring, helping leaders determine the key developmental assignments, facilitating career enhancing visibility. Third, friendship/social support networks which are based on closeness and trust, facilitating work accomplishments for leaders. Day and O'Connor (2003) argue that leadership development involves three types of capital: human, social, and system. In this regard, Day (2000) states that networking activity can provide a wider range of contacts, both inside and outside the organization, which, in turn, enables the leader to have a greater range of information, perspectives, and views. In sport settings, networking activities of the board members and the presidents of sport governing bodies at the national level with their counterparts at the international level help build their leadership experience over time due to the ongoing communication. A study investigated how relationship marketing, specifically networking, was used to create sustainable event impacts in the context of pre-event training for the Sydney 2000 Olympic Games. The results suggested that a relationship-based approach to a major sport event can expand short-term impacts for hosts into longer-term opportunities for tourism, investment, and trade relations (O'Brien and Gardiner, 2006).

ACTION LEARNING

Most studies that address best practice for leadership development conclude that action learning is one of the leading activities in leadership development.

In this process, learning occurs through the process of approaching problems from a learning view, where participants solve problems and develop in the process. For example, in an Olympic Games, reporting a 'tame' problem to the organizing committee needs a quick action to solve it, and thus leaders or managers who work on solving the problem are likely to develop their capability through the process of solving the problem. Marquardt sees action learning activity as:

> A powerful problem-solving tool that has the amazing capacity to simultaneously build successful leaders, teams, and organisations; it is a process that involves a small group working on real problems, taking action, and learning as individuals, as a team, and an organisation while doing so.
>
> (2000: 2)

Reynolds (1998) found that reflection in action learning can provide a deeper awareness when working in collaboration with others – using 'social power', rather than questions and answers focusing on the individual. This can be seen in the organizing committee and sub-committees of large-scale sport events. Thus, a deeper awareness of action learning might increase the individual's capacity to learn although they may not be engaged in a particular type of learning (Gibson and Earley, 2007).

COACHING

The coaching method is used in supporting change by improving individuals' performance with specific leadership competencies and specific problem-solving, and it is seen as "a practical, goal-focused form of personal, one-on-one learning" (Hall et al, 1999: 40). There are two types of coaching methods in the literature (Bluckert, 2005). One type focuses on learning and development to improve performance, while the other focuses on change. Generally, these types of coaching propose that coaches must have different skills and experience (see Laske, 2007). Coaching is, in a sense, the epitome of both off-the-job and on-the-job learning. For many things, we can note that coaching helps staff, volunteers, and members: (1) understand social, political, and cultural contexts to develop behavioural skills that fit the dominant culture; (2) facilitate experience in terms of guiding individuals through a transient organization culture; and (3) help staff, members, and volunteers become more committed and confident (Gray, 2007; Hall et al, 1999).

JOB ASSIGNMENTS

Job assignment activity is one of the experiential learning types. There are various of types of job assignments, including job transitions, e.g. proving yourself with unfamiliar responsibilities; task-related characteristics, e.g. creating change; and obstacles, e.g. adverse business conditions (Day, 2000). Byham et al (2002) argue that for an effective use of job assignments as a leadership development activity, various questions should be considered. These questions include whether it provides challenges that individuals need to function effectively, develops the competencies required, provides insights into specific traits or behaviours that can help to keep the individual on track, provides experience in different organization areas, provides a realistic (pre)view of executive life, provides exposure to different scenarios, gives top managers a chance to observe individuals, and asks whether a given assignment fits the individual's needs. It is worth noting that if the aim of a job assignment activity is not a developmental purpose, the major focus of this activity will be 'performance', which means that learning from mistakes and failure may or may not be considered as a source of development.

JOB ROTATION

Leadership job rotation is used to develop individuals who have a leadership role across all organizational structures by placing them in new jobs or different work settings under the guidance of new superiors in the same or other sport organizations. Leadership job rotation helps leaders increase their portfolio of knowledge and skills. Avolio (2004) states that some of the specific benefits of job rotation include seeing problems from another unit's perspective, owning knowledge about the independent linkages between units, and a developing a framework for understanding problems from multiple perspectives. The outcomes of job rotation include: improving knowledge and skills, a stronger belief in the value of viewing problems from different perspectives, higher mutual respect for other functions, and the need for collaboration (Campion et al, 1994). For example, prior to an Olympic Games, managers rotate across several divisions or committees. Managers can rotate for two years in total prior to the event, including a few months in each of the following committees: communication and public affairs, games operations, venues and infrastructure, villages and games services, transport, human resource, culture, ceremonies, and education. Certainly, those managers will improve their portfolio of knowledge and skills required to run an Olympic Games effectively.

EVALUATION OF LEADERSHIP LEARNING AND DEVELOPMENT

Research on leadership learning and development has various weaknesses to consider. One noted criticism is that in the past 25 years there has been a significant shift towards more informal leadership development methods and activities, such as on-the-job, action learning approaches to management development. Mabey and Finch-Lees (2008) identified several reasons for this shift, including the delayering of organizations, the withdrawal of centralized human resource career management, cost-cutting, more entrepreneurial styles of management, and the advent of more transactional psychological contracts between employer and employee. Consequently, sport organizations are increasingly conferring coaching interventions on their senior management level in recognition of the need for individualized support in crises and difficult times in sport organizations. This proposes that formal leadership development methods and activities are not available to all managers and leaders in sport organizations. Importantly, managers need to focus on self-development as human resource departments are shrinking.

Another criticism concerns the potential of transfer of leadership skills that was conceptualized in institutional leadership and management development discourse. Although leadership researchers emphasize the need for specific leadership skills (Megheirkouni, 2017; Megheirkouni et al, 2018; Quarterman, 1998), there is no agreement on a single framework or model to generalize it, for example, to all sport leaders in all sectors (Megheirkouni and Roomi, 2017). Some researchers argue that the reasons could be due to the different approaches to leadership and management training across countries, such as European countries (Ramirez, 2004; Estevez-Abe et al, 2001; Thomson et al, 2001). Besides, patterns of leadership and management development can be moderated by the influence of size and sector (Charlesworth et al, 2003; Geppert et al, 2002; Gray and Mabey, 2005; Newman, 2001; Patton and Marlow, 2002; Tamkin et al, 2006).

Another criticism is that although there is a growing body of research that tackles management development in specific relation to diversity, especially from a feminist perspective (e.g. Megheirkouni, 2014; Megheirkouni and Roomi, 2017), the bulk of research on leadership development perceives the topic of leadership as an abstract, asexual, non-raced, and disembodied individual (Mabey and Finch-Lees, 2008).

Research on leadership learning and development also has several strengths. The current chapter does not represent or address a single unified theory of leadership learning and development, but rather presents the major strengths of several works on leadership learning and development. First, the debate on best practice for leadership development is an interesting debate with general significance that has consequences across the field of leadership development practices. There are certain leadership development practices and approaches which will invariably help sport organizations improve performance and achieve competitive advantage. There is, therefore, a clear link between leadership development practices and performance.

Second, our view of a 'systematic learning and development programme cycle' is presented to help, for example, sport organizations move away from ad hoc, unevaluated training, and replace it with an orderly sequence of leadership learning and development activities. However, some researchers argue that this sort of cycle is not necessarily the most appropriate method to use as it does not focus adequately on learning and may have fitted the 1960s mood for efficiency (Harrison, 2009; Sloman, 2001). Yet, this cycle can provide an answer to sport organizations that are searching for good and sound leadership development in an uncertain world, particularly as the cycle reflects a systematic approach to learning and to development. Given that learning needs may be identified by the individual, by the organization, or in partnership, this would apply to each of the following steps in the circle (Torrington et al, 2014). The cycle helps identify and determine factors influencing leadership development in different stages.

SUMMARY

This chapter has distinguished between and defined three terms: education, training, and development. For a better understanding of learning and development of sport leadership, this chapter discussed learning theories and approaches and has addressed the four learning styles of individuals: activist, reflector, theorist, and pragmatist. This chapter emphasized that sport leaders and managers may learn along different paths. For a better understanding of the transfer process of learning and development to sport organizations, this chapter highlighted the potential application of learning and development initiatives within systematic cycle that includes four stages: identifying and analysing learning and development needs, designing and implementing learning and development programmes, transferring learning and development, and evaluating outcomes. Based on comprehensive reviews of leadership development methods and activities provided by key studies in the field of leadership and its development (e.g. Conger, 1992; Cacioppe, 1998; Conger and Benjamin, 1999; Fulmer et al, 2000; Hartley and Hinksman, 2003; Hernez-Broome and Hughes, 2004), this chapter addressed the leading leadership development methods and activities that have been accepted in the literature: 360-degree feedback, coaching, job assignments, action learning, job rotation, and networking. This chapter also evaluated the strengths and weaknesses of leadership learning and development research.

GENERAL QUESTIONS

1. How do you define education, training, and development?
2. How do people learn important leadership behaviours and capabilities?
3. What are the impacts of internal and external environments of sport organizations on the learning and development of sport leaders?
4. What are the necessary ingredients for systematic progress in sport leadership development programmes?
5. Analyse the links between business strategy and leadership development, using examples from national and international sport settings to support your answer.
6. Why do sport organizations need to have learning and development strategies?
7. What terminology from what is explained above is likely to be used to describe you in five years? Why?

OPEN DISCUSSION QUESTIONS

1. Can you share examples from your experience of education, training, and development in sport leadership?
2. Which one of education, training, or development is essential for successful sport mega event leaders? Why?
3. List some likely future trends in leadership learning and development in the sport and event industries. Which developments do you expect to be prevalent, and why?
4. In what ways have the objectives of leadership development best practices changed as sport organizations have become more diverse?

SELF-ASSESSMENT AND SHARED ASSESSMENT

1. Based on Honey and Mumford's model, select your strongest style and identify three different learning activities that best fit this style for you.
2. Select your weakest style and identify three different learning activities that best fit this style for you.
3. Compare your strongest and weakest styles with your colleagues' styles and identify reasons for these differences or similarities.

Case Study 17.1: Women's Leadership Development

The Women and Leadership Development Programme (WLDP) was a three-year pilot programme designed to develop selected women leaders in UK sport organizations. It was supported by UK Sport, the British Olympic Foundation, and the Central Council of Physical Recreation, and managed by UK Sport. Based on the evaluation of both outcomes and processes by the management team and evaluator, results can be summarized in the following points: First, it sought to evaluate and report the achievement level of key performance indicators identified by the management team in order to: (a) develop leadership behaviour, capabilities, and confidence of all participants; (b) provide development opportunities through the adopted programme; (c) support change in all participants; and (d) support and build strong networking among participants. Second, this programme evaluated the mentoring process in all stages. Third, it attempted to encourage participants to provide feedback, suggestions, and recommendations for the future.

The WLDP, launched in 2006, was divided into pilot and major stages. A formative stage was added to the evaluation of the first two years of the programme. The evaluation of the programme in 2009 revealed that 70 per cent had progressed in their positions or roles in less than three years. All participants reported that the training sessions had a significant impact. Also, 87 per cent revealed that their confidence had increased in leadership. Furthermore, all participants reported that they extended their relationship at the national and international levels through the programme.

Questions

1. Identify two advantages and disadvantages of the WLDP.
2. To what extent do sport leadership development programmes enable women to succeed in positions that are commonly stereotyped as masculine? Why?
3. To what extent do gender stereotypes affect the effectiveness of sport leadership development programmes? Why?

Source: Based on UK Sport. (2016). 'Women in Leadership Programme launched'. News, *UK Sport*. [online]. 31 August 2006. Available at: https://www.uksport.gov.uk/news/2006/08/31/women-in-leadership-programme-launched. See also, Megheirkouni, M. and Roomi, M. (2017). Women's Leadership Development Programmes in a Sports Setting: Factors Influencing the Transformational Learning Experience of Female Managers. *European Journal of Training and Development*, 41(5), 467–484. https://doi.org/10.1108/EJTD-12-2016-0085

Case Study 17.2: Linking Leadership Development Methods to Sport Events

Given the mobilization of sport mega events like the Olympic Games and FIFA World Cup at all levels and all directions and the following information, answer the questions that follow.

Leadership network plays an essential role in bringing stakeholders together and obtaining the resources required. Networking activities help managers and leaders learn and improve their capabilities because leaders and managers in large-scale sport events can learn through communication, regardless of the form of network (formal or informal). Leadership learning and development via networking activities may not only occur through formal and informal communication within the event, but it may begin from the moment, for example, cities submit their applications to host the event until they deliver it.

The leadership and management of organizing committees (see, for example, the structure of the organizing committees of Olympic Games: https://olympics.com/ioc/olympic-games-organising-committees) need to assess not only the progress and implementation of the plans and strategies before hosting the games, but also the performance of all staff operating within their committees every 24 hours and daily as the event progresses in order to ensure avoiding any serious mistakes or at least reducing the aggravation of unexpected problems that can affect the event itself. Adopting 360-degree feedback or part of any other types of assessments can have positive implications on both leadership effectiveness and leadership learning and development.

Given the importance of sport mega events, different types of problems are expected to happen prior to and during the event, and thus learning occurs through finding appropriate solutions. This assumes that leaders and managers of sport mega events learn from the action, and action learning activities are linked to major sport events.

Job assignment does not necessarily mean that someone is 'assigned' to do the job. In other words, managers or even leaders may seek out and volunteer for assignments. For example, heading up a task force to study the efficacy of the TfL *Play Book* map-based software package that up to 400 people were using at the height of the 2012 Olympic Games to access data and models for all 1,300 traffic signals affecting the Olympic Route Network. This assumes that an assignment is linked to leadership and management of sport mega events.

Overall, a leader can learn through one-on-one interactions or group interactions with other leaders who have experience in the field, particularly when they work to meet the requirements of their sport organizations. Indeed, it is known that the organizing committees of sport mega events include leaders and managers who work individually and in groups prior to, during, and after an event. Thus, formal coaching can be used for leadership development prior to and during sport mega events.

Questions

1. Can you link any other development methods and activities with sport mega events?
2. Why do you think leadership development methods and activities should be implemented in the sport and event industries?
3. Can you give examples of a particular method or activity and the purpose of its use in the sport and event industries?
4. Can the content of leadership development methods and activities be transferred from one sport organization or event to others? Why, or not?

SELF-ASSESSMENT 17.1: LEARNING STYLES

David, as one of the board members on an athletics governing body, has participated in several on-job/off-job training and development sessions over the last decade. The most important was the leadership development programme for future sport leaders. David has shown a significant interest in the programme objectives. As a result, he has recently moved to another position at the international level, given his knowledge in management. David has noted several characteristics that learners should know in any future training sessions.

Can you match each of the four learning styles to one of the four statements?

(a) Activist; (b) Reflector; (c) Theorist; (d) Pragmatist

1. David emphasizes the role of personal involvement with others (formal and informal communication) for best learning.
2. David believes that learning occurs not only in the classroom, but also through shadowing or observing others, as this helps learners reflect on what they see.
3. David believes that learners must use logic for building general concepts.
4. David emphasizes the ability of learners to determine whether they can apply what they learn into practices.

SELF-ASSESSMENT 17.2: MATCH THE LEARNING STYLE

Identify which learning style best applies to which individual.

1. Johan always takes risks due to his hasty decisions, acts or tries things out without preparing or thinking.
2. Sara listens and observes carefully to all details, reflects not only on her experience, but also on others' experience to understand what is going on and why.
3. Gael collects and integrates data from all directions and builds a well-structured guidance to understand how things work.
4. Melissa values information that can be effectively used for her job assignments.

Suggested Reading

Beard, C. and Wilson, J.P. (2013). *Experiential Learning: A Handbook for Education, Training and Coaching*. (3rd ed.). London: Kogan Page.

Day, D.V. (2000). Leadership Development: A Review in Context. *The Leadership Quarterly*, 11(4), 581–613. https://doi.org/10.1016/S1048-9843(00)00061-8.

Kolb, D.A. (2014). *Experiential Learning: Experience as the Source of Learning and Development*. (2nd ed.). London: Pearson Press.

Megheirkouni, M. and Mejheirkouni, A. (2020). Leadership Development Trends and Challenges in the Twenty-First Century: Rethinking the Priorities. *Journal of Management Development*, 39(1), 97–124. https://doi.org/10.1108/JMD-04-2019-0114.

Megheirkouni, M. and Roomi, M.A. (2017). Women's Leadership Development in Sport Settings: Factors Influencing the Transformational Learning Experience of Female Managers. *European Journal of Training and Development*, 41(5), 467–484. https://doi.org/10.1108/EJTD-12-2016-0085.

Ryan, R. (2007). *Leadership Development: A Guide for HR and Training Professionals*. London: Routledge. https://doi.org/10.4324/9780080561288.

Sadler-Smith, E. (2006). *Learning and Development for Managers: Perspectives from Research and Practice*. London: Blackwell.

Schunk, D.H. (2012). *Learning Theories: An Educational Perspective*. (6th ed.). London: Pearson.

References

Allen, S.J. (2007). Adult Learning Theory and Leadership Development. *Leadership Review*, 7(1), 26–37.

Allinson, C.W. and Hayes, J. (1996). The Cognitive Style Index: A Measure of Intuition Analysis for Organizational Research. *Journal of Management Studies*, 33(1), 119–135. https://doi.org/10.1111/j.1467-6486.1996.tb00801.x.

Armstrong, S.J. (1999). Cognitive Style and Dyadic Interaction: A Study of Supervisors and Subordinates Engaged in Working Relationships. PhD thesis, University of Leeds. Available at: https://ethos.bl.uk/OrderDetails.do?uin=uk.bl.ethos.365540.

Avolio, B.J. (2004). *Leadership Development in Balance: MADE/Born*. New York. Psychology Press. https://doi.org/10.4324/9781410611819.

Bandura, A. (1978). The Self-System in Reciprocal Determinism. *American Psychologist*, 33(4), 344–358. https://doi.org/10.1037/0003-066X.33.4.344.

Bluckert, P. (2005). The Foundations of a Psychological Approach to Executive Coaching. *Industrial and Commercial Training*, 37(4), 171–178. https://doi.org/10.1108/00197850510602060.

Borthick, A.F., Jones, D.R. and Wakai, S. (2003). Designing Learning Experiences within Learners' Zones of Proximal Development (ZPDs): Enabling Collaborative Learning On-Site and Online. *Journal of Information Systems*, 17(1), 107–134. https://doi.org/10.2308/jis.2003.17.1.107.

Byham, W.C., Smith, A.B. and Paese, M.J. (2002). *Grow Your Own Leaders: How to Identify, Develop, and Retain Leadership Talent*. Upper Saddle River, NJ: Prentice Hall.

Cacioppe, R. (1998). An Integrated Model and Approach for the Design of Effective Leadership Development Programs. *Leadership and Organization Development Journal*, 19(1), 44–53. https://doi.org/10.1108/01437739810368820.

Campion, M.A., Cheraskin, L. and Stevens, M. (1994). Career-Related Antecedents and Outcomes of Job Rotation. *Academy of Management Journal*, 37(6), 1518–1553. JSTOR: https://www.jstor.org/stable/256797.

Charbonneau, D., Barling, J. and Kelloway, E.K. (2001). Transformational Leadership and Sports Performance: The Mediating Role of Intrinsic Motivation. *Journal of Applied Social Psychology*, 31(7), 1521–1534. https://doi.org/10.1111/j.1559-1816.2001. tb02686.x.

Charlesworth, K., Cook, P. and Crozier, G. (2003). *Leading Change in the Public Sector: Making the Difference*. London: Chartered Institute of Management.

Coffield, F., Moseley, D., Hall, E. and Ecclestone, K. (2004). *Learning Styles and Pedagogy in Post-16 Learning: A Systematic and Critical Review*. London: Learning and Skills Research Centre.

Collins, J. (2001). *Good to Great: Why Some Companies Make the Leap ... and Others Don't*. London: Random House.

Conger, J.A. (1992). *Learning to Lead: The Art of Transforming Managers into Leaders*. San Francisco, CA: Jossey-Bass.

Conger, J.A. and Benjamin, B. (1999). *Building Leaders: How Successful Companies Develop the Next Generation*. San Francisco, CA: Jossey-Bass.

Day, D.V. (2000). Leadership Development: A Review in Context. *Leadership Quarterly*, 11(4), 581–613. https://doi.org/10.1016/S1048-9843(00)00061-8.

Day, D.V. and O'Connor, P.M.G. (2003). Leadership Development: Understanding the Process. In: Murphy, S.E. and Riggio, R.E. (Eds.). *The Future of Leadership Development*. Mahwah, NJ: Lawrence Erlbaum. (11–28). https://doi.org/10.4324/9781410608895.

Derry, S.J. (1996). Cognitive Schema Theory in the Constructivist Debate. *Educational Psychologist*, 31(3–4), 163–174. https://doi.org/10.1080/00461520.1996.9653264.

Dewey, J. (1938/1997). *Experience and Education*. New York: Macmillan.

Dixon, N.M. (2000). *Common Knowledge: How Companies Thrive by Sharing What They Know*. Boston, MA: Harvard Business School Press. https://dl.acm.org/doi/book/10.5555/518642.

Estevez-Abe, M., Iversen, T. and Soskice, D. (2001). Social Protection and the Formation of Skills: A Reinterpretation of the Welfare State. In: Hall, P.A. and Soskice, D. (Eds.). *Varieties of Capitalism: The Institutional Foundations of Comparative Advantage*. (e-book: 2003). Oxford: Oxford Academic. (145–183). https://doi.org/10.1093/019 9247757.003.0004.

Fulmer, R.M., Gibbs, P.A. and Goldsmith, M. (2000). Developing Leaders: How Winning Companies Keep on Winning. *MIT Sloan Management Review*, 42(1), 49–59. https:// sloanreview.mit.edu/article/developing-leaders-how-winning-companies-keep-on-winning/.

Geppert, M., Matten, D. and Williams, K. (Eds.). (2002). *Challenges for European Management in a Global Context: Experiences from Britain and Germany*. Basingstoke: Palgrave Macmillan.

Gibson, C.B. and Earley, P.C. (2007). Collective Cognition in Action: Accumulation, Interaction, Examination, and Accommodation in the Development and Operation of Group Efficacy Beliefs in the Workplace. *Academy of Management Review*, 32(2), 438–458. https://doi.org/10.5465/amr.2007.24351397.

Goldstein, I.L. (1993). *Training in Organisations: Needs Assessment, Development and Evaluation*. (3rd ed.). Pacific Grove, CA: Thomson Brooks/Cole Publishing.

Goldstein, I.L and Ford, J.K. (2001). *Training in Organizations: Needs Assessment, Development, and Evaluation*. (4th ed.). London: Wadsworth Thomson Learning.

Gray, C. and Mabey, C. (2005). Management Development: Key Differences between Small and Large Business in Europe. *International Small Business Journal*, 23(5), 467–483. https://doi.org/10.1177/0266242605055908.

Gray, D.E. (2007). Facilitating Management Learning: Developing Critical Reflection through Reflective Tools. *Management Learning*, 38(5), 495–517. https://doi.org/10.1177/1350507607083204.

Hall, D.T., Otazo, K.L. and Hollenbeck, G.P. (1999). Behind Closed Doors: What Really Happens in Executive Coaching. *Organisational Dynamics*, 27(3), 39–52. https://doi.org/10.1016/S0090-2616(99)90020-7.

Harrison, R. (2009). *Learning and Development*. (5th ed.). London: CIPD.

Hartley, J. and Hinksman, B. (2003). *Leadership Development: A Systematic Review of the Literature*. London: National Leadership Centre. Available at: http://www.nursingleadership.org.uk/publications/Systematic%20Review%20-%20Warwick.pdf.

Hernez-Broome, G. and Hughes, R. (2004). Leadership Development: Past, Present, and Future. *Human Resource Planning*, 27(1), 24–32. ProQuest: https://www.proquest.com/docview/224578876.

Honey, P. and Mumford, A. (1989). *Learning Styles Questionnaire*. King of Prussia, PA: Organization Design and Development, Inc.

Ibarra, H. (1995). Race, Opportunity and Diversity of Social Circles in Managerial Managers' Networks. *Academy of Management Journal*, 38(3), 673–703. JSTOR: https://www.jstor.org/stable/256742.

IUCN. (1980). *World Conservation Strategy: Living Resource conservation for Sustainable Development*. Gland: International Union for the Conservation of Nature and Natural Resources (IUCN). Available at: https://portals.iucn.org/library/efiles/documents/WCS-004.pdf.

Jhun, S., Bae, Z.-T. and Rhee, S.-Y. (2012). Performance Change of Managers in Two Different Uses of Upward Feedback: A Longitudinal Study in Korea. *The International Journal of Human Resource Management*, 23(20), 1–14. https://doi.org/10.1080/09585192.2012.657000.

Kaplan, R.E. (2005). Leadership That Is Both Forceful and Enabling. *Leadership in Action*, 25(1), 13–17. https://doi.org/10.1002/lia.1101.

Kolb, D.A. (1984). *Experiential Learning: Experience as the Source of Learning and Development*. Englewood Cliffs, NJ: Prentice-Hall.

Lajoie, S.P. and Azevedo, R. (2006). Teaching and Learning in Technology-Rich Environments. In: Alexander, P.A. and Winne, P.H. (Eds.). *Handbook of Educational Psychology*. (2nd ed.). New York: Routledge. (803–821). https://doi.org/10.4324/9780203874790.

Laske, O. (2007). Contributions of Evidence-Based Developmental Coaching to Coaching Psychology and Practice. *International Coaching Psychology Review*, 2(2), 202–212.

Lave, J. and Wenger, E. (1991). *Situated Learning: Legitimate Peripheral Participation*. Cambridge: Cambridge University Press. https://doi.org/10.1017/CBO9780511815355.

Lawson, K. (2008). *Leadership Development Basics*. London: American Society for Training and Development.

Mabey, C. and Finch-Lees, T.F. (2008). *Management and Leadership Development*. London: Sage.

Manpower Services Commission. (1981). *Glossary of Training Terms*. (3rd ed.). London: HMSO.

Marquardt, M.J. (2000). Action Learning and Leadership. *The Learning Organization*, 7(5), 233–241. https://doi.org/10.1108/09696470010352990.

McGehee, W. and Thayer, P.W. (1961). *Training in Business and Industry*. New York: McGraw-Hill.

Megheirkouni, M. (2014). Women-Only Leadership Positions in the Middle East: Exploring Cultural Attitudes towards Syrian Women for Sport Career Development. *Advancing Women in Leadership*, 34(1), 64–78. https://doi.org/10.21423/awlj-v34.a320.

Megheirkouni, M. (2016). Leadership Development Methods and Activities: Content, Purposes, and Implementation. *Journal of Management Development*, 35(2), 237–260. https://doi.org/10.1108/JMD-09-2015-0125.

Megheirkouni, M. (2017). Leadership Competencies: Qualitative Insight into Non-Profit Sports Organisations. *International Journal of Public Leadership*, 13(3), 166–181. https://doi.org/10.1108/IJPL-11-2016-0047.

Megheirkouni, M. (2018). Insights on Practising of Servant Leadership in the Events Sector. *Sport, Business and Management*, 8(1), 134–152. https://doi.org/10.1108/SBM-01-2017-0001.

Megheirkouni, M., Amarachi, A. and Shehu, J. (2018). Transformational and Transactional Leadership and Skills Approach: Insight on Stadium Management. *International Journal of Public Leadership*, 4(4), 245–259. https://doi.org/10.1108/IJPL-06-2018-0029.

Megheirkouni, M. and Roomi, M. (2017). Women's Leadership Development Programmes in a Sports Setting: Factors Influencing the Transformational Learning Experience of Female Managers. *European Journal of Training and Development*, 41(5), 467–484. https://doi.org/10.1108/EJTD-12-2016-0085.

Nadler, L. and Nadler, Z. (Eds.). (1990). *The Handbook of Human Resources Development*. (2nd ed.). New York: John Wiley and Sons.

Newby, T. (1992). *Cost Effective Training: A Manager's Guide*. London: Kogan Page.

Newman, J. (2001). The New Public Management, Modernization and Institutional Change: Disruptions, Disjunctures and Dilemmas. In: McLaughlin, K., Osborne S.P. and Nicholson, N. (Eds.). *Executive Instinct: Managing the Human Animal in the Information Age*. New York: Crown. (76–92). https://doi.org/10.4324/9780203996362.

Nickerson, R.S., Perkins, D.N. and Smith, E.E. (1985). *The Teaching of Thinking*. Hillsdale, NJ: Erlbaum. [e-book: 2014] https://doi.org/10.4324/9781315792538.

O'Brien, D. and Gardiner, S. (2006). Creating Sustainable Mega Event Impacts: Networking and Relationship Development through Pre-Event Training. *Sport Management Review*, 9(1), 25–47. https://doi.org/10.1016/S1441-3523(06)70018-3.

Ornstein, R.E. (1977). *The Psychology of Consciousness*. (2nd ed.). New York: Harcourt Brace Jovanovich.

Parent, M.M. (2008). Evolution and Issue Patterns for Major-Sport-Event Organizing Committees and Their Stakeholders. *Journal of Sport Management*, 22(2), 135–164. https://doi.org/10.1123/jsm.22.2.135.

Parent, M.M. and Séguin, B. (2008). Toward a Model of Brand Creation for International Large-Scale Sporting Events: The Impact of Leadership, Context, and Nature of the Event. *Journal of Sport Management*, 22(5), 526–549. https://doi.org/10.1123/jsm.22.5.526.

Patton, D. and Marlow, S. (2002) The Determinants of Management Training within Smaller Firms in the UK: What Role Does Strategy Play? *Journal of Small Business and Enterprise Development*, 9(3), 260– 270. https://doi.org/10.1108/14626000210438580.

Quarterman, J. (1998). An Assessment of the Perception of Management and Leadership Skills by Intercollegiate Athletic Conference Commissioners. *Journal of Sport Management*, 12(2), 146–164. https://doi.org/10.1123/jsm.12.2.146.

Ramirez, M. (2004). Comparing European Approaches to Management Education, Training, and Development. *Advances in Developing Human Resources*, 6(4), 428–450. https://doi.org/10.1177/1523422304268378.

Reynolds, M. (1998). Reflection and Critical Reflection in Management Learning. *Management Learning*, 29(2), 183–200. https://doi.org/10.1177/1350507698292004.

Rogers, C.R. (1969/1983). *Freedom to Learn*. Columbus, OH: Merrill.

Sadler-Smith, E. (2006). *Learning and Development for Managers: Perspectives from Research and Practice*. London: Blackwell.

Schoenfeldt, E.L. (1996). Goal Setting and Feedback as a Posttraining Strategy to Increase the Transfer of Training. *Perceptual and Motor Skills*, 83(1), 176–178. https://doi.org/10.2466/pms.1996.83.1.176.

Sloman, M. (2001). Hardier Laurels, Please. *People Management*, 7(25), 39.

Talavera, A.M., Al-Ghamdi, S.G. and Koç, M. (2019). Sustainability in Mega-Events: Beyond Qatar 2022. *Sustainability*, 11(22), 6407. https://doi.org/10.3390/su11226407.

Tamkin, P., Mabey, C. and Beech, D. (2006). *The Comparative Capability of UK Managers. Skills for Business Research Report 17.* Brighton: Institute of Employment Studies. Available at: https://www.employment-studies.co.uk/resource/comparative-capability-uk-managers.

Taylor, T. Doherty, A. and McGraw, P. (2015). *Managing People in Sport Organizations: A Strategic Human Resource Management Perspective*. (2nd ed.). Oxford: Routledge.

Thomson, A., Mabey, C., Storey, J., Gray, C. and Isles, P. (2001). *Changing Patterns of Management Development*. Oxford: Blackwell.

Torrington, D., Hall, L., Taylor, S. and Atkinson, C. (2014). *Human Resource Management*. (11th ed.). London: Pearson Education.

VandeWalle, D. (2004). A Goal Orientation Model of Feedback-Seeking Behaviour. *Human Resource Management Review*, 13(4), 581–604. https://doi.org/10.1016/j.hrmr.2003.11.004.

Wilson, J.P. (Ed.). (2005). *Human Resource Development: Learning and Training for Individuals and Organizations.* (2nd ed.). Derby: Kogan Page.

Yip, J. and Wilson, M.S. (2010). Learning from Experience. In: Van Velsor, E., McCauley, C.D. and Ruderman, M.N. (Eds.). *The Center for Creative Leadership Handbook of Leadership Development* (3rd ed.). London: John Wiley and Sons. (63–96).

INDEX

Note: **Bold** page numbers refer to tables; *italic* page numbers refer to figures.

Printed in Great Britain
by Amazon

50096773R00163